The Filmmaker's Guide to Digital Imaging

The Filmmaker's Guide to Digital Imaging

For Cinematographers, Digital Imaging Technicians, and Camera Assistants

Blain Brown

Focal Press
Taylor & Francis Group

NEW YORK AND LONDON

First published 2015

by Focal Press
70 Blanchard Road, Suite 402, Burlington, MA 01803

and by Focal Press
2 Park Square, Milton Park, Abingdon, Oxon OX14 4RN

Focal Press is an imprint of the Taylor & Francis Group, an informa business

Notices
Knowledge and best practice in this field are constantly changing. As new research and experience broaden our understanding, changes in research methods, professional practices, or medical treatment may become necessary.

Practitioners and researchers must always rely on their own experience and knowledge in evaluating and using any information, methods, compounds, or experiments described herein. In using such information or methods they should be mindful of their own safety and the safety of others, including parties for whom they have a professional responsibility.

Product or corporate names may be trademarks or registered trademarks, and are used only for identification and explanation without intent to infringe.

Library of Congress Cataloging in Publication Data
Brown, Blain.
The filmmaker's guide to digital imaging : for cinematographers, digital imaging technicians, and camera assistants / Blain Brown.
pages cm
1. Digital cinematography. I. Title.
TR860.B76 2014
777'.6--dc23
2014008397

ISBN: 9780415854115 (pbk)
ISBN: 9781315777160 (ebk)

Typeset in Bembo Book by the author.

Printed and bound in India by Replika Press Pvt. Ltd.

Bound to Create

You are a creator.

Whatever your form of expression — photography, filmmaking, animation, games, audio, media communication, web design, or theatre — you simply want to create without limitation. Bound by nothing except your own creativity and determination.

Focal Press can help.

For over 75 years Focal has published books that support your creative goals. Our founder, Andor Kraszna-Krausz, established Focal in 1938 so you could have access to leading-edge expert knowledge, techniques, and tools that allow you to create without constraint. We strive to create exceptional, engaging, and practical content that helps you master your passion.

Focal Press and you.

Bound to create.

We'd love to hear how we've helped you create. Share your experience:
www.focalpress.com/boundtocreate

Focal Press
Taylor & Francis Group

DEDICATION

For my wife, Ada Pullini Brown, who makes it all possible, and Osgood, who keeps things calm.

contents

introduction

IT'S A WHOLE NEW WORLD

Not since the introduction of sound has the world of filmmaking changed so radically and rapidly. In just a few years, digital acquisition and delivery has utterly revolutionized how we do things. Companies that had been making top quality video gear for decades were joined by companies that had been making the best film cameras and with some brilliant engineering and software design, came up with cameras that did things that would have been thought impossible (or at least highly unlikely) just a few years previous. Two results came out of this: first, cinematographers gained all sorts of new tools to work with: cameras, software, monitors and much more; but along with that came a whole raft of new things to learn. Becoming a cinematographer and improving in the field has always involved a great deal of learning and years of practical experience, but for the most part, once you learned your craft you were pretty much set. Sure there were always new toys to play with: lenses, lighting instruments, cranes, grip equipment and more (and of course you were always striving to be better and better at your profession). But these were improvements on existing technology — not so difficult to master. Digital, however, is a whole new bag of beans. Whether you are a film cinematographer transitioning to digital or just coming into the field, there is a huge mass of information to absorb.

There are two ways to approach being a digital filmmaker: you can either work constantly to learn everything you can about cameras, sensors, software and techniques or you can just say "I push the red button to record, right?" Since you are reading this book, I'm going to assume you have chosen the first option. Let's get started.

sensors & cameras

THE DIGITAL SIGNAL PATH

Let's take a look at how the image is acquired and recorded in modern digital cameras; just a quick overview and then we'll get into the details later in this and other chapters.

The lens projects the scene image onto the *sensor* which reacts to light by producing voltage fluctuations proportional to the levels in the scene. Variations in voltage are analog so the first process that must happen is to convert this signal to digital. This is done by the *Analog-to-Digital Converter* (*ADC* or more casually as the *A-to-D Converter*).

DIGITAL SIGNAL PROCESSOR

The data from the ADC then goes to the *Digital Signal Processor* (*DSP*) in the camera. Now that the video image is a stream of *digital code values* (*bits*) rather than an analog electronic signal (thanks to the ADC), the DSP applies various algorithms which both condition the signal for further use and also apply any modifications that we may want. These might include such things as color balance, gamma, color modification, gain and so on, which can be controlled by switches/buttons on the camera (commonly called *the knobs*) or, more commonly, menu selections in the camera controls, all of which are discussed in greater depth in the next chapter.

The DSP actually does a couple of different jobs, some of these operations may include the *Color Correction Matrix transform, Gamma Correction, linear-to-log conversion, knee adjustment* — all of which we will explore in more detail. Most cameras that shoot *RAW* record the image without any of these adjustments such as color balance, changes in contrast and so on; these adjustments are recorded separately as *metadata* (see chapter *Metadata & Timecode*), there are some exceptions which we'll get into later. By the way, RAW is not an acronym, it doesn't stand for anything. Also, writing it as all caps is an industry wide convention. RAW is something we'll be talking about a great deal as it has become an important part of motion picture production.

MATRIX ENCODING

The matrix will be covered in depth in the chapter *Digital Color* but we need to briefly mention it here so that we can talk about what happens in the front end of the camera. If you have used an older *HD* (*High Def*) camera or even a few current ones, you will know that there are menus called *Matrix*, which are used to make adjustments to the color of the image — corrections that are much more specific than the very broad overall warm/cool and magenta/green toning we call *White Balance*.

HD AND UHD

We're going to be talking about two types of cameras: *HD* (*High Def*) and *UHD* (*Ultra High Def*). High Def cameras were basically the first generation of cameras that surpassed the old *Standard Def* (*SD*) that was around pretty much since the beginning of television; it was 480 horizontal lines (US) and 576 horizontal lines (Europe). High Def is considered to be anything that has more "def" than SD but 720 lines is generally considered to be the minimum to be "High" def. HD has several formats, but the most commonly known are 1920x1080 pixels and 1280x720. Ultra High Def cameras are the current generation; they are capable of recording at much higher definition as we'll see soon.

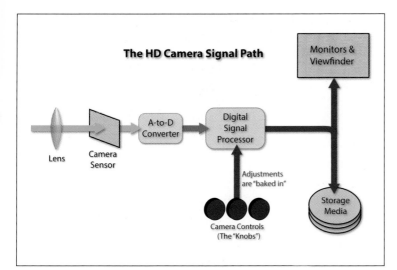

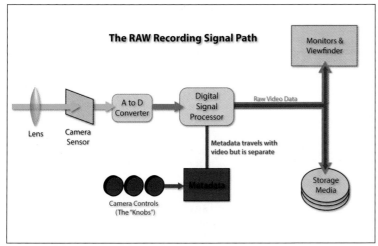

Figure 1.1. (Left, above) The signal path of a traditional video camera includes the "knobs," or in-camera controls of the image which make adjustments which are then *baked in* to the image as it is recorded.

Figure 1.2. (Left, below) The recording path of a camera that records RAW — adjustments to the image are not baked in, but are recorded as metadata alongside the image.

HD Recording

Traditional High Def (HD) cameras employ a basic scheme as shown in Figure 1.1. The digital image flow starts at the image sensor as photons from the scene are focused by the lens onto the photo receptors. There are several types of sensors which we will look into later in this chapter, but all sensors work on the same principle: they convert a light image (photons) formed by the lens (optics) into an electronic signal (electrons). Video sensors are essentially analog devices which produce an electrical signal that is then converted to digital form in the *ADC*.

The digital signal then travels to the camera's internal signal processor, the *DSP* or *Digital Signal Processor* (Figures 1.1 and 1.2.). For most traditional HD cameras, the same signal that is recorded is also sent to the viewfinder and any external monitor outputs, although some viewfinders were reduced in resolution. Cameras of this type were first used around the year 2000. Traditional HD cameras have many adjustments that could be made to the image either with switches, selection wheels and dials or in menus — "the knobs." Changes could be made to gamma (also known as the midtones or mid-range), color, the highlights (knee), shadows (toe) and other aspects of the image. Once these changes were selected the video was recorded that way; we call it *baked in* — once it is recorded in this manner, it is not easy to change it later.

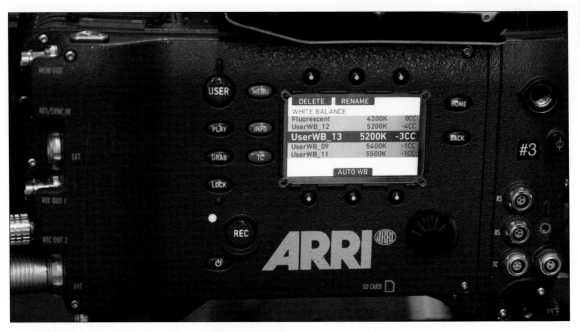

Figure 1.3. An *Arri Alexa* set up for camera tests. In this case, the color balance values are being adjusted in the menus. What is interesting about most (not all) modern cameras such as this is how few buttons, switches and knobs there are. Even the menus are not particularly complicated when compared to video cameras of the past.

RAW VS. BAKED IN

The second revolution came a few years later with the introduction of the *Viper Filmstream* from Thompson, followed soon after by the *Dalsa* and *Arri* digital cameras and later on the *Red One*. These were the first systems to output RAW and also employed *tapeless* recording (digital files directly to a hard drive or flash memory, not to video-tape). The last few years have brought a nearly complete changeover at the professional level to shooting and recording RAW video in a tapeless workflow. Filmmakers who struggled with video tape that had drop outs, jammed or otherwise malfunctioned won't miss them at all. As we have mentioned, RAW image acquisition means that the data that comes off the sensor is recorded with only minimal "non-artistic" transformations or sometimes none at all (depending on the camera and user selection).

Most cameras still allow you to make changes in the color matrix, the gamma, and other important image characteristics, but the big difference is that these manipulations are not actually recorded as part of the video signal — instead they are only saved as *metadata*, essentially this metadata is a sort of commentary on the video scenes, they can be freely changed later on. RAW data is regarded as being a "digital negative." When shooting on film, the negative just records what comes in the lens — it is later on in the print that decisions are made about precise color balance, adjustments in exposure, etc.

While cameras that shoot RAW do have some image adjustments available, video software developer Stu Maschwitz puts it this way: "Adjusting image settings on a digital cinema camera is like arranging furniture to look nice in the moving van." There are, however, good reasons to make adjustments on the set, if only so that the DP and Director have an image on the monitor that somewhat reflects their artistic intentions for the scene. Also without this look added by the DP and director, those viewing the image later on would have no idea what the creative team on the set intended. Finally, the look established in the files sent to the editor (even if that is no look at all) are going to be viewed for weeks or months by the director, editor and others. People tend to just sort of "fall for" that look and may completely forget what the original intentions were. As we'll discuss later on, techniques have been developed to ensure that the Director of Photography (or even the director) still have a major influence over the look of the project, even if he or she is not present during the post production process.

RAW CAMERA SIGNAL PATH

In cameras that shoot RAW, the signal path is not the same as traditional HD cameras (Figure 1.2). What is recorded on the media storage (hard drive, flash card or whatever) is just the RAW signal without any "creative" adjustments. This is what makes cameras that shoot RAW so different from older cameras. It means that important image characteristics such as ISO, white balance, gamma, highlight and shadow alterations and color transformations can be freely altered later on without any degradation of the image. There are some exceptions to this depending on manufacturer; for example some cameras do bake in ISO or white balance at the time of shooting. This is what makes it impossible to make an exact definition of what shooting RAW means. Many DPs also caution against thinking that just because you shoot RAW means that "everything can be fixed later." This is as dangerous as beginning filmmakers who sometimes say "We'll fix it in post."

It is important to note, however, that some aspects of the recording are a permanent part of the image: frame rate, compression ratio and time base (i.e. 24 FPS) cannot be altered once the scene has been shot, at least not without a lot of work. As previously mentioned, in many cases, the RAW data is recorded in *log mode* (see the chapter *Linear, Gamma, Log*) and often with some degree of compression — Red cameras, for example, have a minimum compression of 3:1, which Red has determined to be "visually lossless."

VIEWING STREAM

From the DSP, the signal splits: it is sent both to the recording section of the camera and to the monitoring outputs. In many cases, the viewing output is not the same as is being recorded and different outputs on the camera may be in various formats. For example, some camera viewfinders can't display 1080 HD video, so they are actually being sent something like 720 HD, for example.

Monitor output from the camera may be *SDI* (*Serial Digital Interface*) HDMI, *composite* or *component* video. High end pro cameras generally have a variety of outputs for different purposes.

In the case of the Red camera, for example, the monitoring path converts 16-bit RAW sensor data to white balanced 10-bit 1080 RGB 4:4:4 video. This image is modified by the ISO, white balance or other color space adjustments and provides monitor and viewfinder feeds. Other types of cameras offer different monitoring signals but some down conversion of monitoring is typical. A few cameras have a traditional optical viewing system like a film camera; in other words the operator is looking at the actual scene.

PIXELS

Pixel stands for *picture element* or *pix-el* (no relation to *Jor-El* as far as we know). The term originated in the 1960s and its exact source is not known. A true pixel is effectively color information for a single point. A pixel is not a fixed size. For example, the same image might have very small pixels when displayed on a computer monitor, but the same pixels will be quite large when projected on a theater screen.

Figure 1.4. (Above) Magnifying an image on a display reveals the pixel structure. It is important to understand the difference between pixels and photosites (Figure 1.12). Photosites are physical things in the camera sensor. Pixels are what happens when data from the photosites are interpreted into colors.

The reason we don't perceive these larger pixels as visible elements is viewing distance — in the theater, the viewer is much farther away, which is why when camera tests are being projected, you will often see imaging professionals walking up to the screen and observing it at close range (Figure 1.4). Of course, the smaller the pixels (and thus more of them in the image) the sharper and cleaner the look of the image; this is the basic idea of image resolution, although there is much more to resolution than just how many pixels there are. All else being equal, more pixels would mean more resolution, but then all else is seldom equal. In HD and UHD video, pixels are square. We're going to talk about *photosites* in a moment — photosites (Figure 1.12) and pixels are not the same thing.

RESOLUTION

The resolution of a device (such as a digital monitor or camera sensor) is sometimes defined as the number of distinct pixels in each dimension that can be displayed or captured. In some cases, this is expressed in *megapixels*, at least in the world of digital still cameras (*DSLRs*) — a megapixel being one million pixels. The term megapixels is almost never used in discussing video cameras. In some cases, the measure of the sensor may be different from the output of the camera. There can be some differences of opinion in how to count the pixels of a sensor.

However pixel count is not the only factor in determining resolution; contrast is also an important element. Image processing software developer Graeme Nattress says this in his paper *Understanding Resolution*: "Our overall perception of detail depends not just on the finest image features, but also on how the full spectrum of feature sizes is rendered. With any optical system, each of these sizes is interrelated. Larger features, such as the trunk of a tree, retain more of their original contrast. Smaller features, such as the bark texture on a tree trunk, retain progressively less contrast.

Resolution just describes the smallest features, such as the wood grains, which still retain discernible detail before all contrast has been lost." He adds "Resolution is not sharpness! Although a high resolution image can appear to be sharp, it is not necessarily so, and an image that appears sharp is not necessarily high resolution. Our perception of resolution is intrinsically linked to image contrast. A low contrast image will always appear softer than a high contrast version of the same image. We see edges and detail by the contrast that edges make."

DIGITIZING

The key elements of digitizing are *pixels-per-frame*, *bits-per-pixel*, *bit rate* and *video size* (the digit of file for a given time frame). Digitizing is the process of converting analog information (such as from the video sensor) into digital bits and bytes.

Digitizing involves measuring the analog wave at regular intervals: this is called *sampling* and the frequency of the interval is called the *sampling rate* (Figures 1.5 and 1.6). As you can see, if the number of samples per video line is low, the sampling is very crude and doesn't give a very accurate representation of the original signal. As the frequency of the sampling increases, the digital conversion becomes more accurate. Once the minimum sampling rate that will accurately represent the analog signal has been determined, the actual sampling rate that is used is generally at least twice that rate. The reason for this is the *Nyquist Theorem*.

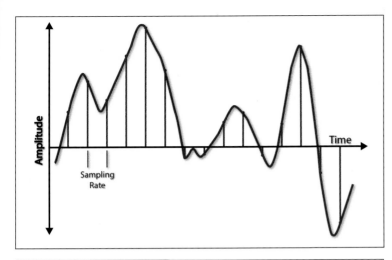

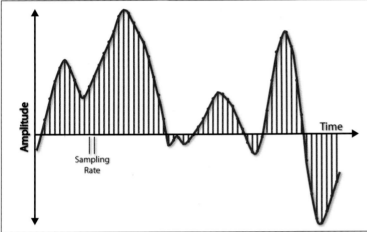

Figure 1.5. (Left, top) Digitizing at a low sample rate gives only a rough approximation of the original signal.

Figure 1.6. (Left, below) A higher sample rate results in digital values that are much closer to the original signal.

Nyquist Limit

The *Nyquist Limit* or *Nyquist Theorem is a* term you will hear mentioned frequently in discussions of digital sensors and video data. No need for us to go into the mathematics of the theorem here, but it states that the sampling rate of an analog-to-digital conversion must be *double* the highest analog frequency. In video, the highest frequencies represent the fine details of a sampled image. If this isn't the case, false frequencies may be introduced into the signal, which can result in *aliasing* — the dreaded stair-step, jagged effect along the edges of objects. Some people mistakenly think they need twice as many pixels as resolution. But because sampling theory refers to the frequency of the video image, which is made up of a line pair, you need as many samples as lines, not twice as many samples as lines.

OLPF

Optical Low Pass Filters (OLPF) are used to eliminate *Moire* patterns (Figure 1.7) so they are sometimes called *anti-aliasing* filters. They are made from layers of optical quartz and usually incorporate an IR (infrared) filter as well, because silicon, the key component of sensors, is most sensitive to the longer wavelengths of light — infrared. The reason a sensor will create moiré is primarily due to the pattern of photosites in a *Color Filter Array* (Figure 1.12)— although all types of sensors (including black-and-white) are subject to aliasing. When a photograph is taken of a subject that has a pattern, each pixel

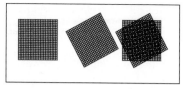

Figure 1.7. An example of how aliasing causes a *Moire* pattern to occur. Here, the *Moire* appears as circles.

is exposed to one color and the camera calculates (interpolates) the information that is remaining. The small pattern of photosite filters is what causes moiré — details smaller than the pixels are interpreted incorrectly and create false details. The trade-off of using an OLPF is a very slight softening of the image. For this reason, they are sometimes removed and in some few cameras, they can be internally changed by the user to select different "grades" of filtering. They work by cutting off the highest frequencies thus smoothing out any detail that is finer than the pixels.

Graeme Nattress puts it this way: "*Optical low pass filters (OLPFs)* or *Anti-Alias* filters work in two passes, each layer splits the light in two either horizontally or vertically, so by combining them together, you get vertical and horizontal filtering. Aliasing is what occurs when too high a frequency (too detailed information) enters a sampling system." Low pass filters are specifically tailored to the sensor they are used with to adjust to differences in photosite pitch, size, etc. Because of this they are a part of what makes cameras from different manufacturers distinct.

DIGITAL SENSORS

At this time, the dominant technologies used in video cameras are *CCD* and *CMOS*, although it is an arena in which we can expect many technological innovations in the future, as all camera companies constantly engage in research and development in this area. Both types of sensors have advantages and disadvantages in image quality, low-light performance and cost. Since their invention at Kodak in the early 1970s, digital sensors have steadily improved in all aspects of their performance and image reproduction as well as lower costs of manufacturing.

CCD

CCD stands for *Charge Coupled Device*. A CCD is essentially an analog device — a photon counter; it converts photons to an electrical charge and converts the resulting voltage into digital information: zeros and ones. In a CCD array, every pixel's charge is transferred through a limited number of output connections to be converted to voltage and sent to the DSP as an analog electrical signal (voltage). Nearly all of the sensor real estate can be devoted to light capture, and the output's uniformity (a factor in image quality) is fairly high. Each pixel is actually a *MOSFET* (*Metal Oxide Semiconductor Field Effect Transistor*) which is a type of transistor that can be both an amplifier and a switcher.

So how do all those millions of pixels output their signal through a relatively few connector nodes? It's a clever process that was actually conceived at the very inception of the digital image sensor. The idea that a silicon chip can react to light and produce an electrical signal is very old indeed. Take a look at an older model light meter, the venerable *Spectra Professional* (Figure 1.9). It is simply a silicon chip that reacts to light by producing a small voltage output, which is measurable. It is, in essence, a sensor with a single photosite. What was new about the idea of an image sensor was a way of using a large number of mini-sensors together and being able to efficiently output their signals. Imagine if all those millions of pixels needed to be wired up individually — it would be quite a soldering job!

Working at AT&T Bell Labs, George Smith and Willard Boyle came up with the idea of a *shift register*. The idea itself is simple, it's like a bucket brigade: each pixel registers its charge and then passes it to the next pixel and so on down the line until it reaches the output connection. Their first demonstration model was only eight pixels, but it was enough to prove the principle which cameras still use today. They were awarded a Nobel Prize for their invention. Other companies developed the ideas and in 1975 Kodak used the concept in the first digital camera which used a 100x100 CCD sensor.

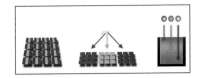

Figure 1.8. (Above) Three principal types of sensors: single-chip, three-chip and Foveon.

FRAME TRANSFER CCD

A disadvantage of the shift register design is that after the exposure phase, during the *readout phase*, if the readout is not fast enough, error data can result due to light still falling on the photosites; this can result in *vertical smearing* of a strong point light source in the frame. Also, the sensor is basically out of action as an image collection device during readout. A newer design that solves these problems is the *frame transfer CCD*. It employs a hidden area with as many sites as the sensor. When exposure finishes, all of the charges are transferred to this hidden area and then readout can occur without any additional light striking the photosites and it also frees up the sensing area for another exposure phase.

CMOS

CMOS stands for *Complementary Metal Oxide Semiconductor*. In general, CMOS sensors are lower in cost than CCDs because the manufacturing process is simpler and there are fewer components involved. They also tend to use less power in operation and have long been capable of higher rates of *readout* (transferring the image data to the processing sections of the camera). A variation on CMOS is the *Back-illuminated CMOS*. Developed by Sony, this type of sensor changes the internal arrangement of layers to improve the chances of a photon being captured, thus improving low-light performance.

In a CMOS sensor, each photosite has its own charge-to-voltage conversion capacity, and the sensor often also includes amplifiers, noise-correction, and digitization circuits, so that the chip outputs a *digital* signal as bits (which still needs processing). These additional functions increase the complexity and reduce the total area available for light capture. With each pixel doing its own conversion, uniformity tends to be somewhat lower than in a CCD, but the sensor chip can be built to require less off-chip circuitry for basic operation.

OTHER TYPES OF SENSORS

There are a few other types of sensors which are not used as much in digital cameras. *Foveon* sensors have three primary colors on each individual pixel arranged vertically on top of each other thus eliminating the need for a color filter array. *Junction Field Effect Transistors (JFET)* are similar to CMOS sensors but use a different type of transistor. *LBCAST* stands for *Lateral Buried Charge Accumulator and Sensing Transistor array*.

3-CHIP

Since the early days of television up to the introduction of UHD, most video cameras used three separate sensors (usually CCD) for the red, green and blue components. This arrangement is capable of very high quality images. Since there is only one lens the image needs to be split into three parts, which is accomplished with prisms and *dichroic filters* as shown in 1.10.

It is critical that all three light paths be the same length so that they focus at the same plane. The sensors must be precisely aligned so that they line up properly when combined into a single color image.

Figure 1.9. The classic *Spectra Professional* (with the dome removed for illustration) is basically a single photosite sensor — it produces voltage when light hits it.

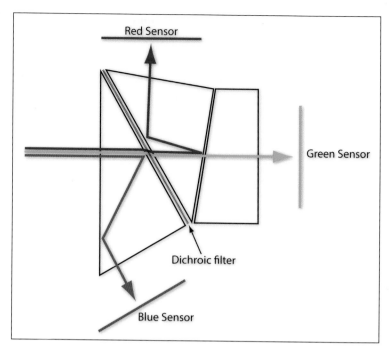

Figure 1.10. Sensor arrangement of a *three-chip camera*. *Dichroic filters* and prisms separate the red, green and blue components of the image.

Red Sensor

Green Sensor

Dichroic filter

Blue Sensor

PHOTOSITES

Digital cameras, whether designed for video, still photos or both, use sensor arrays of millions of tiny *photosites* in order to record the image (Figure 1.12). Photosites are basically photon counters — they react to the amount of light hitting them and output voltage proportionate to that. They sense only photons, which have no color and by the same token photosites have no "color." What do we mean when we say photons have no color? They produce color by affecting the cones of our eyes at different wavelengths; we'll talk about this in more detail in *Digital Color.*

Pixels and Photosites Are Not the Same Thing

It is easy to think that photosites are the same thing as pixels but they are not; the process is a bit more complicated than that. The output from photosites are collected together, unprocessed, to form camera RAW images. In most sensors, output from adjoining photosites are combined in ways that vary between manufacturers. Joseph Goldstone, Image Science Engineer at *Arri*, puts it this way "There can be

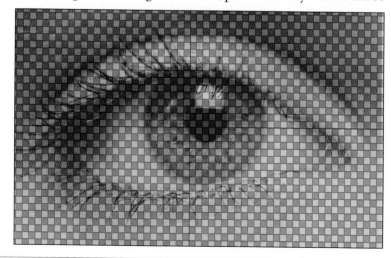

Figure 1.11. An image with a Bayer filter arrangement superimposed.

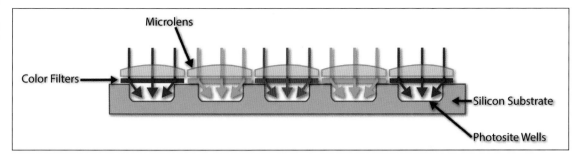

Figure 1.12. Red, green and blue photosites of a typical single chip, color filter array sensor.

a 1:1 relationship between the array (or arrays, if you have a 3-chip camera) of photosites and the array of RGB image pixels, but there doesn't have to be. There are purists who say that the best and most "true" images result when the relationship is 1:1, but there are plenty of good-looking images out there where this isn't true." He cites the Arri *Alexa* as an example. "Tons of episodic TV is shot on an Alexa where the photosite array is 2880 x 1620, and the photosites are simultaneously deBayered and downsampled at a ratio of 3:2 to produce a 1920 x 1080 image — this happens inside the camera if you are getting HD video out of the BNC connectors. Or, if you are shooting a feature on an Alexa and recording ArriRAW, you can use an ArriRAW converter to both deBayer and to uprez to 3840 x 2160 which is referred to as 4K."

Pixels can be thought of as the processed result of the data from the photosites. In a display (such as a monitor) pixels are composed of *sub-pixels* —red, green and blue which can be varied in intensity to form a wide range of colors.

MAKING COLOR FROM BLACK-AND-WHITE

Photosites are unable to distinguish how much of each color has come in, so they can really only record monochromatic grayscale images. To capture color images, each photosite has a filter over it which only allows penetration of a particular color of light — although this differentiation can never be absolute, there is always some overlap. Virtually all current digital cameras can only capture one of the three primary colors in each photosite, and so they discard roughly 2/3 of the incoming light — this is because filters work by rejecting wavelengths that don't match the color of the filter. As a result, the processing circuits have to approximate the other two primary colors in order to have information about all three colors at every pixel.

BAYER FILTER

The most common type of color filter array is called a *Bayer filter*, or *Bayer filter color array*. Invented by Dr. Bryce Bayer at Kodak, it is just one type of *CFA* (*color filter array*) (Figures 1.13 and 1.14) but it is by far the most widely used in cameras. The sensor has two layers:

- The *sensor substrate* which is the photosensitive silicon material, it measures the light intensity and translates it into an electrical charge. The sensor has microscopic cavities or wells, which trap the incoming light and allow it to be measured. Each of these wells or cavities is a photosite.
- *The Bayer filter* is a color filter array that is bonded to the sensor substrate. The sensor on its own can only measure the number of light photons it collects; since photosites can't "see" color; it is the filters that differentiate the wavelengths that result in color.

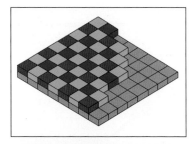

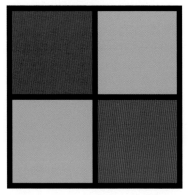

Figure 1.13. (Top) Arrangement of a Bayer filter on a sensor.

Figure 1.14. (Above) The most significant aspect of the Bayer filter is two green photosites for each red and blue. This is a typical arrangement only, some camera companies arrange them differently.

Even with the tremendous advances in nanotechnology, it is still impossible to make the photosites sit precisely next to each other — inevitably there will be a tiny gap between them. Any light that falls into this gap is wasted light, and will not be used for the benefit of exposure. The *microlens* array (as shown in Figure 1.12) sitting on top of the sensor aims to eliminate this light waste by directing the light that falls between two photosites into one of them or other. Each microlens collects some of the light that would have been lost and redirects into the photosite.

DEMOSAICING/DEBAYERING

There is one obvious issue with Bayer filters or anything like them: they are a *mosaic* of color pixels — not really an exact reproduction of the original image at all. *Demosaicing*, also known as *deBayering*, is the process by which the image is put back together into a usable state. In this process the color values from each pixel are interpolated using algorithms. Figure 1.11 shows a simulation of what an unde-Bayered image looks like. Some software applications allow limited control over this stage of the process. For example, in *RedCine-X Pro* you can choose from *1/16, 1/8, 1/4, 1/2 Good, 1/2 Premium* or *full deBayer* (Figure 1.15). This selection is made as you dial in your export settings. So, what quality of deBayer is sufficient to produce an image that is best for your purposes?

According to Graeme Nattress: "Full deBayer is necessary to extract 4k resolution for 4k footage. It also makes for the best 2k when scaled down. However, if you're going direct to 2k, the half deBayer is optimized to extract to the full 4k and scale down to 2k in one step, and hence is much quicker. If you're just going to 2k, then the half is fine, but you may get a percent or two more quality going the full debayer + scale route." (Graeme Nattress, *Film Effects and Standards Conversion for FCP*). In RedCine-X Pro there is also a deBayer selection named "Nearest Fit." This setting automatically selects the deBayer setting that is closest to the output resolution you select for that export. DP Art Adams puts it this way: "A good rule of thumb is that Bayer pattern sensors lose 20% of their resolution right off the top due to the deBayering algorithm blending colors from adjacent photosites into distinct pixels."

Color Interpolation

The most striking aspect of the basic Bayer filter is that it has twice as many green sites as it does red or blue. This is because the human eye is much more sensitive to green light than either red or blue, and has a much greater resolving power in that range.

Clearly it is not an easy task to make a full color image if each photosite can only record a single color of light. Each photosite is missing two thirds of the color data needed to make a full color image; also, the filters cannot do an absolutely precise job of separating the colors so there is always going to be some "bleed" and overlap, but with sophisticated algorithms, most cameras do a surprisingly good job of color interpretation.

The methods used for *deBayering* are quite complex. In very simplified terms, the camera treats each 2x2 set of photosites as a single unit. This provides one red, one blue and two green photosites in each subset of the array, and the camera can then estimate the actual color based on the photon levels in each of these four photosites. Figure 1.14 is an example of a 2 x 2 square of four photosites, each

photosite contains a single color — either red, green or blue. Call them G1, B1, R1, G2. At the end of the exposure, when the shutter has closed and the photosites are full of photons, the processing circuits start their calculations.

If we look at the demosaicing of each 2x2 square, here's what goes on: for the pixel at G1, the green value is taken from G1 directly, while the red and blue values are inferred from the neighboring R1 and B1 photosites; in the simplest case, those photosites' values are simply used directly. In more sophisticated algorithms, the values of multiple adjacent photosites of the same color may be averaged together, or combined using other mathematical formulae to maximise detail while keeping false color artifacts to a minimum.

Based on the Bayer pattern, if the photosite in the center is green, the surrounding photosites will be made up of two blue photosites, two red photosites and four green photosites. If it is a red photosite in the center, it will have four blue photosites and four green photosites around it. If it is a blue photosite in the center, it will be surrounded by four green photosites and four red photosites. In general, each photosite is used by at least eight other photosites so that each can create a full range of color data.

This description is a typical example only, the method used for this color interpolation is proprietary to each manufacturer and is thus a closely guarded secret. Improvements in this process are a big part of how digital cameras keep getting better and better, along with improvements in sensors, compression and other factors, including post-production processing.

Effective pixels

So what happens to the pixels right at the edge of a sensor? — they don't have all the accompanying pixels needed for interpolation. If they are the very edge pixel, they don't have as many surrounding pixels from which to borrow information, so their color data is not quite as accurate. This is the difference between actual pixels and effective pixels.

The actual number of pixels on a sensor is the total number of pixels. However, not all of these are used in forming the image. Those at the edge are ignored by the camera in forming the image, but their data is used by those further from the edge. This means that every pixel used in forming the image uses the same number of pixels to create its color data. Many of the "extra" pixels are behind the chip's *aperture mask*, so they don't receive light. But they still gen-

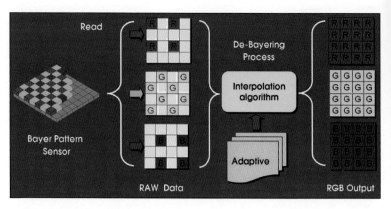

Figure 1.16. The Sony F-65 deBayer process diagram. (Courtesy of Sony).

erate a "dark current" signal that varies with temperature (among other things), and these "black" pixels are used for on-chip black-level control and adjustment. That's why you'll see different actual vs. effective numbers even on 3-chip cameras that don't use a CFA.

This is why in camera specifications you may see something like "effective pixels 10.1 million, total pixels 10.5 million." These extra 400,000 pixels in the total megapixels are the ones used to create color data information, but are not used in forming part of the final image.

HOW MANY PIXELS IS ENOUGH?

Counting how many pixels a sensor has can get a bit complicated. You might think that a sensor listed as 2 MP would have 2 megapixels for each channel: red, green and blue. In most cameras, this is not the case. Similarly, for cameras with Bayer filters, there are twice as many green photosites as there are red, or blue — how is this counted? Each camera company has made choices as to how to come up with a total count; there is no industry-wide standard. However, unlike digital still cameras, the megapixel count is rarely used when discussing the camera. Instead, the number of pixels measured across the horizontal axis is used — 1920, 2K, 4K, 5K, etc.

5K FOR 4K

Some cameras can now shoot at 5K, 6K and beyond. There are currently no displays or projector for this type of footage, so why? It can be thought of as "oversampling." One popular use for this larger format is to shoot a frame larger than is intended for the final output, this leaves some room on the edges for repositioning, steadying shaky footage and other uses. In film, it was common practice to shoot larger formats such as 65mm or Vistavision for VFX (visual effects) shots. This ensured that there would be no degradation quality in the many steps of post-production. 5K, 6K and above can function in this manner as well.

SONY TAKES A DIFFERENT PATH

On their F65 camera (Figure 1.18), Sony uses a different type of sensor design. They are able to achieve a tighter *pitch* (the distance between photosites) without using smaller pixels by using a different pattern that packs them more densely (Figure 1.17). With this scheme, they are able to achieve what they term an 8K sensor. On the F65, Sony calls it a mosaic pattern, not a Bayer pattern. Other Sony cameras use different types of sensors, and have different color filters in front of them.

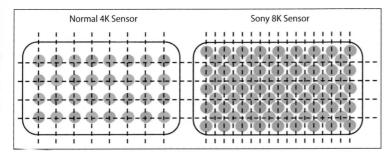

WHAT COLOR IS YOUR SENSOR?

So what is the color balance of a digital sensor? The short answer is that, unlike film stock, which comes in either daylight or tungsten balance, camera sensors don't have a "color balance." Yes, all cameras allow you to choose a preferred color temperature or to automatically "white balance" to adjust to daylight, tungsten, overcast, fluorescent, etc, but these are electronic corrections to the signal — they don't actually affect the sensor itself.

On some cameras, this color correction is "baked in" and is a permanently part of the image. As we know, cameras that shoot RAW may display the image with corrected color balance, but in fact, this is just the metadata affecting the display — the RAW image remains unaffected and any desired color balance can be selected later in software and only needs to be baked in at a later time (there are some exceptions to this, as we'll see). However, that being said, some camera sensors do have a color balance that they are optimized for — this is called their "native" color balance, just as their "built in" sensitivity is referred to as their *native ISO*. Some are known to have slightly different responses at various color temperatures. What is the native ISO or white balance of a sensor is generally determined by what setting requires the least amount of gain (electronic amplification) to be applied. This results in the least noise.

For example, the native color balance for the *Dragon* sensor used in some RED cameras is 5,000 degrees Kelvin, but of course can be electronically compensated for any color temperature in the range 1,700 to 10,000 Kelvin — as we know, this is recorded in the metadata when shooting RAW images. White Balance presets are available for Tungsten (3200K) and Daylight (5600K) lighting; the camera can also calculate a color neutral White Balance value using a standard white card/gray card technique.

Canon takes the approach that color balance is baked in by applying gain at the time of shooting; see the chapter *Codecs & Formats* for a discussion of their logic in choosing this path.

CANON'S APPROACH TO SENSORS

Canon uses a color filter arrangement but the sensor is actually outputting essentially four 2K streams, one for the red pixels, one for the blue pixels, and two streams for green pixels — *Gr* and *Gb*. The second green signal is placed in the signal where the *alpha channel* (transparency or opacity) would normally go in other implementations. These signals are then multiplexed together to form *RMF* (*Raw Media Format*) files. (Figure 1.19).

ALEXA NATIVE COLOR TEMPERATURE

The following is from Arri and is used with their permission. "*What is the native color temperature of Alexa's sensor?* The short answer is that while Alexa does not really have a 'native' color temperature, the

Figure 1.18. (Above) The Sony F-65 at a camera checkout. The recording module is mounted on the back and a *TVLogic* monitor is set up for the camera assistant. (Courtesy of DIT Sean Sweeney).

point at which the lowest overall gain is applied to the red, green and blue pixels is at 5600 degrees Kelvin, yielding the lowest possible noise in the image. However, since Alexa has an amazingly low noise level anyway, the difference in noise between 3200K and 5600K is so minimal as to not be relevant in most shooting situations. So choosing the color temperature can be dictated by other factors, such as the cinematographer's preference or the availability and/or cost of tungsten or daylight lighting instruments.

"For the long answer, we have to start with the birds and the bees, or in our case, with celluloid and silver halide crystals. Film stocks are balanced for either a tungsten (3200 degrees Kelvin) or a daylight (5600 degrees Kelvin) light source. To achieve this, film manufacturers carefully tune the chemistry of the individual color layers. A grey card filmed under the respective lighting conditions should also result in a grey image after development. Thus each film stock has a given color temperature 'baked-in,' which is sometimes also called the 'native' color temperature of that film stock. If you need a different color temperature, you change film stocks.

"The way light is converted to an image is different for film and sensors. In order to display a grey card as grey, digital cameras have to carefully balance the gain (amplification) applied to the red, green and blue (RGB) signals. The response of a digital camera to incoming light of different colors is determined by the response behavior of the filter pack (IR, OLPF, UV), the photocell, the Bayer mask inks and the image processing. Even though the properties of the filter pack, photocell and Bayer mask inks are chosen with the best color balance in mind, there are other factors that also influence the color balance of the signal coming from the sensor, including an optimization for highest sensitivity, widest dynamic range and lowest noise. The proper balance between all those requirements is not only dif-

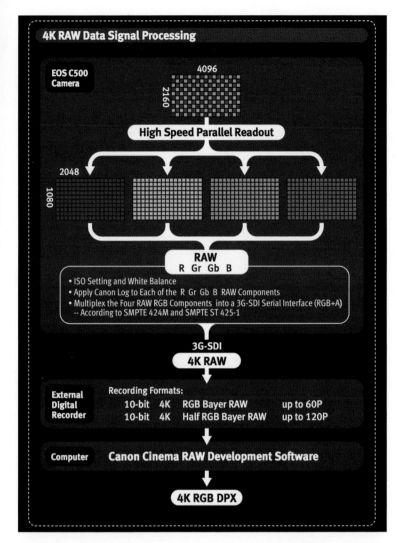

4K RAW Data Signal Processing

EOS C500 Camera

4096
2160

High Speed Parallel Readout

2048
1080

RAW
R Gr Gb B

- ISO Setting and White Balance
- Apply Canon Log to Each of the R Gr Gb B RAW Components
- Multiplex the Four RAW RGB Components into a 3G-SDI Serial Interface (RGB+A)
  -- According to SMPTE 424M and SMPTE ST 425-1

3G-SDI
4K RAW

External Digital Recorder

Recording Formats:
10-bit   4K   RGB Bayer RAW   up to 60P
10-bit   4K   Half RGB Bayer RAW   up to 120P

Computer   **Canon Cinema RAW Development Software**

4K RGB DPX

Figure 1.19. Canon's sensors output red and blue channels, and also two different green channels. These are multiplexed into a 4K RAW image which can then be processed into video. RAW data is not really viewable, so it is not considered to be "video." Also note that Canon's process applies ISO at White Balance early in the process, unlike most other cameras. (Diagram courtesy of Canon).

ficult to achieve, but also one of the factors that differentiates the various models of digital cameras.

"Since one can neither create a separate sensor for each color temperature situation, nor readily change them if one could, digital cameras have to cover a variety of color temperatures with one sensor. For any given color temperature, a sensor will deliver an unequal amount of red (R), green (G) and blue (B) signal. In order to balance the three colors for different color temperatures, digital camera manufacturers use different amplification settings for red and blue, while keeping green un-amplified. Let's look at the actual settings the *Arri Alexa* uses to illustrate this.

"When using Alexa to capture a grey card lit with a tungsten source (3200K), the signals from the red and blue pixels have to be amplified by the following amounts to make a neutral grey:

R — 1.13x

G — 1.00x

B — 2.07x

"Shooting the same chart, but now lit with a daylight source (5600K), will put more blue and less red light on the sensor. So we can apply less amplification to the signal from the blue pixels but need a little more amplification for the signal from the red pixels:

Figure 1.20. Menu selections on a Sony F55. There are still a few buttons but they mostly relate to menu selections. Notice also the selection called *MLUT*. This is Sony's *Monitor LUT* for on-set viewing.

R — 1.64x

G — 1.00x

B — 1.37x

"So, for tungsten, Alexa uses a little more amplification in the blue channel, and for daylight a little more in the red. And for those who are still reading and want more: even though the red and blue amplifications are equal at 5000K, daylight (5600K) has the mathematically lowest overall noise gain, measured as the square root of the sum of the squared gains."

SENSOR SIZE AND DEPTH-OF-FIELD

Sometime people confuse the size of the sensor and resolution. For our purposes in this discussion, the physical dimensions of the sensor are the most relevant. This is because the size of the sensor has an important effect on the cinematic storytelling: it is a major factor in determining *depth-of-field* — the range of area in front of the camera that is in focus. In visual storytelling, it is a useful tool in directing the viewer's attention, among other things. It also contributes to the effect of making a scene look more "film like."

On the other hand, sensor size does not necessarily correlate to number of pixels. Some very small sensors (such as in cell phones or pocket cameras, for example) have very high pixel counts. This can be problematic in that the individual pixels must then be much smaller and closer together. This means that each pixel will "collect" less light (lower ISO) and be susceptible to cross-talk and contamination from adjacent pixels resulting in noise. Larger pixels (generally associated with larger sensors) also usually have greater dynamic range as well. Sensor size can also result in a *crop factor*, meaning that it affects the apparent focal length of the lens.

SHUTTERS

Shutters are always necessary in any type of photography, either still or motion. If the film or sensor was always exposed to the light of the image, it would record the movement in the scene all the time, meaning that the shot would be blurred. Also, there would be much less control over exposure — light would be constantly flooding onto the sensor.

Spinning Mirror

Still cameras had many different types of shutters: *leaf, focal plane, guillotine*, etc. but modern motion picture film cameras almost universally use a *spinning mirror*. In its most basic form it is a half-circle (180°) so as it spins, when the mirror is out of the light path, light reaches the film and the image is projected onto the film emulsion. When the mirror rotates into the light path, it reflects the image up into the viewfinder. While the optical path is closed off by the shutter, the camera advances the film to the next frame. If the film was moving while light was coming in, the result would be a total blur.

Rolling Shutter and Global Shutter

Only a few digital cameras have this rotating mirror shutter; since the imaging medium (video sensor) doesn't need to move between frames as film does, it isn't really necessary. This results in smaller and lighter cameras, but it does have a drawback — video sensors don't necessarily expose the entire frame all at once. Instead, they scan the image up to down (or the opposite). For an object that is moving, it will have moved in the time between when the top of the frame was recorded and shutter closes. Figure 1.21 is an example.

This can have several negative results, including the *jello effect* —a smearing of the moving object or *partial exposure* with a very short duration light source such as a flash or lightning. There are some post production software fixes for this, but of course it is always better to avoid the need for this sort of repair. One approach to preventing this problem is to add a rotating shutter to the camera like the ones used in film cameras. This has the added benefit of providing an optical viewfinder instead of a video one — many cinematographers prefer to view the scene optically.

In video, what is called the shutter is not generally a physical device; it is how the pixels are "read." In general, CCDs have a *global shutter* and CMOS sensors have *rolling shutters*. A *global shutter* controls incoming light to all the photosites simultaneously. While the shutter is open, the sensor is collecting light, and after the shutter closes, it reads the pixel charges and gets the sensor ready for the next frame. In other words, the CCD captures the entire image at the same time and then reads the information after the capture is completed, rather than reading top to bottom during the exposure. Because it captures everything at once, the shutter is considered *global*. The result is an image with no motion artifacts. A *rolling shutter*, on the other hand is always active and "rolling." It scans each line of pixels from top to bottom, one at a time, which can result in the jello effect.

NOISE

Noise is not the same as *film grain* in appearance — some people make the mistake of trying to imitate the look of film by introducing video noise. There is always going to be some noise present in any electronic device — it's just an unavoidable consequence of the physics involved. It is especially a problem at the low end (darkest areas of the image). This is because as the actual signal (the image) gets lower in brightness, it becomes indistinguishable from the electronic noise. As we'll see in the chapter *Exposure*, some cameras are capable of giving warning signs when parts of the image are "in noise." Since noise is most visible in the darker areas of the image there are two consequences: first, an underexposed image will be noisy (just as happens with film negative) and second, at some point the level of noise overwhelms the detail in the image.

Figure 1.21. (Above) This famous picture by Jacques-Henri Lartigue is a vintage still photo of course, but it illustrates the problem of a shutter interacting with motion in the frame. The type of shutter on this camera traveled vertically from bottom to top so by the time the top part of the frame was exposed, the car had traveled a bit farther. This is the concept behind the "jello effect." The leaning spectators show us that he was panning the camera during the exposure.

Beyond this inherent background, the primary cause of noise becoming visible in the image is *gain*, which is electronic amplification. This can be a result of using a higher ISO, underexposing and compensating later or even by color compensation in white balance, which may result in certain color channels being amplified more than others. Charles Poynton, color scientist, consultant and writer, says "Sensitivity and noise are two sides of the same coin. Don't believe any specification that states one without the other. In particular, don't believe typical video camera specifications." A standard measure of noise is the *Signal to Noise* ratio (abbreviated *S/N* or *SNR*, which is usually expressed in *deciBels* (*dB*). As DP Art Adams succinctly puts it — "When it comes to sensors, you don't get anything for free."

ISO IN DIGITAL CAMERAS

ISO (*International Standards Organization*), refers to a number representing *sensitivity* — meaning how much light is needed to produce an acceptable image. Note the term "acceptable" — it is of course possible to shoot an image in very low light conditions and try to "fix it in post," but the result will usually be noisy, low resolution and with strange contrast ratios.

Cameras have a "native" ISO which is just the design parameter of the sensor — what the camera would ideally expose at without any alterations such as gain — which is nothing more than electronic amplification of the image signal. It is the amount of exposure that just fills the photosite, not over or underfilling them. When we express gain as *dB* (*deciBels*), every +6 dB increase represents a *doubling* of the level which means we can also express it in *f/stops*, as every increase in the f/stop equals a doubling of the exposure and a decrease of one stop cuts the exposure in half.

+6 dB = 1 f/stop of exposure

+12 dB = 2 f/stops of exposure

+18 dB = 3 f/stops of exposure

If +6 dB is like adding an f/stop, +3 dB is like adding a 1/2 stop of exposure and +2 dB is like adding 1/3 an f/stop.

The catch is that when you amplify the image signal you are also amplifying the noise, so turning up the gain inevitably results in a picture that is degraded, although camera makers have made huge strides and in most cases, small increases in gain still result in usable images. However, gain is to be avoided if possible.

As the Red camera company puts it, "With Red, the native ISO speed describes the recommended starting point for balancing the competing trade-offs of noise in the shadows and clipping in the highlights. This does not necessarily reflect anything intrinsic to a camera sensor itself or the performance of cameras by different companies. It is a reflection of the sensor design, signal processing and quality standards all in combination."

With cameras that shoot RAW, these changes to ISO are recorded as metadata and the real change in exposure takes place in post-production. High end Canon cameras are slightly different in this regard as we'll discuss later. DP Art Adams say this about native ISO for his own uses: "What I do is look at the noise floor on a waveform monitor. I have some idea of how much noise I like, and I can judge noise pretty well just by looking at the thickness of the trace on a Leader or Tektronix waveform monitor [See Figures 1.22 and 1.23]. I let the camera warm up, put the body cap in, do whatever black compensation operation is necessary to minimize noise (*APR* on the

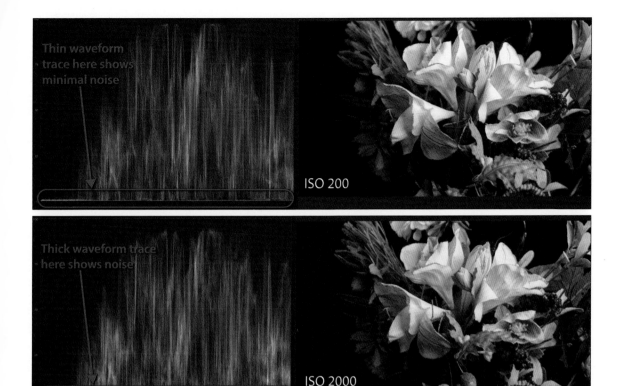

Thin waveform trace here shows minimal noise

ISO 200

Thick waveform trace here shows noise

ISO 2000

F55/F5, for example), and look at the thickness of the waveform trace at different ISOs.

When I find an ISO that gives me the width of trace that I want I verify the noise level by putting a lens on the camera, underexposing the image and looking at the shadow noise. If I'm happy with that level of noise then that's my new ISO. Where ISO is placed is based entirely on noise level and personal taste. The gain coming off the sensor may seem to indicate it is "natively" 160, or 200, or 320, but if the signal is quiet enough you can put middle gray wherever you want by changing the ISO around and seeing if you like the noise level."

DP David Mullen poses this question: "As sensors and signal processing gets quiet enough, the issue of 'native' sensitivity matters less than what is the highest ISO rating you can give it before the noise becomes objectionable. The [Red] *Dragon* sensor is quieter than the [Red] *MX* sensor so it can be rated faster than the MX sensor, but since there is more highlight information at low ISOs compared to the MX, it probably has a lower 'native' sensitivity. So should a sensor that can be rated faster with less noise be called less sensitive? Sort of makes you question what 'native sensitivity' actually means."

IR AND HOT MIRROR FILTERS

Some cameras require an additional *IR* (*Infrared*) or *Hot Mirror* filter when shooting outdoors. The reason for this goes beyond just lighting conditions. Sensors can sometimes see things humans can't perceive, such as an excessive amounts of Infrared. In normal circumstances, IR is a small proportion of the light hitting a sensor. In low light situations, this amount of infrared at the sensor is overpowered by the rest of the spectrum and isn't a problem.

Figure 1.22. (Top) A frame from a Red camera at ISO 200. Minimal noise is shown at the bottom of the display, especially in the far left part of the waveform monitor — in the black and near black regions of the frame, the waveform trace is very thin. For more on understanding waveform monitors, see the chapter *Measurement*.

Figure 1.23. (Above) The same shot with the ISO cranked up to 2000 on the Red. The waveform trace in the black regions is now a very thick line, indicating lots of noise in the darkest areas. Some noise is also visible in the other parts of the frame; shown by a slight fuzziness throughout the waveform trace. There is noise throughout the frame, it just shows up more in the darkest parts of the shot.

This is an enlarged portion of the original frame and even so, the noise is barely visible. This illustrates the usefulness of the waveform monitor in checking for noise. On a large monitor and certainly on a cinema screen, the noise will be visible.

Unfortunately, when shooting outdoors, *Neutral Density (ND)* filters are usually necessary to reduce the amount of light to a manageable level. Although ND filters are designed (ideally) to introduce no coloration (that's why they are *neutral* density) they usually do allow infrared light to pass. Unfortunately, despite the best efforts of filter makers and some highly advanced production techniques, few ND filters are truly 100% neutral. Testing before you shoot is advised.

Manufacturers of film stocks made very low sensitivity (low ISO) films for these situations — as low as 50 ISO. Digital cinema cameras rarely go this low. Traditional HD cameras often had an ND filter wheel and a color filter wheel to accommodate different lighting color situations and light levels. While ND filters work fine for reducing the amount of light to a workable level, they have a drawback — they don't affect infrared equally. The result is that the proportion of visible light compared to IR is changed; the ratio of IR is higher than normal. This can result in red contamination of some colors. IR filters and hot mirror filters are similar in their effect but not exactly the same thing. A hot mirror is a *dichroic filter* that works by reflecting infrared light back, while allowing visible light to pass.

The choice of an IR filter is camera-specific, as different cameras have different IR sensitivities. Camera with built-in NDs typically have filters that are designed with that camera's IR response in mind. That doesn't mean that IR filtration is never necessary for cameras with internal NDs, or when shooting without NDs: some cameras show noticeable IR pollution (especially under IR-rich tungsten light) even with no ND. As always, it's worth testing before an important shoot with an unfamiliar camera. A reddish color on black fabrics is often a telltale, but not always, some cameras show IR pollution more in the blue channel.

the digital image

COOKIE DOUGH AND THE HISTORY OF HD

There are two basic methods used in acquiring video data. The analogy is cookie dough: do you want it raw or baked? They are both delicious and satisfying but in very different ways. First a bit of history — many people are surprised to learn that *High Definition* (*HD*) actually started as long ago as the 1970s but back then it was *analog HD* video. In the 1980s, several companies introduced video equipment that recorded digitally, followed soon by digital cameras which comprised what we now know as High Def video.

DIGITAL *HD*

The traditional HD camera method was used from the introduction of digital HD until the "modern" cameras were introduced in the first few years of the 21st century. We'll call the older units "HD cameras" and refer to the "HD signal" — these include the *CineAlta* series, starting with classic *Sony F900*, Panasonic's *Varicam* and many others. These cameras recorded High Def video, which is only imprecisely defined. In general, HD video is considered to be anything with a resolution greater than SD (480 lines in the US, Japan and a few other countries; 576 in most of the rest of the world). This would include 720P video such as Panasonic's *Varicam*, but for the most part, HD is 1920x1080 — 1920 pixels horizontally and 1080 pixels vertically.

In most cases, these cameras recorded to specially formulated video tape in various sizes; the exceptions included XDCam which recorded onto video disks and then later models recorded onto flash memory cards (Sony *SxS* cards).

THE KNOBS AND ULTRA HIGH DEF

As we touched on briefly in the first chapter, the distinguishing feature of these HD cameras was that they had lots of what color scientist Charles Poynton calls "the knobs" (Figure 2.1) In other words, by using knobs, selection wheels, switches and menus, the operator has a great deal of control over the image — in ways that are going to be the subject of this and later chapters *Digital Color* and *Image Control & Grading*. All of these image manipulations: ISO, gamma, frame rate, shutter speed, color balance, color matrix, black gamma, knee control and others were applied to the video signal and recorded directly to the tape or other media. As we know, this method is called "baked in" — the recorded signal had all of those changes that were made in the camera — changing them later ranged from difficult to very difficult, sometimes impossible.

The next major step in video had several aspects: one of them was resolutions greater than 1920x1080 — the big jump was to 4K video. Now that monitors and projectors have standardized at the 16:9 aspect ratio (a result of the second generation of HD), in order to achieve a wider format such as 2.35:1 or 2:1, for example, you have to reduce the height of the frame (so-called letterboxing). Since the height of the frame is not necessarily constant, the horizontal dimension is a better way to define resolution. With this method, HD at 1920 is just a bit under 2K. This new generation of video is acquired primarily at 4K (at least for now) and it is technically called *UHD* (*Ultra High Def*). In this book, any reference to High Def or HD means the older standard of 1920x1080 recorded with or without changes "baked in."

HAVE SOME RAW

The second major aspect of UHD/RAW is that in most cases the various manipulations of the image are not recorded "baked in." In fact, most UHD cameras have far fewer knobs and switches and their menus are substantially simpler (with the exception of the original Red One, which had a hugely complex menu structure). To clarify, these cameras offer almost all of the image options that HD cameras did; the big difference is that instead of being recorded as part of the signal, these image transformations are recorded separately from the video stream — as metadata, which means "data about data."

It's a simple concept: instead of actually changing the video, you just add some "notes" to it which basically say to the editing software or monitor "when you show this clip, add these modifications to it." See the chapter *Metadata & Timecode* for a more in-depth discussion of metadata. When video is recorded this way, it is called RAW. As previously noted, the capital letters have no meaning as an acronym, it is just a convention that has been adopted by most of the companies that use it, such as RedRAW, ArriRAW. Some things cannot be handled this way and are still part of the recorded image, these include frame rate, bit depth and shutter angle.

DEFINITIONS

Before we go on, let's clarify the terminology. The terms *RAW*, *uncompressed* and *video* sometimes get used a bit loosely. RAW isn't really video yet, not until it is processed in some way, either in the DSP or in some other software or hardware later down the line. It isn't video because it is not really viewable. At any stage during processing, one or more types of compression may be applied to the data. Saying that the images are uncompressed is separate from whether it is RAW or not. For example, *log encoding* is a form of compression — it is frequently applied to RAW data, but not necessarily.

So what is the precise definition of RAW? Surprisingly, there can be some debate particularly when it comes to specific cameras and how they work. Art Adams puts it this way, "The key thing to remember is that 'raw' means that the actual RGB values from the photosites are preserved: they aren't converted into pixels, or deBayered or demosaiced, which would happen if you stored the footage as *ProRes*, for example. Log and linear don't really factor into whether footage is classified as RAW or not. All that's happening is that the luminance information is being completely retained (linear) or compressed in a way that is visually lossless to a great extent (log).

Figure 2.1. (Left) An example of the "knobs" on a traditional HD video camera, a Sony F900. In this case they are switches, of course. In cameras that shoot RAW, these have largely been replaced by menu selections that control only the metadata, not the baked in image.

Figure 2.2. (Above) Another example of "the knobs" — a Sony *Camera Control Unit*, commonly known as a *Paintbox*. With it nearly all of the camera functions can be controlled, including gamma, knee, detail, white balance, black balance, master black and iris. Since this was for traditional HD cameras, once these functions were set on the camera, they were "baked in" to the recording.

The information retained has not been demosaiced. The only thing that makes footage 'raw' is if the color information is still in an un-demosaiced state. Beyond that... well, there's a lot going on under the hood in each raw format. The idea some people have, that all the sensor information is being stored in its entirety in some pristine state, simply never happens. And it certainly never happens in a way that's completely common to all formats."

Mitch Gross of Convergent Design takes a similar view, "To me the most important bit of info is that RAW just means 'non-deBayered.' It may have a gamma curve applied, it could be linear or log, it could have a white point set, it may have gains applied (analog or digital), and it may be compressed. But if it isn't de-Bayered it can still be called RAW."

DIGITAL NEGATIVE

Think of RAW as a *digital negative*. For folks who didn't come up in the world of film imaging, this might take a bit of explaining. The film negative is neutral: it is only capable of recording what came in through the lens. Of course, the film emulsion has some characteristics that alter the image in some ways; mostly ways that the eye finds entirely pleasant. This means that when you make a print from the film negative you have a pretty wide range of creative choices. For those of you who have gone through the print phase of making a movie or commercial, you know the steps: you sit there with a print timer (a highly skilled individual who is an expert at film exposure and coloring — the equivalent of a video colorist) and make choices about each shot — the exposure and color balance. Notice we don't say scene; it is shot by shot, because as hard as we try to be consistent from shot to shot, there are always going to be some variations.

Then a print is made and the DP and director sit through another timing session where they again ask for some variations for creative reasons. Usually by the third print, all three are agreed on a creative end point for the project. At that time, a print is made; or actually an *internegative* is made for the print output for theatrical release. But the thing is, that is not necessarily the end of the road. You can always go back to that original negative and make a whole new print with different creative decisions. Undoubtedly, you have heard of films that have been restored from the original negative. We've all seen magnificent restorations of classic films such as *Gone With The Wind*, *Casablanca* and others. Now here's the tricky question: when a new generation of colorists go back to that original negative and make a new print, how do we know that they are printing the film in accord with the artistic intentions of the cinematographer who shot the film? After all, that DP was the one who was hired and entrusted with making the images (in collaboration with the director and art director, of course) and they are the ones whose artistic intentions must be respected, of course (thankfully, the age of "colorizing" *Casablanca* has passed!) Well, the short answer is we don't. Fortunately, the people who engage in these sorts of restorations are almost always the kind of people who go to great lengths to preserve the intentions of the original artists.

However, to a great extent the DP on a film project can include their artistic intents into the negative. They can do this with exposure and with color; both color balance overall and with individual color within the scene. There are some "tricks" that DPs use to ensure that people later down the line can find it difficult to mess with their images; these include having some "reference white" and "reference black" in the frame. So what does this mean for those of us who now shoot RAW video? Can people further down the line alter our artistic intentions by changing the image in substantial ways? You bet they can.

What does this change? The basic idea of RAW is to simply record all of the data that comes off the sensors, essentially unchanged. Metadata is recorded at the same time and it can record artistic intentions about color, tonal range and so on, but metadata can be changed or just ignored later down the line..

Like a photographic negative, a RAW digital image may have a wider dynamic range or color gamut than the eventual final image format is capable of reproducing, as it preserves most of the information of the captured image. The purpose of RAW image formats is to save, with minimum loss of information, data sent directly from the sensor, and the conditions of the image capture — the metadata, which can include a wide variety of information such as white balance, ISO, gamma, matrix, color saturation and so on. The metadata can also include archive information such as what lens was used, what focal length, f/stop, time of day and (if a GPS unit is used at the time of shooting) the geographic coordinates of the shooting and other slate data such as name of the production, etc.

RAW image files can in essence fill the same role as film negatives in traditional film-based photography: that is, the negative is not directly usable as an image, but has all of the information needed to create a final, viewable image. The process of converting a RAW image file into a viewable format is sometimes called *developing* the image, in that it is analogous with the motion picture film process that converts exposed negative film into a projectable print.

With a motion picture negative, you can always go back to the original. If you shot the negative right to begin with, you can make substantial changes to the print, now or in the future. If five years from now, you decide you want to make the look of the print very different (within the limits of what is possible in making a film print, which is far more limited than what you can do with the digital image). You can do the same with RAW; it is archival and non-destructive, and you can manipulate the image later. Such alterations at the time of processing, color correction or anywhere along the line result in fewer artifacts and degradations of the image; this includes compensating for under or over-exposure. A drawback is that RAW files are usually much larger than most other file types; which means that cameras often need to impose lossy or lossless compression to avoid ridiculously large sizes of captured files.

A widespread misconception is that RAW video is recorded completely uncompressed — most cameras record it with *log encoding*, a type of compression, but there are some exceptions. Both with film negative and shooting RAW, it is important to remember that while you have a wide degree of control over the image, it is still not magic — avoid the myth of believing that we can "fix it in post." There are many types of RAW files — different camera companies use variations on the idea. RAW files must be interpreted and processed before they can be edited or viewed. The software used to do this depends on which camera they were shot with. Also, RAW files shot with a Bayer-filter camera must be *demosaiced/debayered* (the mosaic pattern imposed on the image by the Bayer filter must be interpreted), but this is a standard part of the processing that converts the RAW images to more universal JPEG, TIFF, DPX, DNxHD, ProRes or other types of image files.

One problem with RAW is that every company has their own version of it and there is no standardization. Adobe has been trying to suggest that the industry should come together to agree on common standards — a common file format to store their proprietary RAW information in a way that wouldn't require special apps or plugins. The Red company calls their version *Redcode RAW (.r3d)*, Arri calls theirs *ArriRAW*, Adobe uses *CinemaDNG* (digital negative); Arri-RAW is similar to CinemaDNG which is also used by the *Black Magic* cameras. DNG is based on the TIFF format, which is a very high quality image with little or no compression. Standardization is also hampered by the fact that companies want to keep their proprietary information secret and don't publish the inner workings of their RAW formats.

Some Sony cameras also shoot 16-bit RAW which is part of what they call *SRMaster* recording. Although RAW formats vary from company to company, there are some commonalities, mostly based on an ISO standard which includes:

- A header file with a file identifier, an indicator of byte-order and other data.
- Image metadata which is required for operating in a database environment or content management system (CMS).
- An image thumbnail in JPEG form (optional).
- Timecode, Keycode, etc, as appropriate.

Specifics of RAW will be discussed in the chapter *Codecs & Formats*.

CHROMA SUBSAMPLING

Most camera sensors operate with red, green and blue (*RGB*) information. An RGB signal has potentially the richest color depth and highest resolution, but requires enormous bandwidth and processing power and creates huge amounts of data. Engineers realized that there is also a great deal of redundant information: every channel contains both *luma* data (the black-and-white gray tone values of the pictures) and *chrominance* data: the color values of the image. Color scientists long ago discovered that most of the information we get from an image is actually in the black-and-white values of the picture, which is why in most situations we get almost as much from a black-and-white picture as we do from a color picture of the same scene — it's just inherent in how the eye/brain works. Each channel in an RGB video signal carries essentially the same gray tone values, so you are eating up bandwidth and processing power with three redundant black-and-white images.

Another basic fact of human vision is that a great deal of our vision is centered largely in the green region of the spectrum. This means that the green channel in video is similar to the luminance information. You can try this yourself in any image processing software: take an average photo and turn off the red and blue channels. The green channel by itself is usually a fairly decent black-and-white photo. Now try the same with the other channels — they are often weak and grainy by themselves.

Chroma subsampling is the name for a form of data reduction that works with *color difference* signals. In this technology, the *luma* signal (black-and-white brightness or *luminance*) is sampled at a different rate than the *chrominance* signal (color). Chroma subsampling is denoted as $Y'CbCr$. Y' is the *luma* component while Cr and Cb are the color difference signals. Y represents *luminance*, which is actually a measure of lighting intensity, not video brightness levels, while Y'

is *luma*, which is the weighted sum of the red, green and blue components and is the proper term to use in this context. "Weighted" as it refers to luma means that it is *nonlinear*.

You will notice that there is no *Cg* or *green* channel. It is reconstructed from the other channels. Green doesn't need to be sent as a separate signal since it can be inferred from the luma and chroma components. The editing, color correction software, or display device knows the distribution of the luminance gray tones in the image is from the Y' component. Very crudely put — since it knows how much of the image is blue and red, it figures the rest must be green so it fills it in. It's actually quite a bit more complicated than this, but that's the basic idea.

For luma (grayscale values), the engineers chose a signal that is 72% G, 21% R, and 7% B, so it's mostly comprised of green, but it's a weighted combination of all three colors that roughly corresponds to our own perception of brightness (see *Digital Color* for more on human vision). To simplify a bit, the color information is encoded as B-Y and R-Y, meaning the red channel *minus* luminance and the blue channel *minus* luminance. This is called *color difference* encoded video — the Cb and Cr. There are subtle technicalities, but none that we need to go into in this brief overview. This method of encoding is sometimes called *component video*; it reduces the requirements for transmission and processing by a factor of 3 : 2.

Because the human visual system perceives differences and detail in color much less than in gray scale values, lower-resolution color information can be overlaid with higher-resolution luma (brightness) information, to create an image that looks very similar to one in which both color and luma information are sampled at full resolution. This means that with chroma subsampling, there can be more samples of the luminance than for the chrominance. In one widely used variation of this, there are twice as many luma samples as there are chroma samples, and it is denoted 4:2:2, where the first digit is the luma channel (Y') and the next two digits are the chroma channels (Cb and Cr) — they are sampled at half the rate of the luminance channel.

Video that is 4:4:4 has the same chroma sampling for color channels as for luminance. There are other variations — for example, Sony's *HDCam* cameras sample at 3:1:1. You may occasionally see a fourth digit, such as 4:4:4:4; in this case the fourth number is the *alpha channel*, which contains transparency information. There are others as well, such as 4:2:0 — see Figure 2.3 for a visual representation of these varieties. For our purposes, we can say that a 4:4:4 signal has more data. In any case, a 4:4:4 signal is going to be better in color depth and possibly in resolution as well — with the proviso that as always, it requires more processing power and storage. Some widely used chroma subsampling schemes are listed here. There are of course, more variations than we can go into here.

4:4:4 — All three components are sampled at 13.5 MHz, meaning there is no compression of the chroma channels, however the signal might still be compressed in other ways.

4:2:2 —Four samples of luminance associated with 2 samples of Cr, and 2 samples of Cb. The luminance sampling rate is 13.5 MHz; color component rates are 6.75 MHz. The active picture bit-rate is 167 MBp/s for 8-bit, and 209 MBp/s for 10-bit sampling.

4:1:1 - The luminance sample rate here is still 13.5 MHz, but the chrominance sample rate has dropped to 3.375 MHz. The active picture bit-rate for both 4:2:0 and 4:1:1 is 125 MBp/s.

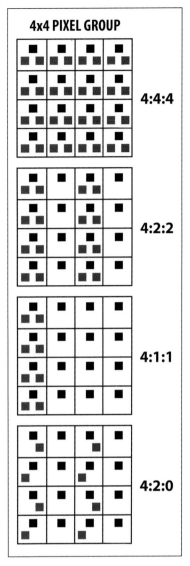

4x4 PIXEL GROUP

4:4:4

4:2:2

4:1:1

4:2:0

Figure 2.3. The operation of various forms of *subsampling*. The black blocks represent the luminance channel, which is why there is no green channel.

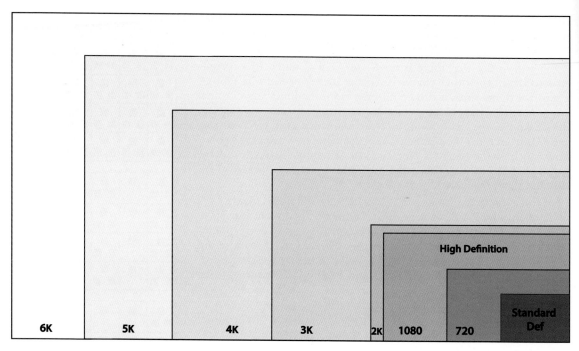

| 6K | 5K | 4K | 3K | 2K | 1080 | 720 | Standard Def |

Figure 2.4. The resolution of *Ultra-High Def* at 4K and above is vastly greater than *Standard Def* and even *High Def* (1920x1080).

4:2:0 – This is like 4:2:2, but doing what's called vertically subsampled chroma. This means that, while the luminance sampling rate is 13.5 MHz, and each component is still sampled at 6.75 MHz, only every other line is sampled for chrominance information.

TYPES OF VIDEO

In ancient times there were only a few varieties of video: basically *NTSC* (American system) and *PAL* (European system) and a variation on PAL used in France, parts of Africa and the Soviet sphere called *Secam*. The introduction of HD video and its acceptance worldwide has led to some standardization, but video itself — at least in the origination formats, comes in a variety of sizes and shapes.

HIGH DEF

Surprisingly, there is no hard and fast definition of what exactly "High Def" is. As a general usage, it is basically anything that has more resolution than SD video, which is 525 lines in NTSC and 625 lines in PAL. Thus 720 video is High Def (although not strictly considered HD by some broadcast organizations). Although there are many variations, the most commonly used high def formats are 1280x720 (720) and 1920x1080 (1080). The numbers refer to the number of pixels horizontally and vertically. As in standard def the suffix "P" indicates progressive while "i" indicates interlaced (which is no longer used). In broadcasting, 1920x1080 dominates for cable television, Blu-Ray discs and in television sets while 1280x720 is still sometimes used in broadband web-based distribution.

ULTRA HIGH DEF

While there are still many high def cameras being made and used, especially at the consumer level, the high end professional cameras have gone beyond 1920x1080. Most people refer to it as *Ultra High Def* (UHD). Some still just call these formats "high def" although this is not technically accurate. In any case, it is much more common to refer to the video by its resolution, such as *2K video, 4K* video and so on. (Figure 2.4)

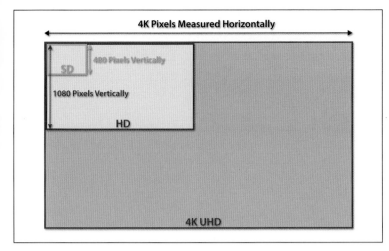

Figure 2.5. *Standard Def* and *High Def* digital video were generally referred to by their vertical dimension. For example 1920x1080 (*HD*) video is commonly called "1080." The problem with this is that video can be acquired and displayed with different vertical dimensions to achieve different aspect ratios. For this reason, *Ultra High Def* (*UHD*) is referred to by the horizontal dimension, such as 4K and 8K. As with many things digital, 4K is not exactly 4000, either in acquisition or display.

There is another change in the naming of video formats: "1080" and "720" refer to the *height* of the format. The problem is that the height of a frame is highly variable. It was a similar problem with 35mm film. While the width of 35mm film has remained unchanged from the time of Thomas Edison until today (with some small variations in the width of the image on that film, from Academy format up to Super35, which is really just a return to the *Silent Aperture* used in Edison's time), the height of the frame has changed a great deal — the result of a constant hunger for "wider" formats (Panavision, Cinemascope, 1.85:1, 2.35:1, etc.). None of these is actually wider film — they are all (with the exception of anamorphic, which is an optical trick, and 70mm which didn't last long as a theatrical format) the same width — what really changes is the height of the frame. As with *letterboxing* on television — the frame is made to appear wider by making it shorter. This applies to video as well, when you change the aspect ratio of the frame, you mostly just cut off the top and bottom.

For this reason, it makes more sense to use the width of the frame as nomenclature, which is made easier since video no longer really consists of scan lines (a vertical measurement only) but of pixels, which can be quantified as either height or width. Thus when we talk about 2K video (a widely used format in theatrical projection), it means a frame that is approximately 2,000 pixels wide (actually 2,048) while 4K video is 4,096 pixels wide. This means it doesn't get complicated (in terms of names) when you change the aspect ratio to a taller or shorter frame. Fortunately, the high def era has also brought about a wider standardization of aspect ratio: 16x9 is almost universal in television sets, in broadcast and on Blu-Ray discs and so on. This is a modern format and can more definitively replace the always changing film formats that were constrained by what was basically a late 19th/early 20th century implementation.

The presentation formats (theaters, televisions, disc players, etc.) need to be somewhat standardized — because millions of people who buy TVs and media players, or thousands of theater owners as well as post-production facilities, invest in the equipment and it needs to remain more or less stable for some time. The origination formats (cameras and editing hardware) can be more flexible. Just as theatrical movies were nearly all projected in 35mm — they were originated on 35mm film, 65mm, 16mm or high def video. Although there is a debate as to how much resolution is "enough" — there is an upper limit to how much fine detail the human eye can

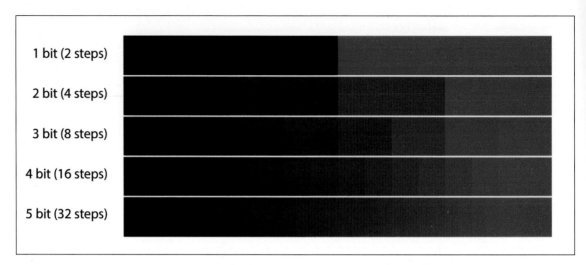

1 bit (2 steps)	
2 bit (4 steps)	
3 bit (8 steps)	
4 bit (16 steps)	
5 bit (32 steps)	

Figure 2.6. The more bits-per-channel, the more gradations of tone can be rendered.

perceive, there is no question that higher resolution capture formats are better for post production and final viewing. How far cameras will go in terms of resolution remains to be seen; digital still cameras have made huge advances in sensor resolution — some still cameras go as high as 80 megapixels per frame. What is sufficient resolution for image capture always entails understanding the final size for which it will be used: an image created strictly for a mobile phone clearly does not make the demands on resolution that are involved for something that is going to be shown on a large theatrical screen. Even when considering screen size, the viewing distance is a crucial factor. To really appreciate (and perceive) ultimate image resolution, it is necessary to sit no more than two to three screen heights away from the display/screen. This means that if the screen is 20' high, for example, then the ideal viewing distance would be less than 60' away, so always have a tape measure with you at the movies.

It is important to distinguish between the resolution of an image (how good it is at portraying fine detail) and other factors such as the brightness range it can represent: they are different factors and while they often improve side-by-side as manufacturers develop their technology, they are not necessarily connected. Along with dramatic increases in resolution with the introduction of 4K and higher video, the improvements in the brightness range video cameras can handle has been equally revolutionary.

BIT DEPTH

Bit depth is not the same thing as *bit rate*. *Depth* refers to how many bits of data are recorded *per pixel*. We'll discuss this more extensively in the chapter *Codecs & Formats*. By way of example, most consumer video equipment is 8 bit, while high-end professional equipment may be 12 or 14 bits per pixel. This gives you more to work with and has huge implications for workflow, ability to achieve the image you want to and issues such as dynamic range and color accuracy but it also means that you have a lot more data to deal with. One thing to watch out for is that bit depth is counted in two different ways. One of them is bits total and the other is bits-per-channel, which includes the Red, Green and Blue channels and, in some cases, also the Alpha channel which is transparency data.

Deep Color refers to anything above *True Color* (24 bit) and we're talking about *billions* of colors but at some point it is not really about how many colors, it is really about the grayscale reproduction and

Bits Per Channel	Steps Per Channel	Total Colors	Examples
1	2	8	
2	4	64	
3	8	512	
4	16	4,096	
5	32	3,2768	
6	64	262,144	
7	128	2,097,152	
8	256	16,777,216	DVD/Blu-Ray, 5D, TV, Computer
9	512	134,217,728	
10	1,024	1,073,741,824	ProRes, DNxHD(x), DPX 10-bit
12	4,096	68,719,476,736	DCP, ArriRAW, RedCode RAW
16	65,536	281,474,976,710,626	F65 RAW, DCDM, DSM

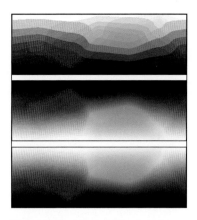

Figure 2.7. (Above) The top figure shows very low bits-per-channel and it exhibits visible *banding* because there are large jumps from one gradation of the color to the next (exaggerated for illustration here). Middle and lower figures show 16 and 24 bits per channel and the difference is obvious — there are much finer and more subtle changes in color.

Table 2.1. (Left) Bits-per-channel and how it affects the total number of colors that can be displayed. Think of the number of colors as the degree of subtle variations that are possible.

the ability to represent subtle changes in tone. When we refer to grayscale in a context like this we mean the changes of tone within a particular color channel.

BIT RATE

Bit rate is the measure of how many bits can be transferred per second. Higher bit rates generally mean better quality images but also much larger files. While media storage is measured in bytes (big "B") MegaBytes (MB), GigaBytes (GB), TeraBytes (TB), PetaBytes (PB) and perhaps ExaBytes (EB), data rates are measures in bits per second (small "b"). Several bit rates are used in serial digital video: For (archaic and outdated) standard definition applications, as defined by SMPTE 259M, the possible bit rates are 270 Mb/s, 360 Mb/s, 143 Mb/s and 177 Mb/s. 270 Mb/s is the most commonly used. For high-def applications requiring greater resolution, frame rate, or color depth than the HD-SDI interface can provide, the SMPTE 372M standard defines the *dual link interface*. As the name suggests, this interface consists of two SMPTE 292M (HD-SDI) connections operating in parallel. The dual link interface supports 10-bit, 4:2:2, 1080P formats at frame rates of 60 Hz, 59.94 FPS, and 50 FPS, as well as 12-bit color depth, RGB encoding, and 4:4:4 color sampling. 3G-SDI transmits the same 2.97 Gb/s data as Dual Link but is able to do it with only one connection. There is also Quad-Link SDI for 4K video. For more on SDI, see the chapter *Data Management*.

FRAME RATES

So film is 24 frames per second and video is 30, right? It would be great if the world was that simple, but unfortunately it's not. Yes, film has been shot at 24 frames per second since about 1929. Before that it was more commonly shot at from about 14 to 18 FPS, but since cameras were mostly hand cranked before then, it was really just an approximation. It was the introduction of sync sound that brought about standardization: in order for sound to be synchronized, cameras and projectors have to be running at a constant rate. Thomas Edison maintained that 46 FPS was the slowest frame rate that wouldn't cause eye strain. In the end 24 FPS was chosen as the standard. It was not, as is often said, for perceptual or audio reasons. Interestingly, some filmmakers now believe that 48 FPS is the ideal frame rate, while others advocate frame rates of 60 FPS and even 120 FPS.

When video was invented, 30 FPS was initially chosen as the standard rate, to a large extent because the power supply of the US runs at a very reliable 60 *hertz* (cycles per second or *Hz*) and electronic synchronization is a fundamental part of how video works both in cameras and on TV sets. In Europe, on the other hand, 25 FPS was chosen as the television standard because their electrical systems run at 50 Hz, which is simpler in many ways.

The intention to run video at 30 FPS soon ran into problems, it turned out with color that there was interference with the subcarrier signal. To solve the problem, engineers shifted the frame rate slightly to 29.97. As a result of this, when 24 FPS film is converted to video, the actual frame rate turns out to be 23.976. Some post people make the point that 23.98 (the rounded off value) is not the same as 23.976 in that some software applications (particularly Adobe products) handle them in slightly different ways.

You will also see such frame rate designations as 60i or 30P. These refer to *interlaced* or *progressive* video. Again going back to the old days of NTSC video, the engineers decided that the televisions of the day would let the eye see the top of the frame as blank as the electronic scan got down toward the bottom of the frame, causing visible flicker. To solve this, they had the scan skip to every other odd-numbered line, then start over again at the top and do the even lines. This is called *interlaced* video. With modern displays, this is no longer necessary, as they don't use an electron beam scanning across the screen to produce the image, so now video is nearly all *progressive*. Also, interlaced video was difficult to rescale or process in postproduction; an important factor in abandoning it for progressive.

THE FILM LOOK VS. THE VIDEO LOOK

Film at 24 FPS has a distinctive look that most people consider to be cinematic in appearance; on the other hand, 30 FPS has a "video" look. The primary reason for this is that we have become accustomed to 24 frames per second. In reality, when we see film projected, we are seeing 48 FPS. This is because projectors have a blade which interrupts each frame and makes it the equivalent of two frames. Film also has an impressionistic feel — it doesn't actually show us every detail. For this reason it has been the practice for some time in video to shoot dramatic material at 24 FPS and sports at 30 FPS (actually 23.98 or 29.97).

HIGH FRAME RATE

High Frame Rate (HFR) for distribution is still in the trial stage, however it was tried many years ago in film. *Showscan*, developed by effects wizard Douglas Trumbull, ran 70mm film at 60 FPS; if you've ever seen it, you know it is an amazing experience. *The Hobbit* was the first major studio example of a film shot and shown at a high frame rate, in this case 48 FPS. The future of HFR remains to be seen, as does the future of 3D.

ULTRA HIGH SPEED

One type of camera dominates the high speed market: the *Phantom* line of cameras, which are capable of frame rates up to a remarkable 10,000 frames per second plus, resulting in some amazing footage. The result is obvious — high speed camera jobs require far more storage space for the data, with an equivalent increase in the amount of time needed to download, transcode and make output drives. Extremely high frame rates can only be sustained for a few seconds of recording time.

Figure 2.8. A *Phantom Flex* high speed camera being prepared for a dolly shot. The camera is capable of frame rate up to 1,445 FPS at 2.5K resolution and up to 10,750 FPS at lower resolution. (Courtesy of *Love High Speed*).

A LITTLE MATH REVIEW

We need to do a quick review of some of the very basic math and terminology we need to know to understand video. You'll probably already know most of this, but it never hurts to review. Don't be afraid, it's not nearly as scary as it seems. Most of it is actually surprisingly simple.

CARTESIAN COORDINATES

Just about everything we'll discuss about video signals can be expressed as a 2D or 3D diagram with co-ordinates. They are called *Cartesian co-ordinates* after their inventor, philosopher *René Descartes* (Figure 2.9). The simple version is a two axis diagram where X is the horizontal axis and Y is the vertical axis. In a three-dimensional version, the third axis is Z. Where they meet is called the *origin* or (0,0,0). The diagram may or may not have negative values, which are down from the origin (negative Y values) or the left of the origin (negative X values); the same applies to the Z dimension. It's important to label what each axis represents and what the units are — they can be 0 to 1 or 0 to 10,000 or whatever you want: *volts, candelas-per-square-meter, pizzas*.

POWER FUNCTION

The *power function* is important in video; you might also know it as "to the power of," or the *exponent*. It is represented as a smaller number raised to the power number, such as 3^2 which "three squared" or "three to the power of two." In this example, 3 is the *base* and 2 is the *exponent*. It means that the base (3) is multiplied by itself once, resulting in 9. An exponent of 2 is called "squared." An exponent of 3 (as in $5^3 = 125$) is called "cubed." Figure 2.10 show the graph of two powers: functions X^2 and $X^{1/2}$.

The *base* can be any number, positive or negative, and so can the *exponent*. A negative exponent is a little different — it results in a number smaller than the base. For example, $10^{-1} = .1$ and $10^{-6} = 0.000001$. Plotting power functions on a graph, we find that a positive power function is a line that curves upward and an exponent of less than one produces a line that curves downward.

Figure 2.9. The Cartesian co-ordinate system can represent values in two or three dimensions.

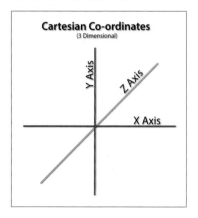

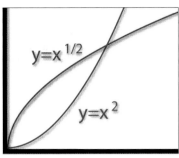

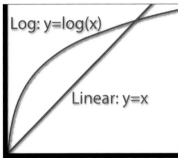

Figure 2.10. (Above, top) Two examples of *power functions* or *exponents*.

Figure 2.11. (Above, bottom) *Linear* vs. *log* functions. Linear is a straight line; x=y. The log function results in a curve that changes slope.

Figure 2.12. (Right, above) Trying to graph powers of ten is almost impossible because the jumps are so large.

Figure 2.13. (Right, below) Portraying the same series of numbers by using the *log* of each number results in manageable and easily readable graphs. This had enormous implications for data storage. In this very simple example, the log of 10 is 2, the log of 100 is 3, and so on.

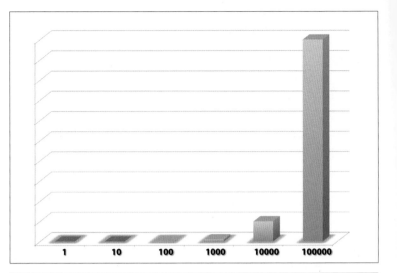

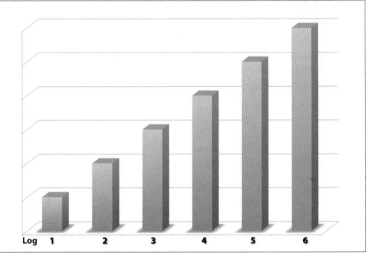

Logs

With a series of numbers, it often happens that the numbers get very large very quickly, which makes them hard to deal with and certainly hard to graph. A simple additive series such as 1, 2, 3, 4, 5, 6, etc. would be pretty easy to graph. On the other hand, the series 10^1, 10^2, 10^3, 10^4, 10^5, 10^6, etc. would be very difficult to graph. It goes 10, 100, 1000, 100,000, 1,000,000 (Figure 2.12). If we make a graph that can accommodate the value of 10^8 for example, then the lower values would be impossibly small to read. If we make it so that the lower values are easy to read, then the larger values would be "off the chart." The reality is that we graph and visualize things largely based on what will fit on a sheet of paper.

Scientists and engineers use *logarithms*. The *log* of a number (in base 10) is the exponent needed to raise 10 to that number. For example the log of 1000 is 3, because 10^3 = 1000; this is in base 10, meaning that 10 is the base number. There are, of course, other bases for logs, such as binary logarithm base = 2, often used in computer science. In our graphing example above, our graph in log base 10 would go 1, 2, 3, 4, 5, 6 — a whole lot easier to graph! (Figure 2.13). It makes many calculations much easier as well. Logarithms are now a huge part of video recording, due their power to "compress" large numbers and also because human vision operates in a logarithmic way.

Scalar Multiplication of a Matrix

$$2 \cdot \begin{bmatrix} 1 & 8 & -3 \\ 4 & -2 & 5 \end{bmatrix} = \begin{bmatrix} 2 \cdot 1 & 2 \cdot 8 & 2 \cdot -3 \\ 2 \cdot 4 & 2 \cdot -2 & 2 \cdot 5 \end{bmatrix} = \begin{bmatrix} 2 & 16 & -6 \\ 8 & -4 & 10 \end{bmatrix}$$

Dot Product Multiplication of Two Matrices

$$A = \begin{bmatrix} 1 & 2 \\ 3 & 4 \end{bmatrix}, \quad B = \begin{bmatrix} a & b \\ c & d \end{bmatrix}$$

$$A \cdot B = \begin{bmatrix} 1 & 2 \\ 3 & 4 \end{bmatrix} \cdot \begin{bmatrix} a & b \\ c & d \end{bmatrix} = \begin{bmatrix} 1 \cdot a + 2 \cdot c & 1 \cdot b + 2 \cdot d \\ 3 \cdot a + 4 \cdot c & 3 \cdot b + 4 \cdot d \end{bmatrix} = \begin{bmatrix} a + 2c & b + 2d \\ 3a + 4c & 3b + 4d \end{bmatrix}$$

Figure 2.14. (Above) A simple 3x3 matrix.

Figure 2.15. (Left, above) *Scalar multiplication* of a matrix simply multiplies each component or *scales* it.

Figure 2.16. (Left, below) *Dot product multiplication* of *matrices* is a bit more complex, but it's still just simple arithmetic. In this example, there are two matrices: A and B, shown in the top row. The lower row shows the process of dot product multiplication of these two matrices.

MATRIX

A matrix is an ordered array of numbers arranged in rows and columns; each number (or symbol or expression) is called an *element* or an *entry* (Figure 2.14). We know it's a matrix because it is enclosed in brackets. A matrix is defined by how many rows and columns there are, such as a 2x3 matrix, or an 8x8 and so on.

There are many useful things you can do with matrices (which are a branch of *linear algebra*) but in the handling of video signals, the most common operation is to multiply two matrices. This is called *matrix multiplication* or a *dot product*. A matrix is denoted with a capital letter. *Scalar multiplication* is very simple. You multiply each element of the matrix by a scalar factor, in this example, 2 (Figure 2.15):

For our purposes, the operation most often used is the *dot product,* which is a little more complex. In this case the elements of the rows in the first matrix are multiplied with corresponding columns in the second matrix, as in this example (Figure 2.16). It looks a bit complex, but it's really just basic arithmetic. Most of the time when dealing with video, a 3x3 matrix is used, for the simple reason that we are generally dealing with three channels: Red, Green and Blue. As we will see later, this is directly related to the idea of matrix on a video camera, which is a way to control the color of the image.

MEASUREMENTS

It is important to know the terminology of various measurements we use in talking about video, light, data transmission/storage and exposure. Here's a quick review of some of the most commonly used metrics. In most cases, the *SI (metric units)* are used, with a few exceptions such as *foot-candles*, which are sometimes used by cinematographers who started in the film era. At one time, light meters measured only foot-candles and it was commonly used to discuss the lighting of a scene.

LIGHT

The measurement of light can get surprisingly complex, with metrics for *radiance, luminance, illuminance, luminous flux* and many more (Table 2.2). We don't need to go into all of these but there are some basic measurements that are essential to understand.

- *Foot-candle.* A foot-candle is the amount of light generated by one standard candle measured at one foot away. Classic light meters such as the *Spectra* measured in foot-candles.
- *Foot-lambert.* This is a non-SI unit. A *foot-lambert* is $1/\pi$ *candela-per-square foot*, or 3.426 *candela-per-square meter*.

1 Foot-candle = 10.76 Lumens/m^2
1 Foot-candle = 1 Lumen/ft^2
1 Lux = 1 Lumen/ m^2
1 Lux = 0.093 Foot-candles
1 Foot-lambert = 1 Lumen/ft^2
1 Foot-lambert = 0.3183 Candles/ft^2

Table 2.2. Commonly used light measurement values.

- *Lumen* is a measure of the total amount of visible light from a source. It is an SI unit.
- *Lux* is one lumen per square meter, so it is the SI equivalent of a *Foot-candle*. It is roughly one tenth of a *foot-candle*.
- *Candela*. An SI unit, it is the output of one standard candle.
- *Candela-per-square-meter* (*cd/m^2*) or *nits*. This is a measure of luminance. It is one candela spread over a square meter. Because *candelas-per-meter-squared* is a bit of a mouthful, the colloquial shorthand is the *nit* (*nt*) — from the Latin *nitere*, to shine.

METER, MILLIMETER, MICROMETER, NANOMETER

The *English system* of measurement (inches, feet, yards, etc.) which is no longer standard in England, or in any country except the US, Liberia and Burma; it is not much used in video (other than focus marks on lenses). The metric system (or more formally, *SI — Le Système International d'Unités*) is preferred for nearly every measurement, certainly in science and engineering. A *meter* (or *metre*) was originally one-ten millionth of the distance from the Equator to the North Pole — it is about 39 inches or very roughly a *yard*.

A meter can be divided into one hundred *centimeters* and a *centimeter* is divided into ten *millimeters*. Smaller than that are *micrometers* (1/1000 of a millimeter) and *nanometers* (1/1000 of a micrometer) which is *one-billionth* of a meter. Finally, ten *angstroms* make up one nanometer.

To get a grasp on these sizes, a millimeter is about the size of the lead in a pencil and a water molecule is about one nanometer in width and a human hair is roughly 75,000 nanometers (*nm*). We will most frequently encounter nanometers as they are used to describe wavelengths of light. For example, the range of human vision in wavelengths extends from about 390 to around 750 nanometers — we look at this more deeply in the chapter *Digital Color*.

MEASUREMENT OF TIME

Time is an element in video measurement as timing is critical to the video signal. In SI units, a *millisecond* is one-thousandth of a second, a *microsecond* is one millionth of a second and a *nanosecond* is one-billionth of a second.

DIGITAL

Everyone knows the *bit*, which is a digital/electrical state of on or off. It has only two possible values: 0 or 1, (at least until we get cameras that contain *quantum processors*). A *byte* is 8 bits which results in 256 possible combinations — 0 to 255. A byte doesn't have to be 8 bits but this is by far the most widely used implementation.

Of course a *kilobyte* is 1000 bytes (rounded off from 1024), a *megabyte* is 1000^2 or 1,000,000; *gigabyte* is 1000^3 or 1,000,000,000, *terabyte* is 1000^4 or 1,000,000,000,000 and a *petabyte* is 1000^5 (1000 *terabytes*, 10^{15} *bytes*) or 1,000,000,000,000,000. Individual frames of video now are frequently many megabytes in size and 500 megabyte and terabyte size hard drives are practically a minimum requirement. Finally a *digital word* is a defined number of bits used by a particular digital process, such as 16-bit, 32-bit or 64-bit. As an example, the *Cineon* video compression format developed by Kodak is based on 10 bits per channel, contained in a 32-bit *word*, with two bits not used.

Just to keep track of some symbols that are frequently used in video calculations, here's a quick review — the Greek letter, its English name and its most common usage in the context of video applications, formulas and calculations. Of course, in discussions of other subjects the same Greek letters will have different meanings.

α = Alpha (opacity)
γ = Gamma (gamma)
λ = Lambda (wavelength)
Δ = Delta (change or difference)
ρ = Rho (reflectance)
τ = Tau (transmittance)
Φ = Phi (flux)

DeciBels

A *deciBel* (*dB*) is a commonly used measure of power or intensity — most frequently *gain* (increase of a signal) or *attenuation* (decrease of a signal). It is a logarithmic scale. As an example: going from 10 dB to 20 dB is the same as increasing the power from 10 to 100; and from 20 to 30 is an increase from 100 to 1000. See Table 2.3.

A change in power by a factor of 10 is a 10 dB change. A change in the ratio by a factor of 2 is roughly 3 dB. DeciBels are used in, among other things, measuring noise in video sensors and, of course, audio.

Dynamic Range		
Factor (power)	deci-Bels	Stops
1	0	0
2	3.01	1
3.16	5	1.66
4	6.02	2
5	6.99	2.32
8	9.03	3
10	10	3.32
16	12.0	4
20	13.0	4.32
31.6	15	4.98
32	15.1	5
50	17.0	5.64
100	20	6.64
1,000	30	9.97
1,024	30.1	10
10,000	40	13.3
100,000	50	16.6
1,000,000	60	19.9
1,048,576	60.2	20
100,000,000	80	26.6

Table 2.3. Power, deciBels and stops compared in measuring dynamic range. F/stops are based on powers of 2 and deciBels are logarithmic.

measurement

MEASURING THE IMAGE

Measuring the video signal rose to a high art in the realm of television. Since the earliest days, a usable video signal depends on careful control of timing, amplitude and frequency. In order to make sure the equipment in the TV studio stayed up to spec and delivered a reliable image to home televisions, engineers developed sophisticated standards and tools for measuring and controlling them.

Analog video equipment in particular required constant maintenance and adjustment. Digital video has somewhat simplified parts of the process in terms of broadcast and maintaining video cameras but for us on the set, measurement of the video signal is important, especially when it comes to exposure and color. Video has always been unforgiving in terms of exposure error, even more so than film. New sensors and video formats have somewhat reduced these critical limits, but controlling how the scene is recorded is still critical to getting the best possible image.

Since the DIT is often something of the *video engineer* on the set, we're going to go into the technical aspects of the digital signal measurement and control a little more deeply than if this were purely a cinematography book. Figure 3.1 shows many of the tools available for this. There is, however, a great deal more to video engineering than can be covered within the scope of this book.

THE SIGNAL

We need to know when our signal is good and when it isn't. Fortunately there are some excellent tools that are readily available and should definitely be on every professional set in some form or another. They are the *waveform monitor* and the *vectorscope*. They are usually combined in the same unit as an external box. Also, many pro monitors have a waveform monitor display built in and nearly all types of editing and color correction applications have software waveforms and vectorscopes.

When shooting film, there is one tool that is, for the cinematographer, absolutely essential — the light meter. Indeed, a cinematographer can't do their job without it. It is still very important, but the waveform is also critical to doing the job properly. In some ways the light meter and the waveform do the same job, but the waveform monitor gives us so much more information as well. Let's look at them one at a time.

THE WAVEFORM MONITOR

On video shoots, the light meter is still useful, and sometimes essential — but the waveform monitor is also a reliable reference. Many cinematographers have returned to using the light meter as their primary tool, as is discussed in the chapter *Exposure*.

The waveform monitor can tell us "the truth" about our video even if our monitors (on the set or in the editing room) are not properly calibrated; or on location when viewing conditions are bad and it is difficult to get a good idea of the condition of the image even from a very good, well calibrated monitor.

In short, the waveform displays the *amplitude* of the video signal; this translates into the *brightness* or *luminance* of the signal. According to *Tektronix*, a leading manufacturer of video test equipment: "Many video facilities rely heavily on picture monitors for quality checks at various stages of production and distribution. A picture monitor, after all, displays the final product, the picture. It's a quick and easy means of ensuring that there are no obvious picture impair-

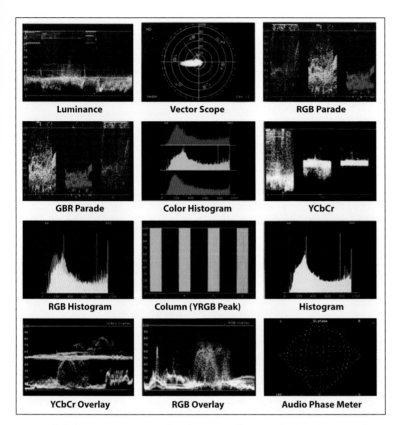

Luminance	Vector Scope	RGB Parade
GBR Parade	Color Histogram	YCbCr
RGB Histogram	Column (YRGB Peak)	Histogram
YCbCr Overlay	RGB Overlay	Audio Phase Meter

Figure 3.1. The types of measurement displays available on a Flanders monitor illustrates most types of measurements used in video plus an audio phase meter.

ments." But picture monitors do not tell the whole story. In fact, relying solely on picture monitors for video quality checks can be an open invitation to disaster. First of all, not every problem with the digital image is obvious on a picture monitor — especially on a small one. Minor problems are easily overlooked. Some cannot be seen at all. For example, a marginal video signal can still produce a seemingly "good" picture on a forgiving monitor. The rule of thumb is that the smaller the monitor, the better things look — often a dangerous illusion. On a small monitor, focus problems, for example, are rarely visible unless they are egregious. This can produce a false sense of security as signal degradations accumulate through various production stages.

To avoid such surprises, you need to look at more than pictures. You need to look at the video signals that convey the picture information through the various devices and interconnecting cables of

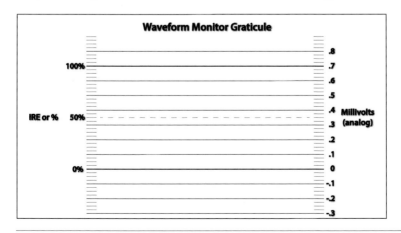

Figure 3.2. The graticule display of a standard HD waveform monitor. Technically, HD is measured in percentage, not *IRE* (*Institute of Radio Engineers*), but many people still refer to IRE values. For practical purposes, they are the same thing: for example, 100 IRE is the same as 100%. Millivolts is an analog (standard def) measurement.

measurement

Figure 3.3. (Right, above) SMPTE 75% color bars as they are seen on a video monitor. The primary and secondary colors are arranged in order of brightness. In the bottom row, second patch from the left is a 100% white patch.

Figure 3.4. (Right, below) The SD color bars as seen on a *waveform monitor,* which measures the voltage of the video signal. Also on the lower row at the right on the color bars is the PLUGE, which can be clearly seen on the waveform signal. Notice how the top line of colors nicely stair step down in brightness level.

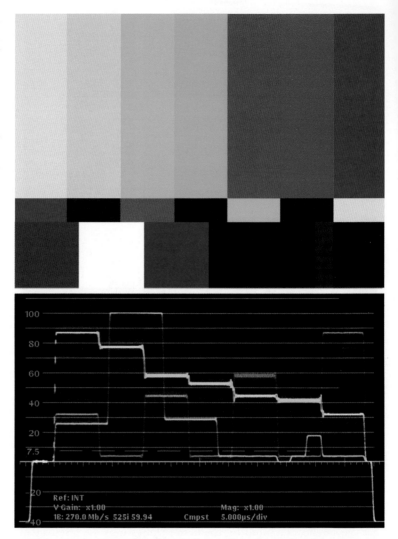

a video system. Specialized instruments have been developed to process and display these signals for analysis. The *waveform monitor* is an instrument used to measure luminance or picture brightness. The *vectorscope* is required for quality control of video chrominance, especially in more complex systems. When properly used, these tools allow you to spot signal problems before they become picture problems. You can make certain that the signals are optimal, rather than marginal and problematic. Plus, with regular video system testing, you can catch minor degradations and performance trends that indicate a need for system maintenance. This allows you to avoid costly failures, both in equipment and in program production or distribution." Waveform examples are shown in Figures 3.2 and 3.4.

TEST METHODOLOGY

Textronix, puts it this way: "There are two somewhat differing ideas used in testing video. Our approach is to test characteristics of a specific signal to ensure that it meets certain artistic or technical requirements. Or, we may test the characteristics of individual pieces of equipment or several pieces in the video signal path to determine that signal distortions introduced by this equipment are acceptable — or, at least, minimized." (Textronixs: *Video Measurements*).

GRATICULE

The *graticule* (Figure 3.2) of waveform monitors has markings for both IRE (*Institute of Radio Engineers*) units and *millivolts*. Technically, IRE units apply only to *composite* video signals: a value of zero IRE equaled zero volts and 100 IRE is peak white. The alternate scale is from -.3 to +.8 volts, with .7 volts being peak white video. In HD video we use percentage, but since 0 to 100 is the same in IRE or percent, it makes little practical difference and many people still say IRE when referring to signal level. Waveforms have markings above pure white (100%) and below pure black (0%) — there are relevant parts of the video signal below zero (in particular, the sync or blanking signal in analog composite video, which goes to minus 40 IRE).

FLAT OR FILTERED

The video signal has components in addition to luminance/brightness and the waveform monitor can also display *chrominance* or the color component signal. This is called *Y/C*, where Y is luminance and C is chrominance. Sometimes the chrominance signal can be useful but often it confuses the picture and makes it more difficult to see pure luminance, particularly when judging exposure, which is what we are most often doing with a waveform monitor on set. Viewing the waveform "flat" is easier to read as the chrominance signal is turned off.

CALIBRATION

The most fundamental adjustment is to make sure the wave display is properly positioned on the graticule. This is easily done with a test signal display — color bars generated by the camera (Figures 3.3 and 3.16) being the most readily accessible on the set.

LINES DISPLAYED

It is possible to select whether to have the display represent the entire picture or a single line of video, which the user can select. Some also allow the selection of a single field, which only applies to interlaced video, of course, as progressive video doesn't have fields.

LOOP THROUGH

Although most waveforms offer a loop-through, it is always a good idea to make the waveform monitor the first device in the chain, just as the picture monitor that the DP uses should never be placed down the line, where the picture accuracy might be degraded. Important caution: some scopes require *termination*, which means that a 75 ohm resistor has to be on the output of the last device in the chain.

PICTURE MONITOR

Many waveform monitors are switchable to be able to display the picture that is being measured; in some cases, the waveform display can be overlaid on top of the picture, in other cases, the picture can either be full screen or a small insert screen in the corner. While this isn't usually a high-quality image, it is useful to have it there.

EXTERNAL SYNC

All video requires time synchronization, it is critical to a usable video signal. The waveform monitor can take an external sync source, such as a separate *sync generator* (Figure 3.5), however they usually take sync from the video input they are displaying. The same applies to most video equipment: they can either generate their own sync signals or accept an externally generated one. In studios, there is sometimes

Figure 3.5. The *LockIt* box by *Ambient* is a widely used external sync generator for multi-camera uses. (Courtesy of Ambient Recording, GmbH).

a central sync pulse generator for all the equipment. This is often critical when shooting multiple cameras, especially when doing live switching from one camera to another — without sync, switching might produce a visible glitch. Multiple cameras can also be synced or *genlocked* by running a *BNC* cable from the *Genlock Out* port of the master camera to the *Genlock In* of a slave camera and daisy-chaining additional cameras.

SETUP/PEDESTAL

Setup or pedestal is really more of a standard def issue, but you should be aware of what it means. In NTSC video, the designers didn't have much faith in tube broadcasting equipment and televisions to properly display the very dark parts of an image. To counter this, they set "black" as 7.5 IRE, which is called the *pedestal* or *setup* level. It is no longer needed in the digital world but it is still used in some cases. Most software and waveform units allow setup to be turned on or off.

It is important to remember that when it comes to video, what constitutes "pure black" is not always the same. In 8-bit video, pure black is not zero, it is 16, although that is still 0%. It is the same at the top end: "pure white" is not 255, it is 235, and again, this is 100% white. Anything under 16 is called *superblack* and anything over 235 is *superwhite*. This is called *studio-swing*; when the full range from 0 to 255 is used, this is called *full range* or *extended range*. We'll discuss these concepts in more detail later on in the chapter *Linear, Gamma, Log*.

TYPES OF DISPLAY

Most waveform/vectorscope units and software displays are capable of showing the signal in several formats; all of which have their own uses and all are useful at some point or other in the production and post production workflow. Some units can show several types of display at the same time and this is user selectable to adapt to various situation and needs. Different technicians have their own favorites for each situation.

LUMINANCE

This is the most basic of displays: it is a trace of the luminance/ brightness/exposure of the picture (Figure 3.6). For setting exposure levels this is often the quickest to use. Pure luminance shows only the Y levels; some turn it off when exposure is the primary concern. Since it is capable of showing both luminance (Y) and chrominance (C), it is called Y/C display. Luminance display may not show when an individual color channel is clipping.

OVERLAY

Overlay shows the R,G,B traces but overlaid on each other. To make this readable, the traces are color coded to represent each channel in its own hue. (Figure 3.7)

RGB PARADE

Parade view shows the luminance of the red, green and blue components shown side by side (hence *parade*). Many technicians say that they "make their living with parade display." Its value is obvious: rather than just showing the overall luminance levels of the frame, it shows the relative values of the different color channels; this means that judgements can be made about color balance as well as just luminance. (Figure 3.8). It shows color balance and also when individual color channels are clipping.

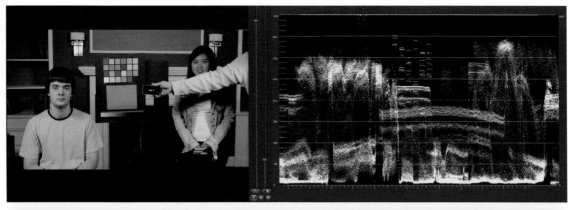

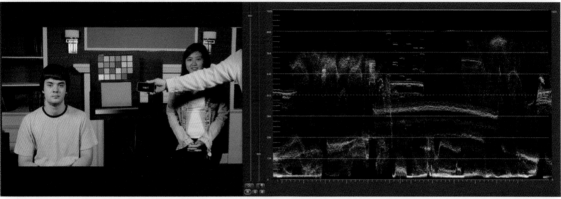

YCᴮCᴿ

This display is a bit trickier to interpret; it shows luminance first, followed by the color difference signals: Cb and Cr. Cb is blue minus luma and Cr is red minus luma. The two color signals will be markedly different from the left hand luma reading — it contains the entire luminance range of the picture, where the Cb and Cr only reflect whatever color might be in the picture. Since the luminance is removed from these two signals, they are much smaller than the luma signal. In practice it is seldom used on the set.

When interpreting the YCbCr signals, remember that in 8-bit black is 16, and white is 235 (although it may be converted internally for display), and you want your signal to fall in between those limits. YCbCr is both a color space and a way of encoding RGB information. The output color depends on the actual RGB primaries used to display the signal.

Figure 3.6. (Top) A frame shown with *luminance (luma)* only waveform — this is just the grayscale values of the image.

Figure 3.7. (Middle) *RGB overlay* which shows all three signals at the same time.

Figure 3.8. (Bottom), *RGB parade* is probably the most widely used display as it also shows the relative color balance of the scene and whether or not a particular channel is clipping

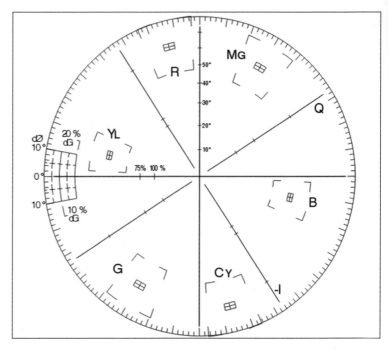

Figure 3.9. The graticule display of a vectorscope. Boxes indicate where the trace should fall for the primary and secondary colors when SMPTE color bars are displayed on the camera.

HUE/PHASE

Phase is what we also call *hue*, or what many people mean when they use the word "color" casually. "Color" has too many meanings to be useful for engineering purposes. Hue is represented as a circle (just like the color wheel) and the "color" can be precisely described as degrees around this circle; video engineers use the term *phase* to refer to the relative position of hue on the vectorscope.

THE VECTORSCOPE

The vectorscope (Figure 3.9) is a bit more specialized than the waveform — it only measures the color signal, but when it comes to color, it is an invaluable instrument. Figure 3.10 shows a shot displayed on the vectorscope. We can see that this scene is heavy in red/yellow with some blue and cyan as well. It shows us no information

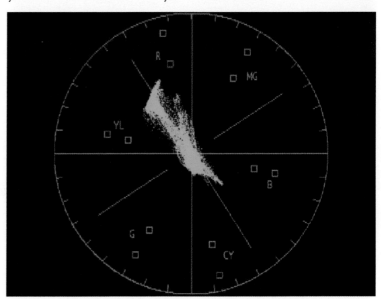

Figure 3.10. A typical image shown on the vectorscope. We can see that this frame has a good deal of red and some blue with not too much of the other colors.

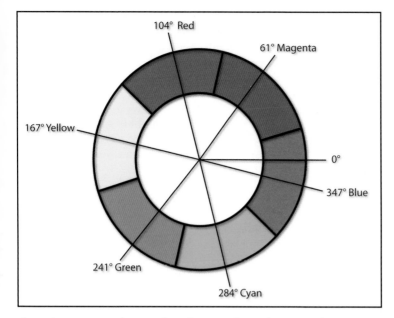

about luminance; that is what the waveform does. On the set or in a postproduction suite the two are used together. The vectorscope display is basically the color wheel but of course, this being video, it is called *phase*. It starts at the 3:00 position, which is zero degrees. The other positions are:

> Magenta: 61°
> Red: 104°
> Yellow: 167°
> Green: 241°
> Cyan: 284°
> Blue: 347°

These are in some respect "centers" of the color. In reality, we deal with all the subtle gradations of these colors, not just the pure hue; this is why a mathematical description is important — when it comes to digital signal handling, terms like "chartreuse" don't mean much.

So, going around the circle is one dimension. The other dimension is how far the trace is from the center. Distance from the center is usually thought of as the measure of *saturation*, but in fact this is not entirely accurate. Distance from the center can be saturation or

value or a combination of the two (See *Digital Color*). This is why the *arrowhead display* is so useful (Figure 3.21). This means that a pure black-and-white frame will appear as a dot in the center of the screen. A monochromatic blue scene that had no other color in it at all would be a dot that is shifted to the right, for example.

One display you will see and use frequently is color bars on the vectorscope. All color bars (and there are several, which we'll look at later) have the primary colors red, green, blue and the secondary colors magenta, cyan, yellow. The vectorscope has boxes for where each of these hues should display on the graticule (Figure 3.9).

COLOR BARS IN DETAIL

On the old style *SMPTE color bars* test chart (Figure 3.14); the top two-thirds of the frame are seven vertical color bars. Starting at the left, the bars are 80% gray, yellow, cyan, green, magenta, red, and blue. The color patches are at 75% intensity — commonly called "75% bars."

In this sequence, blue is a component in every other bar — as we will see in calibrating monitors, this is a very useful aspect. Also, red is on or off with every other bar, while green is present in the four left bars and not present on the three on the right. Because green is the largest component of *luminance* (brightness) this contributes to the stair step pattern which descends evenly from left to right when viewing on the *waveform monitor* (Figure 3.4).

Below the main bars is a strip of blue, magenta, cyan, and white patches. When a monitor is set to "blue only," these patches, in combination with the main set of color bars, are used to calibrate the color controls; they appear as four solid blue bars, with no visible distinction between the bars and the patches, if the color controls are properly adjusted. We'll look at this calibration procedure in more detail in a moment — calibrating the monitors on the set is one of the most critical steps of preparing for the day's shooting.

The lower section of the standard SMPTE color bars contains a patch of pure white (100%) and a series of small patches of black and near black, called the *PLUGE*, which stands for *Picture Line-Up Generation Equipment*. It was developed at the *BBC* as a way to make sure all the cameras throughout the building were calibrated to the same standard. It was produced by a signal generator in the basement and sent to all the studios so that engineers could calibrate equipment.

USING THE PLUGE IN MONITOR CALIBRATION

In SMPTE color bars, the PLUGE is underneath the red primary color bar (Figure 3.14). It comprises three small vertical bars, a right most one with intensity just above the saturated black level, a middle one with intensity exactly equal to saturated black, and a left most one with intensity just below saturated black (or "blacker than black"). The PLUGE is critical to properly setting the bottom blacks on a monitor. Think of it this way: if all there was to go by was a "black" patch, we could easily set the monitor controls to make it appear black, but how would we know if we had set it so it's just black or did we maybe go too far and make it darker than pure black? It would still appear the same on the monitor — black is black on a display screen.

By having these patches that are just barely above black we can set the level so that it's black but not "too black" — which would affect the values of the rest of the picture as well: the middle tones and the highlights as well as the dark regions. When a monitor is prop-

Figure 3.13. A monitor calibration probe by *xRite*. Calibration probes function by quantifying how far the monitor output deviates from known standards, thus allowing you to adjust the monitor to bring it back to standard.

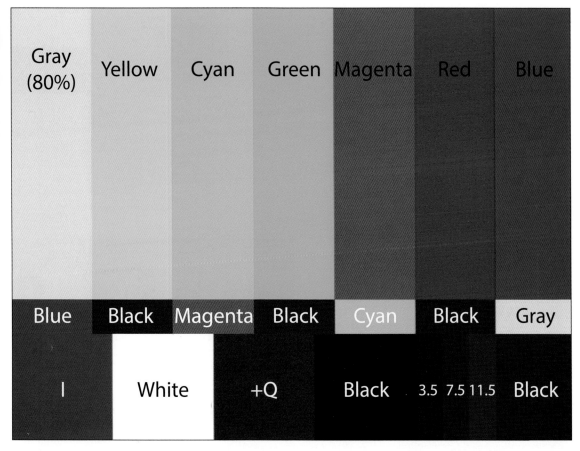

Gray (80%)	Yellow	Cyan	Green	Magenta	Red	Blue
Blue	Black	Magenta	Black	Cyan	Black	Gray
I	White	+Q	Black	3.5 7.5 11.5		Black

erly adjusted, the right hand pluge bar should be just barely visible, while the left two should appear completely black. It's an ingenious solution to the problem of setting the levels. The original PLUGE generator devised at the BBC used only -4% and +4% bars on a black background, but that left a fairly wide range of settings that could look correct. Absolute precision was not considered as important as having a system that could be used quickly and easily. Adding a -2% and +2% bar makes the pattern more precise, but is a bit more difficult to calibrate, because when the -2% bar disappears the +2% is often just barely visible. If you wish, you can just use the outer +/-4% bars as more of a "quick and dirty" method.

Increasingly, *probes* are used for calibrating monitors (Figure 3.13). These are electronic sensors which are temporarily attached to the surface of the monitor. The probe software then displays a series of test patches on the display and the probe measures them and allows adjustment of the monitor. These probes range in price from tens of

Figure 3.14. The traditional SMPTE color bars. Lower right between the two pure black patches is the *PLUGE*. The I and +Q patches are from the now disused *NTSC* color system, however they still appear on some vectorscopes.

Figure 3.15. The PLUGE is valuable for monitor calibration. Between two pure black patches are sections that are at 3.5, 7.5 and 11.5 IRE.

measurement

Figure 3.16. HD color bars are substantially different from SD bars. They include a Y-ramp (luminance from 0% to 100%) as well as 40% and 75% gray patches. The PLUGE is different as well in that it is measured in percentage instead of IRE. Technically IRE values don't apply to HD signals. This set of color bars was developed by *ARIB*, the *Association of Radio Industries and Businesses*, a Japanese industry group. They have been standardized as *SMPTE RP 219-2002*.

thousands of dollars to relatively affordable. Mike Sippel, Director of Engineering at Fletcher Camera puts it this way "a probe doesn't so much perform adjustment of a monitor as it allows you to quantify the extent to which the monitor deviates from a known standard luma or color representation. The probe software 'knows' what a particular color or gray swatch is 'supposed' to look like (in terms of emissive wavelength values) under a particular calibration reference (like Rec.709) and displays offset values describing what the monitor is actually displaying as compared to what it's supposed to be displaying. You can then use the monitor controls to manually align the picture so the displayed values equal the correct values, or in some cases the software can talk to the monitor and automatically tell the monitor the adjustments to make to square itself up against the target." Many technicians and facilities also employ independent contractors who specialize in monitor calibration.

In the bottom section are two patches that represent the "I" and "Q"signals. These relate to no longer used *NTSC* video, which has been replaced by *ATSC* (*Advanced Television Systems Committee*) video so we won't go into them in great detail. Suffice it to say that they relate to the NTSC color signal and the color burst. The "I" line has become associated with skintone values (Figure 3.29). It is pure co-incidence that this line is near where most skin tones fall on the vectorscope.

There is another form of bars, called *100% Color Bars*, or RGB pattern, which consists of eight vertical bars of 100% intensity, and does not include the other patches or luminance patterns. Like the SMPTE standard (75%) pattern, the color order is white, yellow, cyan, green, magenta, red, and blue, but with an additional column of saturated black. This pattern is used to check peak color levels and color saturation as well as color alignment. The 100% pattern is not as common or as useful as the SMPTE standard 75% pattern, but many pieces of test equipment generate both patterns, and can be selected to generate either one. Many pro cameras can be set to generate a 100% pattern for calibration to broadcast or recording equipment, especially in a multi-camera installation.

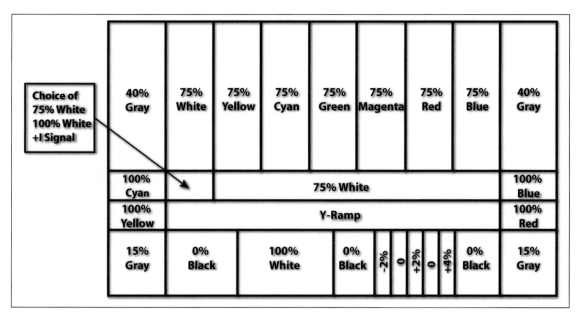

The following table represents the color bars shown in the figure:

Choice of 75% White 100% White +I Signal	40% Gray	75% White	75% Yellow	75% Cyan	75% Green	75% Magenta	75% Red	75% Blue	40% Gray
100% Cyan		75% White							100% Blue
100% Yellow		Y-Ramp							100% Red
15% Gray	0% Black	100% White		0% Black	-2%	0	+2%	0	+4%	0% Black	15% Gray

Figure 3.17. Anatomy of the ARIB/SMPTE HD color bars.

Although color bars were designed to calibrate analog video equipment in the standard def world, they remain widely used within digital video — although the form of the bars is different. SMPTE HD color bars are standardized as *ARIB* or *SMPTE RP 219-2002* (Figures 3.16 and 3.17).

The HD color bars have a few additional features, including a wide patch of 100% white and a *Y-ramp* or *luminance* ramp. The version of the pluge for this pattern is -2% black, 0% black, +2, another 0% black and then +4% black as narrow bands, then on both sides are larger patches of 0% black. At the ends of the bottom row are two patches of 15% gray. In the middle band, next to the long 75% bar and the Y-ramp are two patches of white which can alternately be used for I signal 100% or 75% white patches if needed.

LEGAL AND VALID

There are both technical limits to a broadcast signal and statutory limits set by government or quasi-government agencies that help to ensure that a signal you send out basically won't mess up somebodies television reception. These standards specify that the signal must stay within a certain range. A signal that stays within these limits is called *legal video*. *Valid* means it remains legal even when displayed in a different color space. For example, if a color difference signal is translated in an RGB format and remains within legal limits, it is called a *valid* signal.

TYPES OF WAVEFORM MONITORS

There are several types of external and internal waveforms. An external unit is the original form and most often they are a combination of waveform display and vectorscope, either switchable or with several displays shown simultaneously. Software waveform/vectorscopes are generally lower in resolution and response time but they are improving with every new release of the applications. The reason for this is simple: software designers want to devote most of the processing power to the user experience and picture quality. Waveform displays that are built into picture monitors sometimes have resolution so low they are approximations at best, however this is often "good enough" for our purposes on the set.

USING THE WAVEFORM ON SET

The waveform has many uses on a set and even more in the video engineering lab, but the two that are most commonly used are camera setup and checking lighting and exposure.

MEASUREMENT IN CAMERA SETUP

Setting up the camera is done with *test charts* and *patterns*. They differ in that test patterns are generated by the camera itself. These include the color bars and others such as these on the Red cameras.

- Luma ramp
- Chroma ramp
- Focus pattern/multiburst
- Chip chart
- Black field
- White field

These patterns cannot be recorded but are output to the viewing monitor, waveform and vectorscope — they are used in checking for problems with the signal path or monitoring.

CHANGING THE LOOK

As we change the look of the image with gamma, color space, matrix and other controls, we can use the waveform and vectorscope to see exactly what is happening to the picture with much greater precision than just on the picture monitor. This particularly applies to any safe limits in luminance, chrominance and gamut we are trying to adhere to — the waveform/vectorscope will show if changes we are making are taking it out of limits.

EXPOSURE ON THE WAVEFORM

As we are lighting a scene, setting the aperture and shooting, there is no more accurate and precise representation of exposure than the waveform and we'll discuss its use for this is in the chapter *Exposure*. Remember that exposure has two components: overall exposure and balancing exposure within the scene. See *Cinematography: Theory and Practice 2nd Edition* and *Motion Picture and Video Lighting 2nd Edition*, (both by the same author as this book) for much more on exposure theory, lighting and setting the camera. Reading a waveform trace for exposure takes a bit of practice but perhaps the most important aspect is easy to understand and watch for — clipping. For an example see Figure 3.20.

CLIPPING

Clipping is not necessarily the same thing as video reaching 100%; in fact the clipping level is adjustable on some cameras. Clipping means that the video device has reached the "saturation level" and no longer shows gradations of white at the upper levels. It's easy to spot on the waveform trace: it is when the signal "flatlines" at the top. There can be clipping of the luminance and also clipping of chrominance, which can be due to oversaturation of a particular channel or overexposure of a color channel. A viewing/monitoring *LUT* may make a signal appear to be clipping when it really isn't. See *Image Control & Grading* for a more detailed discussion of LUTs.

Clipping is a simple concept: at some point a digital device reaches its saturation level — it can't handle any more. Once it reaches this point, any additional signal results in no change in the signal. The real problem is this: any signal that is clipped has "no information," meaning that nothing can be recovered, nothing can be "saved."

  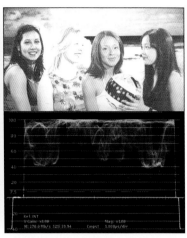

Once a signal is clipped, it's gone. There is no magic hardware or special software that can fix it. Sometimes very small areas of a picture are clipped with no ill effect on the image; sometimes it may even be a deliberate artistic choice.

Historically, video has always had trouble with the highlights and digital video generally has had less latitude in the high end than in the low end, one of the reasons film has hung in there so long as a capture medium. Camera makers are constantly working to improve highlight capture performance in sensors and they continue to make ... t in the meantime, "pro-... e most important jobs of ... o be watching a waveform

... y want your blacks to be ... dark region equivalent of ... eristic look on the lumi- ... hing the tonal range into ... observe by displaying any ... np will show it best) on an ... g the image from normal ... overexposed. This can be ... ure or in color correction/ ... ghtness.

... hart at normal, under and ... that all tones do not move ... sure changes; specifically, ... cally. With overexposure, ... ther until they flatline in ... loser together means that ... resents the original image ... ses, that's what we want ... riginal. When we get cre- ... course, but to start with, ... e digital image, our goal is for the recorded image to be a true representation of what was on the set or on the test chart. In *log encoded* video, the steps will remain equal all the way up to the clipping point. At the bottom end, there is nearly always some compression of the steps near black as sensors tend to behave this way as the signal approaches the noise floor.

Figure. 3.18. (Left) The *DSC Labs Cambelles* at normal exposure. The whites of the surf are very near 100% and the darkest areas are under 7.5 IRE.

Figure 3.19. (Middle) The *Cambelles* underexposed. On the waveform not even the lightest parts of the image get above 50 IRE and the entire image is crushed down to lower levels.

Figure 3.20. (Right) The *Cambelles* severely overexposed. Many parts of the image are now clipping (flat-lined at the top) and there are almost no areas of the image below 50 IRE.

Clipping of whites and crushing of the blacks will be apparent in all types of waveform displays, but for simplicity, most of our illustrations here employ luminance only waveform displays.

USING THE VECTORSCOPE ON THE SET

There are safe limits for what we can do with luminance in order to end up with a good image and there are also limits for what we can do with color. In order to monitor this, we use the vectorscope in various displays. As with the waveform monitor, it can be used to check the camera, set it up for a particular look and to monitor the image during shooting.

Color limits vary according to what standard or color space you are using, simply because every color space and video format treats color differently. For example, a vectorscope display of a standard color chart will appear markedly different when Rec.709 (HD) is chosen than when ITU 601 (a different standard) is selected.

For various technical reasons, 100% saturation is generally not used in test charts and patterns — they cannot be properly printed using standard inks and printing techniques. For this reason, some vectorscopes can display at either 75% saturation or at 100%. Naturally, you need to be sure you are using the correct settings to match the test pattern or chart you are using at the time.

COLOR BARS ON THE VECTORSCOPE

The vectorscope display has boxes for the primary and secondary colors (Figure 3.9). When color bars are generated from the camera or other source, the trace should fall into those boxes — if it doesn't something is wrong. If the trace is rotated clockwise or counter clockwise, then phase (hue) is off. If they are too near the center or too far from the center, then saturation is too low or too high. Changing the hue in color correction software will also shift them in one direction or another. As we will see, most printed test charts are not set up for 100% saturations on colors, as they are impossible to print properly. Some test cards set saturation at 50% and the vectorscope is then set to 2X gain to give an accurate reading.

WHITE BALANCE/BLACK BALANCE

When the camera is aimed at a neutral gray card or neutral white target, white balance is readily judged on the vectorscope. Since a truly neutral test chart has no color bias in any direction, its trace should appear as a dot in the middle of the vectorscope — the image has luminance, but no chroma at all.

If the dot is not in the center, this means the white balance of the camera is off. If the dot is shifted toward blue, it probably means that the lighting on the test patch is daylight (blue) balance and the camera is set for tungsten. If the dot is shifted toward the red/yellow, it usually means the opposite: the lighting is tungsten and the camera is set for daylight balance. See Figure 6.14 in *Digital Color*. Many technicians also use the parade waveform to judge color balance, as it shows the relative balance between the three color channels. We'll look at an example of this in a later chapter.

Black balance is also very important. Most cameras include an automatic black balance function. If you were to do it manually, you would cap the lens so that no light at all is reaching the sensor, then make sure the dot is in the center of the vectorscope.

GAMUT

A primary concern with video is staying within the limits of *gamut* (which we'll discuss in greater detail in *Digital Color*), particularly as defined by the rules and by the limits of equipment. Some vectorscopes have displays and warnings that help with this, some of them patented by Tektronix and used in their units. Some software will give warnings when gamut limits are exceeded.

ARROWHEAD

The *arrowhead* display (Figure 3.21) shows chrominance in a way that makes interpretation of gamut easier. The display shows when RGB amplitude values exceed specified limits. Although this particular display is not used a great deal on the set, it is useful to know what it is and how to use it.

DIAMOND DISPLAY

The *diamond display* shows RGB gamut limits (Figures 3.22 through 3.24). It is arranged as two diamonds, one atop the other. The left hand side of both diamonds is green. The upper right side is blue and the lower right side is red. For a signal to be properly within gamut, all the traces must be within the G-B and G-R diamonds. There are two dashed lines on the edges of the diamonds. The inside line is for 75% signals and the outer edge is for 100% signals.

Excursions outside these lines are, of course, "illegal." This display can be useful in color balancing. With a monochrome target, such as a gray card, the trace should be a straight vertical line. If the line bends toward the left, the image is too green, such as it might be with fluorescent lighting. If the trace bends to the top right, it is too blue; bending to the lower right is too red. It is also a good tool for analyzing black balance: correct black balance will show a dot at the connecting point of the two diamonds. Errors in black balance (meaning that it is not purely black) will show up as a stretched dot in the direction of the color channel that is too strong. A variation is the *Split Diamond*, which makes it easier to see problems in the black regions of the image.

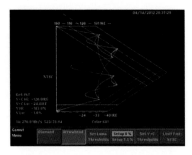

Figure 3.21. The *arrowhead display* is another way of viewing color; it is used for judging when colors are out of gamut. It is proprietary to Tektronix waveform monitors. The innermost "arrowhead" is 100 IRE. (Courtesy of Tektronix).

Figure 3.22. (Left, top) How the diamond display and split diamond display are formed. (Courtesy of Tektronix).

Figure 3.23. (Left, bottom) Examples of bad signals as they would display in diamond mode. (Courtesy of Tektronix).

Figure 3.24. (Below) Gamut error shown on the diamond display. Each diamond represents the gamut limits. (Courtesy of Tektronix).

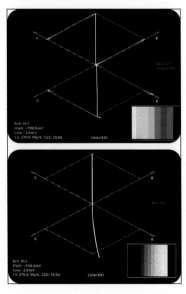

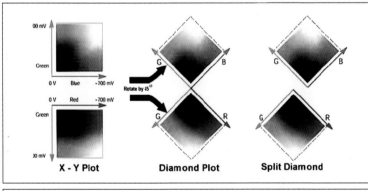

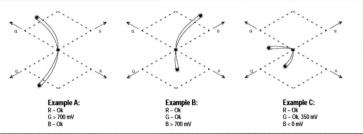

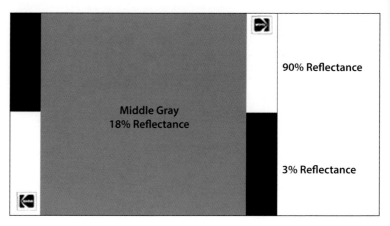

Figure 3.25. The *Kodak Gray Card Plus* includes a 90% white patch and a 3% black patch as well as the middle gray card.

90% Reflectance

Middle Gray
18% Reflectance

3% Reflectance

VIDEO TEST CARDS

Color bars are internally generated by the camera, which means that they tell us nothing about the scene we're shooting, the lighting, lens color and flare characteristics or even camera setup modifications. To evaluate these, we need something external — *test charts*, also called *test cards* or *calibration targets*.

THE DECEPTIVELY SIMPLE NEUTRAL GRAY CARD

The 18% Gray Card has been an essential and absolutely necessary tool for still photographers and cinematographers for decades. In the Ansel Adams *Zone System*, the grayscale from black to white is divided into sections or zones, each one representing a piece of the continuous scale. Traditionally, it is divided into eleven zones from zero to 10, with 0 being pure black and 10 being pure white. Adams used Roman numerals to designate the Zones. There are several important landmarks we can reference: Zone 0 is theoretical pure black, but Adams considered Zone I to be the darkest "useful" Zone; he felt that Zone 0 was a theoretical minimum.

At the other end Zone X is theoretical maximum white, but zone IX is the usable, practical top end. (We'll see later how this is analogous to concepts in video: superblack and superwhite). He termed Zone II through VIII to be the textural range: meaning they were areas of the grayscale in which you could still detect some texture and detail — these are also useful concepts in video exposure.

A useful reference point is *middle gray* — Zone V. This is *perceptually* halfway between black and white. This is because human vision is not *linear*; it is actually *logarithmic*. We perceive increases in brightness unevenly — at the dark end of the grayscale we can discriminate small changes in brightness, at the high end of the scale it takes very large changes in luminance for us to perceive a difference. This logarithmic change applies to most human perception; for example it is why loudness is defined in terms of *deciBels* (*dB*) which are logarithmic units as we'll see in *Linear, Gamma, Log*.

THE NEUTRAL PART

Notice that part of the name is "neutral" — as the name implies, it is designed and manufactured to be free of any color tint. This aspect of the card is extraordinarily useful when it comes to color balance and grading; in particular for white balancing the camera before shooting. Some DPs prefer to use the gray card for camera white balancing since it is likely to be more color neutral than a sheet of white paper or even the white side of the card. Some companies also make specialized white cards for white balancing cameras.

The other side of the gray card is 90% diffuse white. The primary reason for this is that 90% reflectance is the whitest white that can be achieved on paper. Like the gray side, it is color neutral and is widely used as a target for white balancing cameras, although many people prefer the gray side for this purpose. It is dangerous to use just any old piece of white paper that's lying around for white balancing a camera. The reason for this is simple — next time you go to a stationary store, take a look at how many dozens of "white" paper they have, none of them exactly matches the others. Worse, the "bright white" papers are made with bleach and other products that may cause them to fluoresce in the non-visible spectrum and this will lead to unexpected results.

How a Gray Card Can Help You Nail Color Balance and Exposure

One problem cinematographers have dealt with since the earliest days is getting the lab (or colorist) to process the image in a way that matches what the DP intended when they shot it on the set. This is particularly true of *dailies*. In the longform workflow (meaning projects that take more that a couple of days to shoot, such as feature films) dailies are usually produced without the supervision of the cinematographer, since they are done overnight, when the crew is (hopefully) getting some sleep before the next shooting day begins. When the DP couldn't be present for dailies, all sorts of devices were used to get the colorist to understand what was intended. Failure to do so can cause directors and producer to panic when they see dailies that do not reflect what the DP really intended, with all sorts of negative consequences, such as people getting fired.

In film, the colorist threads up the negative and then views it on a monitor — they really have no idea what the DP was trying to accomplish: is the scene supposed to be dark and shadowy? Bright and crisp? Blue and sinister or warm-toned orange? Toward the darker side or lighter? DPs send notes to the colorist, call them on the phone, send sample photos from magazines, photos from the set, all sorts of things.

These all work, sort of, but there is a simpler and more direct method that is purely technical and calls for no subjective, artistic vision on the part of the dailies colorist (who is often one of the lowest paid people in the facility). In film based production "shooting the gray card" is a standard procedure on sets and has been for a long time; it is still important when shooting video.

Certainly, using an *Auto White Balance* feature on a camera is a gamble. Especially when shooting difficult lighting conditions such as fluorescent, proper white balancing will save difficulty later. When the camera is set up and the scene is lit, a camera assistant holds a neutral gray card in front of the lens and the operator shoots it at the f/stop calculated by the cinematographer to give an ideal exposure for the card. Once the colorist has this on their monitor, the rest is simple and quick. He or she places the exposure of the card at the prescribed level for middle gray on the waveform monitor (which is not going to be at 50% on the waveform monitor — more on that later) and then looks at the vectorscope and places the small dot the card produces at the exact center, which means it is neutral gray. With this, the image will be what the cinematographer intended — or at least what they shot. If those two things aren't the same, then it is not the colorist's fault.

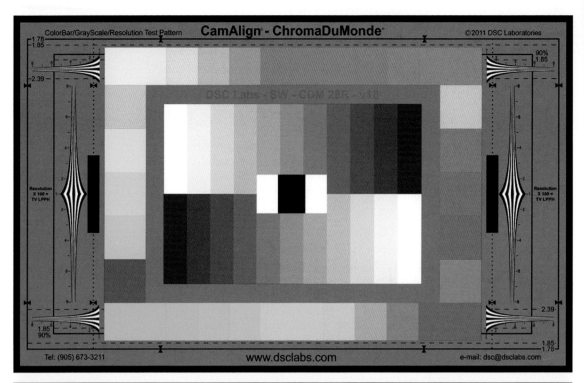

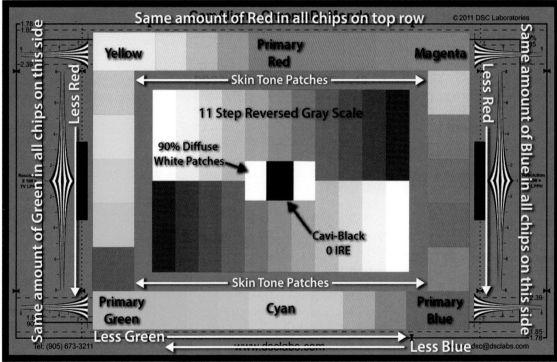

Figure 3.26. (Top) The *DSC Labs ChromaDuMonde™* test target — an extraordinarily useful tool. For technical reasons, the color patches are not at 100% saturation.

Figure 3.27. (Above) A *ChromaDuMonde™* dissected.

WHY ISN'T 18% GRAY ALSO 50%?

A logical person is going to assume that middle gray is going to fall at exactly 50% on the waveform monitor. It would be a nice, neat world if it did, but, it doesn't. When log encoding or gamma correction is applied, middle gray falls at anywhere from 38 to 46 IRE. First of all that's a pretty big range and it's also quite a way from 50%. We're going to go into why this happens in the next chapter. In

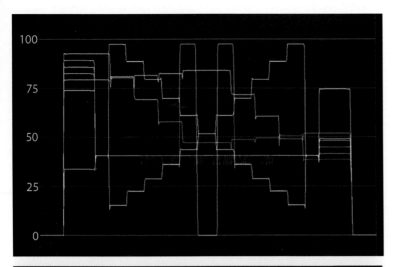

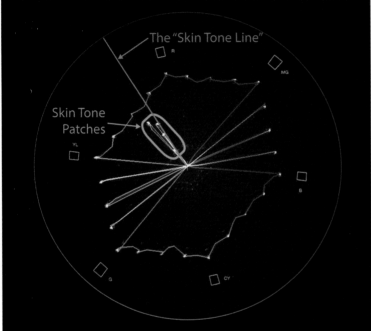

Figure 3.28. (Top) The *ChromaDu-Monde*™ on the waveform monitor in Final Cut Pro X. Notice that the Cavi-Black gets all the way to zero — a reliable reference. The white patches do not go to 100% as expected, but to 90%. You can also see the luma (brightness) distributions of the various color patches and skintone patches.

Figure 3.29. (Left) The *ChromaDu-Monde*™ on the vectorscope. The color patches are distributed evenly as you would expect, however notice that they do not reach "the boxes" on the graticule. This is because the DSC charts are designed to show full saturation when the vectorscope is set at 2x gain and Final Cut Pro (unlike professional vectorscopes) does not have a setting for "times two."

Also note how the skin tone patches fall very close to each other despite the fact that they are skin tones for widely varying coloration. In fact, human skin tone varies mostly by luminance and not by color.

The "Skin Tone Line" is a co-incidence. In the outdated NTSC system, it was the "I" line and it just happens that most skin tone colors fall *approximately* along this line. It is a handy reference but it is no substitute for a good eye and a well calibrated monitor.

Rec.709, middle gray is 40.9%. For now, it is enough to understand that the video signal is not linear — video data, especially from cameras that record log encoded video, is manipulated in various ways in order to extend the dynamic range and this results in the value for middle gray being pushed down the scale. It varies because different camera companies use different math in their digital signal processors and even present the user with several different choice. Understanding how this works is actually going to be a big part of learning how the video signal works in cameras, in color correction software and indeed in all aspects of image acquisition and processing.

18% GRAY: LEGEND OR MYTH

There's another complication as well. One that can prove severely mind-boggling for old-time photographers who trained in the Zone system and later transferred those skills and knowledge to film and electronic cinematography. Hold onto your hat: middle gray isn't 18% and light meters don't read 18% as middle gray. In reality,

Figure 3.30. The *DSC Labs One-Shot* includes gray, white and black patches, the primary and secondary colors and skin tone samples. It is designed for quick field use when you might not have time to set up and light a full test chart such as the *Chroma du Monde*.

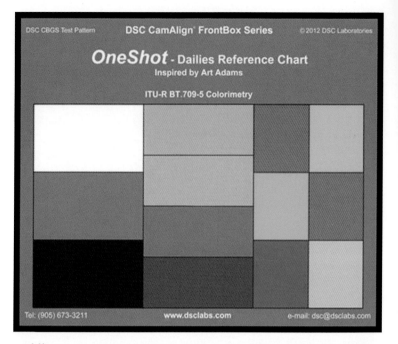

middle gray is 12% to 15% on reflectance light meters (depending on the manufacturer). We'll come back to this in the next chapter. Don't give up all hope, however, in the end what really matters is that there is one standard that is well known and agreed on; one measuring stick that everybody can easily refer to. Does it really matter that a meter is one ten-millionth of the distance between the equator and the North Pole? Not really; what counts is that everybody has a reference they agree on, a common standard, even if it is no longer a platinum bar in a vault in Paris. These days, it is the distance light travels in a vacuum in 1/299,792,458th of a second — try turning that into an iPhone app!

So for now at least, don't panic. As Charles Poynton puts it "Close enough for jazz." Gray cards and 18% gray areas on test cards are still very important and useful; cinematographers should absolutely know how to use them if you really care about controlling your images and getting predictable results.

CALIBRATION TEST CHARTS

The need to calibrate cameras goes back a long way. We previously talked about the invention of the PLUGE at the BBC as a way to make sure all the cameras in their many studios were calibrated to the same standard. In the days of tube cameras, calibration was a constant task as the image could change based on age of the tubes, temperature, etc. Cameras are more stable in these digital days but there are still lots of things that can happen to an image, for better or worse: lighting, exposure, compression, recording format, camera settings — the list goes on and on. All of these make in front of the camera calibration test charts absolutely essential.

DSC LABS TEST CHARTS

Without a doubt the top-of-the-line, the Lamborghinis of test charts are those from *DSC Labs* in Toronto. In particular, the *ChromaDuMonde*™ is the ultimate — you will see this chart in use on virtually every professional set using video cameras, in every rental house and in use by cinematographers and camera assistants everywhere.

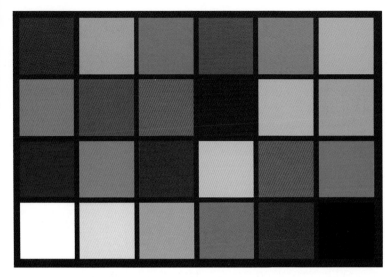

Figure 3.31. (Above) The *DSC Labs Cambelles* is an excellent reference for skin tone and color. Because it is standardized and manufactured to exacting standards it can be a constant in different camera tests, where actual people subjects may vary.

Figure 3.32. (Left) The *X-Rite Color-Checker* card. Many people still refer to it by the original name: *Macbeth ColorChecker*. The actual color values are shown in Figure 6.31 in *Digital Color*.

The anatomy of this chart is shown in Figures 3.26 and 3.27. It consists of an 11 step crossed gray scale and 28 color patches which include primaries, secondaries and four typical skin tone patches. One of the most useful and important features is in the center — called the *Cavi-Black*, it is a hole in the chart which is backed by a black velvet-lined box. This forms something that is truly black, zero IRE — an extraordinarily useful point of reference. When aligning a scene on the waveform monitor, having a reference that we absolutely know where it belongs on the waveform monitor is a huge help. On either side of the Cavi-Black are 90% white patches, the most reflective that can be achieved with printed materials. Many people still refer to white patches such as this as 100% white — it isn't. So when people refer to a white patch as 100% white just keep in mind that it is close to 100%, but not really. The background of the entire chart is 18% neutral gray — another important reference point for exposure. Also included are resolution trumpets and framing marks for 1.78 (16x9), 1.85 and 2.39.

The chart is glossy, which gives deeper blacks and thus more contrast. Glossy also means that reflections and glares are readily visible and can be dealt with; this also means that careful positioning and lighting of the card is important as glares and reflections will most definitely interfere with proper use of the test target.

THE ONE SHOT

Cinematographer and author Art Adams, who consults for *DSC Labs*, suggested a design for a quick field reference test chart. Called the *One Shot*, it consists of black, white and middle gray patches, the primary and secondary colors and four typical skin tone patches (Figure 3.30). Adams points out that if one is setting up a camera, grayscale references are vital for adjusting exposure, but tell you little about alterations made in the color matrix — these are much more easily tracked in the color patches and especially the skin tone areas. Since it is for quick use where an elaborate lighting setup is impractical, it is matte.

Blogging at ProVideoCoalition.com, Adams writes about this chart: "In the old days we shot an 18% gray card to tell a film dailies timer where we wanted our exposure placed and what color we wanted dailies to be. Now that film is being replaced by HD a simple gray card is no longer enough, because while film colors are fixed by

Figure 3.33. The *Siemens Star* is an excellent way to judge focus but there are several other focus targets from various companies.

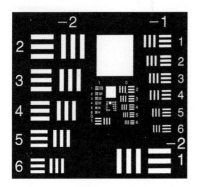

Figure 3.34. An early version of a method for judging resolving power: the *1951 USAF Resolution Test Chart*.

emulsion, video colors are not. A gray card in video doesn't communicate anything about accurate color. That's why I designed the *DSC Labs OneShot* dailies reference chart.

The *DSC Labs OneShot* is intended to give a colorist the most information possible without taking up a lot of time on set. The chart contains white and black chips for white and black balancing (yes, black has a color, and if it's not right your entire image will suffer); an 18% gray chip for exposure; four common flesh tone references; and the Rec.709 primary and secondary colors, at 50% saturation. This chart is only truly usable for Rec.709 colorimetry, which is HD colorimetry. We're working on a digital cinema version, but for now this will do as dailies are frequently viewed in Rec.709.

The Rec.709 primaries and secondaries are printed at 50% saturation because it is impossible to print them at full saturation: their colors, as seen properly on a monitor, are more saturated than modern printing technology can reproduce. The primaries and secondaries are perhaps the most important references on the chart. It is certainly possible to neutralize the image using only white and black references but this doesn't necessarily mean that color will be accurate after doing so: the camera's matrix generally doesn't affect neutral tones (white, black and gray) but it always affects colors. White balance means that neutral tones will appear white, but says very little about how red, green, blue, cyan, yellow and magenta are rendered." We'll be discussing Rec.709 in detail later on.

THE MACBETH /XRITE COLORCHECKER

Although most people still call it the *Macbeth* color checker chart (the original name), it is actually now made by the *xRite* company (Figure 3.32). Originally designed for still photographers whose work would end up in print, it is still used in video. It works fine if you have it as a reference on a still photo shoot — it is photographed and then the person producing the end product (such as a catalog) also has one to compare to under tightly controlled illumination conditions— this is how it was used in photo production for print. In the case of video, it is very unlikely that the video colorist would have one. Even if they did, how would they view it? Color correction suites are very dark. Would they take it out into the hall and look at it under fluorescent? Although its color and grayscale values are known (Figure 6.31), they are not so easy to place on the vectorscope/waveform monitors. However, the chart does have its uses, especially if a spectrometer or other calibration device is involved. Despite these limitations, it is still used by many people who do find it a helpful visual reference.

SKIN TONE

Because the reproduction of skin tones is such an important subject, nearly all camera tests will include a human subject. For even tighter calibration, images of people have long been used for this as well. In the early days of film, *China Girls* were a widely used standard. This

Figure 3.35. (Right) The *Koren* lens test chart. (Courtesy of Norman Koren).

Figure 3.36. (Below) A resolution test painted on the end of a U.S. Air Force runway.

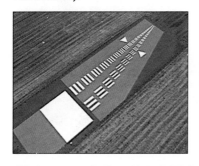

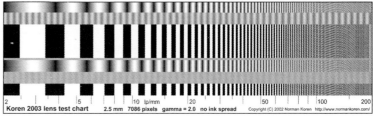

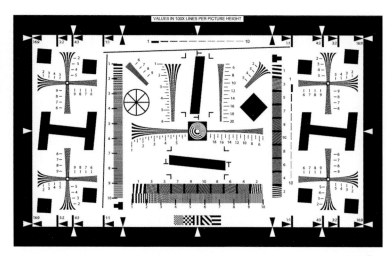

Figure 3.37. The *ISO 12233* test chart has both horizontal and vertical lines but also includes tilted lines and objects for measuring edge definition. (Courtesy of Stephen H. Westin of Cornell University Light Measurement Laboratory).

has nothing to do with ethnicity, they are called that because they were hand painted on porcelain (China). They provided a stable and repeatable image of skin tone for calibrating film processing equipment. A newer test reference are the *Cambelles* by *DSC Labs* (Figure 3.31). Carefully calibrated and printed, it has four models with typical and representative skin tones. When shooting camera tests, it is always important to include a live person in the frame along with charts — skin tone is both a useful guide and reproducing it well is always an important goal. Actual skin reacts to light in a way that no test chart can.

WARM CARDS

While a white target or neutral gray card are used for setting *white balance*, the result will be technically correct, but not always aesthetically pleasing. Since people almost always look better with a slight warm tone to the image, we don't always want a purely technical white balance. Because cameras adjust white balance by adding the opposite of the color they see on the reference target, photographing a slightly blue card will result in a warmer image. To make this easier, there are *warm cards*. Instead of being neutral white or gray, they are made in varying degrees of slightly blue, so that when they are used as the color balance test target, the image will be adjusted accordingly. They usually come in sets with grades such as Warm 1, Warm 2, etc.

MEASURING IMAGE RESOLUTION

Image resolution can be measured in various ways. One widely used method quantifies how small and close together lines can be to each other and still be visibly resolved — this is the method used to test the resolution of lenses, camera sensors and other components of the imaging chain. Sometimes the goal is to test individual components (such as a lens) or to test the entire system as it works together. Resolution units can be tied to physical sizes (e.g. lines per mm, lines per inch), or to the overall size of a picture (lines per picture height).

RESOLUTION TEST CHARTS

A resolution of 10 *lines per millimeter* means 5 dark lines alternating with 5 light lines, or 5 *line pairs* (*LP*) per millimeter (*5 LP/mm*). Photographic lens and film resolution are most often quoted in line pairs per millimeter; some charts are measured in *lines per picture height* (*LPHH*). Some tests are expressed in lines, while some are in line pairs. Moreover, the results might also be in lines per picture height

Figure 3.38. How an MTF test works: the original test chart has lines that decrease in size and spacing. The final reading shows how the system loses the ability to resolve them sharply as they decrease and how it is measured to produce a final result: the Modulation Transfer Function. The central concept is that no imaging system can perfectly reproduce reality — but some are better than others.

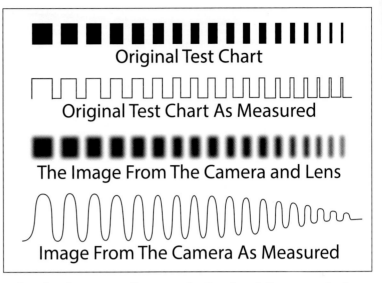

Original Test Chart

Original Test Chart As Measured

The Image From The Camera and Lens

Image From The Camera As Measured

rather than lines per millimeter. The fact that different standards are in use is of little consequence — what really matters is that if you are comparing two lenses or two cameras, that the same test chart and measuring standards are employed; otherwise it is very much an "apples and oranges" situation. (Figure 3.35)

MODULATION TRANSFER FUNCTION

In optical testing, it is important to consider more than just a single link in the chain such as the lens or the sensor. A lens can be quantified in terms of how many line pairs per millimeter it can resolve, but a single number isn't really the whole story: it is important to measure the lens not only in the center (where lenses are almost always at their best) but also at the corners (generally lower resolution) and at different f/stops.

A lens usually has a "sweet spot" in the f/stop range where it is best. Most often this is near the middle of its range and resolution falls off as the aperture opens up or closes down to the ends of the range. Sometimes lenses are even optimized for particular ranges. But beyond lenses, it is important to evaluate the interaction of the lens, the sensor, the digital processor, the compression scheme and so on, in other words to test the entire system as a whole, which in the end is what really matters. If you have a great camera with a substandard lens, then you're never going to get the best results.

The method used for this more comprehensive measure of resolution is called the *modulation transfer function* (Figure 3.38). In the simplest terms, it involves photographing a test chart of line pairs and then measuring how much the image degrades as it passes through the image chain.

linear, gamma, log

Figure 4.1. Human vision has an extremely wide dynamic range but this can be a somewhat deceptive measurement. It's not "all at once," the eye adapts by altering the iris (the f/stop) and by chemically adapting from *photopic* (normal lighting condition) to *scotopic* vision (dark conditions). The actual *instantaneous range* is much smaller and moves up and down the scale.

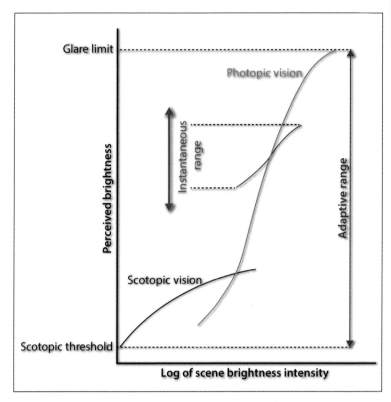

DYNAMIC RANGE

Brightness range, dynamic range and *luminance range* are terms for the same concept: how much variation there is in the luminance levels of a scene and then how accurately the imaging system is able to reproduce those levels. Any scene we look at has a specific brightness range, which is a result of the combination of how much light is falling on the scene and how reflective the objects are. Also, some things in the scene don't reflect light so much as they generate their own light: lamps, a fire, windows, the sky, etc. The eye can perceive an enormous range of light values: about 20 stops. It does this in two ways: first the iris opens and closes just like the aperture in a lens. It also changes its response by switching from *photopic* vision (the cones, better when there is lots of light) to *scotopic* vision (the rods, which are good in low light situation). But at any one time (barring changes in the eye) we can see a range of about 6.5 stops (there is not much scientific agreement on this). How these factors interact to create the dynamic range of human vision is shown in Figure 4.1.

The difference between the darkest part of a scene and the brightest part can be enormous, especially in exterior scenes. If there is something dark and in shadows in the scene and then there are brightly lit clouds, the difference can easily be as much as 20 stops or more. Twenty stops is a ratio of 1,000,000:1. As with all scenes, how reflective the objects are is a key factor in addition to the different amounts of light falling on areas of the scene — think of a black panther in a cave and a white marble statue in full sun, in the same frame. Even with the amazing range the human eye is capable of, there is no way you can really see both at the same time. You can shield your eyes from the glare of the marble statue and let them adapt to the dark and see the panther in the mouth of the cave or you can squint and let your eyes adapt to the light and see the marble statue but you'll never be able to see both of them at the same time.

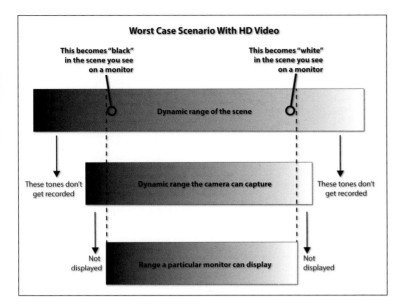

Figure 4.2. Because the camera and then the monitor are not always capable of reproducing the extreme dynamic range of some scenes, the tonal range is represented differently in each step of the process. Fortunately there have been huge strides in making cameras that have amazing dynamic range.

Film and video have dynamic ranges that are limited by technology. Color scientist Charles Poynton states "*Dynamic Range* according to the definition used by sensor designers, is the ratio of exposure at sensor saturation down to exposure where noise fills the entire lowest stop. Consider whether that sort of dynamic range is a useful metric for you." In other words, your mileage may vary.

Until recently video was far more limited than film, but new cameras are rapidly closing that gap, even exceeding that range. Traditional HD video (up until the introduction of the *Viper*, *Red One Genesis*, *Alexa* and now many others) was limited in range. The problem is illustrated in Figure 4.2 — *Worst Case Scenario HD Video*. The dynamic range of the scene may be quite large. However the camera can only pick up a limited portion of that brightness range (we're assuming that the camera exposure was set right in the middle). This means that something that was just very light gray in the scene will be recorded by the camera as being pure white, because that brightness value is at the top end of what the camera can "see." At the low end, something that is just dark gray in the scene will be recorded by the camera as being pure black.

The same process is repeated when the recorded images are displayed on a monitor that has even less range than the camera: image information is lost at both ends of the scale. In old fashioned analog video, especially in early TV, the cameras had ridiculously limited dynamic range. As a result old TV studios were lit with very "flat" lighting: no deep shadows or even slightly bright highlights were allowed as they would simply turn to harshly glaring highlights and deep murky shadows. Even though it was a classic age in terms of the programs, the cinematography was uniformly bland and dull — it was the only way to deal with the limitations of the technology. These days, of course, with the newest cameras, there is some truly outstanding cinematography being done on programs produced for cable TV. The same problem happened to film when color came in: *Technicolor* film had a limited dynamic range and it also required huge amounts of light due to the chemistry of the emulsion but also because the image was being split by prisms and sent to three separate pieces of film, resulting in severe loss of light. There was some outstanding cinematography done in the Technicolor era but for the

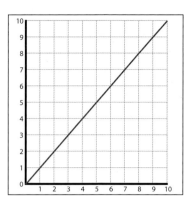

Figure 4.3. Linear response on a Cartesian diagram: every increment on the X-axis results in an equal change on the Y-axis.

most part it was marked by bland, dull low-contrast lighting, much of it " flat front lighting" which is something DPs avoid today. This was a huge step down from the black-and-white era, of course. The same cinematographers who had produced stunning, high contrast, moody images in black-and-white were now working in color — it's not that they didn't know how to do great lighting, of course they did, it was just the limitations of the new medium that forced them into it.

LINEAR RESPONSE

If an "ideal" film was truly linear, it would have an equal increase in density for every increase in exposure: doubling the amount of light in the scene would exactly double the brightness of the final image (Figure 4.3). The problem is that linear response means some brightness ranges exceed the limits of the film (Figure 4.4) — parts of the scene that are too bright just don't get recorded: they come out as pure, featureless white on the film (in video, we call this clipping): no detail, no texture, no separation. The same happens with the very dark parts of the scene: they are just a featureless dark blob on the negative. Instead of subtle shadows and gradations of black tones, it's just pure black with no texture. Simply put, since the brightness range of many scenes exceeds what cameras and displays are capable of, a purely linear response puts some areas of the scene off the scale at the extremes. Even with the most advanced new cameras, this will always be a problem in cinematography; after all, not even the human eye can accommodate the brightness range of the real world without adaptation.

An Ideal and a Problem

You may have heard that video cameras are "linear," meaning that they have that one-to-one correspondence between the input (scene brightness values) and the output (pixel brightness values). It just means that there is no alteration of the data in the transition.

At first glance this seems ideal — for every change of brightness levels within the scene, there is a corresponding change in the output levels from the photosites. Sound great, after all, accurate reproduction of the scene is what we're after, right? If only life was so simple, everything would be easy.

Because the brightness range of the real world is often huge, no current sensor, monitor or projector can accommodate that great a brightness range. The human eye can accommodate a ratio of 100:1 under static conditions (without adaptation with the iris or changing chemically from scotopic to photopic or vice versa). So we have certain hard limits to what brightness range we can record and use — as cameras and displays evolve, in the end it will not be the equipment that is the limiting factor, it will be human vision. In regards to a sensor, we call that upper limit *clipping*, as we talked about previously; camera manufacturers call it *full well capacity* or *sensor saturation*. Full well capacity simply means that each photosite (well) has absorbed as many photons as it can take. Our starting point is pure black, 0 IRE and the dynamic range of the sensor is measured between black and the upper limit of clipping. With the best new cameras, this can be quite an impressive range of up to 14, 15 stops or more, but even so, many scenes, especially exteriors with bright sunlight and deep shade exceed this dynamic range. This means that there are many instances where a linear recording of a scene exceeds the dynamic range that sensor/recording system (or indeed, the eye) is capable of.

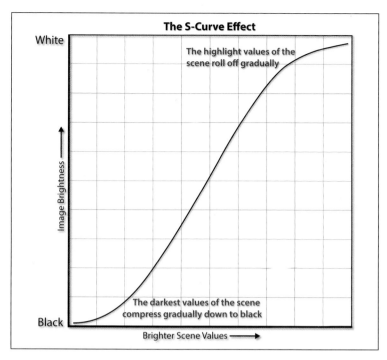

The S-Curve Effect

White

Image Brightness →

The highlight values of the scene roll off gradually

The darkest values of the scene compress gradually down to black

Black

Brighter Scene Values ——→

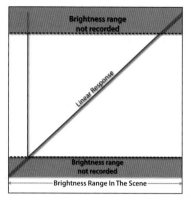

Brightness range not recorded

Linear Response

Brightness range not recorded

Brightness Range In The Scene

Figure 4.4. (Above) Unlike the gentle roll-off of highlights and shadows in the film S-curve, a purely linear representation means that the shadows and highlights fall beyond what the medium is capable of reproducing.

Figure 4.5. (Left) The S-curve in film. The gentle curve of the shadow reproduction and the falloff of the highlights is a form of compression that extends the dynamic range. This works because human perception is far more sensitive to the middle range than to the extremes.

LINEAR AS SCENE REFERRED

We've talked about some of the problems with linear, but don't lose sight of the fact that it is still an ideal to which we aspire in image acquisition — the ultimate goal is accurate representation of the scene as it actually appears in the real world; artistic interpretations aside, of course. In this context, the term is *scene-referred*, which means that the tonal scale and color of the actual scene are reproduced in the image to whatever extent the sensor is capable of doing so.

Color scientist Charles Poynton defines it like this: "If an imaging system has a direct, deterministic link from luminance in the scene to image code values, in color management technology, the image data is said to be *scene referred*." The opposite is when the imaging characteristics of the final display device (monitor, home theater or cinema projector) are used as the reference: "If there is a direct, deterministic linkage from image code values to the luminance intended to be produced by a display, the image data is said to be *display referred*." (Charles Poynton, *Digital Video and HD, Algorithms and Interfaces*, 2nd edition). This also turns out to be a crucial concept in the second half of the *ACES* process which will be discussed more extensively in the chapter *Workflow*; as we'll see, *ACES* is a method of dealing with images in both *scene referred* and *display referred* methods at different points in the image chain.

THE CLASSIC S-CURVE IN THE IMAGE

Let's take another look at how film responds to light before we get into video. The reason for this is that it illustrates the concepts in a very simple way and also that video engineers have spent a great deal of time trying to get video to behave like film. Figure 4.5 shows the *response curve* of a typical film negative, they're always an S-shape. The reason for this is that on film, the highlights "roll off," meaning that after a certain point the graph is no longer a straight line. Adding more and more light eventually has less and less effect. This is because the silver crystals in the film emulsion get saturated and stop responding.

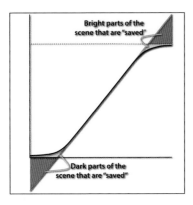

Figure 4.6. An illustration of how the S-curve "saves" the extreme shadows and highlights.

A similar phenomenon happens in the shadows (left hand part of the graph). As photons begin hitting the silver crystals during exposure, the emulsion doesn't immediately respond so the line stays flat for a while. This happens due to latency in the silver crystals response to light: they don't immediately respond when a few photons fall on each crystal. It takes many photons to get the chemical change started and even then, it happens slowly. This causes the *toe* of the film curve to start out flat, then slowly curves up, eventually becoming the straight line portion of the curve, or the midtones.

Think of it like trying to push start a stalled car. When the car is at a stand-still, it takes a lot of effort to get it moving at all. Then, even when it starts moving slowly you still have to push hard to get it going faster. Once it's rolling along, fairly minimal effort will keep it going. In the highlights, the silver crystals eventually reach a saturation point, but they do so gradually; as more and more photons pour in, the chemical response starts to slow down, slows even more and then stops entirely. The result is the *shoulder* of the film curve.

One would think that this inertia at the low end and fall-off in response at the high end would be a real problem because they make the response non-linear. After all, isn't the goal of "ideal" exposure to reproduce the real world scene as closely as possible? A non-linear response curve isn't really "accurately" reproducing the scene in front of the camera.

As it turns out, this S-curve is one of the biggest advantages film has over video, and the lack of it is one of the biggest obstacles to overcome in video. As Art Adams puts it in his on-line article *Hitting the Exposure Sweet Spot,* "The S-curve does what our eyes do naturally: it stretches out the mid-tones, so they are the same distance apart that they would be if the camera only captured six stops, and compresses the highlights and shadows, which is where our eyes are least sensitive to differences in tonality. We can cram the steps together in the highlights and shadows, making them less contrasty, because the mid-tones are where we pay the most attention."

You may be wondering why such a detailed discussion of film in a book that is entirely about digital image making? Well, the curve is an absolute essential concept to understand in video. It is one that you will be using in the menus of digital cameras, in LUTs, in color correction and in post-production of video projects.

FILM GAMMA AND VIDEO GAMMA

What is gamma? It is an important concept in both film and video and something we deal with frequently at the camera, in post, in delivery — everywhere. Some people think that gamma just means contrast and nothing more, but this isn't really true. Certainly changing the gamma does affect the contrastiness of the image, but there's a lot more to it than; also, there are other factors that alter the contrast of an image; we'll talk about those a little later. First we need to take a quick glance at gamma in film — it's a bit different. In film, gamma is the slope of the middle (straight line) portion of the curve. Clearly a steeper line is more contrasty — the Y value (image brightness) changes more quickly for every unit of change in the X value (scene brightness). A slope that is less steep means that pixel brightness changes at a slower rate than image brightness, which results in midtones with less contrast. For this reason it was very easy to tell the difference between low, medium and high contrast film stocks simply by looking at the response curves.

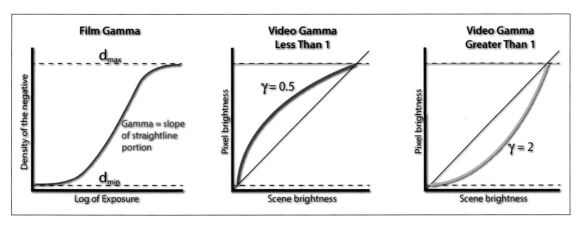

| **Film Gamma** | **Video Gamma Less Than 1** | **Video Gamma Greater Than 1** |

Figure 4.7. (Left) In film, *Gamma* is the slope of the straight line portion of the curve, the midtones.

VIDEO GAMMA

Video gamma is a *power function*, which takes the form of a curve. As you can see in Figures 4.8 and 4.9, it can be a upward curve or a downward curve, depending on whether the value is greater than or less than 1 (a gamma of 1 would be a straight line). For a visual illustration of gamma, see the chapter *Image Control & Grading*.) In video, it mostly comes down to how much pixel brightness results from X amount of electrical input. If we change the gamma, the pixels can be made to appear brighter or darker — it's the same original electrical signal; it's just by changing the shape of *transfer function* (the response curve) that we make the pixels appear brighter or darker.

Gamma has been part of video since the earliest days. The reason for this is that most early televisions were *cathode ray tube* (*CRT*) displays, which have an inherent gamma curve of their own — it's just part of the physics of how they work. Their display of red, green and blue is non-linear. Called the *Optical-electronic conversion function* (*OECF*), it averages to a power function of about 2.4. Displays designed and used for various purposes differ slightly, from about 2.2 to 2.6, depending on, among other things, the brightness of the typical environment in which they will be used, the reason for this is discussed in *Picture Rendering* at the end of this chapter.

Figure 4.8. (Middle) Video gamma is a power function, a curve. A gamma less than one results in an upward curve.

Figure 4.9. (Right) A video gamma of greater than one forms a downward curve.

THE COINCIDENCE

Human vision perceives brightness in a non-linear fashion; it works out to a gamma of about .42, which is, by amazing coincidence, the inverse of 2.4 (1/2.4=.42). As a result of this, engineers realized very early in the development of television that cameras must include something at the front end to compensate for this; it is called *gamma correction* (Figure 4.10). Recall that in the first decades of television, images went directly from the camera to the control room, to broadcast towers to people's televisions. In short, gamma encoding at the camera is the inverse of the gamma characteristics of CRT monitors — the two cancel each other out. Modern flat panel displays such as *LED*, *plasma*, *LCD*, *OLED*, don't have this non-linear nature, and CRTs are no longer even being made, so it would seem that this gamma correction is no longer needed. However, there are decades worth of gamma corrected RGB video already in existence, so even the newest displays still incorporate this correction.

While CRTs came by their gamma naturally due to physical factors, flat screen displays need a *Look Up Table* (*LUT*) to achieve the proper gamma correction (see *Image Control & Grading*) for more on LUTs). There used to be quite a bit of variation in gamma correction, but there has been a tendency to standardize on 2.2 for monitors.

Figure 4.10. Gamma correction in traditional video — the gamma curves of the camera and the monitor are the inverse of each other and thus cancel out.

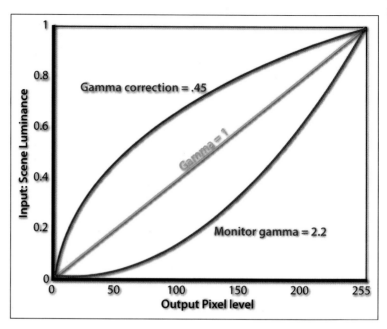

REC.709

The term *Rec.709* (or *BT.709*) appears in discussions of HD video all the time. It comes up in several different places in this book because it is not just one thing: it's actually a collection of specifications that define traditional High Definition video up to 1080. Basically modern video as we know it now came along with cameras like the Viper, Red, Genesis, Alexa and all the others that created *Ultra High Def*. Historically Rec.709 replaced *NTSC* and *PAL* (remember them?). The Rec.709 specifications include a color space, a gamma curve, aspect ratios, frame rates and many engineering details we don't need to get into here.

The official name is *ITU-R Recommendation BT.709* but most often it is referred to as *Rec.709* but you'll also see it Rec 709, Rec709 and Rec. 709. *ITU* is the *International Television Union* which is sort of the United Nations' version of *SMPTE* (*Society of Motion Picture & Television Engineers*) in the US, the *EBU* (*European Broadcast Union*) or *ARIB* (*Association of Radio Industries and Businesses*) in Japan, all of which are organizations that create standards so that everybody's video signal plays nice with all the rest. It has been officially adopted as a standard so technically it is no longer a "rec," but it is unlikely that the terminology in general use will change anytime soon.

Rec.709 is WYSIWYG or "what you see is what you get." It was designed to be *display referred*, meaning that the contrast range that comes out of the camera sensor is *mapped* to standardized contrast range designed to suit specified display devices. In order to do this it brings all color values into a fairly limited range: in fact the range that could be accommodated by monitors and displays at the time Rec.709 was standardized, although there have been some tweaks and adjustments along the way.

You will primarily see Rec.709 talked about in two ways: one as a *color space*, which we'll look at in the chapter *Digital Color* and in this chapter you'll see it discussed as a gamma curve (Figure 4.11). Almost every time a color space or response correction curve is described, it usually includes a comparison to Rec.709, which is why we need to go into it a bit thoroughly.

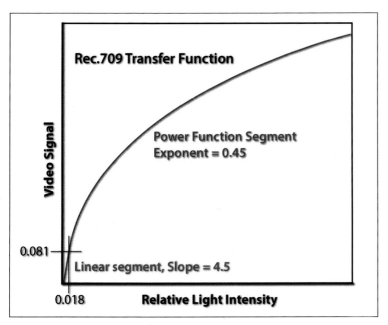

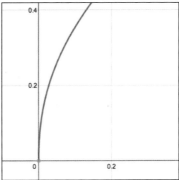

Figure 4.11. (Left) The Rec.709 transfer function is mostly a power function curve but there is a small linear portion at the bottom.

Figure 4.12. (Above) As Poynton indicates, the problem with a pure power function for Rec.709 is that it approaches vertical as it gets near zero, which would cause infinite gain and noise in the dark portions of the scene. This is sometimes a problem with some mathematical functions — they "blow up" at near zero.

Table 4.1. (Left, below) The basic formula of Rec.709 transfer function.

THE REC.709 TRANSFER FUNCTION

Because the dominant form of video display at the time was CRT monitors, Rec.709 correction "prepares" video so that it will appear correctly on that type of display. To really oversimplify a bit, it is the red line labeled *Power Function Segment = 0.45* in Figure 4.11. Since this is a technical guide to digital imaging we have to go the extra distance and point out that it is slightly more complicated. Here's the actual spec:

Linear (L) to Rec. 709 (V)	
Condition	Value
0.000 ≤ L < 0.018	V = L×4.50
0.018 ≤ L ≤ 1.000	V = 1.099×L0.45 − 0.099

Don't panic! It's not as complicated as it seems. All it means is that response below 0.018 is *linear*: a straight line of slope 4.5. Above 0.018, the response is a power function with the exponent 0.45. By the way, in case you were wondering, the 0.018 has nothing to do with 18% gray. Technically, Rec.709 has only a five stop range but tweaks such as knee and black stretch can extend this a bit. Most HD cameras can generate signals that are "legal" meaning that the video signal levels stay within the range 0% to 100%. However, each camera company adds their own little twists to try to conform to Rec.709 and they don't always produce the same result; you will hear the term "Rec.709 *compliant*" meaning "kinda, sorta." In his article *HDTV Standards: Looking Under The Hood of Rec.709*, Andy Shipsides writes "In other words, monitors conform to the gamma standards of Rec.709, but cameras generally do not. This is a big reason why setting two cameras to Rec.709 mode doesn't guarantee they will look the same. Different gamma means different contrast and dynamic range. Contrast is just half the equation, of course; the other half is color." We'll discuss this aspect of Rec.709 in *Digital Color*. The bottom line is that in the newer cameras that shoot RAW video, viewing the images in Rec.709 is just an approximation of the actual image. This does not mean that Rec.709 video no longer has a place in shooting. It is often used when video has to be output

Figure 4.13. Output options on the *Arri Alexa*. *Legal* keeps everything in the range of 0-100%. *Extended* ranges from -9% to 109%. *Raw*, of course, outputs everything.

Figure 4.14. Based on the work of Weber and Fechner, psychologist S.S. Stevens proposed that physical stimuli are *exponential functions*. Other researchers prefer to see brightness perception as logarithmic; it's a question of how experimental data is interpreted. In either case, the essential point is that human perception of brightness levels is nonlinear, which has important implications for how we process and display film and video images.

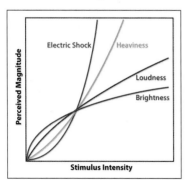

quickly for near immediate use with little or no grading. One might ask, what is the linear portion at the bottom for? Poynton explains it this way, "A true power function requires infinite gain near black, which would introduce a large amount of noise in the dark regions of the image." By infinite gain, he means that the power function curve becomes vertical near the origin. (Figure 4.12).

Some cameras have a Rec.709 output either for viewing or for recording when little or no post-production color correction is anticipated. These are usually not "true" Rec.709 but are designed to look reasonably good on a Rec.709 display. Arri puts it this way: "Material recorded in Rec.709 has a display specific encoding or, in other words, 'what you see is what you get' characteristics. The purpose of a display specific encoding is to immediately provide a visually correct representation of the camera material, when it is screened on a certain display device. This is achieved by mapping the actual contrast range of the scene into the contrast range that a display device can reproduce." Arri also offers their Rec.709 *Low Contrast Curve (LCC)*, which they explain like this, "To enable productions to shoot in Rec.709 color space without the sacrifice of too much highlight information, Arri provides a special *Low Contrast Characteristic (LCC) Arri Look File* that can be applied to change the standard Rec.709 output."

STUDIO SWING LEVELS, FULL RANGE AND LEGAL VIDEO

Rec.709 also incorporates what are called *legal levels*; also known as *studio swing* or *video range*. *Range* or *swing* in this context really means *excursion*, as in how the signal level travels between *reference black* and *reference white*. In 8-bit video, the minimum code value is 0 and the maximum is 255. You would think that 0 represents pure black and 255 represents pure white. In *legal levels*, *video range* or *studio-swing*, however, black is placed at code value 16 and reference white is at 235 (64-940 in 10 bit). Code values from 0-16 and from 236-255 are reserved as *footroom* and *headroom*. When this system is not used and the video signal uses all code values from 0-255 (0-1023 in 10 bit) it is called *full swing* or *extended range*. Figure 4.13 shows Arri's version of *Extended* — it goes from -9% (IRE) up to 109% (IRE). We'll be coming back to the concept of headroom and footroom soon; they turn out to be fundamental to *Cineon*, *OpenEXR* and *ACES*.

An example of this general idea can be seen on the menu of an *Arri Alexa* (Figure 4.13). It offers three options for *Output Range*: *Legal*, *Extended* and *RAW*. The *Legal* setting will output video at 0-100% and *Extended* goes from -9% up to 109%. *Extended* can, however, push your video into *Illegal* ranges on the waveform. As another example, *DaVinci Resolve* has a LUT called *Legal Output Levels*.

THE CODE 100 PROBLEM

There is another consequence of the non-linear nature of human vision. It is called the *Code 100 problem* and we will find that it has huge implications for digital video. Scientists who study perception rely on measurements of the *Just Noticeable Difference (JND)* — the smallest change in input levels that an average person can detect. These perceptual studies are based on averages of many observers. Most human modes of perception are logarithmic or exponential in nature: our ability to sense changes in perception changes as they become more extreme (Figure 4.14).

This applies not only to brightness levels but also to sound level, pressure, heaviness, pain and others. Let's take a simple example:

weight. Anyone can sense the difference between a one pound weight and a two pound weight. On the other hand, not even the guy who guesses your weight at the state fair can detect the difference between a 100 pound weight and a 101 pound weight. In both examples, the difference is the same: one pound, but the percentage change is vastly different: from one to two pounds, the difference is 100%. The difference between 100 and 101 is only 1%.

For our purposes here, human perception of brightness is the relevant issue. Whether it is logarithmic in response to change or exponential is a matter of debate among vision scientists. It all comes down to how they interpret the data of many different studies. In practice, it doesn't make a great deal of difference — the key point is that our perception of light levels is not linear.

THE ONE PER CENT SOLUTION

The human visual system can perceive a one per cent difference in brightness value; this is the *Just Noticeable Difference*. Let's say we're dealing with 8-bit material, so the code values go from 0-to-255 (256 code values total). Figure 4.15 shows the problem — in the darkest part of the image (lower code values) the difference between, for example, *CV* (*code value*) 20 and 21 is 5% — far more than the minimum discernible difference. The result of this is that there are very big jumps in brightness from one code value to the next. This leads to *banding,* (which is also known as *contouring*) in the shadows (Figure 2.7 in *Digital Image*).

At the brighter end of the scale, the differences can be much smaller, such as only a 0.5% difference between CV 200 and 201 — much smaller than is perceptible. This means that a lot of these code values are wasted. If the visual difference between two code values is not perceivable, then one of them is unnecessary and it is a waste of space in the file and in the data storage, which becomes a real issue when shooting RAW, and especially in 3D, high speed, multi-camera or other situations where a great deal of video is recorded.

There are two ways to deal with this issue. One of them is to have lots of bits at the sensor/processor level; this is how DSLRs deal with it. Another way is to have the spaces between the levels be unequal — putting the light values/code values at the bottom end closer together and making them farther apart at the top end; as we will see, the steps are made unequal in spacing but are still *perceptually equal,* meaning that the eye still sees them as equal. This can be accomplished either through *gamma encoding (power function)* or through *log encoding,* which we will discuss in more detail in the next section as it has become a major factor in digital video. To help us prepare for the discussion of these techniques of gamma and log encoding, let's take a look at the traditional HD controls; which are in fact largely the same as have been used on video cameras for many decades.

GAMMA CONTROL IN TRADITIONAL HD

We have already discussed the meaning of gamma in the video signal and how it differs from film gamma. In HD cameras, *Gamma* (sometimes called *Coarse Gamma*) is a key adjustment that is available to the operator. Typically, the gamma was preset to .45 and could be adjusted up or down from there, depending on the desired image. As you would guess, raising the gamma to something like .55 gives an image that is overall contrastier, while lowering the Coarse Gamma to .35 gave you a lower contrast image.

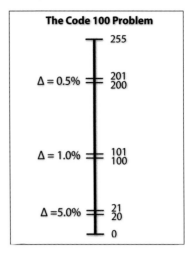

Figure 4.15. The *Code 100* problem in digital video in an 8-bit system. Because human perception of the *Just Noticeable Difference* in lightness is a ratio (percentage) rather than an absolute value the number of digital code values needed to efficiently portray the gray scale is not uniform as we move up and down the brightness scale.

Figure 4.16. (Below) The *Knee Control* function in video alters the *slope* of the highlight response. The *Knee Point* determines where this alteration begins.

Figure 4.17. (Bottom) B*lack Stretch* or *Black Gamma* controls alter the slope of the shadow region to help preserve some detail in the shadows.

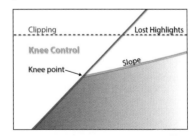

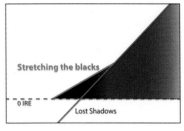

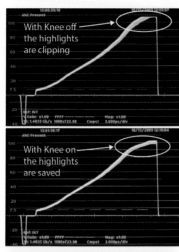

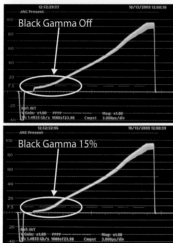

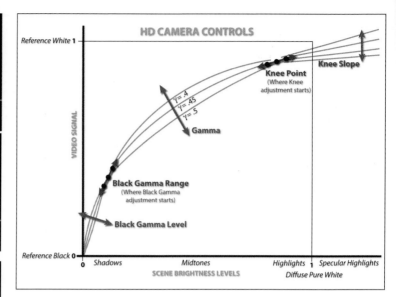

Figure 4.18. (Top) The image with the highlights clipping.

Figure 4.19. (Second down) With *knee control* turned on to preserve the highlights without clipping.

Figure 4.20. (Third down) The signal with *Black Gamma* off.

Figure 4.21. (Fourth down) With *Black Gamma* at 15%, the dark areas of the scene have been made darker; what a DP might call "crunchier shadows."

Figure 4.22. (Right) Image controls on traditional HD cameras (otherwise known as "the knobs") allow the operator to control different parts of the image separately. (After a diagram by Charles Poynton).

KNEE CONTROL

Knee Control adjustment in most cameras usually consists of two separate adjustments: *slope* and *knee point*. *Slope* is the angle of the response in the highlights or knee, Figures 4.18 and 4.19. Obviously, a lower angle means that changes in brightness only slowly change the image brightness; you could call it lower contrast. A steeper slope means that image brightness changes very quickly, in other words higher contrast. Most often this is used to accommodate for some bright highlights in the scene, such as a window or lamp shade. The *Knee Point* control lets the operator to select where on the curve the slope adjustment kicks in. Knee control is rarely used in UHD video.

BLACK STRETCH/BLACK GAMMA

In the toe (shadow regions) a similar strategy is used. Different camera companies use different terminology but *black stretch* or *black gamma* are typical names for this function. It alters the slope of the curve at the lower end to make it more or less contrasty. These illustrations are simplified and diagrammatic, of course, the actual changes to the curve are a bit more complex and vary from camera to camera. Figure 4.20 and 4.21 shows Sony's *Black Gamma* curves and resultant frames. All three of the HD gamma controls are shown in diagram form in Figure 4.22.

ANOTHER APPROACH

Just bending and stretching the knee and shadow areas can achieve a good deal but in the end it is a limited approach and can result in some images that look a bit unnatural. Over the years camera manufacturers have come up with even more sophisticated ways of extending the dynamic range of video cameras. Each company has their own names and terminology. Each has their own secret sauce; in some cases even more secret than what comes on a Big Mac.

HYPERGAMMA/CINEGAMMA/FILM REC

Camera manufacturers have developed several versions of gamma encoding variously called *Hypergamma*, *Cinegamma*, *Video Rec*, *Film Rec* or *low contrast curve* (depending on the camera), which is designed to extend the dynamic range of the camera. These gamma curves are usually measured in a percentage, with the range of Rec. 709 as

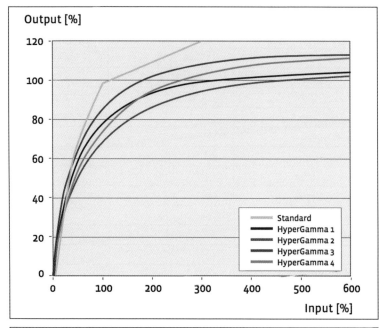

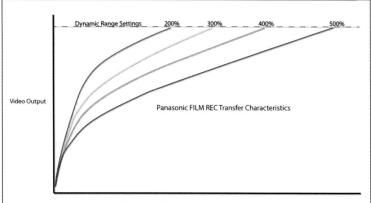

Figure 4.23. (Left, top) Sony's *HyperGamma* curves as compared to video with the Rec.709 curve applied which here they call *standard* — the yellow line. This chart uses Sony's older method of naming gamma curves; see the text for their new system. (Courtesy of Sony).

Figure 4.24. (Left, below) Panasonic's *Film Rec* curves. They are denoted as the percentage by which they extend the dynamic range.

a base 100%, with typical settings of 200%, 300%, 400% and so on. The higher the dynamic range, the flatter the curve and the lower the contrast, which means that color correction will be necessary and it also makes the use of exposure aids such as zebras difficult or impossible. *Panasonic's Film Rec* (Figure 4.24)was originally designed for shooting video that was to be transferred to film in post-production.

According to Sony, "HyperGamma is a set of new transfer functions specifically designed to maximise the latitude of the camera, especially in highlights. It works by applying a parabolic shaped curve to the gamma correction circuit, so that the huge dynamic range of Sony CCDs can be used in the final recorded picture, without the need for the cameraman to adjust any settings in the camera. This approach also means we do not use any knee, thus removing the non linear part of the transfer characteristic as HyperGamma is a totally smooth curve. This means you remove any traditional issues which occur because of the non-linearity, especially in skin tones, and improve the dynamic range in one step.

"On lower end Sony cameras there are four HyperGamma curves as standard, two of which are optimized for 100% white clip in a TV workflow (HG 1 and 2), and two for the 109% white clip generally used in traditional film style workflow (HG 3 and 4). Having

linear, gamma, log

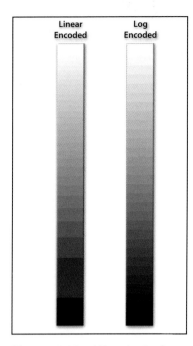

	Linear Encoded	Log Encoded

Value	Code Range	Total # Values
Max White	16,384	
One Stop Down	8,192-16,383	**8,191**
Two Stops Down	4,096-8,191	**4,095**
Three Stops Down	2,048-4,095	**2,047**
Four Stops Down	1,024-2,047	**1023**
Five Stops Down	512-1,023	**511**
Six Stops Down	256-511	**255**
Seven Stops Down	128-255	**127**
Eight Stops Down	64-127	**63**
Nine Stops Down	32-63	**31**
Ten Stops Down	16-31	**15**
Eleven Stops Down	9-15	**6**
Twelve Stops Down	5-8	**3**
Thirteen Stops Down	3-4	**1**
Fourteen Stops Down	1-2	**1**

Figure 4.25. (Above) A linear encoded grayscale distributes the tones unevenly (left). Log encoding distributes the tones more evenly. (Right) The gray scale steps in this case represent the number of code values in each stop.

Table 4.2. (Right) Based on a 14-bit sensor, this chart shows that the first few stops down from maximum white hog most of the available code values, while the darkest part of the image contain so few code values that they are not able to accurately depict the subtle gradations of one — resulting in *banding* in the image. Experiments have shown that around 60 to 70 code values are needed per stop for proper representation of the image. Derived from calculations made by Art Adams.

chosen your white clip point, two curves are available to either optimize for maximum highlight handling (HG 2 and 4) or for low light conditions (HG 1 and 3)." (Sony, *Digital Cinematography With Hypergamma*). Higher end cameras have as many as eight HyperGamma curves (Figure 4.23). They are different than knee adjustments in that the changes to the curve starts down toward the middle, so they generate a more "holistic" compression of the highlights as opposed to the somewhat unnatural look of knee and black stretch.

SONY HYPERGAMMA TERMINOLOGY

Sony now uses a naming format for hypergamma that includes the *range*. For example, HG8009G30 has a dynamic range of 800%, a middle gray exposure of 30% and a white clip level of 109%. HG (HyperGamma) 800 (dynamic range), [10]9 white clip level and G30 (middle gray exposure level at 30%).

Sony HG4609G33 has an extended dynamic range of 460%, a white clip of 109%, and a middle grey exposure level of 33%. This means that the name of the HyperGamma actually includes Sony's recommendation for exposure: they want you to expose your middle gray at a particular IRE value (in this case 33 IRE), which will then give you the indicated percentage of dynamic range.

GAMMA IN RAW VIDEO

When shooting RAW, gamma is just metadata, you aren't really changing the image at all until you bake it in, which you do have to do at some point. An example of how this is done is how Red cameras handle this. Their color science has been evolving since the introduction of the first *Red One* and offers several selections: *RedGamma 2*, *RedGamma 3* and a log version: *Redlogfilm*. These are different look profiles for viewing on set and for conversion as the RAW files are imported to editing or color software; as with all metadata, you're not stuck with them, but they do offer a starting point for the final look and guidance for the postproduction process.

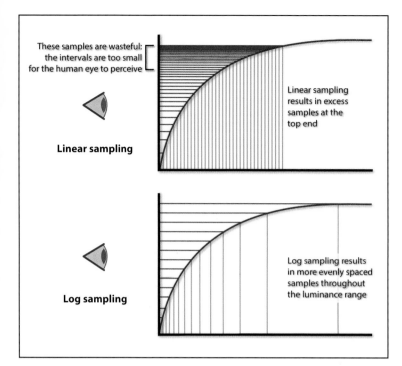

These samples are wasteful: the intervals are too small for the human eye to perceive

Linear sampling

Linear sampling results in excess samples at the top end

Log sampling

Log sampling results in more evenly spaced samples throughout the luminance range

Figure 4.26. Linear sampling wastes codes values where they do little good (upper diagram), while log encoding (lower diagram) distributes them more evenly — in a way that more closely conforms to how human perception works. Based on a diagram by Steve Shaw of *Light Illusion*.

THE INEFFICIENCY OF LINEAR

In addition to potentially losing data at the top and bottom of the curve, linear video reproduction has another problem — it is extremely inefficient in how it uses *bits per stop*. Table 4.2 shows how Art Adams calculates the output of a 14 bit sensor, which has 16,384 bits per channel. It shows the code values in terms of f/stops. Recall that every f/stop is a doubling of the previous value (or half the previous value if you're going down the scale) — the inefficiency is obvious in the table and the problem is clear — the four stops at the top end of the scale (the highlights) use up 15,356 bits, most of the available bits!

As Adams puts in his article *The Not-So-Technical Guide to S-Log and Log Gamma Curves* (*Pro Video Coalition*) "As you can see, the first four stops of dynamic range get an enormous number of storage bits- -and that's just about when we hit middle gray. This is the origin of the "expose to the right" school of thought for 'RAW' cameras: if you expose to the right of the histogram you are cramming as much information as possible into those upper few stops that contain the most steps of brightness. As we get toward the bottom of the dynamic range there are fewer steps to record each change in brightness, and we're also a lot closer to the noise floor." (*Expose to the right* will be discussed in more detail in the chapter *Exposure*.)

There's another problem. Experiments have shown that around 60 to 70 code values per stop is ideal. In this example, many stops at the bottom have less than this and stops at the top have much more.

Figure 4.26 is a diagram devised by Steve Shaw of *Light Illusion* which illustrates this problem. The top part of the figure shows that not only are there an excessive number of bits used up in the highlights, but also the divisions are too small for the human eye to perceive and so are wasted. The point of these examples is that there is more to the problem than just bending the top of the curve down to save the highlights.

Figure 4.27. *Gamma curves* and *log curves* are different mathematically but are somewhat similar in their effect on video levels in the recorded image. Both, however, are dramatically different from a purely linear response. Remember that gamma curves created by camera manufacturers are rarely a simple exponent function; most of them have a *secret sauce*, in some cases, very secret.

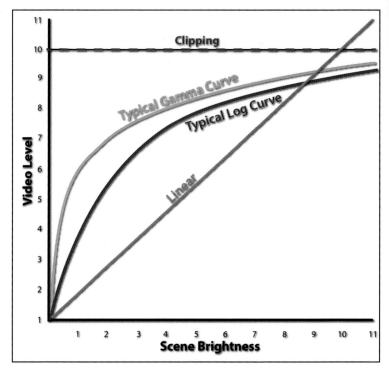

LOG ENCODING

Fortunately, there is a solution to this inefficiency: *log encoding*. It is similar in concept to gamma in that it reduces the slope of the response curve in order to extend the dynamic range to stretch the brightness values that can be captured and recorded without clipping. The difference between the two is self-evident: instead of applying a *power function* to the curve, it uses a *logarithmic* curve. Figure 4.27 shows this in graphic form.

As we learned in *A Little Bit of Math*, a key element of log scales is that the spacing of the values is not even, as we see here along the vertical Y-Axis. As you can see, it's pretty much like magic — a lot of problems are solved with this simple mathematical translation. Log curves and power function curves look somewhat alike when graphed and they do operate in similar ways, but there are mathematical and "behavioral" differences which can be exploited by camera and software designers and each can be used for specific purposes.

Brief History of Log

So where does this idea of log encoding for video come from? It's origin was a Kodak project in the 1990s which was a system for converting film to video. Although it was a complete system with a scanner, workstations and a laser film recorder, it was the file format that has had a lasting influence on image production. The system and the file format were called *Cineon*. Kodak's engineering team decided that a film image could be entirely captured in a 10 bit log file. It was intended as a digital intermediate (*DI*) format, not one to be used for delivery, CGI or anything else. As it was about origination on film and ultimately for printing on film, the entire system was referenced to *film density* numbers — which is the key value needed to understand and transform film negative. We'll talk about Cineon in more detail when we get to the *Academy Color Encoding Specification*.

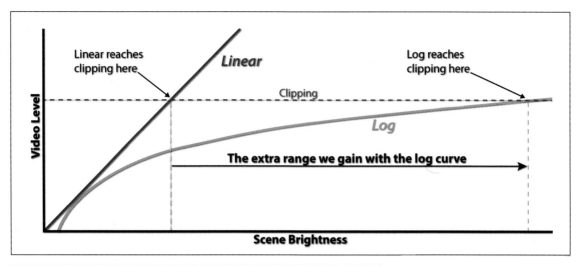

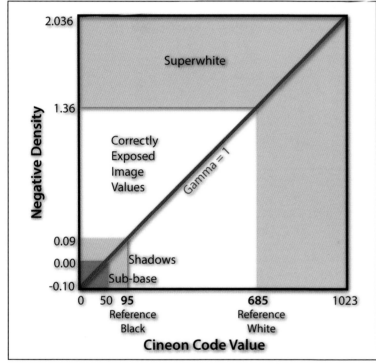

Figure 4.28. (Above) How log encoding provides extra dynamic range.

Figure 4.29. (Left) The "correctly exposed" image values occupy only a part of the entire range of *Cineon* code values. *Reference Black* is placed at CV 95 and *Reference White* is at CV 685 thus allowing headroom for superwhite and footroom for sub-black values.

SUPERWHITE

Film and video have a crucial difference. In 8-bit video computer graphics, "pure white" is all channels at maximum: 255, 255, 255 but in the film world, what we might call pure white is just a representation of "diffuse white" or brightness of a piece of illuminated white paper (about 90% reflectance). Because of the shoulder of the S-curve, film is actually capable of representing many values of white much brighter than this. These are *specular* highlights, such as a light bulb, a candle flame or the hot reflection of sun off a car bumper, for example.

If we stuck with 0-to-255, then all the "normal" tones would have to be pushed way down the scale to make room for these highlights that are above diffuse white. Kodak engineers decided on a 10-bit system (code values from 0-to-1023) and they placed diffuse white at 685 and black at 95 (Figure 4.29) — just as legal video goes from

Figure 4.30. *Rec.709* and *Cineon*. By placing *reference white* at a lower code value, extra headroom is allowed for highlights and specular reflections. The same is true at the bottom where code value 64 is taken as pure black, allowing for some footroom below that value.

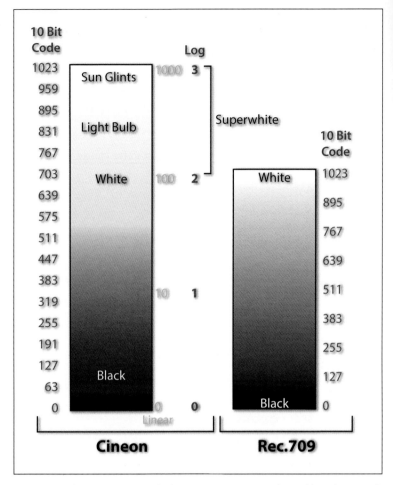

16-235 (8-bit) 64-940 (10-bit) or –9% to 109%. The values above reference white are thus allowed for and are called *superwhite*. Similarly, there are code value levels below *Reference Black* that allow some *footroom*, in the digital signal.

What You See Is Not What You Get

One important aspect of log encoded video is that it is *not* an accurate representation of the scene when viewed on a monitor — this is both its strong point and a limitation. Since it is essentially compressing scene values in order to get them to fit into the recording file structure, a log encoded on a monitor will look washed out, pale and low contrast (Figure 4.31). While most cinematographers can adapt to viewing this, it tends to freak out directors and producers and may not be especially useful for other crew members as well. It can also make lighting decisions more difficult and affect other departments such as set design, wardrobe and makeup. Of course, the fact that the log encoded images are not really "ready for prime time," means that the image must be color corrected at some later time, certainly at the time of final grading (Figure 4.32). In the meantime, it is often useful to have some sort of temporary correction for viewing purposes.

There are good reasons to have an accurate view on the set monitors — or at least one that is close to how the scene will appear. This is usually in the form of a *LUT* (*Look Up Table*) which we'll talk about in *Image Control & Grading*. Rec.709 is WYSIWYG because it is *display-referred*, meaning it is set up to be compatible with most

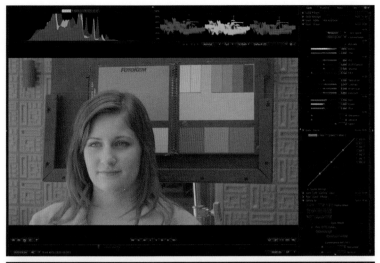

Figure 4.31. (Top) A Red camera shot displayed in *RedLogFilm* — a log space. The image is dull and low contrast by design. Note the waveforms in upper center: nothing reaches 0% at the bottom or 100% at the top; they don't even come close. This also shows in the histogram in the upper left. As shown here, the log image is not really viewable insofar as it is not an accurate representation of the scene — it is not intended to be.

Figure 4.32. (Below) The same shot with *RedColor* and with *RedGamma3 LUT* applied. This LUT is Rec.709 compatible, meaning it is designed to look good on a Rec.709 display. Notice especially the difference in the parade waveforms. This is a problem as it means that the log image is not only dull and low-contrast but also the waveform monitor and vectorscope are no longer accurate as relates to the actual scene values.

monitors and projectors; for this reason, just doing a quick, non-permanent conversion to Rec.709 is output for use on the set. Some cameras have a Rec.709 monitor viewing output just for this purpose — it has no effect on the recorded files. There are other viewing modes besides Rec.709, some of them custom built for the project. It is also important to remember that viewing the scene in log mode, you may not be able to make accurate exposure decisions, particularly with tools such as zebras or false color. There are different ways to deal with this and we'll discuss them in the chapter *Exposure*.

Log and *RAW* — Two Different Things

Log and RAW are two different things; however, many cameras that shoot RAW actually record the data log encoded — in most high end cameras, the sensors produce more data (higher bit depth) than is feasible to record using current technology. Just keep in mind that you can record RAW that isn't log or log that isn't RAW, but for the most part, they go hand-in-hand.

Some cameras do have the ability to record RAW uncompressed; however this can be likened to drinking from a fire hose — while there may be important reasons for recording uncompressed RAW data, it is important to understand the implications of the torrents of data that will be generated. As with a firehose — you better be sure

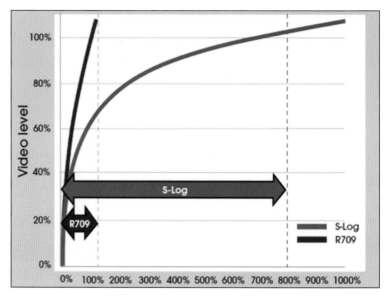

Figure 4.33. Sony's curve for S-Log as compared to Rec.709. (Courtesy of Sony).

you're really that thirsty. Other recording options include Rec.709 or *P3*, which is a wide gamut color space that is part of the *DCI* (*Digital Cinema Initiative*) and so is an industry wide standard.

PROPRIETARY LOG CURVES

Camera companies employ log curves extensively in recording image data; each manufacturer has designed one or more log encoding schemes which are part of their "secret sauce" in the quest for a better camera. Red cameras have *RedLogFilm,* Arri uses *Log C,* Canon cameras employ *C-Log* and Panavision has *Panalog.* The manufacturer's graphs of these encoding schemes are shown here and actual results of some of them are shown in Figures 4.33 through 4.38.

SONY S-LOG

S-Log comes in three versions, S-Log1, S-Log2 and S-Log3. DP Art Adams on S-Log: "Because code values never quite reach the extremes of black and white S-Log looks really flat because normal shadow values in a scene never reached the minimum code number for black. For that reason they looked too bright, or milky. S-Log2 appears to rectify that problem by storing shadow values farther down the curve so that the darkest tone the camera can possibly see is mapped very close to the log curve's minimum recordable value. By making blacks black again the log image actually looks fairly normal on a Rec.709 monitor. The highlights are still crushed because they are heavily compressed by the log curve for grading, but the image otherwise looks 'real.' It's less likely to cause people to panic when walking by the DIT's monitor." Sony says "S-Log3 is a log signal with 1300% dynamic range, close to Cineon Log curve. This does not replace S-Log2 and S-Gamut3. It is added as another choice."

As you will see from the following brief descriptions of various camera companies approach to log, they start from different assumptions about what is important in imaging and how best to achieve that. It is important to understand these differences and how best to use them as you use them on the set — it is not unlike testing, evaluating and using different film stocks. Table 4.3 shows the IRE and code values of S-Log1, S-Log2, and S-Log3. Keep in mind that in HD /UHD, IRE and % on the waveform are the same measurement, although % is the technically correct designation.

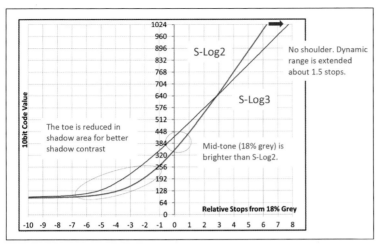

Figure 4.34. (Left, top) A comparison of S-Log2 and S-Log3. (Courtesy of Sony).

Table 4.3. (Left, below) Black, middle gray and 90% white figures for S-Log1, S-Log2 and S-Log3.

	0% Black		18% Gray		90% White	
	IRE	10-Bit CV	IRE	10-bit CV	IRE	10-bit CV
S-Log1	3%	90	38%	394	65%	636
S-Log2	3%	90	32%	347	59%	582
S-Log3	3.5%	95	41%	420	61%	598

SONY S-GAMUT

S-Gamut is a color space designed by Sony specifically to be used with S-Log. Since an S-Gamut conversion to Rec.709 can be a bit tricky, Sony has several conversion LUTs to be used with color correction software and makes them freely available on their website.

ARRI LOG C

Arri's *Log C* is based on the Cineon print density curve and is meant to be used with a Cineon based LUT for translation (Figure 4.35). According to Arri "Material recorded in Rec.709 or P3 has a display specific encoding" or in other words "what you see is what you get" characteristics or display referred. "These characteristics map the actual contrast range of the scene to the total contrast range the display device is able to reproduce. The purpose of these encodings is to directly provide a visually correct representation of the cap-

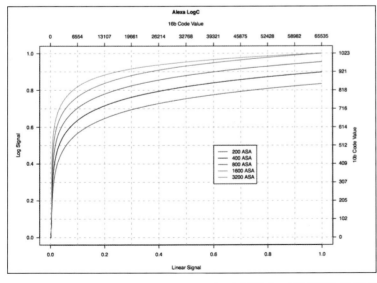

Figure 4.35. Arri Log C is not a single function but is actually a set of curves at different ISOs. (Courtesy of Arri).

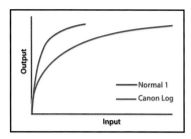

Figure 4.36. (Above) *Canon Log* vs. normal output. (Courtesy of Canon).

Figure 4.37. (Right) *Canon Log C* changes in dynamic range as ISO is set for different values. This is similar to the response of film. (Courtesy of Canon).

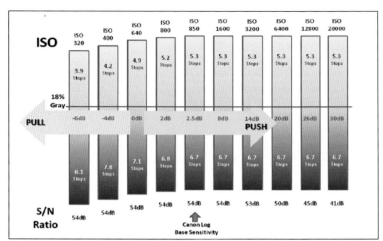

tured material, when it is screened on HDTV monitors (Rec.709) or digital cinema projectors (DCI P3). Because of this requirement, these display specific encodings provide somewhat reduced choices in color grading. The Log C curve is a logarithmic encoding of the scene, meaning that the relation between exposure measured in stops and the signal is constant over a wide range. Each stop of exposure increases the signal by the same amount. The overall shape of the Log C curve is similar to the exposure curves of film negatives. Because of fundamental differences between a sensor and negative film, however, the color characteristics remain different." (Arri Group, *Log C and Rec.709 Video*, *Arri White Paper*).

Log C is not a single transfer function, it is actually a set of curves for different ISO settings. All of these curves map 18% middle gray to code value 400 (out of 1023 on the 10-bit scale). Arri goes on to say:"The maximum value of the Log C curve depends on the EI value. The reason is quite simple: When the lens is stopped down, by one stop for example, the sensor will capture one stop more highlight information. Since the Log C output represents scene exposure values, the maximum value increases." Arri is adamant that, in their implementation of log encoding, changing the EI (Exposure Index) does not change the dynamic range; however it does affect how the total range is distributed above and below middle gray. This can be a useful tool for the cinematographer who may need to accommodate scenes where there is some crucial detail either in the highlights or in the shadows.

Arri's Alexa FAQ includes this note: Question:"*Does Alexa's exposure latitude change with different Exposure Index (EI) settings?* Answer: No, it does not. Most digital cameras have the greatest exposure latitude at a specific EI setting (often called the 'sweet spot'). Choosing an EI setting that is higher or lower than the optimal setting will result in a sometimes surprisingly large loss of exposure latitude. Alexa is unique in that its exposure latitude of 14 stops stays constant from EI 160 to EI 3200." Canon and other camera makers take a different approach to this aspect of log encoding, which is why extensive testing is important to get to know the cameras.

Canon-Log

Commonly referred to as *C-Log* (*Canon-Log*), it behaves in slightly different ways depending on the ISO setting (Figure 4.37). "As a result of its operation, exposure latitude/dynamic range can be extended up to a maximum of 800% by raising the camera's *Master*

Canon C-Log			
Image Brightness	8-bit CV	10-bit CV	Waveform
0% — Pure Black	32	128	7.3%
2% Black	42	169	12%
18% Middle Gray	88	351	39%
90% 2.25 Stops Over Middle Gray	153	614	63%
Maximum Brightness	254	1016	108.67%

Table 4.4. Code and waveform values for Canon C-Log.

Gain setting. Canon states that this will yield a still acceptable noise level of 54 dB." (Larry Thorpe, *Canon-Log Transfer Characteristics*.) As previously mentioned Canon takes a different approach to its RAW encoding in that it is partially baked in, meaning the color channels have gain added to them in order to achieve the correct color balance for the scene and then this is recorded as baked in data.

PANALOG

Panavision's chief digital technologist John Galt, in the white paper *Panalog Explained,* summarizes: "Panalog is a perceptually uniform transfer characteristic that internally transforms the 14-bit per color linear output of the Genesis A/D converters into a quasi-logarithmic 10-bit per color signal that enables the RGB camera signal to be recorded on 10-bit recorders." Galt explains that although the Genesis sensor is 14-bit, the recorder is only capable of handling 10-bit data; many high end cameras share similar characteristics. Panalog in comparison to other curves is show in Figure 4.38.

REDCODE

Red cameras record using *Redcode RAW* codec, which has the file extension *.R3D* and is, as the name states, a RAW format. It is a variable bit rate lossy (but visually lossless) wavelet code with compression ratios selectable from 3:1 to 18:1. It is *intraframe* with four channels: 2 for green and 1 each for red and blue.

As a wrapper format, it is similar to Adobe's *CinemaDNG*. Because it is a *wavelet* codec, as are *CineForm RAW* and *JPEG 2000*, the artifacts which may be the result of lossy compression are not like the "blocking" that occurs with heavy JPEG compression. We'll discuss wavelet, JPEG and other forms of video file compression in the chapter *Codecs & Formats*.

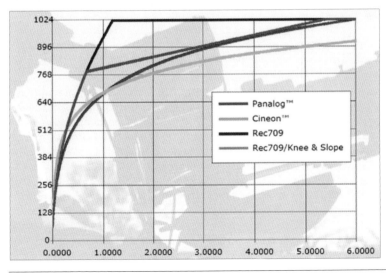

Figure 4.38. A comparison of Panalog, Cineon, Rec.709 and Rec.709 with typical knee and slope applied. (Courtesy of Panavision).

linear, gamma, log

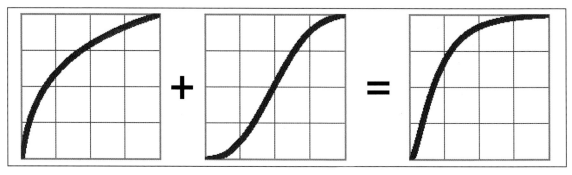

Figure 4.39. With Red cameras, the gamma setting may also be comprised of other tonal curves. To give images the toe and shoulder characteristics of film tones, *REDgamma3* (right) and similar settings are the net result of both a standard log curve (left) and a contrast curve (middle). The contrast S-curve causes shadows and highlights with more pleasingly roll off into pure black and white, respectively, and improves contrast and color saturation within the more visually important mid-tones. (Courtesy of Red).

RedCode RAW stores each of the sensor's color channels separately prior to conversion to a full color image. This brings advantages in control over color balance, exposure and grading in post-production. As with other RAW formats, these adjustments are stored as separate metadata until they are baked in at some point; this means that adjustments are non-destructive — in other words, reversible.

RED LOG

Like all camera manufacturers, Red has constantly sought to improve their color space, log and gamma and they have gone through several generations of their software/firmware for Red cameras. This is from the company: "*REDlog* is a log encoding that maps the original 12-bit R3D camera data to a 10-bit curve. The blacks and midtones in the lowest 8 bits of the video signal maintain the same precision as in the original 12-bit data, while the highlights in the highest 4 bits are compressed. While reducing the precision of highlight detail, the trade off is that there's an abundance of precision throughout the rest of the signal which helps maintain maximum latitude.

REDlogFilm is a log encoding that's designed to remap the original 12-bit camera data to the standard Cineon curve. This setting produces very flat-contrast image data that preserves image detail with a wide latitude for adjustment, and is compatible with log workflows intended for film output." (Figure 4.39)

18% GRAY IN LOG

If you ever studied still photography, you probably learned that 18% gray (middle gray) is half way between black and white and that light meters are calibrated to 18% gray as being the average exposure of a typical scene. Now why is middle gray 18% and not 50%? Because human perceptual vision is logarithmic, not linear. The Kodak 18% gray card is probably one of the most widely used and trusted tools in photography and film shooting. So we can depend on the gray card, light meters and expect that 18% gray will read as exactly 50% on the waveform monitor, right?

Not exactly, except for one part: 18% reflectance (actually it's 17.5%) is middle gray *perceptually*, but it turns out that incident meters are calibrated according to *ANSI* (*American National Standards Institute*) at 12.5% (with some small variations between different manufacturers). Reflectance (spot) meters are calibrated at around 17.6%, again with variation among manufacturers. Even Kodak acknowledges this in their instructions packaged with the Kodak Gray Card: "Meter readings of the gray card should be adjusted as follows: 1) For subjects of normal reflectance increase the indicated exposure by 1/2 stop." The instructions have since been updated to: "Place the card close to and in front of the subject, aimed halfway between the main light and the camera." Due to the *cosine effect*, holding the card at an angle has the effect of reducing the reflectance of the card, which in effect forces the meter to increase the exposure by roughly 1/2 stop. (For more on the cosine effect in lighting, see *Motion Picture and Video Lighting* by the same author.)

How middle gray reads on the waveform monitor is a more complex topic, but an important one to understand. Despite some lack of precision, middle gray/18% is still a very important part of judging exposure and testing cameras and gray cards in particular are widely used and trusted. Just because there is some confusion about exact numbers doesn't mean they aren't useful — after all, when it comes to exposure, there are shades of gray.

In Rec.709, the transfer function placed middle gray at 40.9% (generally rounded off to 41%). It assumes a theoretical 100% reflectance for "white" — which is placed at 100 IRE (100% on the waveform monitor) but as we know, that isn't possible in the real world, where the 90% reflectance is roughly the high end. If you put a 90% reflectance (such as a Kodak white card) at 100% on the WFM, 18% gray will wind up at 43.4%, OK call it 43%. Red values are higher? Alexa values are lower? Neither Red's 709 nor Alexa's 709 curves precisely follow the Rec.709 transfer function. In neither case can we assume that 18% gray hits 41% when we set the camera up to its nominally correct exposure level. The same is likely to be true for any camera with a non-Rec.709 curve (Figure 4.40)

In both the Red and the Alexa cases the recommended values are those the manufacturer says will render the optimum exposure for the way they've set up their cameras to work. Red's FLUT adds considerable S-curving, both in shoulder and toe in film terms, and does interesting and seemingly appropriate things in the midtones, but strict 709 it ain't. Likewise Alexa, which rolls off from the 709 curve quite early on — which gives that delightful tonal scale rendering, but again it isn't the straight Rec.709 curve. Since log curves aren't meant to be WYSIWYG, the manufacturer can place 18% gray wherever they think they get the most dynamic range out of the curves. More often than not they place it farther down the curve to increase highlight retention, but this is not always the case.

The bottom line is that, barring artistic considerations, no matter where the manufacturer places middle gray it will most likely be moved toward about 41% in the grade, because the grade is where we make the image look good on a Rec.709 display.

VARIATION IN LOG CURVES

When it comes to log encoded video, however, all bets are off as far as white point and middle gray — the engineers at camera manufacturers have made considered decisions about what seems to work best for their sensors and their viewpoint about what is the "best" image data to be recorded. The point of log is to push the highlight values down to where they can be safely recorded, leave room for specular highlights and bring the darkest values up above noise, and this naturally has an effect on the midtones as well. Where 18% falls in terms of the waveform monitor and code values varies according to camera manufacturers as each of them has their own philosophy of what works best for their cameras. Figure 4.40 shows the waveform and code values for middle gray and 90% white for several log encoding schemes. None of them places 18% middle gray even close to 50%. Not surprisingly, the white point is much lower than it is in Rec.709, as this is a goal of log encoding — to preserve the highlights and make room available for specular highlights/superwhite.

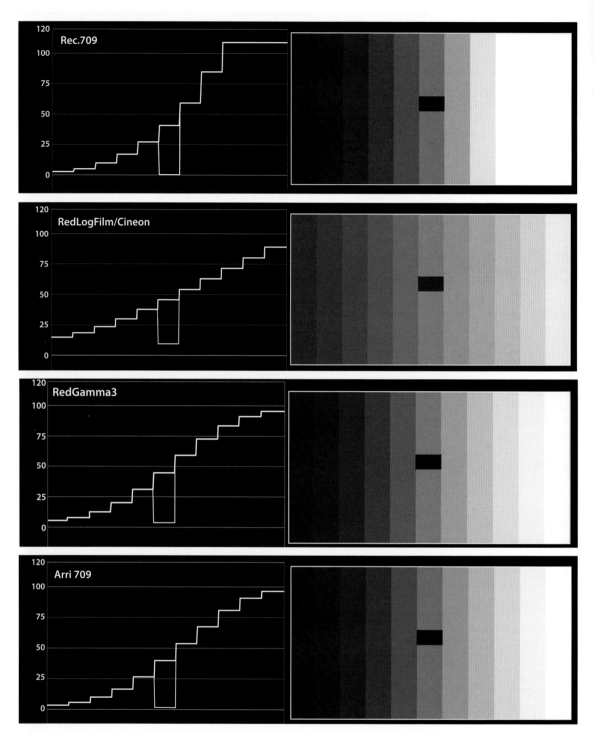

Figure 4.40. (Top) *Rec.709* doesn't have the dynamic range to represent all eleven steps of this grayscale, as the waveform shows. These computer generated grayscales have a range from five stops above to five stops below 18% middle gray (11 stops total), so the right hand white patch is brighter than 90% diffuse white as it would be on a physical test chart. All of the grayscales are copyright Nick Shaw of *Antler Post* in London and are used with his permission.

Figure 4.41. (Second down) *RedLogFilm/Cineon* keeps the black level well above 0% and the brightest white well below 100% with steps that are fairly evenly distributed.

Figure 4.42. (Third down) *RedGamma3* shows all the steps but they are not evenly distributed, by design. The middle tones get the most separation as they are where human vision perceives the most detail.

Figure 4.43. (Bottom) In *Arri 709* the middle tones get the most emphasis while the extremes of the dark and light tones get much less separation between the steps. Black comes very close to 0% on the waveform.

filmmaker's guide to digital imaging

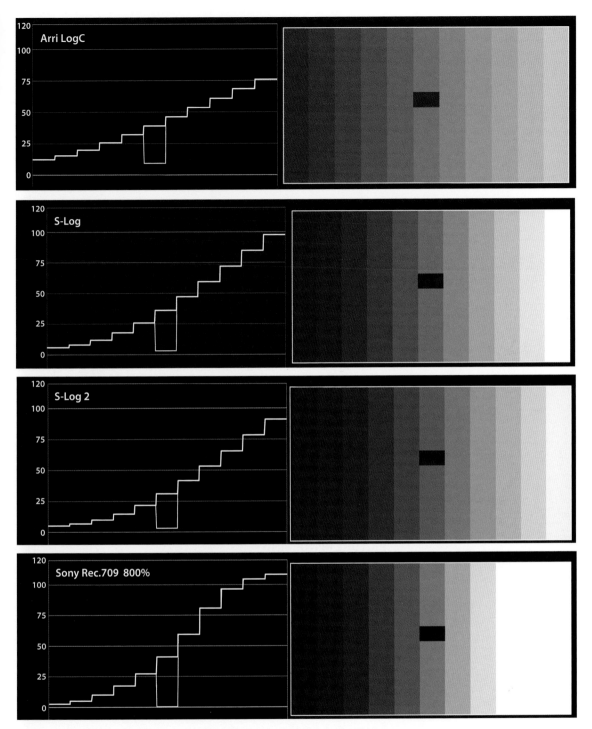

Figure 4.44. (Top) Arri's *LogC* is a much flatter curve, with the brightest patch (five stops above 18%) down at 75% and 18% gray well below 50% (as is true of all of these curves).

Figure 4.45. (Second down) *S-Log* from Sony, shows a distribution similar in some ways to *Cineon* but keeps more separation in the highlights while crushing the dark tones very slightly more. The brightest white patch gets very near 100%.

Figure 4.46. (Third down) *S-Log2* crushes the black a bit more but still doesn't let pure black reach 0% and keeps the brightest white patch well below 100%.

Figure 4.47. (Bottom) *Sony Rec.709 at 800%* actually places the brightest white patch above 100% on the waveform but with little separation. The mid tones get the most separation and the darkest tones are somewhat crushed. Unlike "regular" 709, there is still separation at the high end but like Rec.709, pure black goes very close to 0%

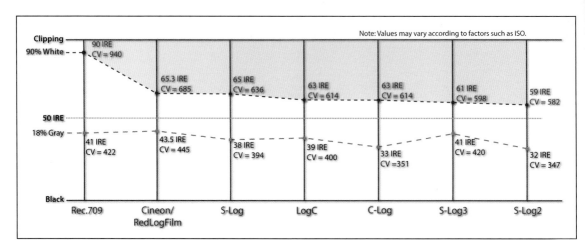

Note: Values may vary according to factors such as ISO.

Figure 4.48. Relative values for 90% diffuse white and middle gray of *Rec.709, Cineon, LogC, C-Log and S-Log 1* and *2*. The values for where 90% diffuse white (the red dotted line) is placed change as much do the values for 18% middle gray. Values are show in IRE and Code Values (CV).

Several log and Rec.709 curves from various cameras are shown in Figures 4.40 through 4.47. Notice that Arri 709 and Sony 709 at 800% work differently than "original recipe" Rec.709; an illustration of how the Rec.709 standard has been adapted and updated over the years.

Of course, the log curves from each camera are quite different in how they reproduce the grayscale; none of them puts the brightest white step at 100% or the pure black at 0%. The sample grayscales, which were created by Nick Shaw of *Antler Post* in London, show five stops above and five stops below middle gray, with a pure black patch in the center; each step of the scale goes up or down by a full stop. He says that he created these samples because "many people were not aware that the same level on a waveform meant something different depending on what camera was being used and what monitoring LUT was loaded." He adds these additional notes:

1. Each camera's log curve is quite unique.
2. Each camera's "video" (Rec.709) curve is also unique.
3. Sony Rec.709 (800%) is the only camera curve to reach 0%.

PICTURE RENDERING

In his seminal book, *Digital Video and HD Algorithms and Interfaces (2nd edition)*, Charles Poynton brings another factor into the mix — human perception of "colorfulness" (color saturation), tone scale and contrast are different depending on the light level of the viewing conditions. We perceive lightness and color differently at very low light levels than we do at high light levels — this is a key factor in what is called *picture rendering* and it has substantial implications for how we prepare video for viewing on a monitor or projector.

Poynton proposes this thought experiment: imagine a field of tulips at noon — the colors are intense and highly saturated. Now imagine the same field of flowers in the dimness of twilight — the colors are desaturated and the apparent contrast is lower. It's the same flowers, the same scene; only our perception of the appearance has changed. Technically, the differences of perception at low light levels is called the *Hunt Effect*, for color scientist R.W.G. Hunt, who first described it in his book, *The Reproduction of Color*.

If we stay all the way until the even lower levels of moonlight, the flowers will lose nearly all their color in our perception of their appearance. This is because in very dim light, our vision changes from the *cones* in our eye (*photopic vision*) to the *rods* (*scotopic vision*) which is mostly black-and-white. The main reason for this is simple:

Table 4.5. Picture Rendering

Display	Gamma
Office Computer	2.2
Home Theater	2.4
Cinema Projector	2.6

there are three kinds of cones, each type sensitive to a different wavelength. But there is only one type of rod; in essence they are monochromatic in nature.

Beyond differences of the light levels of the live scene itself, our perception of appearance changes with the light levels of the viewing environment and of the display device. For example, a noontime scene might be illuminated at the very high level of 30,000 *candelas-per-meter squared* (30,000 *nits*) when we shoot it but it might be projected in a dark cinema with the whites on the screen at 30 nits: a ratio of 1000:1. Clearly this will require some adjustment of the image for our perception of appearance to match that of the original scene. This is accomplished by changing the *gamma* of the image, which alters the appearance of colorfulness (saturation) and tone scale (Figure 4.50). On the other hand, a candle lit scene which is illuminated at 30 nits on the set, could be projected in a cinema at 30 nits and it would require no alteration at all. The result of this is that computer monitors (usually used in a fairly bright environment), home television (usually a fairly dark or medium light level) need a different gamma than a very dark cinema. (Table 4.5). Clearly, the darker the environment, the higher the gamma to achieve correct picture rendering.

This especially affects the preferred gamma for theatrical display since theaters are a very dark environment. Poynton puts it this way: "The dilemma is this: we can achieve mathematical linearity, or we can achieve correct appearance, but we cannot simultaneously do both! Successful commercial imaging systems sacrifice mathematics to achieve the correct perceptual results."

Another aspect of picture rendering is our perception of what is *white*. It turns out that what we see as pure white in an image can vary widely; the eye and brain are easily tricked in this regard. This applies to our perception of tone scale and contrast as well. Film emulsion had its own version of picture rendering built into the chemistry; in HD video, the Rec.709 specification also deals with this issue. Picture rendering is taken into account in the *ACES* workflow, which we'll discuss in the chapter *Workflow*.

Figure 4.49. A simulation of how human perception of contrast and saturation changes at different levels of brightness. At top is a scene in full sun, the colors are bright and intense. At bottom is how they would appear in very low light such as twilight — the objects are not nearly as colorful. This is only a simulation because cameras do not react to changing light levels in the same way human vision does.

exposure

EXPOSURE THEORY

Frankly, exposure can get pretty technical, so it's important to grasp the basic concepts first before we plunge into the world of exposure control for technical and artistic purposes. Let's take a look at exposure the simple way just to ease into it. As a camera person or DIT you may think you really understand exposure (and you may well do) but it is also very possible that there's a lot more to it than you may have thought.

This introduction is a bit simplified, but it will provide a working understanding of exposure that is useful without being too technical. First of all, there is one notion that has to be put away right now: some people think of exposure as nothing more than "it's too dark" or "it's too light" — that's only part of the story. There are many other important aspects of exposure that are vitally important to understand.

WHAT DO WE WANT EXPOSURE TO DO FOR US?

What is it we want from exposure? More precisely, what is "good" exposure and what is "bad" exposure? Let's take a typical scene, an average one. It will have something in the frame that is very dark, almost completely black. It will also have something that is almost completely white, maybe a white lace tablecloth with sun falling on it. In between, it will have the whole range of dark to light values — the middle tones, some very dark tones, some very light tones.

From a technical viewpoint, we want it to be reproduced exactly as it appeared in real life — with the black areas being reproduced as black in the finished product, the white areas reproduced as white, and the middle tones reproduced as middle tones. This is the dream.

Now of course, there will be times when you want to deliberately under or overexpose for artistic purposes, and that is fine. In this discussion we are only talking about theoretically ideal exposure, but that is what we are trying to do in the vast majority of cases anyway. So how do we do that? How do we exactly reproduce the scene in front of us? Let's look at the factors involved.

THE BUCKET

Let's talk about the recording medium itself. In film shooting it is the raw film stock; in video it is the sensor chip, which takes the light that falls on it and converts it to electronic signals. For our purposes here, they are both the same: exposure principles apply equally to both film and video, with some exceptions. They both do the same job: recording and storing an image that is formed by patterns of light and shadow that are focused on them by the lens. In this context, we'll only mention film exposure when it serves the purpose of illustrating a point or highlighting an aspect of general exposure theory.

Think of the sensor/recording medium as a bucket that needs to be filled with water. It can hold exactly a certain amount of water, no more, no less. If you don't put in enough water, it's not filled up (underexposure). Too much and water slops over the sides and creates a mess (overexposure). What we want to do is give that bucket the exact right amount of water, not too much, not too little — that is ideal exposure. So how do we control how much light reaches the sensor? Again, in this regard, video sensors are no different from film emulsion.

CONTROLLING EXPOSURE

We have several ways of regulating how much light reaches the film/sensor. The first is the *iris* or *aperture*, which is nothing more than a light control valve inside the lens. Obviously, when the iris is closed down to a smaller opening, it lets less light through than when it is opened up to a larger opening. How open or closed the iris is set for is measured in f/stops (we'll talk about that in more detail later). Remember, the film or sensor wants only so much light, no more no less (they're kind of dumb that way). If our scene in reality is in the bright sun, we can close down the iris to a small opening to let less of that light through. If our scene is dark, we can open up the iris to a wider opening to let in all the light we can get — but sometimes this will not be enough. There are other things that control how much light reaches the image plane, which we'll talk about.

CHANGE THE BUCKET

There is another, more basic way to change the exposure: use a different bucket. Every video sensor has a certain sensitivity to light; it's part of their design. This means that some are more sensitive to light and some are sensitive. It is rated in *ISO* which stands for *International Standards Organization*. (In film, it was previously called *ASA* for *American Standards Organization*.) Although the acronym has many other uses (because the organization publishes standards for all sorts of things) in the world of cameras, it signifies a "rating" of the sensitivity of the camera/sensor; the two must be thought of as a unit because some aspects of ISO are actually handled in the *Digital Signal Processor* and elsewhere in the camera circuitry, not just exclusively in the sensor. In some cases, the term *EI* (*Exposure Index*) is used to indicate the sensitivity of the recording medium. The difference is that while *ISO* is derived from a specific formula, *EI* is a suggested rating based on what the manufacturer believes will give the best results.

A sensor with a low sensitivity needs lots of light to fill it up and make a "good" image. A high-speed film is like using a smaller bucket — you don't need as much to fill it up. A low-speed sensor is like a larger bucket — it takes more to fill it up, but on the other hand we have more water. In the case of film and video images "having more water" in this analogy means that we have more picture information, which in the end results in a better image. As we'll see later on this is one important difference between how film and HD cameras work and how most cameras that shoot RAW work.

THE ELEMENTS OF EXPOSURE

So we have several elements to contend with in exposure:
- The *amount* of light falling on the scene. Also, the *reflectance* of things within the scene.
- *Aperture* (*iris*): a light valve that lets in more or less light.
- *Shutter speed*: the longer the shutter is open, the more light reaches the film or sensor. *Frame rate* also affects shutter speed.
- *Shutter angle*: the narrower the angle, the less light reaches the sensor.
- *ISO* (sensitivity). Using a higher ISO film is an easy fix for insufficient exposure, but it involves the penalty of more video noise and an image that is not as good.
- *Neutral Density* (*ND*) filters can reduce the light when it is too much for the aperture and other methods to deal with.

LUX	LIGHTING
100,000 +	Direct sunlight
10,000+	Indirect sun
1,0000	Overcast sky
500	Clear sunrise
200-500	Office lighting
80	Hallway
10	Twilight
5	Street lights
1	Candle at 1 m
1	Deep twilight

Table 5.1. (Above) Typical light levels in various situations. Clearly, there is an enormous range.

Light

Intensity of light is measured in *foot-candles* (in the United States) or in *lux* in metric (*SI*) countries. A *foot-candle* (*fc*) equals 10.76 *lux*. A foot-candle is the light from a standard candle at a distance of one foot (it's like a standard horse). One lux is the illumination produced by one standard candle at a 1 meter. A sensor exposed to a standard candle 1 meter away, receives 1 lux of exposure. Table 5.1 shows some typical lighting levels for common situations. These are just general averages, of course, individual situations may vary greatly, especially when it comes to interiors. Some typical points of reference include:

- Sunlight on an average day ranges from 3,175 to 10,000 fc (32,000 to 100,000+ lux).
- A bright office has about 40 fc or 400 lux of illumination.
- Moonlight (full moon) is about 1 lux (roughly a tenth of a foot-candle).

As you can see from Table 5.1, the brightness range between the darkest situations humans encounter and the brightest situations is over 100,000 to 1 — a fairly amazing range for the eye.

F/Stops

Most lenses have a means of controlling the amount of light they pass through to the film or video sensor; this is called the *aperture* or *iris* and its setting is measured in *f/stops*. The f/stop is the mathematical relationship of overall size of the lens to the size of the aperture.

Stop is a short term for f/stop. On a lens the f/stop is the ratio of the focal length of the lens to the diameter of the *entrance pupil*. This works out to each f/stop being greater than the previous by the square root of 2. *Opening up* one stop means twice as much light is passing through the iris. *Closing down* one stop means that 1/2 as much light is going through.

To be exact, the entrance pupil is not exactly the same thing as the size of the front element of the lens but they are related. An f/stop is derived from the simple formula:

$$f = F/D$$

f/stop = Focal length/Diameter of entrance pupil

F/stops are frequently used in lighting as well, they don't only apply to lenses. In lighting, the fundamental concept is that one stop *more* equals double the amount of light and one stop *less*, means half the amount of light.

If the brightest point in the scene has 128 times more luminance than the darkest point (seven stops), then we say it has a seven stop *scene brightness ratio*. We'll see that this plays an important role in understanding the *dynamic range* of a camera or recording method.

You will sometimes hear the related term *T/stop* (*Transmission stop*). It's the same idea but calculated in a different manner. F/stop is determined by the simple calculation shown above. The drawback is that some lenses transmit less light than the formula indicates. A T/stop is determined by actually measuring the transmission of the lens on an optical bench. T/stops are especially useful for lenses that transmit less light due to their design, such as zoom lenses which may have a dozen or more glass elements. Lenses that are marked in T/stops usually also have the f/stop numbers on the other side of the lens and marked in a different color.

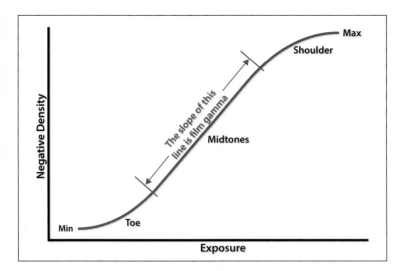

Figure 5.1. The *Hurter and Driffield* (*H&D*) characteristic curve shows the exposure response of a generic type of film — the classic S-curve. The *toe* is the *shadow* areas, the *shoulder* is the *highlights* of the scene. The *straight line* (*linear*) portion of the curve represents the *midtones*. The slope of the linear portion describes the *gamma* (contrastiness) of the film — it is different in video. As we'll see later, although the output of video sensors tends to be linear (not an S-curve like this) it is quite common to add an S-curve to video at some point.

SHUTTER SPEED/FRAME RATE/SHUTTER ANGLE

These three work together in determining exposure. Film cameras (and a few video cameras) have rotating *shutters* that either allow light to reach the recording medium or close off the light. *Frame rate* or *frames per second* (*FPS*) applies to both film and video. Obviously, if the camera is running at a very low frame rate (such as 4 FPS) each frame will get more exposure time. A higher frame rate, such as 100 FPS, each frame will be exposed to light for a much shorter time. When a camera has a physical shutter, the angle may be 180° (open half the time, closed half the time) or may have a variable shutter angle. In conjunction with frame rate, this also affects shutter speed.

THE RESPONSE CURVE

In the 1890s, *Ferdinand Hurter* and *Vero Driffield* invented a way to measure how exposure affected a film negative. The *H&D* diagram is still used today. Figure 5.1 shows a typical H&D response curve for film negative. The X axis indicates increasing exposure. The Y axis is increasing negative density, which we can think of as brightness of the image — more exposure means a brighter image. To the left on the X axis is the darker parts of the scene, commonly called the *shadows*. On the diagram, it is called the *toe*. To the right on the X axis are the brighter parts of the scene — the *highlights*, called the *shoulder* on the diagram. In video, this area is called the *knee*. The middle part, which is linear, represents midtones.

WHY TALK ABOUT FILM?

Why are we discussing film in a book about digital imaging? A couple of reasons. First, the underlying principles are the same for both. Secondly, some concepts, such as the S-curve, still play an important role in video imaging. Also, film makes for more readily understandable explanations, and a little understanding of the history of imaging is valuable no matter what medium you work in.

UNDEREXPOSURE

Figure 5.2 shows underexposure. All of the original scene brightness values are pushed to the left. This means that highlights in the scene are recorded as just light or medium tones. The shadows are pushed down to where there is no detail or separation recorded because the response curve at that point is essentially flat — decreases in exposure at this point result in little or no change in the image brightness.

OVEREXPOSURE

Figure 5.3 shows overexposure — the scene brightness values are pushed to the right. Dark areas of the scene are recorded as grays instead of variations of black. On the right, the scene highlights have no *separation* or *detail* — they are on the flat part of the curve; increases in exposure in the flat part of the curve don't result in any change in the image.

CORRECT EXPOSURE

In Figure 5.4 we see how theoretically correct exposure places all of the scene values so that they fit nicely on the curve: highlights go up to just where the curve flattens and scene shadows only go down to where they are still recorded as slight variations in image brightness.

HIGHER BRIGHTNESS RANGE IN THE SCENE

The problem is more difficult if we consider a scene that has more stops of brightness than the sensor or film can accommodate. Here there is no aperture setting that will place all of the values on the useful part of the curve. If we expose for the shadows (open up the aperture), we get good rendition of the dark gray and black areas, but the brighter scene values are hopelessly off the scale. If we "expose for highlights" (by closing down to a smaller f/stop), we record all the variations of the light tones, but the dark values are pushed completely off the bottom edge and don't record at all; there is no information on the negative, no detail to be pulled out.

TWO TYPES OF EXPOSURE

There are really two ways to think about exposure: overall exposure and balance within the frame. So far we've been talking about overall exposure of the entire frame; this is what you can control with the iris, shutter speed and some other tools, such as neutral density filters, which reduce the total amount of light.

You also have to think about balance of exposure within the frame. If you have a scene that has something very bright in the frame and also something that is very dark in the frame, you may be able to expose the whole frame properly for one or the other of them, but not both. This is not something you can fix with the iris, aperture, changing ISO, or anything else with the camera or lens. This is a problem that can only be fixed with lighting and grip equipment; in other words, you have to change the scene. Another way to deal with it in exterior shooting is to shoot at a different time of day, change the angle or move the scene to another place, such as into the shadow of a building. For more on lighting, see *Motion Picture and Video Lighting* and *Cinematography: Theory and Practice*, both by the same author as this book.

HOW FILM AND VIDEO ARE DIFFERENT

There is one crucial way in which film and video are different. With HD, it is absolutely critical that you do not overexpose the image. This is not as critical with negative film. Film stock is fairly tolerant of overexposure and doesn't do as well with underexposure; HD on the other hand is very good with underexposure, but remember, you will always get a better picture with exposure that is right on the money: this is the crucial thing to remember about exposure.

We should note however, that what we said about film applies only to negative film (which is what we almost always shoot on commercials, music videos, feature films, and short films). There is another type of film called *reversal film* (also known as *transparency* or *positive*

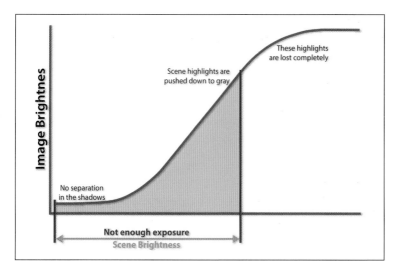

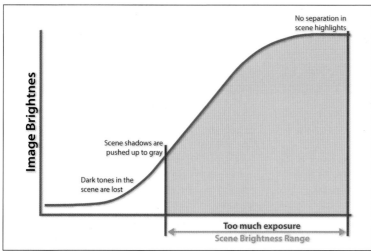

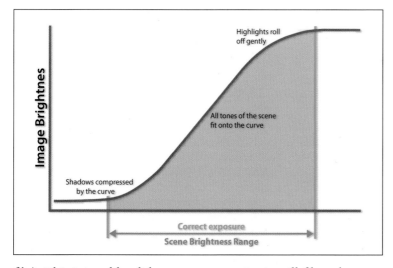

Figure 5.2. (Top) Although the shape of the curve might be different for video, the basic principles remain the same as film, shown here. Underexposure pushes everything to the left of the curve, so the highlights of the scene only get as high as the middle gray part of the curve, while the dark areas of the scene are pushed left into the part of the curve that is flat. This means that they will be lost in darkness without separation and detail.

Figure 5.3. (Middle) With overexposure, the scene values are pushed to the right, which means that the darkest parts of the scene are rendered as washed out grays.

Figure 5.4. (Bottom) Correct exposure fits all of the scene brightness values nicely onto the curve.

film). This is just like slides or transparencies in still film: the same film that ran through the camera comes back from the lab with correct colors, not reversed like negative film. Traditional HD cameras were often compared to reversal film in that they are both extremely intolerant of overexposure.

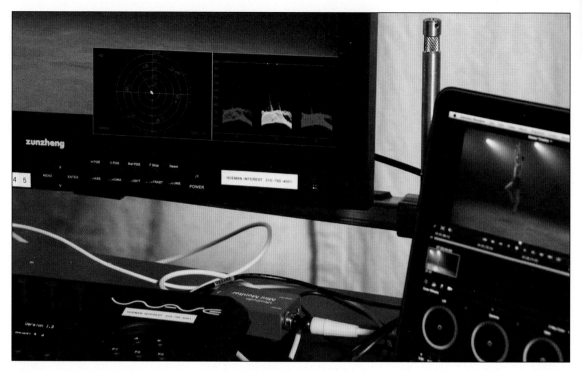

Figure 5.5. On the set, the waveform monitor is often the most direct measure of exposure levels. In this case, it is the *parade display* on a Flanders monitor.

WE'LL FIX IT IN POST

One thing you will hear sometimes, especially on a set is "don't worry, we'll fix it in post." There is nothing wrong with making an image *better* in postproduction: there are many incredible tools you can use to improve the look of your footage. What you don't want to do is take the attitude that you can be sloppy and careless on the set because "everything can be fixed in post." It's simply not true. When it comes to exposure, fixing it in post generally means scrambling to come up with an image that is merely acceptable.

Improving and fine-tuning an image, ensuring consistency of exposure and color and going for a specific "look" in post has always been an important part of the process. It always has been. However, this is not to be confused with "fixing" a mistake, which almost never results in a better image.

THE BOTTOM LINE

Here's the key point: exposure is about much more than just it's "too dark" or "too light." Exposure affects many things: it's also about whether or not an image will be noisy or grainy, it's about the overall contrast of the image, and it's about whether or not we will see detail and subtleties in the shadows and in the highlights. It's also about color saturation and contrast — the colors in the scene will only be full and rich and reproduced accurately when the exposure is correct. *Overexposure* and *underexposure* will *desaturate* the color of the scene; this is particularly important in *greenscreen* and *bluescreen* shooting. In these situations, we want the background to be as green (or blue) as possible, in order to get a good *matte*. This is the main reason we have to be so careful about exposure when shooting greenscreen or bluescreen. Checking exposure of the background is critical when shooting any form of *chroma key*, the generic name for this process.

The bottom line is this: you will get the best image possible only when your exposure is correct. This is true of still photos on film, motion picture film, digital photography and, of course, video.

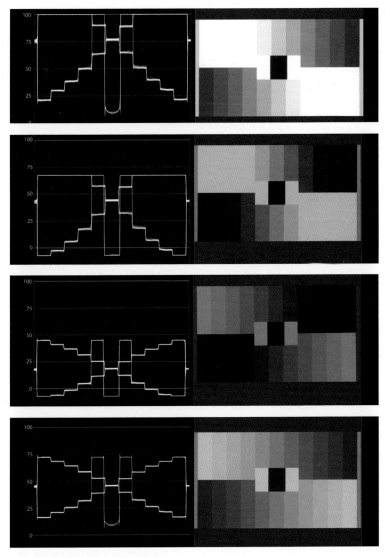

Figure 5.6. (Top) This very overexposed 11 step grayscale shows clipping in the lighter steps and the darkest steps are more gray than they should be.

Figure 5.7. (Second down) Here an attempt has been made to "save" this shot by reducing brightness in post-production. It does nothing to bring back any separation to the clipped steps and reduces the dark steps till they just mush together. Only middle gray is where it should be and that is only because we placed it there in post.

Figure 5.8. (Third down) A severely underexposed frame of the grayscale. Not only are the highlights just mushy gray but the darker tones are crushed — there is much less separation in the steps. The lowest steps are also deeply into video noise.

Figure 5.9. (Bottom) Trying to save this shot by bringing middle gray back up does nothing to bring the separation between the steps; it only serves to make the darkest steps muddy gray, and, of course, the video noise will still be there.

EXPOSURE IN SHOOTING RAW VIDEO

Some people make the mistake of thinking that just because you're shooting RAW video that exposure isn't critical — "It's all captured in RAW so anything can be fixed later." This is a myth of course; you can still screw up the image with bad exposure just as you can with any other type of image acquisition. Underexposure can result in a noisy image and overexposure can cause clipping. Clipped highlights cannot be fixed. There is no magic software, no cute little button you click in post, that will bring detail back into the highlights — clipping means that there is just no information there at all, nothing to recover. There is a difference between "appearing" to be clipped and actual clipping. Sometimes when RAW footage is subjected to a quick down-and-dirty conversion to Rec.709, for example, some of the highlights may appear to be burned out and clipped but when you look at them on the waveform monitor they are very close to the maximum but there still something there — these are highlights that can probably be recovered with proper treatment in color correction software. This is why the waveform monitor is so important as a reference: viewing footage on a less than stellar monitor or even seeing them under unfavorable viewing conditions can be misleading.

Figure 5.10. (Top) The classic method of incident metering — hold the meter at the subjects position and point the dome at the camera. Technically it is called the "Norwood Dome."

Figure 5.11. (Above) Using the same Sekonic meter as a reflectance/spot meter allows the DP to check the exposure levels of different parts of the scene based on a combination of the lights hitting the objects and their inherent reflectance. It is also the only way to effectively meter objects that generate their own light, such as a lampshade, a neon lamp or a campfire.

VIDEO EXPOSURE

The same principles of exposure apply to video; the same ideas of the *curve*, *toe* and *shoulder*, also apply, although in video the highlights are called the *knee* and the darkest parts of the scene (called *toe* in film) are simply referred to as *shadow* areas.

Figures 5.6 through 5.9 illustrate test shots of an 11 step grayscale. In the overexposed frame (Figure 5.6) the highlights are clipped — no information there; just burned out white. Notice that in the underexposed frame (Figure 5.8) all the tones are *crushed* together. Simply making it brighter in post will not restore a full range of tones. The result will be dull and flat with video noise. Figure 5.7 and 5.9 show the fallacy of the attitude that "We'll fix it in post." Some things can't be fixed in post, they can only be made less bad. In the chapter *Measurement*, Figures 3.18, 3.19, and 3.20 show the *Cambelles*, standardized test subjects made by DSC Labs. They illustrate the same principle: proper exposure gives you a full range of tones from black to white, and the tones are rendered as they appeared in the scene. This is the constant balancing act of exposure: to get the middle tones right without losing the dark tones to underexposure or the light tones to clipping.

THE TOOLS

When shooting film (as different from video), the two most basic tools of the cinematographer's trade are the *incident meter* and the *spot meter*. There is a third type of meter, the *wide angle reflectance meter*, but it has extremely limited use in film; it is a holdover from the days of still photography. This type of meter gave you a general reading of the average reflectance of the entire scene but little else. It only read the light as it was being reflected off the scene and one had to be very careful in how you pointed it.

THE INCIDENT METER

The incident meter does not always work as it should with traditional HD cameras. If you haven't made any changes to the image with camera controls, then an incident reading will be pretty much accurate, but if you have changed any of those settings it will not be. This is not as much of a problem with cameras that shoot RAW and record log encoded video, as discussed in the next chapter. The *incident meter* measures scene illumination only — in other words: the amount of light falling on scene. To accomplish this purpose, most incident meters use a hemispherical white plastic *dome* that covers the actual sensing cell (Figures 5.10 and 5.11).

The diffusing dome accomplishes several purposes. It diffuses and hence "averages" the light that is falling on it. Unshielded, the dome will read all of the front lights and even some of the side-back and back light that might be falling on the subject. Many people use their hand to shield the back light off the reading and use a combination of hand shielding and turning the meter to read the backlight and usually the key, fill, side lights, and back lights separately.

The classical practice, however, is to point the hemisphere directly at the lens and eliminate only the backlights, then take a reading exactly at the subject position. Reading key, fill, and backlight separately is in fact only a way of determining the ratios and looking for out-of-balance sources. In most instances, reading the key light is what determines the exposure — how the lens aperture will be set. The key light, crudely put, is the main light on the subject, whether it's an actor or a can of dog food. Later we will look at applications that go beyond the simple classical approach and are useful in dealing with unusual situations. Most meters that are used with the diffusing dome also come with a *flat diffusing plate* that has a much smaller acceptance angle (about 45° to 55°). This means that the angle of the light falling on the plate has an effect on the reading, just as it does in illuminating a subject.

The flat plate makes taking readings for individual lights simpler and is also useful for measuring illumination on flat surfaces, such as in art copy work. Incident meters are sometimes also supplied with a *lenticular* glass plate that converts them to wide acceptance reflectance meters, which can read the *reflected* light of an entire scene. Lenticular is like glass beads. These see little use on most sets as they have very wide acceptance angles and it is difficult to exclude extraneous sources. For the most part, incident meters are set for the film speed and shutter speed being used and then display the reading directly in f/numbers.

THE REFLECTANCE METER

Reflectance meters, (most frequently called *spot meters*) read the *luminance* of the subject, which is itself an integration of two factors: the *light level falling on the scene* and the *reflectivity* of the subject. It is why they are called reflectance meters.

On the face of it, this would seem to be the most logical method of reading the scene, but there is a catch. Simply put, a spot meter will tell us how much light a subject is reflecting, but this leaves one very big unanswered question: how much light do you want it to reflect? In other words, incident meters provide absolute readouts (f/stops), while spot meters give relative readouts that require interpretation.

Think of it this way: you are using such a meter and photographing a very fair-skinned girl holding a box of detergent in front of a sunset. You read the girl's face: f/5.6, the box reads f/4, the sky is f/22. So where are you? Not only do we not know where to set the aperture, we don't even know if the situation is good or bad. Using a spot meter to set exposure requires a high level understanding of exposure theory. In most cases, spot meters are actually used to check potential problem areas of a scene such as a lampshade or a window which might "blow out" and clip if they're too hot.

A DIFFERENT WORLD OF EXPOSURE

With cameras that shoot RAW, the procedure used by many DPs has changed over time, as we'll talk about in the section *Philosophy of Exposure* later in this chapter. Adjusting the aperture is the most commonly used way of adjusting exposure, but not the only way. *Neutral density filters*, *frame rate*, *shutter angle* (if it's adjustable) and changing the *ISO* or *gain* can all be used to make adjustments, but of course the key element is often adjusting the lighting of the scene.

You can adjust the scene brightness values by adding or subtracting lights, dimmers, nets, flags, scrims, overheads or other grip equipment. There are many options available even when shooting day exterior. You might also deal with exposure problems by changing the frame to exclude the offending objects. Don't underestimate the power of persuasion in convincing the director to change the camera angle or the background to achieve better lighting results. Of course, choice of location and time of day to shoot are powerful factors in the lighting of a scene. See *Motion Picture and Video Lighting*, and *Cinematography: Theory and Practice* by the same author for more information on specific lighting techniques.

SETTING EXPOSURE WITH THE WAVEFORM MONITOR

As we saw in *Measurement*, the waveform monitor is a very precise tool for judging exposure values. It may be built into the camera or monitor or may be a freestanding unit. With HD cameras, the DP would look at the waveform and set whatever values they felt were important. The chapter on *Measurement* contains most of what you need to know about the waveform monitor; in this chapter we'll deal more with their specific use in judging the scene, setting exposure and the general theory of exposure control. With the waveform monitor, the real trick is having some references you can use. You need to pick something in the scene that you know where you want them to fall on the waveform monitor. First, some background.

F/Stops On the Waveform

It would be nice if a one stop change in exposure resulted in a uniform, predictable change on the waveform monitor. Unfortunately, it doesn't quite work that way. If you are shooting straight Rec.709 with no gamma or other adjustments, a one stop change in exposure will be approximately a 20% change on the waveform. This really only applies in the middle part of the curve but it's a general rule of thumb to use as a starting point. In the highlights and shadows there will be less of a change on the waveform. Digital consultant Adam Wilt puts it this way — "If you are shooting with a wider dynamic range, and monitoring that signal without a viewing LUT or other output conversion, then the stop variation will depend on the camera, and possibly where on the brightness scale the signal is. For example, on Alexa, or a Sony's Hypergamma, the brighter your signal is, the less of a change you'll see on the WFM with a 1-stop change. With the Blackmagic Cine Camera in "film mode", on the other hand, you will see something like 10% change at low levels, and about a 13% change at brighter levels." (LUTs are discussed in more detail in *Digital Color* — for now it is enough to know that they can be used to make the scene on the set monitors reflect the look the DP is going for — among many other uses.)

The 18% Solution

A widely used reference value is middle gray (18% reflectance). If you're using a gray card or a DSC chart, you will have something that you know for certain is 18% middle gray. That's the simplest case, so let's deal with that situation for now. Your first instinct might be to place 18% gray at 50 IRE — half way between black and white. After all, it is middle gray.

Unfortunately, it's a bit more complicated than that. There are a couple of factors involved. The main one is that in many cases, you will be feeding a *log encoded* image to the waveform monitor, which we'll talk about in detail in the next chapter. Log encoding changes the signal by lowering the highlights, at least temporarily during recording; they are brought back up in grading. Inevitably this has some effect on the midtones as well, meaning that middle gray is not going to be the same on the set as it will after it is altered by log encoding, Hypergamma, a LUT or other manipulation. Of course, you may be using viewing LUTs on the set, as well for the DP and director viewing monitors. Whether this LUT is being applied to the signal going to the waveform is another matter — obviously it is critical that you know if it is or not. You will always need to be aware if the signal is log, Rec.709, has a modifying LUT or gamma curve applied to it, and so on, as these affect how it appears on the waveform monitor.

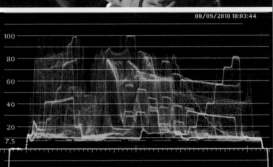
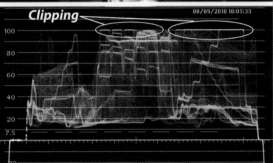

Fortunately, camera companies publish the data for where 18% gray should fall on the waveform, see Figure 4.40 in *Linear, Gamma, Log*. Interestingly, none of these ever come out to be 50 IRE, the logical, expected place for it to fall on the waveform monitor. For many years, cinematographers carried plastic coated pocket cards listing the "safe" frame rates and shutter angles for shooting with HMI lights. Perhaps we have reached a time where they will have to carry cards listing the middle gray IRE/% values for various cameras and the particular gamma or log encoding they are using on a particular scene.

CAMERA EXPOSURE INDICATORS

Since exposure meters won't always give the most accurate guidance when the gamma or other aspects of image (such as knee or toe, for example) have been changed, other exposure guides are needed. Fortunately, professional cameras have several exposure tools. As we'll see in the section *Philosophy of Exposure*, this has changed with the newest generation of cameras.

ZEBRAS

In the viewfinder or appearing on the camera operators monitor, *zebras* have long been a useful tool for judging exposure. Unlike histograms or goal posts, they show you specifically within the frame where there is overexposure or exposure at the specific level you are looking for, such as skin tone.

Zebras indicate a particular IRE level in the scene; however they are useless unless you know what IRE level the zebras are set to indicate. Aside from being useful in judging specific tones for exposure, zebras excel at indicating overexposed areas.

Professional cameras offer the choice of selecting what IRE level you want to set the zebras for and generally have two sets of zebras which can be used in a variety of ways. A fairly common use is to

Figure 5.12. (Left) Normal exposure on an HD camera. Notice the proper skin tones, the correct color saturation in the chart, and how all segments are shown on the gray scale. These images are from a latitude test on an HD camera.

Figure 5.13. (Right) At just two stops overexposed, the skin tone is blown out, the color saturation is severely reduced and there is no *separation* visible in the lighter tones on the gray scale. *Clipping of the highlights* appears on the waveform monitor as a flatline at the top of the signal. This is at only plus two stops of exposure and already it has exceeded the *latitude* (*dynamic range*) of the HD camera. This is an older camera; more current cameras have more dynamic range.

Figure 5.14. (Top) Normal exposure with the zebras (70% and 100% in this example) and shown on the waveform monitor.

Figure 5.15. (Above) The same scene very overexposed with zebras and the waveform. On this Sony camera, the two types of zebras are shown as opposite diagonal angles.

target one set of zebras for midtones (such as typical skin tone) and the other set for dangerous overexposure, such as 90, 100 or even 108 IRE. Cameras use different methods for differentiating the two sets of zebra stripes (and usually offer the option of turning one or both of them off). In some cases, one set of stripes is diagonal and the other set is the opposite diagonal; some are horizontal, some are "crawling ants" and so on. Figures 5.14 and 5.15 show a method used by Sony — the sets of zebras are diagonal lines tilted in opposite directions. It is important to be sure you know what the protocols are for the camera you are using and be sure you know what levels the zebras are set for. If you are using zebras, it will be an important part of your camera prep and setup procedures to check what levels they are set to.

HISTOGRAM

The histogram is probably the simplest tool around for analyzing an image. It is somewhat primitive but can be very effective, especially for a very quick look at the overall exposure of a shot. It is also nearly ubiquitous: even the simplest consumer still cameras have histogram displays. It is basically a distribution diagram of the tones in our scene: on the left hand are the dark tones and on the right side of the diagram our light tones. (Figures 5.16 through 5.18.)

A normal scene properly exposed will have a more or less even distribution of tones from dark to light and won't be too much pushed up against the left or right sides. The distribution of tones in the middle will change based on the scene; it's the light or dark tones pushing up against the extreme limits that you really want to watch out for.

TRAFFIC LIGHTS AND GOAL POSTS

These are particular to Red cameras and provide very general but useful information. They are basically warning systems to alert the operator to percentages of the picture that are either in clipping or in "noise" at the bottom end — meaning underexposed. They may seem simplistic, but are in fact well suited to the new exposure

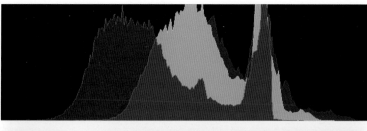

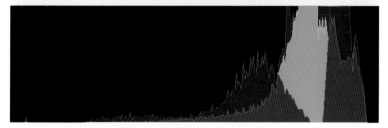

Figure 5.16. (Top) Histograms can be a very useful tool for judging exposure. The top figure shows a fairly normal distribution of highlights, midtones and shadows.

Figure 5.17. (Middle) An underexposed shot — all tones are pushed to the far left.

Figure 5.18. (Bottom) An overexposed shot, with all tones pushed far to the right.

needs of shooting RAW and log. Even though this method of shooting allows a good deal more room for error, that doesn't mean that making errors in exposure is any more of a good idea than it was with traditional HD recording.

Goal Posts

Red's explanation of their *Goal Posts,* (Figure 5.19) is this: "In order to quickly balance the competing trade-offs of noise and highlight protection, Red cameras also have indicators at the far left and right of their histogram. Unlike the histogram though, these are not affected by the ISO speed or look setting, and instead represent RAW image data. The indicators are depicted as vertical bars to each side of the histogram, and are often referred to as the "goal posts," since the aim is usually to achieve a histogram which doesn't hit either side.

The height of each goal post reflects the fraction of overall pixels that have become either clipped (on the right), or near the capabilities of the camera to discern real texture from noise (on the left). The full scale for each goal post represents a quarter of all image pixels. In general, the left goal post can be pushed up to about 50% height and still give acceptable noise, but even a small amount on the right goal post can be unacceptable, depending on where this clipping appears in the image."

Traffic Lights

In addition to the *Goal Posts*, Red provides another indicator of the crucial indicator of clipping — the so-called *Traffic Lights*, shown in Figure 5.20. These indicators show what color channels (Red, Green, Blue) have some areas that are being clipped. Some people see these indicators and assume they mean *Go, Caution, Stop*. Not so at all. Unfortunately, calling them traffic lights reinforces this misconception.

exposure

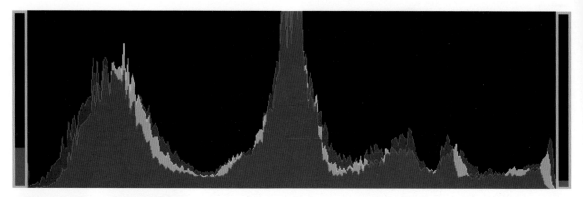

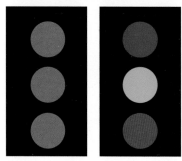

Figure 5.19. (Top) Red's *Goal Posts* are also very helpful in judging exposure. They are the two vertical stripes at the far right and left of the histogram. The height of the bar on the right indicates what percentage of pixels are clipped or in noise. The bar on the left indicates what percentage of pixels are in noise. Full scale of these indicators is only 25% of total pixels, not all of them as you might expect.

Figure 5.20. (Above) Two views of the *Traffic Lights* on a Red camera. It is important to note that they are not red, yellow, green as you would expect in real traffic lights. They are not the equivalent of *Go, Caution, Stop*. What they actually mean is that when about 2% of the pixels *in a particular color channel* have reached clipping, the corresponding light turns on.

Notice for example that the third color is not yellow, but blue. The real meaning is that when about 2% of the pixels in a *particular color channel* have reached clipping, the corresponding light turns on. It's one of those things that are wonderfully precise in scientific terms but still require a great deal of human interpretation to be used properly. Good news, we have delayed the takeover by the machines for at least a few months! Sleep well, Sarah Connor.

According to Red: "When about 2% of the image pixels for a particular color channel have become clipped, the corresponding traffic light for that color channel will light up. This can be helpful in situations where just the red channel has become clipped within a skin tone, for example. In that case, the right side goal post would be much lower than it would appear otherwise, since all three channels haven't become clipped."

Adam Wilt has this to say about these tools "The traffic lights seem interesting but in the end, how valuable is it really to know that '2% of pixels in that channel' are clipping? In my Red work, I find them useful as 'idiot lights': I can tell at a glance if there's a *possibility* I might be getting into trouble. They don't replace a careful study of the histogram; what they do is say, 'hey, buddy, you *might* want to take a closer look here...' and they say it even when I'm too busy to be focusing on the histogram, because I'm focusing instead on movement and composition.

"Same with the Goal Posts, they are halfway between the see-it-in-a-flash 'idiot lights' of the traffic lights and the study-intensive histogram. They show me (a) I have stuff in the scene that exceeds the range of the capture system at either or both ends of the tonal scale, and (b) by comparing their relative heights, I can see quickly if I'm losing more shadow details, or more highlights, or if I've balanced the losses equally (assuming that's what I want, of course).

"I use 'em all: traffic lights as a quick-and-dirty warning, goal posts as a highlights/shadows balancing indicator, and the histogram or an external WFM to see in detail what the signal is doing. The traffic lights and goal posts don't show me anything I can't get from the histogram or WFM, but they show it to me very quickly, with a minimum of focus and concentration required on my part to interpret the results. It's nice to have choices."

False Color Exposure Display

Many pro cameras and field monitors now offer the choice of *false color*, which displays different tonal ranges coded in various "false" colors (Figure 5.21). As with any color code system, it's worthless unless you know the key. Although different camera companies use their own set of colors, they usually have some commonalities. False

color displays can usually be turned on or off either in menus or with assignable buttons on the exterior of the camera that can be assigned to any one of several different camera controls depending on the wishes of each individual user). Once you get to know them, they can be a useful guide to exposure, but they can also interfere with viewing the scene while operating the camera. For this reason, many cinematographers use them only when lighting the scene and while determining the proper exposure for the scene and not while shooting the scene, when they might be a distraction for the operator.

Figure 5.21. False color display in Adam Wilt's *Cine Meter II* iPhone app. Unlike most cameras, the color code is user adjustable — the value range can be selected for each color.

RED FALSE COLORS

Red cameras have two false color selections: *Video Mode* and *Exposure Mode*. Video mode false colors are shown in Figure 5.22. *Exposure Mode* is a more simplified method which is used with RAW image viewing. Most of the image will appear as a grayscale but purple will be overlaid on any parts of the image that are underexposed and red will be overlaid on any overexposed regions of the frame. Since this applies to the RAW data, it indicates over and underexposed regions of the frame regardless of the current ISO or look settings. Since it is simpler, it can be less confusing to look at than video mode false colors; choosing which mode to use for viewing can depend on whether it is used only in preparing the shot (while lighting) or if an exposure mode or *focus assist* (*peaking*) is going to be used while operating the actual take.

COMPARING RED EXPOSURE MODES

Table 5.2 shows the specifications of the three Red exposure modes — *Video Mode*, *Zebra Mode* and *Exposure Mode*. Zebra and Video Mode are based on IRE or RGB values, which is a relative scale based on the output signal sent to the monitor, not necessarily the actual values of the recorded scene. Red says "It is most useful when assessing direct output via HD-SDI, or whether the current ISO and 'look' are a good starting point for post-production."

Figure 5.22. False colors can give more precise exposure information about individual portions of the image, but only if you know the code! At top is the grayscale including *superblack* and *superwhite*. Below that is the color code for Red camera false colors, then Alexa's color code and finally the Red camera *Exposure Mode* at bottom.

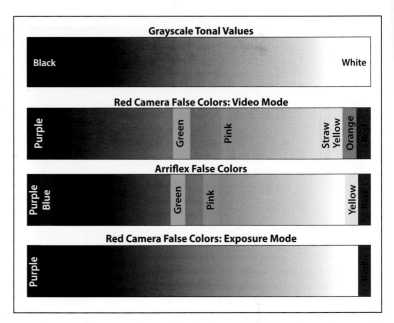

Red puts it this way: "As with other IRE-based modes, zebra mode is only applicable for the current ISO and look settings (such as with HD-SDI output) — not for the RAW image data. If anything is changed in post-production, the indicators won't be representative of the final output tones. In those situations, zebra mode is therefore more of a preview and output brightness tool than an exposure tool." Despite this, they can still be useful in some circumstances. In general, most exposure tools are measuring the image with the various adjustments to the look already applied.

RAW in this context, is an absolute scale based on the output of the sensor. It is not necessarily related to the viewing image in terms of brightness values. Red says:"This is most useful when trying to optimize exposure and looking toward post-production." This is, of course, the basic concept of shooting RAW vs. shooting video that is more or less "ready to go." Shooting with the image adjusted to roughly where you want it to be can be thought of as "HD style" shooting, where gamma, knee and black values are adjusted with "the knobs."

Shooting RAW/Log, as we have talked about, is not oriented toward producing a final image, but is more about producing a "digital negative" that has great potential for fine-tuning and adjustment further down the line. As we will see, this is the fundamental concept of the ACES workflow as well. As we have discussed elsewhere, the downside of this is that the images are not directly viewable and this makes using exposure tools like zebras and histograms pretty much useless — they can still be used as approximations but they are not really accurate.

With a Red camera the exposure mode you choose will determine what type of false color schemes you see displayed in the viewfinder. Red sums up their overall recommendation for using these tools:

Table 5.2. Red's Exposure modes and specifications. Notice that *Video Mode* and *Zebra Mode* are only applicable in IRE (Rec.709, not RAW).

RED EXPOSURE MODES	Basis	Levels	Adjustable?
Exposure Mode	RAW	2	No
Video Mode	IRE	9	No
Zebra Mode	IRE	1-3	Yes

Figure 5.23. (Top) A frame from a Red camera in standard mode. (Courtesy of the Red Digital Cinema Camera Company).

Figure 5.24. (Below) The same frame in *Exposure Mode*: red indicates clipping (overexposure) and purple shows parts of the frame in noise (under nominal exposure). (Courtesy of the Red Digital Cinema Camera Company).

"First, in *Exposure Mode*, use the purple and red indicators to adjust your lighting or lens aperture. The strategy is usually to achieve an optimal balance between clipping from overexposure and image noise from underexposure. With most scenes, there can be a surprising range of exposure latitude before excessive red or purple indicators appear.

Then if necessary, in video or zebra mode, use the other tonal indicators to fine-tune how the scene will appear via HD-SDI, or to adjust your suggested look when sending footage for post-production. The zebra and video modes are also an objective way to assess LCD preview brightness under varied ambient light."

ARRI ALEXA FALSE COLORS

The Arri Alexa has similar false color codes but they are a bit simpler (Figures 5.22 and 5.25). Arri's color code has fewer steps which some find makes it easier to read in the viewfinder or monitor. Green is middle gray (38% to 42%) and Pink is average Caucasian skin tone (52% to 56%). Red (which they call *White Clipping*) is 99% to 100% and Purple, which they call *Black Clipping*, is 0% to 2.5%.

Figure 5.25. Numerical values and colors of the *Arri Alexa False Color* system. (Courtesy of Arri).

What	Signal Level	Color
White clipping	100% - 99%	red
Just below white clipping	99% - 97%	yellow
One stop over medium gray (Caucasian skin)	56% - 52%	pink
18% medium gray	42% - 38%	green
Just above black clipping	4.0% - 2.5%	blue
Black clipping	2.5% - 0.0%	purple

Figure 5.26. (Right) At top is a Red frame two-and-a-third stops underexposed.

Figure 5.27. (Right, below) Red's *FLUT* in use. A FLUT of 2.3 has been applied, bringing the shot back to fairly normal exposure. In this case, the FLUT has been applied in *Assimilate Scratch*.

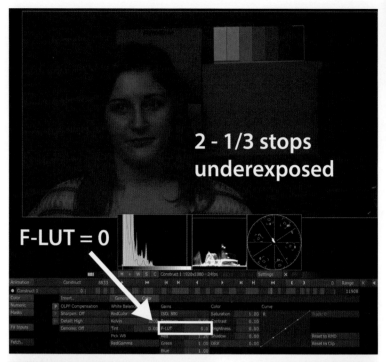

F-LUT

FLUT or *F-LUT* is specific to Red cameras. It stands for *Floating Point Look Up Table*. According to the Red company: "FLUT™ is a new control (for very fine ISO/mid grey adjustments without inducing clipping) and an underlying technology that facilitates all of the above, and indeed was necessary to make the new color and new gamma curves work." It was devised by Graeme Nattress, a mathematician who is a prolific innovator in the field of image processing software. He advises "FLUT is fine control over ISO, so ISO 320 +1 is the same as ISO 640. Similarly ISO 800 -1 is the same as ISO 400. Generally set rendering intent with ISO then fine-tune, if necessary on the FLUT." See Figures 5.26 and 5.27 for an example of FLUT in use on an underexposed shot. FLUT is enumerated in f/stops; so a FLUT of 1.0 is the same as opening up one stop on the lens — except it is a more fine tuned increase or decrease in exposure since it doesn't affect all areas of exposure equally.

A FLUT of .3 is the same as 1/3 f/stop and so on. ISO is generally measured in 1/3 stops. FLUT doesn't allow anything that is not actually clipped (i.e. 12-bit value = 4095) to actually clip. They will get crushed up towards 4095, might actually reach 4094, might in extreme circumstances get quantized up to 4095, but that's it.

PHILOSOPHY AND STRATEGY OF EXPOSURE

We've looked at the many tools available for judging exposure. But what about the basic philosophy of exposure — it's not a purely mechanical, by-the-book procedure — every experienced cinematographer has their own way of working, their own favorite tools and bag of tricks. As with just about everything in filmmaking, it's not about the right way or the wrong way — it's about achieving the desired final product, which is always several steps away down the line. Ultimately, it's all about what appears on the cinema screen or the home television.

There are adjustments to be made for individual cameras, artistic preferences and so on. We know the basic goal — to get an image that will yield the best results in the end. An individual cinematographer will develop methods that work for them based on experience, testing and the feedback they get from viewing dailies or looking at the footage on the set.

Don't Let It Clip, but Avoid the Noise

Homer (not Homer Simpson, the other one) wrote about two mythical sea monsters on each side of the Strait of Messina, a dangerous rocky shoal on one side and a deadly whirlpool on the other. Called *Scylla* and *Charybdis*, they are the origins of the terms "between a rock and a hard place" and "on the horns of a dilemma." In shooting video, our Scylla and Charybdis are *clipping* at the brightest areas of the scene and *noise* in the darker parts of the scene. Technically, clipping is *sensor saturation*; camera manufacturers refer to it as *well overflow*, in reference to the wells of the photosites. It's the point at which the photosite has absorbed all the photons it is capable of handling and any additional photons make no difference in the output of the sensor; instead they go into the *overflow drain*.

As we saw in the first chapter, the *noise floor* is not the same as the lower black limit. It is the level of sensor output with the lens capped — no photons hitting the sensor at all. In this condition, there is still some electrical output from the photosites; simply because all electrical systems have some degree of randomness. There is noise everywhere in the sensor, but it is usually most noticeable in the darkest areas of the image. .

The Red camera company summarizes it this way: "Optimal exposure starts with a deceivingly simple strategy: record as much light as necessary, but not so much that important highlights lose all texture. This is based on two fundamental properties of digital image capture:

Noise. As less light is received, image noise increases as we discussed in the chapter *Sensors & Cameras*. This happens throughout an image with less exposure, but also within darker regions of the same image for a given exposure.

Highlight Clipping. If too much light is received, otherwise continuous tones hit a digital wall and become solid white. Alternatively, this might happen in just one of the individual color channels, which can cause inaccurate coloration. Unlike image noise, which increases gradually with less light, highlight clipping appears abruptly once the clipping threshold has been surpassed."

TEXTURE & DETAIL

Some terms you'll hear frequently when discussing exposure are *texture*, *detail* and *separation*. For example, *textured white*, *textured black*, *detail* in the highlights or *separation* in the shadows. These are all essentially the same thing and are important references in exposure. The concepts originated with Ansel Adams, who needed terms to describe how far exposure (negative density) can go before they are just pure black or pure white; soot and chalk as he sometimes called them. *Textured white* is defined as the lightest tone in the image where you can still see some *texture*, some *details*, some *separation* of subtle tones.

Diffuse white is the reflectance of an illuminated white object. Since perfectly reflective objects don't occur in the real world, diffuse white is about 90% reflectance; roughly a sheet of white paper or the white patch on a *ColorChecker* or *DSC* test chart. There are laboratory test objects that are higher reflectance, all the way up to 99.9% but in the real world, 90% is the standard we use in video measurement. It is called diffuse white because it is not the same as maximum white. Diffuse means it is a dull surface (and in this context, paper is a dull surface) that reflects all wavelengths in all directions, unlike a mirror which reflects a beam of light at the same angle it hits the surface.

Specular highlights are things that go above 90% diffuse reflectance. These might include a candle flame or a glint off a chrome car bumper. As we'll see later, being able to accommodate these intense highlights is a big difference between old-style Rec.709 -HD video and the modern cameras and file formats such as *OpenEXR*.

Textured black is the darkest tone where there is still some separation and detail. Viewed on the waveform, it is the step just above where the darkest blacks merge indistinguishably into the noise.

THE DILEMMA

What is a great leap forward for shooting with these modern cameras is also something of a disadvantage — recording log encoded video gives us huge benefits in terms of dynamic range, but it also means the images the camera is outputting and recording are in no way *WYSIWYG* (*what you see is what you get*). In fact, on the monitor, they look awful — low in contrast and saturation. Even worse, they mean that the waveform monitor and vectorscope are not showing us the reality of the scene as it will be in the end result. A commonly used method is to display a Rec.709 conversion of the image on the set monitors. This makes the scene viewable (what we might think of as human readable) but they are only a rough approximation of what is really being recorded and even more distant representation of what the image will eventually look like. Likewise, in a scene with a Rec.709 viewing LUT applied, the waveform monitor isn't telling us the whole story. Not just that they don't always have the benefit of fine-tuned color correction, but that they don't show us what the image will look like after it has been "developed," using the metaphor that RAW data is like a film negative.

Developing, in this case is not a photochemical process, but is the deBayering and *log to linear* conversions that will take place outside of the camera. If you've ever looked at *original camera negative* (*OCN*) you know that it is nearly impossible to comprehend visually; not only is it a negative in that tones are reversed, but also the colors are all opposite and there is a heavy orange mask. Cinematographers have developed the skill of looking at camera negative and getting a sense of what is a *thick* (overexposed) or *thin* (underexposed) image, but any understanding of color is impossible. These concepts come into play as we consider exposure with cameras that record log data either internally or on an external recorder. Some DPs and DITs prefer to have the log encoded image on the waveform monitor and a viewing LUT applied for the monitors.

But how to achieve these goals of having an ideal digital negative? What methods get you there reliably and quickly — speed is always a factor in motion picture production. Three cinematographers highly respected not only for their artistry but also for their in-depth knowledge of technical issues weighed in on this topic at *Cinematographer's Mailing List* (*CML*). They are Geoff Boyle, (founder of CML) David Mullen, and Art Adams.

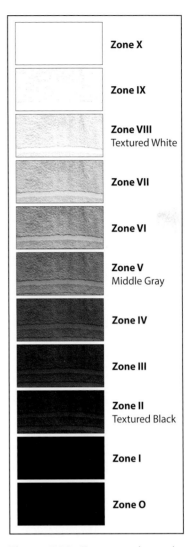

Figure 5.28. Zones as shown by photographing a towel in sunlight. What's important here is the concept of *texture and detail*.

USING LIGHT METERS

Many DPs have returned to using their light meters, both incident and reflectance (spot) meters. This is after years of using them infrequently if at all when shooting HD video, where factors such as gamma, knee, black gamma, etc. altered the image enough to make light meter readings less relevant or even misleading. When shooting RAW/log, the waveform suddenly becomes less precise because the image is displayed at very low contrast. A purely RAW Bayer image is, of course, unviewable for all practical purposes. The good news is that when shooting RAW/log, any alterations you make to the image, are purely metadata, which has the end result of making the light meter readings more accurate. Art Adams puts it this way, "I find myself using an incident meter much more often now. I rough in the lighting and then check it on a monitor and waveform, and then use the incident meter for consistency when moving around within the scene. I still pull out my spot meter occasionally but I'm becoming less reliant on it. The incident meter helps me get my mid-tones right and keep them consistent, and the monitor and waveform tell me about everything else."

METER THE KEY

This is the age old formula for exposing film: use an incident meter (with proper ISO, frame rate, filter factors and shutter angle dialed in on the meter) to read the key light (usually right where the actor is) and set the aperture for that reading (Figure 5.11). This provides an overall average for the scene — it is usually remarkably successful. Art Adams says, "If I have a choice I work strictly by meter. If not I work off the waveform. I use my meter to set proper mid-tones, and the waveform tells me if I'm losing detail in either the highlights or the shadows."

In the same vein, British DP Geoff Boyle states, "I've gone back totally to using my incident meter together with my old Pentax digital spot calibrated with the zone system. I decide where the skin will be and keep it there. Overall with the incident reading, spot checks of highlights, shadows and skin, hang on! That's how I used to shoot film. I have expanded the zone system range by a stop at either end,

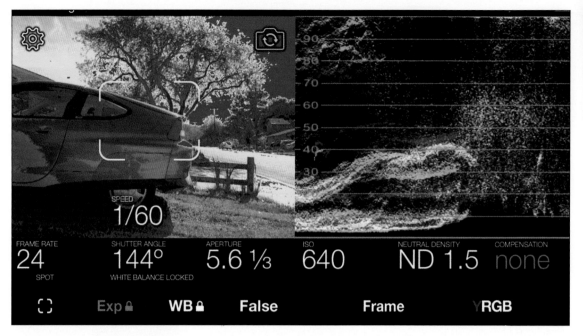

Figure 5.29. Adam Wilt's *Cine Meter II* offers a wide array of exposure tools in an iPhone app. In this case, both an overlay waveform and false colors are displayed. The yellow brackets represent the *spot meter* which can be moved, allowing the user to select what part of the scene is being exposed for. (Courtesy of Adam Wilt).

i.e. where I knew I would get pure white or black I now know I will have detail. I use an ISO for the cameras that I've established from testing works for the way that I work, that sounds familiar as well. Yes, I will use a waveform on some work; it's a great tool there or diamonds [diamond display], but otherwise it's a rare thing for me. For me it's a question of dynamic range, once it gets to 12 stops or more I can relax and get into the pictures rather than the tech."

Here's Art Adams on shooting HD: "The big change for me is that I used to use nothing but a spot meter [when shooting film] but gamma curves are so variable that trying to nail an exposure based on a reflected reading is the true moving target. I can use a spot meter to find out how far exposed a window will be on a scout but it's tough to light using nothing but a spot meter in HD, the way I could in film. Film stocks had different gammas but we only had to know a couple of them; every HD camera has at least 7 or 8 basic variations, plus lots of other variables that come into play."

Waveform Monitors

When shooting HD (Rec.709) the waveform monitor has always been an important tool for making exposure decisions. It was supplemented by zebras and histograms, but those are rough guides at best; the waveform is accurate, precise and gives you information about every part of the scene. The problem, of course, is that if the camera is outputting log/RAW information, the waveform display doesn't reflect the actual image as it is being recorded and will be processed later down the line (Figure 5.31). This output is difficult to judge and for directors may essentially be unviewable on the set; to make any sense of it takes a good deal of experience and mental calculation. As a result, monitors on the set generally display a converted image; most often the log image is converted to Rec.709 by a LUT either internal on the camera, externally through a LUT box or with a monitor that can host LUTs. While this makes it easier to interpret, it in no way shows the real image, particularly the highlights and shadows. Adams says "A LUT may not show the real image but LUTs almost always show a subset of the image that throws away

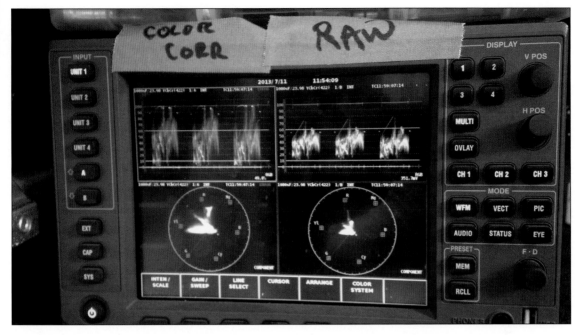

Figure 5.30. DIT Evan Nesbit uses a *quad display* waveform/vectorscope to look at both the RAW video feed from camera and the color corrected image. (Courtesy of Evan Nesbit).

information by applying gamma, etc. I have no problem working off a Rec.709 converted log signal with a monitor and a waveform because I know that if it looks nice on set I can always make it look a lot nicer later in the grade. For example, if the Rec.709 image isn't clipping then I know the log image really isn't clipping. I make the image look nice and then shoot. I do check the log image on occasion but not very often."

Cinematographer David Mullen, says this, "It would be nice to see a waveform display of the log signal while monitoring a Rec.709 image to know exactly how much clipping is going on... but most camera set-ups seem to involve sending Rec.709 from the camera to the monitors so any waveform on the cart would be reading Rec.709. I don't find much value in seeing the waveform reading of the Rec.709 monitor signal if I am recording log or RAW — I can see clipping in Rec.709 with my own eyes on the monitor, so the waveform just tends to tell me what I can already see. I'd rather see a waveform reading of the log signal getting recorded."

PLACING MIDDLE GRAY

When shooting film negative, the prevailing practice is to use the incident meter for setting the f/stop on the lens and using the spot meter to check highlights such as windows, lamp shades, etc. Reading with the incident meter is the same as placing middle gray at 18%. Some cinematographers use a similar method in log/RAW video — placing middle gray at the values recommended by the camera manufacturer; for example, S-Log1 at 38% and C-Log at 32%, with adjustments made for the cinematographers own preference of course.

Art Adams uses this method: "I go for accurate middle gray, or place middle gray where I want it, and see how the rest falls. Midtones are where our eyes are the most sensitive. We naturally roll off the extreme shadows and highlights, just as cameras have been designed to do, so it makes little or no sense to me to base a scene's exposure on the part of the image that our brains naturally compress anyway. I generally expose raw and log based around middle gray using a meter... unless I'm shooting doc-style, and quickly. In

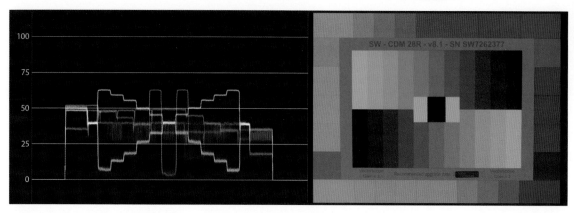

Figure 5.31. Waveform display of a log encoded image of a DSC Labs *Chroma du Monde* with exposure set by placing middle gray at the camera manufacturer's recommended level. The highlights are far below 100% but the important aspect of shooting RAW/log is that you are not necessarily trying to create a final look for the scene — it is a digital negative, not the desired end result.

that case I tend to look at the mid-tones and the highlights together on a waveform. In certain cameras, like any of the Canon C family, throwing the camera into *Cine Lock* mode puts the waveform in that mode as well.

I know that in the C500 the waveform continues to look only at a log representation of the raw signal even if view assist is turned on. Canon's implementation of log pushes blacks fairly far up the scale to the point where I really don't worry about them at all. I find a mid-tone exposure on the waveform that works for me while trying not to clip highlights. It's as much trusting the image by eye as it is judging the waveform monitor with my gut." He also points out that there are different values for middle gray depending on the camera and the log encoding being used (Figure 4.40 in *Linear, Gamma, Log*) and it's important to keep this in mind when setting the exposure to achieve those values. *Cine Lock* is an option on some Canon professional cine cameras that locks out picture controls so that the recorded image is largely unaffected by in-camera manipulation. More importantly, it sets the camera to *Canon Log* (*C-Log*) and the default matrix for *cinema mode*.

Adams adds about the Alexa "Middle gray stays at nearly the same value when toggling between Log C and Rec.709, with the upshot that the Log C image — which is not designed to be viewable on any kind of HD monitor — still looks okay when viewed on a Rec.709 monitor. The bottom line is that middle gray changes very little when toggling between Log C and Rec.709, and this seems to make Log C more "monitor friendly" than other log curves." We'll go into Arri's Log C, Canon's C-Log and the log encoding from other camera companies in the next chapter.

START AT THE BOTTOM OR START AT THE TOP

Placing something pure black in the scene at 0% on the waveform seems tempting but the catch is finding something truly black. At first glance it seems quite a bit safer than trying to select something in the frame to place at 100% white. As we have seen, what is really white is subjective and highly variable. Especially if you are shooting RAW/log and viewing in Rec.709, it is extremely difficult to even determine where the clipping level really is. Even more confounding, is the white object you selected 90% diffuse white, 100% white or something else?

When using the *DSC Labs Chroma du Monde* chart (as discussed in the chapter *Measurement*), the *CaviBlack* (Figure 5.32) is pure black but as we saw, it takes a good deal of innovation to make it truly black; a condition very unlikely to occur in a typical scene or even in an ordinary situation when testing or setting up a camera. Art Adams puts it this way, "Putting something black at the black point is similarly pointless because there's not a lot of real black out there unless it's a dark shadow. Also, if a camera exhibits wide dynamic range but it isn't equally split between highlights and shadows, you'll always have more stops in the shadows, which means putting something black at black results in pushing the exposure way down. Also, if what's black in one frame isn't black in another you end up with the same problems as exposing to the right: inconsistent noise and overall exposure."

Although placing pure black at 0% on the waveform is unlikely to be a useful method on the set, it still has a very useful place in testing, calibrating and comparing cameras, because in a test situation you are better able to place something in the frame that you know to be pure black, such the CaviBlack and it's very easy to know where to place it as you adjust exposure and view the result on a waveform monitor.

ART ADAMS' 45 DEGREE RULE

As for placing diffuse white, (not specular highlights), Adams points out a trick that may be useful. Find the point on the log curve where the slope is 45° — this is usually where the camera company puts 90% diffuse white. Frequently, middle gray will be half of that. This applies to shooting log, of course. He put it this way: "Where to set 'white': typically black and middle gray stay in roughly the same portion of the IRE scale, with white and super white being the moving targets. My rule of thumb, is that your brightest 'textured white' should be placed where the curve goes through a 45 degree angle into the highlights. Beyond that the steps between values decrease dramatically, and that's suitable for highlight rendition but not for holding detail in anything truly important. Textured white is an Ansel Adams reference to the brightest white value in a print where one can still see detail [see Figure 5.28]. Highlights are effectively gone when they flatten out horizontally and show no more steps of brightness. The farther up the flat part of the curve the highlights go the fewer steps will be employed to store them, so try not to push any but the brightest highlights to that edge." (Art Adams, *The Not So Technical Guide to S-Log* at ProVideo Coalition.)

EXPOSE TO THE RIGHT

Expose to the Right (*ETTR*) is popular with digital still photographers and is occasionally mentioned in connection with exposure in digital cinema. The idea is simple — since the dark areas of the image is where there is the most noise, we want to push the exposure as high as we can *without clipping*. On the histogram, the right side is the highlights, so those who use this method try to move the image toward the right on the histogram (Figures 5.33 through 5.35).

This method is not without its critics, however, most of them assert that it is no longer necessary as the noise level of cameras steadily improves. "Exposing to the right results in inconsistent noise from shot to shot, which can be jarring, and also tends to result in less consistency of exposure such that every shot needs its own grade," says Adams. He adds, "Exposing to the right or to the left is great for one shot that stands alone... which almost never happens. When your images sit adjacent to others why would you base their exposures on the things that change the most between them?" Geoff Boyle comments, "I understand the expose to the right camp and I have done

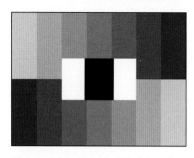

Figure 5.32. The *CaviBlack* is a key feature of the *Chroma du Monde*. It is an open hole in the middle of the chart which is backed by a velvet lined foldout box on the back of the chart. It's a complete light trap and provides a reliable pure black reference in the frame, an invaluable tool for testing and camera setup.

this at times in the past but not anymore." He adds, "ETTR is not a practical method of working for us, every shot having to be graded individually and huge measures taken to match. Equally, whilst you can pull and push film you can't do it on a shot by shot basis." In general, expose to the right is more suited to still photography or specialized situations that only involve a few shots, such as commercials." In practice, cinematographers rarely use ETTR on feature films or long form projects. As an exposure method, it might still be useful for isolated shots, such as landscapes or product shots and on commercials which might consist of only a few shots in the day and thus consistency and efficiency in the grading process are less of an issue.

ZEBRAS

As we have previously discussed, zebras can be operator selected to appear in the viewfinder of many cameras and on some monitors and are a handy, always present (if you choose) check on highlight values and clipping. The problem is they are based on measuring the IRE (luma) value and are thus a bit more difficult to use when shooting log. In cases where you are shooting HD style (that is, basically in Rec.709 mode or WYSIWYG), they are very useful. Adams comments, "If I'm running around then I look at zebras and judge mid-tones in the viewfinder by eye. It's not ideal, but I'm old school enough that I can do it well."

THE MONITOR

During the HD years, you often heard "Don't trust the monitor!" Several advances have changed that. First of all, the kind of high end monitors that are likely to be the DP's main monitor near camera and at the DIT cart have greatly improved in color and tone scale accuracy. Additionally, much more attention is paid to frequent and proper calibration of monitors.

David Mullen puts it like this: "I mainly come to rely on the monitor with occasional double-checks using various devices — meters, waveforms, histograms, just not on every shot. The main point is the feedback loop over time (if this is a long-form project), you check the footage again in dailies, in the editing room, etc., to see if your exposure technique is giving you good results, and sometimes you make adjustments when you find that your day work is a bit too hot or your night work is a bit too dark, etc. I also shoot tests before I begin to see how things look on the set versus later in a DI theater."

One issue that has to be considered when discussing monitors is viewing conditions. A monitor, even a very good one, standing in a brightly lit area outdoors or even on the set, isn't going to give you accurate information. The problem is not the monitor, it is the glare that happens as light comes in from all directions. Also, since your eyes will adjust to the brightly lit conditions, they aren't well adapted to seeing what's on the monitor. This is why you'll see dark hoods around monitors on the set, or at least the grips will set 4x4 floppies or other shades to prevent glare on the monitor. As we'll see in *The DIT Cart*, DITs often work inside a tent when setting up outdoors.

KNOW THYSELF AND KNOW THY CAMERA

Just as you get to know the characteristics of particular cameras and how they respond, you also need to get to know your own inclinations. As David Mullen puts it: "Finally, the old saying 'Know Thyself' can be applied to exposure technique; we know if we have a tendency to overexpose or underexpose in general so we can develop

filmmaker's guide to digital imaging

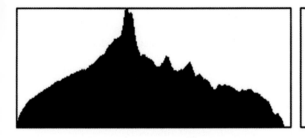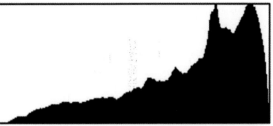

a technique to take that into account." As you go through the feed-back cycle of using your meters, waveform, zebras or whatever it is you use, then setting exposure and viewing the results in dailies, you need to watch what works and what doesn't. Do you have a tendency to overexpose night scenes? Underexpose day scenes? Whatever it is you do, learn from it and bring that self-knowledge back to the set with you next time you shoot. Perhaps you consistently interpret you incident meter in a particular way and tend to set exposure by the waveform in a slightly different way. Despite the accuracy of the tools and the (perhaps illusory) precision of digital it's never a straightforward, mechanical process, there is always an element of human judgement involved; sometime a very large component of "go by the gut," especially in unusual exposure situations.

BLACK MAGIC CAMERA EXPOSURE ADVICE

Blackmagic Design, the maker of *DaVinci Resolve* and several video cameras, offers the following view on exposure with their *Blackmagic Cinema Camera* and *4K Production Camera*. "Why do my RAW shots look overexposed? Answer: The 100% Zebra level in the Display Settings helps you adjust your exposure to ensure that you don't overload the sensor and clip your highlights. It is based on the full dynamic range capability of the *Blackmagic Cinema Camera* and not on video levels. A quick way to ensure you do not allow the sensor to clip any image data is to set your Zebra level to 100%, expose your shot such that zebras start to appear and then back it off until the Zebras disappear. If you have an auto iris lens on the camera, pressing the IRIS button will do this automatically for you by adjusting the lens aperture to keep the white peaks just below the sensor's clipping point.

"If you normally expose your shots based on an 18% gray card at 40 IRE video levels, then your log images will look correct when imported into DaVinci Resolve. However, if you want to maximize your camera sensor's signal to noise ratio, you might expose your shots so the white peaks are just below the sensor clipping point. This may cause your log images to look overexposed when a video curve is applied to the preview, and the highlights you thought were safe will look as though they have been clipped. This is normal and all the details are still retained in the file. If there is a lot of contrast range in the shot, the log images may look fine and not overexposed.

"Shooting in RAW/log captures a very wide dynamic range. However, you might only see the image in the more limited *Video range* (*Rec.709*) when you open the CinemaDNG files in a compatible application. If the camera is not exposed based on 18% or other video related exposure guides, the RAW files will look over or under exposed depending on the dynamic range of the scene. The good news is that you have not really lost any information in your shots. Based on the contrast range of your shot, you can creatively adjust the exposure settings of the DNG file for the look you want using

Figure 5.33. On the left, a fairly normal, typical distribution of tones on the histogram. On the right, an example of *Expose To the Right* — the tonal scale is pushed toward higher exposure, but without clipping.

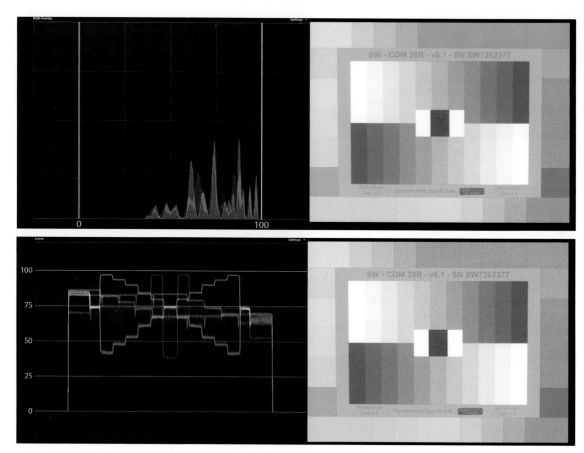

Figure 5.34. (Top) An example of the *Expose to the Right* method on the histogram. The chart looks blown out and desaturated, but in fact, nothing is clipping so the values can be brought back in color correction. The risk is obvious, even a slight increase in exposure will cause some values to clip.

Figure 5.35. (Bottom) The same *Expose to the Right* frame as shown on the waveform. While the high values are dangerously close to clipping, all of the darker values have been pushed up the scale, well away from noise.

software such as *DaVinci Resolve, Adobe Photoshop* or *Adobe Lightroom.* To recover the highlights not displayed in Resolve, use the RAW image settings and adjust the Exposure values so the details you need fit within the video range. Exposing your shot to the point just before the sensor clips, ensures you are getting the best signal to noise ratio for the maximum flexibility during post production.

"Alternatively, you can also base your exposure while using the LCD set to preview in Video dynamic range so there is no need to worry even if you do not have a gray card. Shots exposed this way will then look the same when imported into Resolve and will need very little exposure correction."

DEALING WITH RANGE IN COLOR CORRECTION

Over the years, postproduction professionals have developed many different techniques and types of hardware for dealing with the image and in particular with adjusting color and exposure. As image-making moved into the digital origination as well as post, even more powerful tools for adjusting exposure and color became available. These digital techniques continue to grow and expand. Controlling the image with these methods is covered in the chapter *Image Control & Grading* later in this book. As we'll see, it's not only about making individual shots look good, but also about establishing consistency of exposure and color within scenes and across the entire project. No matter how careful the DP is with exposure and color control, it is inevitable that some adjustments will be needed. Cinematographers put a premium on keeping the need for these kinds of adjustments to a minimum so valuable color correction time can be devoted more toward the artistic and storytelling goals of the project.

HDR

Frequently when shooting outdoors, the contrast ratios can be very high, especially if the sky or very bright areas such as a snow covered mountain are included in the frame. In black-and-white still photography, Ansel Adams developed techniques for dealing with this by altering the chemical development of the negative; something that really isn't practical when shooting color film. With the advent of digital cameras, still photographers developed a method called *High Dynamic Range* (*HDR*). Photographers discovered that if, instead of taking one image of a scene, they took several shots of the same scene at different exposures, they could be combined later on to make a photo that had dynamic range that far exceeded what was possible in a single shot, even with the very best of sensors (Figures 5.36 through 5.39).

How it works is actually fairly simple. Let's say we are faced with a scene that has an extreme contrast ratio (dynamic range): from something very dark to something very bright. An old example is a single scene that has a black leopard in the mouth of a cave and nearby is a white marble statue in full sun. Read with a reflectance (spot) meter, the brightness range is enormous. For the sake of our example, let's say it ranges from F/1.4 to F/128 — an incredibly big spread. There is no video sensor, not even any film stock, that could accommodate such a brightness range. But you could take one exposure at F/1.4 that properly exposes the leopard in the deep shade — this shot would horribly overexpose the marble statue of course. Next you take a shot at F/128 (in reality you would probably have to change the exposure time as well — lenses that close down to F/128 are very rare) — this shot would expose the marble statue properly but of course the cave with the leopard would be pure black - no detail.

In photo software, combining the two shots is almost trivial. With the combined shot you have both the extremes well exposed and thus a photo with an extreme dynamic range. There are a couple of caveats, though. Obviously, you have to deal with the stuff in the middle: the mid-range tones. Neither of the extreme exposures are going to correctly reproduce the parts of the scene that are in the middle of the exposure range. Not a problem: it's easy enough to take additional exposures to fill in. Scenic photographers shooting sunsets (very high brightness in the sky) with dark landscape in the foreground (typically very low brightness values) often take four, five, or more exposures to cover the entire range. I use f/stops in this example for simplicity only; in general, it is better to change the exposure with shutter speed; changing the f/stop alters the depth-of-field.

It doesn't take much thought to reveal the other limitation of this method for motion picture work: if the subject is moving (such as objects or people in action) then it really isn't practical to take multiple exposures of the same scene; in the fraction of a second between exposures they would have shifted slightly or even significantly, resulting in blur in the image.

HDRx

Red's *HDRx* (Figures 5.40 through 5.43) is not a separate file format, it integrates two images per frame: the primary exposure and also an underexposed capture of the same frame to preserve highlight detail. These are dealt with together in software such as *RedCine X Pro*. The primary exposure is called the *A Frame* and the secondary underexposed image is the *X Frame*. According to Red: "It works by

Figure 5.36. (Top) A normal "correctly exposed" frame leaves little detail in the deep shadows or in the highlights; it's an average that doesn't do justice to the extremes.

Figure 5.37. (Second down) An overexposed image sees into the shadows.

Figure 5.38. (Third down) The underexposed frame retains the highlight detail.

Figure 5.39. (Bottom) When combined as an *HDR* image, the frames produce an image with enough dynamic range to accommodate the original scene.

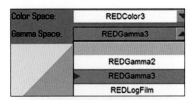

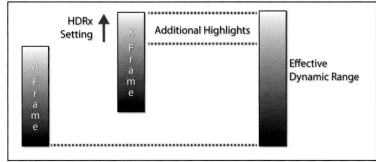

Figure 5.40. (Right) A diagram of how Red's *HDRx* format works.

Figure 5.41. (Above, top) The Red camera menu selections for gamma and log curves.

Figure 5.42. (Above, middle) The same gamma and log selections in *RedCine-X Pro*.

Figure 5.43. (Above, bottom) Red-Cine-X Pro includes menu selections for use with *Red's HDRx*, including *Magic Motion*, which blends the *A* and *X* frames.

recording two exposures within the interval that a standard motion camera would record only one: The primary exposure is normal, and uses the standard aperture and shutter settings (the "A frame"). The secondary exposure is typically for highlight protection, and uses an adjustable shutter speed that is 2-6 stops faster (the "X frame"). For example, if the A frame is captured at 24 FPS and 1/50 second shutter speed, then specifying 2 stops HDRx causes the X frame to be captured at a shutter speed of 1/200 second." These two frames then need to be combined and the percentage of each that is used in the final shot needs to be variable. Since there is a difference in the motion blur within the frame between shots taken at very different shutter speeds, there is a need to adjust the apparent blur in the shot. This is provided for in Red Camera companies software *RedCine-X Pro* and is called *Magic Motion*. It allows the user to view the blend of the two frames and adjust the ratio between them, thus adapting for different situations. Figure 5.43 shows the menu selections available for this function.

digital color

Color is both a powerful artistic and storytelling tool and a complex technical subject. As with most artistic tools, the better you understand the technical side, the better equipped you will be to use it to serve your creative purposes. Although we'll be delving into the science and technology of color, it is important to never lose sight of the fact that it all comes down to human perception — the eye/brain combination and how it interprets the light waves that come in is the basis of everything we do in this area. As for technology, never forget that when it comes to achieving your artistic and crafts person goals — anything goes; you are never constrained by some "techie" requirement, unless, of course, ignoring that technical aspect is going to interfere with what you finally want to achieve.

THE VISUAL INTERFACE

The eye and the brain work together in visual perception, but let's start with the physiology of the eye — it's important to understand on its own, but it also will give us some clues as to how imaging systems work. The eye has cells that function as receptors, in ways that are surprisingly similar to how video sensors work. First some basic terminology. The primary aspect of light as we deal with it is the wavelength, which is measured in *nanometers (nm)* — one billionth of a meter or 1×10^{-9} meter.

There are two basic types of receptor cells: *rods* and *cones* and they serve two types of vision: *scotopic* and *photopic*. Scotopic vision (the rod cells), is adapted for low light conditions. These cells are most sensitive in a range centered around 498 nanometers (green-blue); this means that low light vision is very poor in color perception.

Photopic cells in the retina do most of the work of color perception; they function mostly in normal light conditions. Just like video sensors, there are three types, each of which is sensitive to different wavelengths. Technically they are sensitive to long, medium and short wavelengths (*LMS*) but they are commonly called the red, green and blue receptors. Because we have two systems of vision that operate at different light levels and we also have an iris that functions in exactly the same way as a camera lens aperture, human visual perception has an extraordinary dynamic range of brightness levels, as we saw in *Linear, Gamma, Log*.

Sir Isaac Newton is the seminal figure in color theory. He cut a small hole in the window shade of his room at Cambridge and placed a prism so that the rays of sunshine were intercepted by it. The pattern it projected onto a white target is the familiar "rainbow" of the color spectrum: Red, Orange, Yellow, Green, Blue, Indigo and Violet, which is easily remembered with the mnemonic Roy G. Biv. However, like Pluto (the former planet, not the cartoon dog), Indigo is no longer officially recognized, so now it's Roy G. Bv.

As is hinted at in Figure 6.2, one of the most interesting things about color is what happens when we mix them. We can select three "primary" colors which just happen to roughly correspond to the sensitivity of the cones and by mixing them create any of the other colors. In the case of light, which is *additive color* (the *subtractive* color system is used with pigmented color such as painting, printing and color filters) the primaries are Red, Green and Blue. Figure 6.2 shows the mixing of long waves (Red) medium waves (Green) and short waves (Blue). The mixing of red and blue results in magenta; mixing blue and green gives us cyan (otherwise known as blue-green) — these are intuitively obvious. These are the secondary colors that we get when we mix *pure* primaries. Not at all obvious or intuitive is

Figure 6.1. (Below, top) Sensitivity curves of the three types of *cones* in the eye. The black line is the response curve of the *rods*.

Figure 6.2. (Below, bottom) The cone's sensitivity curves with color mixing shown: red and green mix to form a perception of yellow; blue and green mix to create a perception of cyan.

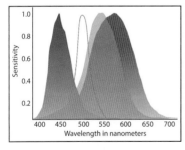

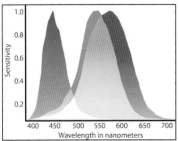

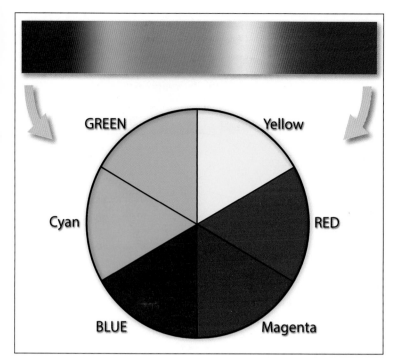

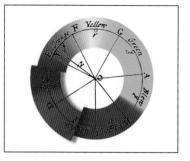

Figure 6.3. (Above) Newton's original diagram (with color added). Note how he shows the Magentas as separate from the rest.

Figure 6.4. (Left) Newton's innovation was to take the spectrum and bend it into a circle. Note that the color wheel has magenta even though it does not appear on the spectrum. The secondaries Cyan and Yellow are mixtures of the primaries on either side of them on the spectrum, but Magenta is a mixture of Red and Blue which are at opposite ends of the spectrum.

what happens when we add green and red together — the result is yellow. Clearly there are all sorts of reds that are not "pure" red — there are many gradations in the region between 620 and 680 nanometers.

Newton's Wheel

Another contribution Newton made to color science was his invention of the color wheel (Figure 6.3). The spectrum is linear, it goes from around 380nm to about 780nm. Around 1666 Newton came up with the idea of bending that spectrum into a circle; it makes the relationship of primaries and secondaries much more clear, but it has another interesting aspect: in order for it to work, two colors that don't really "belong" together are joined: blue and red are far apart from each other on the linear spectrum and here they are near neighbors — between them is their mixture, magenta, which you will notice does not appear in the linear spectrum! In color terminology, the hues from the linear spectrum are called *spectral colors*. In Figure 6.4 you can see that he indicated these *non-spectral* colors; the magentas, as being somehow different from the others.

What Causes "Color"

Our eye/brain visual system, film emulsion and video cameras all work in similar ways when it comes to color: they create the full range of the spectrum by mixing just three primary inputs. It is easy to understand how we see these primary colors: blue light comes into the eye and the blue cones react and send an electrical impulse to the brain which is interpreted as "blue" and so on. However, to call something "blue light" is not really accurate. The photons that make up light have no color, they are just wavelengths. It is our eye and brain that create the sensation of color from what happens in the retina when different wavelengths hit the receptor cells. The same is true of colors that come from mixing primaries — it is an interpretation of the brain.

Figure 6.5. (Above) *Hue,* what most people think of as "color" is measured around the color wheel. *Value* goes from dark to light (Red is used as the example here) and *Saturation* is the "colorfulness" — high saturation is the color very intense and low saturation is the color as a pale tint.

Figure 6.6. (Right) The basic color wheel shows the primary colors: Long wavelengths (Red), Medium wavelengths (Green) and short wavelengths (Blue) and the secondary colors that result form mixing two primaries equally.

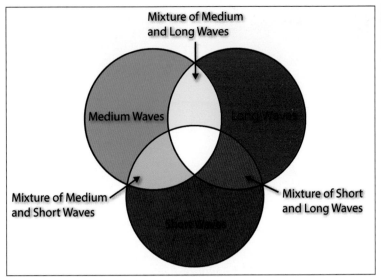

A Color The Brain Invents

But here's the rub: as we saw, magenta doesn't appear on the spectrum at all; it is not one of the colors of the rainbow. On Newton's color wheel, we can see that it is produced by a mixture of red and blue and this is easily demonstrated by mixing red and blue light. On the spectrum, however, red and blue are at opposite ends: red is long waves and blue is short waves, in between them is green. So where do we get magenta, also commonly called purple? The brain invents it. When roughly equal numbers of red and blue cones are firing, the signal they send to the brain is interpreted as magenta. Removing green from white light also creates magenta for the same reason.

Does this mean that magenta/purple is an "imaginary" color because it is "invented" by our brain? As a psychiatrist once told his patient: "It's all in your head." The answer is no and for this we need to understand the definition of what is a color. If humans can't see it, it's not a color. There are some things we call by names that sound like colors but are not: *ultraviolet* and *infrared*, for example. In terms of color science, they are not colors because humans can't see them. Maybe a butterfly can see them (they have the widest perceptual color range in the animal kingdom), but we don't yet make movies for butterflies. Colors are colors because we see them.

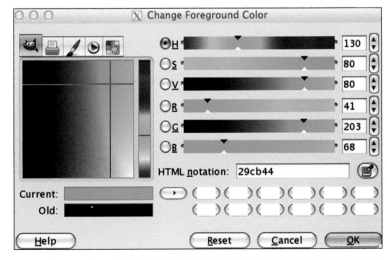

Figure 6.7. A typical color picker in a graphics program — color can be picked through combinations of Hue/Saturation/Value or by mixing different amounts of Red/Green/Blue.

filmmaker's guide to digital imaging

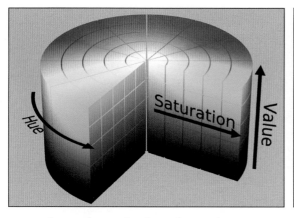
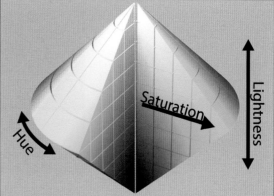

In understanding color for video, we're going to see how this plays out in diagramming and analyzing *spectral* (colors of the spectrum) and *non-spectral* colors — the *purples*, as they are called, with purple being the same as variations of magenta in this context.

COLOR TERMINOLOGY

As we mentioned in *Measurement*, what we commonly call color is more properly termed *hue*. *Value* is how light or dark a color is and *saturation* is how "colorful" it is; in video we more commonly call it *chroma saturation* or just *chroma*. A desaturated color in everyday terms might be called a *pastel*. These terms are the basis for two color models: *Hue/Saturation/Value* (*HSV*) and *Hue/Saturation/Lightness* (*HSL*) which are shown in Figures 6.8 and 6.9. These systems are widely used in computer graphics and sometimes show up in applications used in dealing with video streams or individual frames (such as when adjusting a frame or frames in *Photoshop*, for example); they are widely used in *color pickers* which are always a part of visual software (Figure 6.7).

Derived from the color wheel, it is easy to conceptualize hue as a circle and saturation as its distance from neutral white in the center. This is shown in Figure 6.8; this is a simple visualization of hue, color mixing and chroma saturation decreasing to white (no saturation), however it does not show value/lightness decreasing to black. This is a pervasive problem with illustrating and graphing color models, since there are usually three important axes, it is hard to do it in on the two-dimensional space of paper. All three dimensions are shown in the cylinder of HSV and the double cone of HSL but these are just snapshot views — we're only looking at it from one side which means that important parts of the diagram are hidden.

WHERE'S WHITE?

The color wheel shows us most of the important aspects of color (Figure 6.6). We know that white is an equal combination of all the colors; so what is the precise scientific definition of white? Well, surprisingly, at least in video terms, there really isn't one. White is a somewhat evasive concept. You have probably encountered this problem many times, probably without having to give it too much thought — every time you white balance a video camera. Let's say you're photographing something we know to be white — the back of a *Kodak Neutral Gray* card, for example; it is carefully manufactured to be truly neutral white. We know it is what is says it is, so why do we have to fiddle with the camera to get it to appear just as we see it in real life?

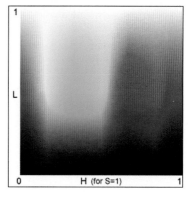

Figure 6.8. (Top, left and right) Two slightly different color models. On the left is *Hue/Saturation/Value* and on the right is *Hue/Saturation/Lightness*.

Figure 6.9. (Above) A two-dimensional representation of *Hue/Saturation/Lightness*.

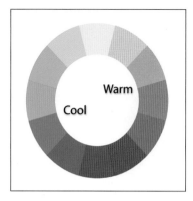

Figure 6.10. (Above) Warm and cool colors. This is a psychological phenomenon; in terms of physics, the color temperature of Blue is "hotter" (higher in degrees Kelvin) than Red but this has little to do with our perceptual reaction to colors.

Figure 6.11. (Right) The filter wheels on a Sony *CineAlta* camera. There are two wheels — *Neutral Density* filters are numbered 1 thru 4 and *color filter presets* are labeled A, B, C and D. On this particular camera both sets of filters are actual glass filters that are rotated in front of the sensor; on many cameras these functions are performed electronically.

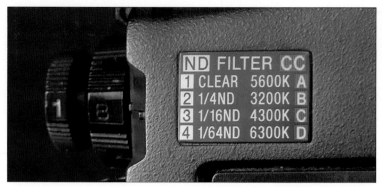

Because its appearance on video depends very much on the *illuminant* of the scene — this is just a fancy term for what lighting we are using on the card. It could be any one of a huge variety, but most often it is one of the three we all know: daylight, tungsten or fluorescent. Aside from tungsten, which is very well defined and for the most part constant, these colors are really just approximations; after all simple observation shows us that "daylight" changes color all day long: dawn is more magenta, mid-day light can vary considerably based on what city or country you are in and just at sunset, the light of the sun is actually tungsten color; which is why when shooting film, we would often "lose the 85" for magic hour shots — the 85 being the 85 correction filter that gave us the proper color balance on tungsten film shot outdoors. So let's define some of these terms and try to get a better handle on the concept of white and how we deal with it in production and post-production.

COLOR TEMPERATURE: THE BALANCES

Even deeper down the rabbit hole — what is daylight? It's not sunlight, which tends to be warmer due to the yellow sun of Earth; it's not skylight, which is very blue, it's a combination of the two. It is a somewhat artificial standard, established back in the fifties when someone went out on the front lawn of the *Bureau of National Standards* in Washington at noon with a color meter. They determined that daylight was 5600K. The units are *K*, for *degrees Kelvin*. The ° symbol is not used with the Kelvin scale.

Many people think this scale was invented by Lord Kelvin, but in fact it is just named in his honor. The Kelvin scale uses the same units as *Celsius*; the difference is that the Celsius scale places zero at the freezing point of water, where on the Kelvin scale, the starting point is absolute zero: -273° C or -459° F. OK, fine, but why are we talking about temperature when the subject of discussion is color? Well, a fellow named Max Planck won the Nobel Prize for figuring out that the color of a *black body* (think a black piece of metal) changes color in proportion to its temperature. If you heat a black body radiator to 3200K it will be the same orange color as the light bulbs we use in filmmaking; in other words, the Kelvin scale is sort of a common sense application of the terms "red hot," "white hot," etc. Here's the funny part: a lower temperature makes the color "warmer," where logic would imply that making it hotter makes it "warmer" in color. On this scale the average color temperature of daylight is 5600K. Consumer cameras (and most DSLRs) have other preset white balances in addition to daylight and tungsten (Figure 6.16). These usually include *open shade*, which is much cooler because it is mostly skylight which is much bluer; the same applies to overcast days, where the warmer direct sunlight is not a factor.

Figure 6.12. (Below) Color Temperature in degrees *Kelvin*. Lower color temperature is Red/Orange; higher color temperature is bluer.

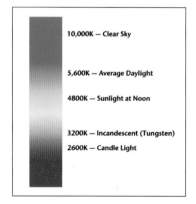

WARM AND COOL

On the warmer end of the scale are things like household light bulbs, candles and other smaller sources which are in the 2000K to 3000K range. All this brings us to the question: what do we mean when we say "warm" or "cool" colors? Clearly it doesn't relate to the color temperature; in fact it works in the opposite direction. Color temperatures above 5000K are commonly called cool colors (blueish), while lower color temperatures (roughly 2,700–3,500 K) are called warm colors (yellow through red). Their relation on the color wheel are shown in Figure 6.10. The color temperatures of black body

Figure 6.13. (Above) This shot was lit entirely by skylight, which is blue. On the left, the camera is set to *Tungsten balance* and the resulting shot is very blue, it looks unnatural. On the right, the same shot with the camera's color balance adjusted to the color temperature of the existing light.

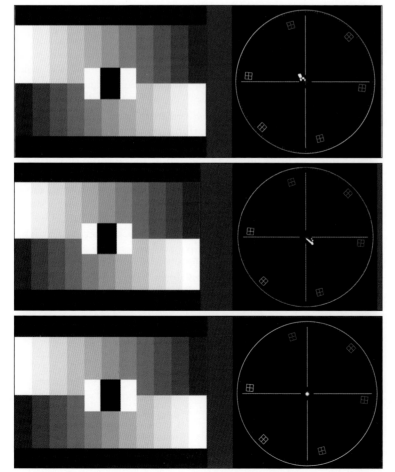

Figure 6.14. (Top) A neutral gray scale with the color balance skewed toward warm light. Notice how the trace on the vectorscope is pulled toward red/orange.

(Middle) The same chart with color balance skewed toward blue — the vectorscope trace is pulled toward blue.

(Bottom) The gray scale with neutral color balance — the vectorscope shows a small dot right in the center, indicating that there is no color at all: zero saturation.

digital color

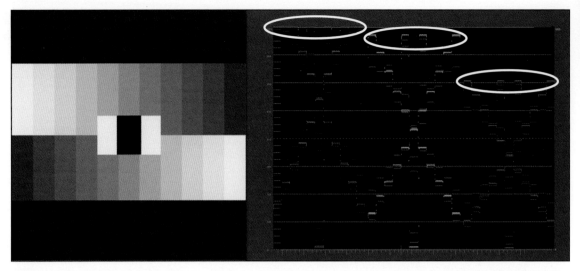

Figure 6.15. *Parade view* on the waveform monitor clearly shows the incorrect color balance of what should be a neutral gray chart. On the waveform, the Red channel is high, while Green is a bit lower and Blue is very low (top end of each channel is circled in this illustration). This is why so many colorists and DITs say that they "live and die by parade view."

radiators are also shown in Figure 6.23; it is called the *black body locus*, meaning that it is a collection of points, not a single instance.

Color temperature is a useful tool but it doesn't tell us everything about the color of a light source; specifically it doesn't tell us anything about how much green or magenta is in a light's radiation. This is a problem because many modern light sources have a lot of green in them, usually a very unpleasant amount, especially for skin tone; these sources include fluorescent tubes, *CFLs* (*Compact Florescent Lights*) and even some *HMIs*. All of these produce light by electrically exciting a gas.

Because color temperature and green (and its opposite magenta) are two different and independent aspects of light, they have to be measured separately. For this reason, color meters will have two scales and output two measurements: one in *degrees Kelvin* and the other in *Color Compensation (CC)* units. Cameras will have similar controls.

As you can see, there's a lot involved in what is "white," but our everyday experience is that white things appear white in all kinds of situations. A white piece of paper will appear white to us whether it's in a fluorescent lit office, a tungsten lit living room or outdoors in the noon day sun. This is because our brain knows that it's white so it just interprets it as white. This can accommodate a wide range of color sources but of course, in extreme conditions under a single color source such as pure red or blue, it does break down and we see the paper as taking on the color of the source. Cameras don't have the ability to adapt in this way: they will record the color of light reflected off the paper just as it is. This is why we have to *white balance* cameras. In older HD cameras, this white balance is baked in, with cameras that shoot Raw, it is recorded in the metadata. Figure 6.13 show incorrect and adjusted color balance.

Most cameras will have preset color balances (Figure 6.16) but it is usually more accurate to do an active white balance on the set. The VFX people will appreciate this as well as they frequently have to artificially recreate the lighting conditions that were on the set. It is

SHADE	DAYLIGHT	FLOURESCENT	INCANDESCENT
Preset to 9,000K	Preset to 5,600K	Preset to 4,500K	Preset to 2,800K
CLOUDY	**FLASH**	**TUNGSTEN**	
Preset to 7,500K	Preset to 5,500K	Preset to 3,200K	

Figure 6.16. Color temperatures of typical camera *presets* in degrees Kelvin.

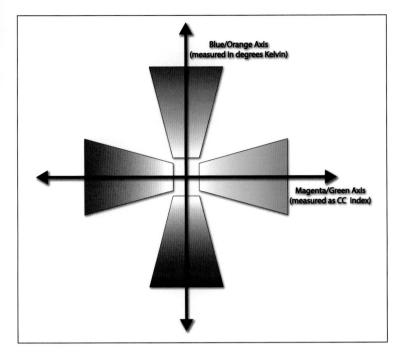

Figure 6.17. The two axes of color: Red/Orange-to-Blue and Magenta-to-Green. They are completely separate and have to be measured separately, which is why all color meters have two different measurements: *Degrees Kelvin* and *CC (Color Correction) Index*.

helpful to understand how a camera accomplishes this (Figure 6.18). It is a process of sensing what light is in the scene and "adding" the opposite (by adjusting the gain of the color channels), so that they balance back to neutral white. In traditional HD cameras (and even in a few RAW cameras) this is done by adjusting the gain on the three color channels. As mentioned in the chapter *Sensors & Cameras*, sensors have a "native" white balance — it is the color balance at which there is the least gain (and therefore the least noise) added. In cameras that shoot RAW, the gain of the color channels is not changed in the camera (except on some Canon cameras), the color balance adjustments are recorded in the camera and the actual changes occur in post-production or at the DIT cart in color grading.

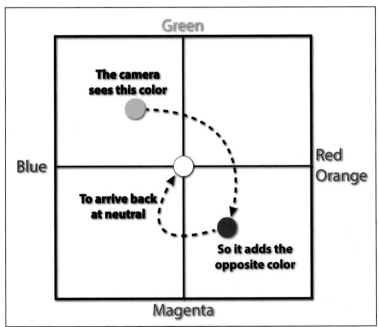

Figure 6.18. How a camera does auto white balance. Notice that it operates on the two color axes: Green-to-Magenta and Blue-to-Red-Orange. In this example the camera "sees" the scene as being lit with blue/green (cyan) lighting, which might be typical of some types of daylight fluorescent tubes. This is why it is important to use a truly neutral white or photo gray card as the target while white balancing — you want the camera to be analyzing *only* the color of the lighting of the scene, not the color of objects within the scene.

digital color

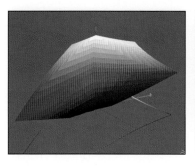
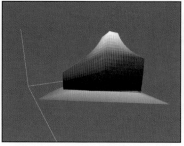
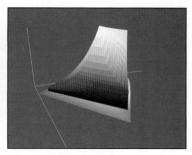

Figure 6.19. (Above, left) sRGB gamut in the L*a*b* color model.

Figure 6.20. (Above, middle) sRGB gamut in the CIELUV color model.

Figure 6.21. (Above, right) sRGB in CIE xyY— the one most often used in video.

We tend to think of this process as purely about tungsten vs. daylight; this is probably because in the days of shooting on film emulsion, the manufacturers made only two types of film: tungsten or daylight. When shooting film in a lighting situation that included green (such as fluorescent in an office) you had only a few choices:

- Turn off the fluorescents and provide your own lighting.
- Put Minus-Green (magenta) gels on the flourescents.
- Filter the lens with a Minus-Green (magenta) filter.
- Shoot a gray card for reference and fix it in post.

As you can guess, this is not always necessary with a video camera, because white balance function on the camera, more properly called color neutral balance (although in many cases, altering the lighting is still the best choice) is capable of removing any color cast that takes the image away from an overall neutral white appearance, which obviously does not apply to creative choices concerning color tone. This includes green/magenta imbalance as well as red/blue (daylight/tungsten) color shifts. Keep in mind, however, that altering the lighting is still often the best choice both creatively and for maintaining control of the elements. Lighting situations, especially those that involve a mixture of different types of sources, are seldom about just getting a mechanically "OK" neutral appearance. This axis is called *tint*, the *magenta/green axis* or *"CC"* meaning *color correction*.

COLOR MODELS

Trying to describe color, especially as a diagram, has a long history, going back to the German writer Goethe, who was the first to attempt to form a complete color system. It's not simple, which is why there are many different *color models*, in addition to dozens of historical models which are no longer used. We have already looked at the HSV and HSL color models but there are others that are relevant to vision and image production. These include $L*a*b*$, *CIELUV*, *YUV*, and *YCbCr*, which is central to component video as discussed in *The Digital Image*. CIELUV and CMYK are not generally relevant to video work. CMYK (Cyan, Magenta, Yellow and K for black) is used only by printers. There are a few others as well, such as the Munsel color system.

LAB COLOR

Technically called $L*a*b*$ (*L-star, a-star, b-star*) is also know as *CIE Lab* but frequently just called *Lab color*. Lab color space has three dimensions: $L*$ for lightness (luminance) and $a*$ and $b*$ for the color component dimensions. It is based on nonlinearly compressed *CIE XYZ* color space coordinates. It can only be accurately represented in a three-dimensional view (Figure 6.22).

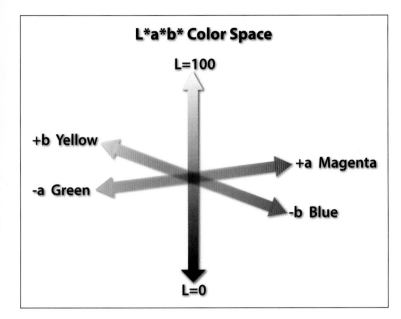

L*a*b* Color Space

L=100

+b Yellow

+a Magenta

-a Green

-b Blue

L=0

Figure 6.22. A representation of *CIE L*a*b** color space. The vertical axis (*L*) is lightness. Axis *a* is green to magenta. Axis *b* is yellow to blue.

THE CIE DIAGRAM

Just about everything in video is acquired and handled in RGB (Red, Green, Blue). Figure 6.19 is a representation of RGB with the axes labeled X, Y and Z. It's a perfectly good model, but it is purely theoretical. What we need is a color model that is based on human visual perception.

This is why the CIE (*International Commission on Illumination* or in French *Commission Internationale de l'Eclairage*) was formed in 1913. They endeavored to employ the latest scientific research into color science to develop international standards for colorimetry. In 1931 they published a formal definition of X,Y, Z color space, and also the standard illuminants A, B and C. Illuminant D6500 was added later in 1964.

THE SPECTRAL LOCUS

Today, you will see the CIE chromaticity diagram everywhere that video color is being discussed (Figures 6.23 and 6.24). It is so significant that we need to examine it in detail. First is the "horseshoe" shape with the various hues. The curved outline of this diagram is really just the spectrum bent into the horseshoe shape. This outer boundary is called the *spectral locus* — it is the line of the pure hues of the spectrum at maximum saturation. Also note that not all hues reach maximum saturation at the same level.

Within the area enclosed by the spectral locus are all of the colors that the human eye can perceive. Recall that one tenet of color science is that if the human eye can't see it, it isn't really a color. As we shall see, sometimes color science strays over that boundary into what are called imaginary colors or non-realizable color, but these are for purely mathematical and engineering reasons.

THE WHITE POINT

In the center is a *white point*, where all the colors mix together to form white. It is not a single point — the CIE includes several white points call illluminants. In the example shown in Figure 6.23, the white point show is D65, which is roughly the same thing (in theory) as a scene lit with daylight balance light. In the US, we consider daylight balance to be 5600K; however Northern/Western

Figure 6.23. The bare bones elements of the *CIE Diagram*: the horseshoe shaped spectral locus, the white points and black body locus, the line of non-spectral purples and the small x and small y axes. Keep in mind that because this is a two dimensional paper diagram, the third axis cannot be shown: it is Y (big Y) which represents luminance. For a three dimensional view that includes the Big Y axis, see Figure 6.21. Also there are many white points, based on the illuminant of the scene.

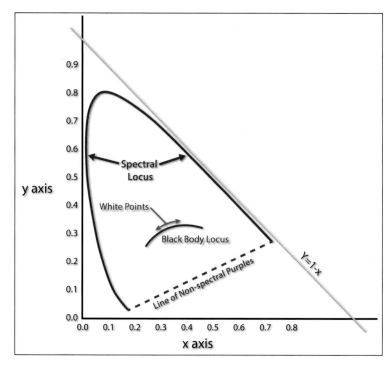

Europe tends to have slightly bluer skies so they have taken 6500K as their standard. In actual fact, every city and region has their own typical ambient color. If you see a painting of Venice (the one in Italy, not the one in California) by the master Canaletto and then visit the city you will see that the pale blue tones that are typical of his paintings are in fact an accurate representation of the color of the atmosphere there. Other CIE Illuminants include A: Tungsten, F2: Cool White Fluorescents, and D55: 5500K. There are several others as well. Although there is no one official standard but D65 is the most widely used as the white point for monitors.

THE BLACK BODY LOCUS

A curved line near the center of the CIE diagram (Figure 6.23) is called the *black body locus*, sometimes called the *Planckian locus*. A few pages ago we talked about how color temperature is measured in degrees Kelvin (K) which is derived from the theoretical heating of a black body to higher and higher temperatures. At some point it starts to glow red, then orange, yellowish white, then white hot and finally bluish. The curve of the black body locus is just the track of that progression plotted on the diagram.

THE LINE OF PURPLES

Along the bottom straight edge is an especially interesting part of the diagram: the *line of non-spectral purples*, commonly called the *line of purples*. Think back to Newton's color wheel, which bent around to join the short wave end of the spectrum (Blues) with the long wave end (Reds) which form magenta and its variations — all of the purples. These are colors that can only be achieved by mixing. Figure 6.23 also shows some other key aspects of the CIE diagram, including the x and y axis. Upper or lower case is important in matters of color science so many practitioners use the terminology "big Y" (luminance) or "little y" (the y axis) to differentiate them.

CIE uses XYZ tristimulus values which correlate to the spectral sensitivities of human vision and are mathematically translated to

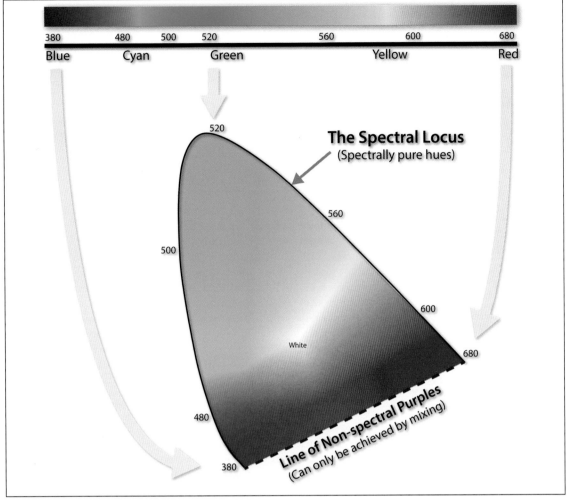

Within the image the following labels appear: 380, 480, 500, 520, 560, 600, 680 along the top spectrum bar; Blue, Cyan, Green, Yellow, Red; and inside the diagram: 520, **The Spectral Locus** (Spectrally pure hues), 560, 500, 600, White, 680, 480, **Line of Non-spectral Purples** (Can only be achieved by mixing), 380.

xyY for the CIE diagram. The reason that they are not x,y, z is mathematical and more technical than we need to get in this discussion (for more on this see Charles Poynton's work, especially *Digital Video and HD Algorithms and Interfaces*, 2nd edition). The xyY numbers are also referred to as *tristimulus values*. A typical set of these are shown in Figure 6.31, which are measured from the standard and widely used *Macbeth* color checker chart. (Although it is now actually the *XRite Color Checker*, it is commonly referred to in the industry as the Macbeth color chart, its original name.)

Using this system, any hue can be defined with two numbers, the x and the y. What is missing obviously is the Y (big Y) axis, which is *luminance*. This is because the CIE diagram is actually three dimensional and can't be completely depicted on two dimensional paper. To see the Y axis we need to view it three dimensionally (Figure 6.25). We run into the same problem we saw before: a three dimensional view can only be partially viewed in diagram form.

GAMUT

The CIE diagram shows all colors that human vision can perceive, but currently no electronic (or photochemical) method yet devised can represent all of them; perhaps some day on the *Holodeck*, but not yet. So within the horseshoe we can place representations of the various degrees of color that cameras, monitors, projectors or soft-

Figure 6.24. The anatomy of the *CIE Diagram*. Not unlike the color wheel, it starts with the spectrum. The *spectral locus* (horseshoe) represents the colors of the spectrum at maximum saturation, with saturation decreasing as you move toward the center, where all colors mix to create white. At the bottom is the *Line of Non-Spectral Purples* (Magentas) which are not spectrally pure in that they can only be achieved by mixing — they don't appear in the original spectrum, just as there is no magenta in a rainbow.

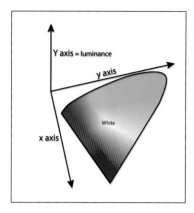 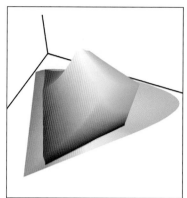 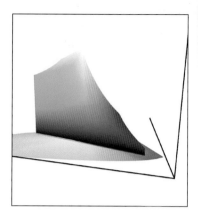

Figure 6.25. (Left) The three axes of the CIE diagram. Since we normally see it on flat paper in 2D, it is easy to forget that there is a third axis: Y (big Y) or luminance.

(Middle and right) Two different views of the same color space, seen from different angles: the gamut of Rec.709 shown on the CIE diagram in three dimensions. The lower you go on the Y axis, the darker the value gets, eventually reaching pure black. Not all colors reach the same height in luminance because some colors are "brighter" than others. Note for example that yellow reaches almost the same level of luminance as white does, which is why life jackets are yellow.

ware can achieve — this is called the *gamut*. The limits of gamut are important measures of a particular camera or a system of color. As with dynamic range (which we usually think of as grayscale range) cameras, monitors and projectors are steadily improving in their gamut range. Gamut is also important in the definition of the color spaces we use, which are standardized and formalized by SMPTE, although they may be initially designed by industry leaders or specialized work committees such as *DCI* — the *Digital Cinema Initiative* (a collaborative effort by the major film studios), a panel of experts convened by the major studios to help facilitate the transition from photo-chemical film to digital as a distribution and presentation medium and also image acquisition. More recently there is the *ACES Committee (Academy Color Encoding System)* which we will talk about in a moment.

Gamut is most easily visualized on the CIE diagram; it is defined by its primaries, usually in the areas of Red, Green and Blue and its white point. Figure 6.26 shows the gamut of Rec.709. It also identifies one of the CIE defined illuminants D65, or 6500K. Once you have defined a gamut, it is easy to tell, either graphically or mathematically when something is *out of gamut*, meaning it falls outside the triangle. As color is passed from one device to another or one color space to another, it is very possible for some color points to be out of gamut. This can be dealt with in a variety of ways: the color can simply be *clipped* (and we've seen how much of a problem that can be in terms of luminance — there is no way of predicting if it will produce an acceptable result), or it can be brought back in through the mathematical operation of a *matrix transform* or by *gamut mapping*, such as with a *Look Up Table (LUT)*. We'll look at these later.

VIDEO COLOR SPACES

Now that we have some basic concepts and terminology, let's look at some color spaces that are used in production, post and distribution. Having a solid understanding of the various color spaces, their potential and their limits is important for cinematographers, colorists, editors, VFX people and those involved in mastering and distribution. Following are some of the most widely used color spaces in HD and UltraHD video work.

Table 6.1. The CIE locations of the R, G, B primaries and the white point of BT.709 (Rec.709) color space.

BT.709	White	Red	Green	Blue
x	0.312	0.64	0.3	0.15
Y	0.329	0.33	0.6	0.06
y	0.358	0.03	0.1	0.79

REC.709 AND REC.2020

HD production has used Rec.709 for many years; it is the official standard for high definition video. Technically it is known as *ITU-R Recommendation BT.709*. It is important to remember that Rec.709 is for the world of HD, where cameras were more limited in dynamic range and gamut. More modern UHD cameras not only have higher dynamic range, they also generally have wider color gamuts. Rec. 709 is still the standard for the great majority of monitors so it is necessary to use it in many situations. Fortunately most camera provide the option of outputting Rec.709 video to the monitors; if they don't it can be accomplished in other ways, such as a viewing LUT, which might be applied through a separate *LUT Box*, by using a LUT applied to the monitor output of the camera or by other means; we'll talk more about these methods in a later chapter, *Workflow*.

Viewing material that is being shot as RAW or log in Rec.709 is not a perfect solution, but it generally serves as at least a guide and makes viewing more comfortable and understandable, particularly for the director and those outside the camera department. Despite the fact that Rec.709 is tied to the appearance of types of monitors that are no longer even manufactured, it has shown resilience in remaining a standard and most likely will remain so for some time. ITU Rec.2020 is the standard for 4K (3840x2160) and 8K (7680x4320) UHD. As shown in Figure 6.27, it has a substantially wider gamut than Rec.709. It has the same D65 white point. There are many new monitors and projectors that have much wider color gamuts than Rec.709.

sRGB

Originally developed for computer graphics, sRGB shares the same primaries and white point as Rec.709, which is fortunate as so much of the video process is done in the realm of computers, often using off-the-shelf displays. However it is important to be aware of what type of display you are viewing the images on.

DCI P3

The *Digital Cinema Initiatives* group was formed in 2002 by a consortium of major studios. Their primary aim was standardization of distribution and theatrical displays for the motion picture industry. The standards they have published include the *P3 color space* (Figure 6.27) and also the *Digital Cinema Package (DCP)* and *Digital Cinema Distribution Master (DCDM)* which standardized files and formats for distribution to theaters. The DCI work group decided on a wide gamut for their standardized color space, in recognition of the amazing advances that have been made in sensors, cameras and projectors in recent years. Their hope was to future proof it as much as possible.

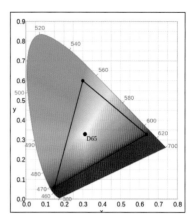

Figure 6.26. The primaries of Rec.709 HD color space as measured on the CIE x,y,Y co-ordinates.

ITU 2020	White	Red	Green	Blue
x	0.312	0.708	0.170	0.131
Y	0.329	0.262	0.678	0.059
y	0.358	0292	0.797	0.046

DCI P3	White	Red	Green	Blue
x	0.314	0.680	0.265	0.150
Y	0.351	0.320	0.690	0.060
y	0.340	0	0.050	0.790

Table 6.2. CIE co-ordinates for ITU Rec.2020.

Table 6.3. The CIE locations of the R, G, B primaries and the white point of DCI P3 color space.

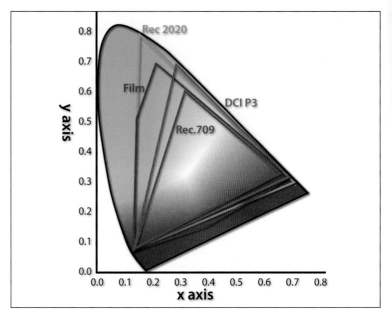

Figure 6.27. The relative *gamuts* of *film*, *DCI P3* and *Rec.709*. This clearly shows the value of the CIE chart in comparing the relative gamuts (limits) of various imaging color spaces. Rec. 2020 is the gamut for UHD video.

AMPAS ACES COLOR SPACE

If the folks at DCI thought big in terms of gamut, the *Science and Technology Council* of the *Academy of Motion Picture Arts and Sciences* (*AMPAS*) decided to go big, big! In formulating the *Academy Color Encoding System* (*ACES*) they actually went outside the gamut of colors encompassed by human vision; it is an ultra-wide gamut. The reasons for this are mathematical and technical, but the result is that the Green and Blue primaries are *imaginary*, *non-realizeable* colors. There are actually two things called ACES — Figure 6.29 is the *color space* of ACES; we're going to talk about the ACES *workflow* later.

OCES Color Space

Another aspect of the ACES workflow is *OCES*: *Output Color Encoding Specification*. Unlike ACES color space, which is *scene referred* (linear to the original values of the scene), OCES is *display referred*, meaning that it is limited to match the gamut of an idealized display device. OCES is not something the typical user will ever deal with but it is useful to know the term and what place it has in the overall system.

COLOR TRANSFORMS

So we have several different color spaces to deal with and inevitably, there is going to be a need to convert footage that is in one color space to another one. In practice this is handled by the software, but it is very useful to have an idea of what is going on under the hood. The basic concept is a *color transform*, usually accomplished with a process known as matrix multiplication. This is why a quick overview of matrix math was included in *A Little Math Review* in *The Digital Image*. It is actually much simpler than it seems. Similar operations are used to convert other RGB spaces back and forth (Figure 6.28). Later on, we'll talk about using a *Look Up Table* (*LUT*).

Figure 6.28. A color transform matrix; in this case the standard transform for converting X,Y, Z color space to Rec.709 color space.

$$\begin{bmatrix} X \\ Y \\ Z \end{bmatrix} \cdot \begin{bmatrix} 3.240479 & -1.53715 & -0.498535 \\ -0.969256 & 1.875991 & 0.041556 \\ 0.055648 & -0.204043 & 1.057311 \end{bmatrix} = \begin{bmatrix} R709 \\ G709 \\ B709 \end{bmatrix}$$

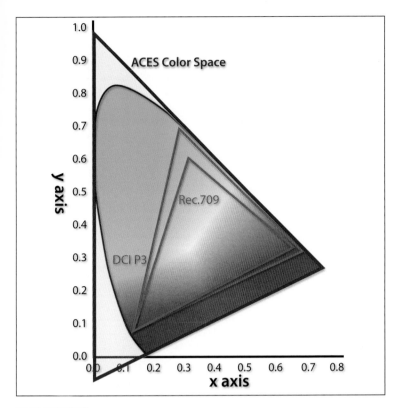

Figure 6.29. *AMPAS ACES* color space is actually larger than the gamut of the human eye. For mathematical reasons, the *ACES* color space includes not only every color the eye can perceive but also color outside the spectral locus. These are called non-realizable or imaginary colors. They basically exist only to make the equations come out right.

THE MATRIX

No, you don't have to choose between the *Red Pill* or the *Blue Pill* (that comes later) — in this context, the *matrix* refers to a mathematical/electronic function that controls how colors are converted from the sensor to camera output. In short, the matrix in the camera controls the way in which the red, green and blue signals from the sensors are combined. It is a mathematical formula that can be altered to suit the needs of the shot and the look you're going for. It is not to be confused with *white balance* — which alters the overall color cast of the scene to adjust to differently colored lighting sources (and sometimes as a creative choice as well). White balance is an overall shift of all colors in one direction or another — usually toward blue (daylight balance) or toward red/orange (tungsten balance) but may also include adjustments for the green in fluorescents, for example. Matrix adjustments generally have little effect on the appearance of whites and neutral colors (such as the gray card).

Art Adams has this to say: " I describe the matrix as adding and subtracting color channels from each other. Not colors, but channels—that's a big difference. Channels are just light and dark, like

Figure 6.30. In the movie it was simple, all you had to do was choose between the Red Pill and the Blue Pill. In the camera matrix you have many more choices: R-G, R-B, G-R, B-G and so on. We're not saying you have to be Neo to figure it out, but it would help.

digital color

Figure 6.31. CIE values of the *Macbeth/xRite* color checker. These refer to the numbers on the x and y axis as well as the Y axis (luminance) which isn't seen in the normal 2D representation of the CIE chart.

Macbeth/xRite Color Checker CIE Values

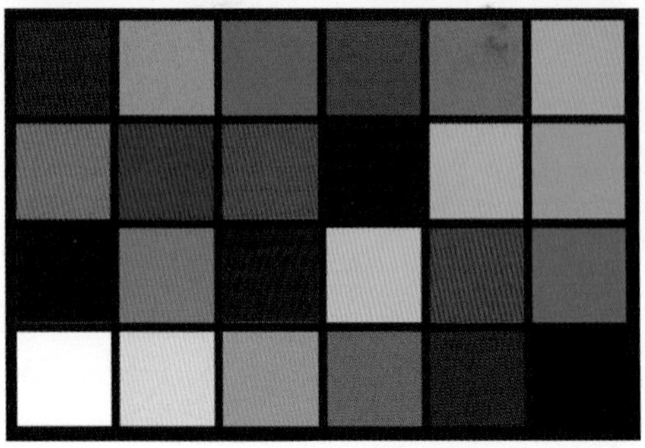

Color Patch	Tristimulus Values		
	x	y	Y
Dark Skin	0.426	0.374	9.83
Light Skin	0.401	0.370	35.7
Blue Sky	0.265	0.288	18.7
Foliage	0.355	0.445	13.3
Blue Flower	0.287	0.273	23.4
Bluish Green	0.276	0.378	42.0
Orange	0.524	0.412	29.6
Purplish Blue	0.226	0.205	11.3
Moderate Red	0.485	0.323	19.4
Purple	0.312	0.239	65.0
Yellow Green	0.392	0.499	43.7
Orange Yellow	0.486	0.444	44.3
Blue	0.196	0.148	58.7
Green	0.319	0.505	23.3
Red	0.567	0.323	12.1
Yellow	0.460	0.474	60.6
Magenta	0.401	0.260	19.2
Cyan	0.206	0.287	18.8
White	0.336	0.352	88.5
Neutral 8	0.333	0.348	58.4
Neutral 6.5	0.332	0.348	35.6
Neutral 5	0.334	0.349	19.5
Neutral 3.5	0.331	0.347	8.7
Black	0.333	0.346	3.1

the black and white negatives from three-strip Technicolor. The dye filters on a sensor's photosites require some overlap so they can reproduce intermediary colors. The way to get pure color is to subtract one color channel from another to remove its influence. Or, if a color is too saturated, you can add some of another channel's color to desaturate it. Do the blue photosites respond a little too much to green, adding a bit of blue to anything that's green? Subtract some of blue's channel from green's channel and you can clear that right up. It's not as simple as this but that's the idea."

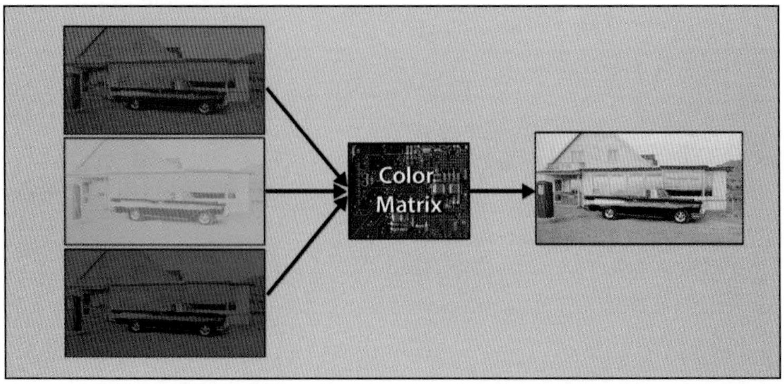

Figure 6.32. A diagram of the matrix concept. In the camera, it combines the inputs from the Red, Green and Blue channels using the same kind of 3x3 matrix math we've seen before. This is not to be confused with *Neutral White Balance*, which shifts all colors in one direction or another. In the matrix, there is much more fine tuned control of color shifts.

filmmaker's guide to digital imaging

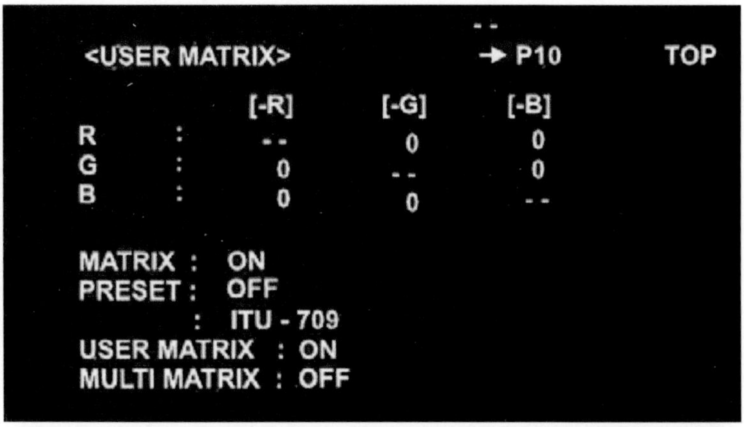

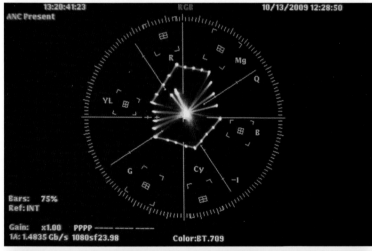

Figure 6.33. A typical menu panel for control of the camera matrix.

As an example, the Sony F3 (which does not shoot RAW but has many other controls over the image) has several matrix presets in the *Picture Look* menu. This camera also offers several preset matrix combinations: in addition to a *Standard* matrix setting, there is a *HighSat* matrix which heightens the saturation of the colors, and a *Cinema* setting which more closely simulates the color tone reproduction of film shooting and several other selections and finally a *FL Light* setting for shooting with fluorescents; and here it is important to remember that fluorescent lighting involves more that just a white

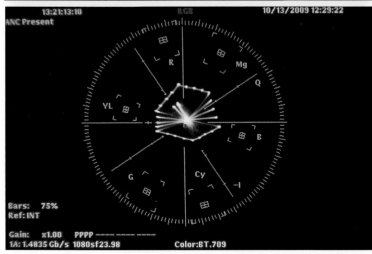

Figure 6.34. (Left, top) The *Chroma du Monde* on the vectorscope in *Rec.709* color space.

Figure 6.35. (Left, bottom) The same chart rendered in a different color space — in this case, NTSC. As you can see, changing the color space can make a big difference in color reproduction.

Figure 6.36. (Top) Color effects of changing various aspects of the matrix.

Figure 6.37. (Bottom) The matrix menus on a Sony camera. Menus and selections vary between camera types and manufacturers. Most cameras allow for matrix setting to be recorded in memory or onto flash memory to be saved by the operator or transferred to other cameras: very useful on a multi-camera job.

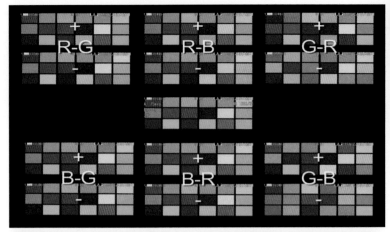

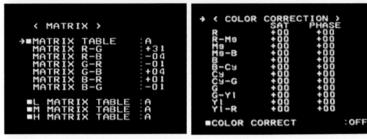

balance setting, which is why there is no matrix preset for *Tungsten* or *Daylight* — those adjustments can be handled adequately with either using the white balance presets or by shooting a gray card or neutral white target under the scene lighting conditions. Many cameras have the ability to store user set matrix adjustments.

Typically, the camera matrix controls are:

- R-G: Red has only its saturation changed, while Green has both it saturation and hue (*phase*) altered.
- R-B: Red keeps the same hue but saturation changes, but Blue changes in both hue and saturation.
- G-R: Green changes only saturation but Red can vary in both hue and saturation.
- The same concept applies to G-B (green-blue), B-R (blue-red), B-G (blue-green).

Most traditional HD cameras have some form of matrix adjustment for hue, contrast and saturation. Examples of matrix adjustment are shown in Figures 6.38 through 6.40. Some have overall controls for saturation (Sony calls it *Level* on the F3) and overall *Phase*, which shifts the hue of the entire picture. More advanced cameras may also have a more fine-tuned adjustment that focuses on small segments of the color spectrum; this is called *multi matrix* on some cameras (such as the Sony *CineAlta* series of cameras) and vector on others. This is the same as *secondary color correction* in post. With these adjustments on the cameras, it is possible to select a segment of the color wheel and make adjustments on it. The selection may be defined by phase (such as 0° to 13°) or by color, such as Blue, Blue-Magenta, etc. This makes it possible to do very specific alterations to the picture: if, for example there is only one red object in the scene (such as an apple), it is possible to change hue and saturation of only the apple without affecting the rest of the scene.

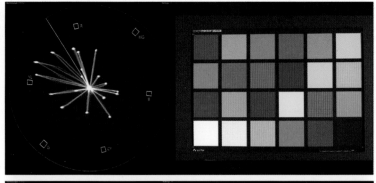

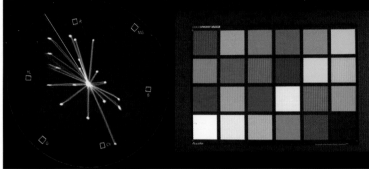

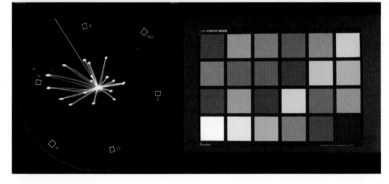

Figure 6.38. (Top) All matrix controls set at zero on a Sony F3 — camera default. The Macbeth Color Checker and its trace on the vectorscope.

Figure 6.39. (Middle) Matrix control R-B set at +99.

Figure 6.40. (Bottom) Matrix control R-B set at -99. There are of course, a vast array of different choices, these are just a couple of examples at extreme settings. They also illustrate the power of the vectorscope in evaluating color on the camera or in post as well as the importance of a properly calibrated test chart — without these, you're really just guessing. There are plenty of people they can hire who are just guessing — you don't want to be one of them.

METAMERISM

Metamerism (pronounced either MET-a-merism or Me-TAM-erism) is a result of the fact that the eye can "see" two objects as the same color even though they are measurably different colors; in other words two spectrally distinct objects create the same tristimulus values. It is an anomaly of the human visual system.

codecs & formats

VIDEO FILE FORMATS

Video can be defined by its compression format, resolution, aspect ratio, color depth, the type of "wrapper" or other criteria. For example we might refer to a clip as "4K video" or "ProRes" or "a 10-bit file." In the end, all of these are important, and people tend to talk about the video in terms that are important to what they are doing with it. For example, a cinematographer or DIT might refer to a video file as variously "24P," "anamorphic," .r3d or "RAW" video — even though all of these are the same video clip; the DIT might refer to it as 4:4:4, while the editor might talk about the same clip as ProRes video and the colorist might refer to it as "12-bit." Everybody is talking about the same piece of video; they are just referring to different attributes of the same shot. To the director reviewing dailies at night; it might matter whether it is a Quicktime .mov file or an MKV file — but probably only in regard to whether their device (computer, iPad, etc.) can play it back.

Also, the file type may change as it goes through the workflow. Red camera files, for example, are often converted almost immediately into some other format for editing. Log files and RAW files have to be converted in order to be viewable in WYSIWYG form. In the early days of high def video, this often depended on what equipment and software could handle the very large video files; this is changing as even very large video files can be edited and processed on computers and with software that is readily available to all professionals (and even students or prosumers), and not just high end editing houses. Video formats that only a few years ago required a 50 or 100 thousand dollar system to even view can now be edited on a laptop! Being able to edit high end video on commonly available computer systems is one of the biggest advances of recent years.

WHAT'S A FILE FORMAT?

A file format is the structure in which information is encoded (stored) in a digital file. When dealing with video, a large amount of data is required to record the video signal accurately, this information is often compressed and written into a *container file*. This section outlines digital video file formats: what they are, the differences between them, and how best to use them. There are many different formats for saving video. Some formats are optimal for capture of video, and some are better suited for editing workflow, and there are many different formats used for delivery and distribution of video.

Video files are significantly more complex that still image files. Not only is there a lot more different kinds of information inside them, but the structure of a video file is much more "mix-and-match." You can tell a lot about most still image files by the file extension (.jpg for example), but that does not hold for video. The file type is sometimes just a container, and could be filled with really low quality web video, or it might have 3-D video and eight channels of theater-quality audio. Additionally there will be timecode and other data such as closed captioning and many other types of information.

ANATOMY OF A VIDEO FILE

While there is a wide range of video formats, in general, each format has the following characteristics:

- *The signal* (both video and audio): This is the actual video and audio data, which has characteristics described in the next section. In this context, audio and video are most often referred to as the *essence*.

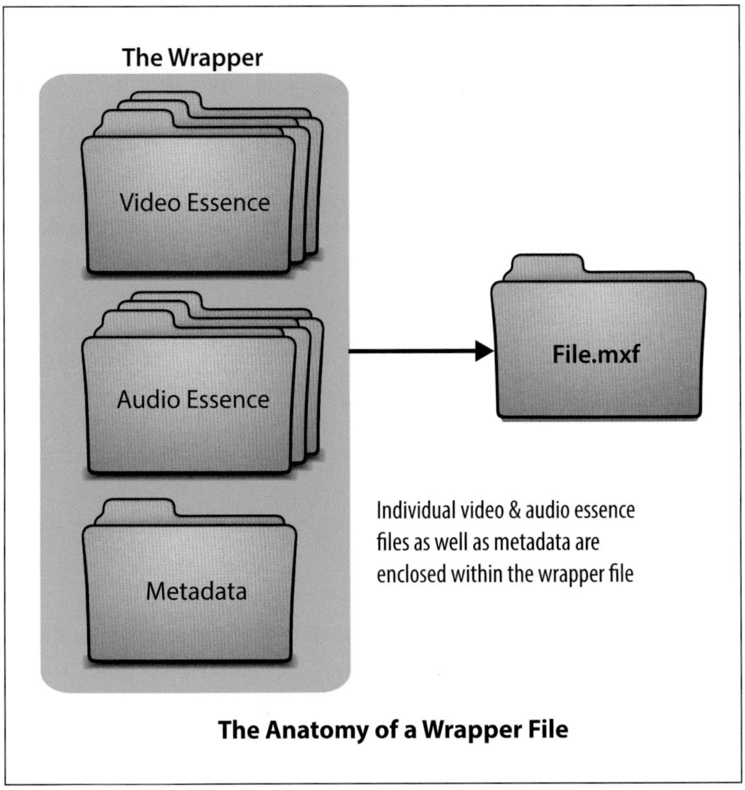

Figure 7.1. How a *wrapper/container* file works. In this example it is an .mxf file, but the same principle applies to other types of wrapper files as well.

The Wrapper

Video Essence

Audio Essence

File.mxf

Metadata

Individual video & audio essence files as well as metadata are enclosed within the wrapper file

The Anatomy of a Wrapper File

- *Container*: the structured file format that contains the signal.
- *Codec* stands for *COmpressor/DECompressor*. It refers to the software or hardware that is used to encode and decode the video signal. Video applications use a codec to write the file and to read it. It may be built-in to the program, or installed separately.

THE CHARACTERISTICS OF A VIDEO IMAGE
Every video file has some attributes that describe what makes up the video signal. These characteristics include:
- Frame size: This is the pixel dimension of the frame.
- Aspect Ratio: This is the ratio of width to height.
- Frame rate: This is the speed at which the frames are captured or played back. Expressed as *frames per second* (*FPS*)
- Bit rate: The bit rate or data rate is the amount of data used to describe the audio or video portion of the file. Measured in per second units and can be in megabytes or gigabytes per second. In general, the higher the bit rate, the better the quality but also the greater the storage requirements and need for higher power equipment.
- The audio sample rate: This is how often the audio is sampled when converted from an analog source to a digital file.

WRAPPERS, STACKS, CONTAINERS AND CODECS
There are some general categories of file types. Some are what is called *wrapper* formats, or more properly *metafile formats* (Figure 7.1) They are just containers that hold video and audio. You are probably familiar with computer files such as Zip or RAR compression. As you know, merely to say that some data is in a Zip file tells you absolutely nothing about what is actually inside: it might be photos,

a database or old emails. Video container types are like that, they just hold the data in a structured way — in other words the container is something the software you are using can understand. *Quicktime* is a typical container format; it has the file extension *.mov*. Quicktime is capable of holding over a hundred different types of codecs. By the same token, Quicktime files might contain High Def video, standard def video, audio, subtitles, second audio program and many other kinds of data, either compressed or uncompressed. Some file types cross over; for example, MPEG-2 is a codec but it can also be a container when audio is included.

STACKS

Some formats use *stacks* instead of wrapper files. A stack is a folder where each image (frame) is an individual file. For example, one Canon camera outputs stacks of .RMF files when in RAW mode. Other cameras work with stacks of .DPX files. Even though they are separate files, most software can automatically put them in the right order. The Arri Alexa creates stacks of .ari files, again only when in ArriRAW mode.

VIDEO CONTAINER FORMATS

Many people assume that a *Quicktime* video file, an *AVI* or an *MKV* is a specific type of video and compression. Because they are *metafile* formats which contain the data (such as the video stream — called the *essence*), along with metadata that is associated with that data stream. Like all things digital, there is a constant evolution. For example .TIFF was designed specifically as a still photo format, but it now sees use as a file type for high def video; in cases where each frame is encoded as a separate file.

- AVI — The standard Microsoft Windows container.
- DVR-MS — Microsoft Digital Video Recording.
- Flash Video (FLV, F4V) — Adobe Systems.
- IFF A platform-independent container format.
- Matroska (MKV) — An open standard/open source container format, not limited to any particular codec or system.
- MJ2 - Motion JPEG 2000 file format.
- MXF — Can hold virtually any type of data stream. It is platform agnostic and supports timecode and metadata.
- QuickTime — A widely used wrapper/container format developed by Apple; capable of holding a wide variety of video/audio streams. Has a .mov extension.
- MPEG program stream.
- MPEG-2 Transport Stream — The *TS* on DVDs and Blu-Ray (*BD*) discs.
- MP4 — Based on MPEG-4 which in turn was based on the Quicktime file format.
- Ogg — Container for the video format Theora.
- RM — Real Media, used as a container for RealVideo.
- ASF— Microsoft's *Advanced Systems Format* for .asf, .wma and .wmv files. Proprietary and patent protected.

Audio container formats include *AIFF* (Apple's *Audio Interchange File Format*, *WAV* (Microsoft's *Waveform Audio File Format*) and *XMF* or *Extensible Music Format*. Some of the video/audio formats deserve discussion in a bit more depth as they are the ones most widely used in video production.

Figure 7.2. The *Kodak Digital LAD Test Image*. *Marcie*, as she is known, is the "Mona Lisa" of digital image testing — it's an image you'll see in many places where digital imaging is the subject. *LAD* stands for *Laboratory Aim Density*. It is a good example of an image in log space — it appears very flat and low contrast. It is not intended to be viewed this way in it's final use; before that it needs color correction.

Note that the gray patch is *not* 18% middle gray. For Cineon, Kodak chose a different middle gray, which has code values 445,445, 445 — this is slightly darker than the standard 18% gray card. This was done for technical reasons relating to print density.

MXF

MXF is a container/wrapper format which supports a number of different streams of "essence," encoded with any one of a variety of codecs, together with a metadata wrapper which describes the material contained within the MXF file.

MXF was intended to address a number of problems with other formats. MXF has full timecode and metadata support, and is intended as a platform-agnostic standard for future professional video and audio applications.

DPX AND CINEON

The DPX and Cineon formats have a long and interesting history. In the 1990s Kodak recognized that there was a need to integrate film imaging with the world of digital, in the form of computer generated images and VFX and also for digital intermediates — where film is scanned to digital to allow for all the image manipulations that can be done in the computer. They developed an entire system of scanners, recorders and accompanying software for this purpose. Although the system was abandoned in 1997, the file format developed for it, *Cineon*, lives on, although it is used in a slightly different way now. It was based on *TIFF* still photo files (*Tagged Image File Format*).

As developed, *Cineon* (file extension *.cin*) was very film oriented. It is not merely a digital picture of a film frame, the file format itself takes into account uniquely filmic properties such as cross-talk between layers. It is based on printing densities, such as a film process would be.

DIGITAL COMPRESSION CODECS

Digital cameras are capable of generating extremely large amounts of data up to hundreds of megabytes per second. As resolution, bit depth and channels increase, the file sizes continue to get larger and larger. To help manage this huge data flow, nearly all cameras and the recording hardware designed to be used with them utilize some form of *compression*. *Prosumer* cameras typically use high compression to make the video files more compact for recording and storage. While this allows footage to be handled even on less powerful computers, the convenience comes at the expense of image quality.

A *lossless* compression system is one that is capable of reducing the size of digital data in a way that allows the original data to be completely restored, byte for byte. This is done by removing redundant information; these procedures benefit from the fact that most real world data (including video) has statistical redundancy. For example, if an area of the image is all pure white, where normally the digital code would be a long list of zeros, the compression algorithm might write a code that means "there is a row of 2000 zeros," which will use only a few bits of data instead of thousands. Compression may be *mathematically lossless* or *visually lossless*, the latter being in the eye of the beholder, of course.

Much higher compression ratios can be achieved with *lossy* compression. With lossy compression, information is discarded to create a simpler signal. These methods take into account the limits of human perception: they try to lose only information that won't be missed by the eye. Lossy compression may be invisible to the eye but can have a negative effect on later generations of duplication. YouTube's billion dollar discovery was that people will put up with insane amounts of compression artifacts and horrible image quality if the video shows a cat playing the piano. That being said, if you remember how bad such video sharing websites were just a few years ago, compared to the HD quality they can deliver now, you can easily appreciate the improvements that have been made in video compression, storage and transmission, even by wireless means.

VISUALLY LOSSLESS

As noted, some codecs are lossy but are classified as *visually lossless*. This goes beyond the pure mathematics that is the basis of most compression procedures and deals also with the vagaries of the human eye and the perception qualities of the eye/brain combination, such as the fact that humans perception is more sensitive to subtle variation in brightness than to variations in color. A compression scheme may be perceptually lossless, in which case the average human viewer cannot distinguish between the original image and the compressed image. Most lossy image and video compression have some sort of quality factor or factors. If the quality is good enough, then the image will be perceptually lossless. What is perceptually lossless is also dependent on the mode of playback: errors that are imperceptible on an iPhone may be obvious on an IMAX screen.

TYPES OF COMPRESSION

There are many types of compression, some are internal to the camera, and may be output differently from different camera connections, some are used primarily post camera (meaning both at the DIT/Loader station and in post production) and some are primarily for distribution/broadcasting/webcasting.

RAW IN ITS MANY FORMS

We talked about RAW in *The Digital Image* as being the unprocessed (not deBayered) photosite data, but there is more to discuss. RAW is really several things that go by the same name:

1. A way that cameras operate.
2. A type of video recording.
3. A method of shooting and workflow.

First, we must deal with a common misconception: that RAW video is uncompressed video. Not strictly true. RAW files are produced by both digital still cameras and most professional digital cinema cameras; in most (not all) cases they involve some form of lossless or visually lossless compression, although it may be minimal or extensive depending on the capabilities of the camera and the internal software/firmware. RAW means that the exposure values of the red, green and blue photosites are recorded without any deBayering (demosaicing). Some systems strain to even play RAW files back at real time speed, particularly those recorded at low compression rates.

Different types of RAW

ArriRAW from the Alexa is uncompressed RAW data (although the camera can output other types of files as well). Red camera files are RAW but compressed with *wavelet compression*. Blackmagic cinema cameras output *CinemaDNG* files. Developed by Adobe Systems as an open format based on the *TIFF* format, *DNG* stands for *Digital Negative* and can be stored as *video essence* in an MXF file.

Canon's Version of RAW

Canon takes a different approach to RAW recording, summarized by Andy Shipsides of Abel CineTech: "Canon RAW is stored in file stacks, similar to ArriRAW or CinemaDNG, and each frame is in an .RMF (RAW Media Format) file. Any given take will be stored in a folder containing stacks of these files. Each frame is approximately 11MB in size, making it larger than just about any RAW format out there. Doing the math, that's about 16GB a minute or 950GB an hour. Remember, this is uncompressed RAW data; most other RAW formats such as Red RAW and F65 RAW (F5 & F55 too) are compressed to some extent. This is an interesting difference, but here's the real kicker.

"Canon RAW is a 10-bit format with baked-in ISO and white balance. That's right, unlike the other RAW formats, Canon is baking-in gain adjustments (ISO/white balance) before outputting the RAW data. You may be scratching your head as to why, so here's a little bit of the logic. Adding gain adjustments at the sensor level produces a consistent stop range above and below the middle grey level, even at high ISOs, and reduces the overall noise in the image. Other cameras do all of this work in post, which means the stop range above or below middle grey changes as you move your ISO. Canon is implementing these adjustments at the sensor level at higher bit depths and then outputting the results. These adjustments are also applying the *Canon Log* curve to the image, which maximizes the range of the final 10-bit file. [Figure 4.37 in *Linear, Gamma, Log* shows how the dynamic range changes at different ISOs.]

"So is Canon RAW actually RAW? It is, in the sense that the image is not deBayered before you get it – this step is still done in post. You can think of using Canon RAW as being a bit like ordering a steak medium rare."

Chroma Subsampling

We covered *chroma subsampling* in *The Digital Image*. It is not technically a form of compression but rather data reduction. The engineering term is the somewhat brutal *chroma decimation* but for our purposes it has the same effect as compression: not only in determining how many hard drives you have to buy, but also about the speed with which the camera electronics can handle the data and pass it on to

Figure 7.3. Two implementations of inter-frame compression in MPEG-2, showing both an *Open GOP* and a *Closed GOP*. *Open* means that reference can be made to frames outside the GOP while *Closed* refers only to frames within the GOP.

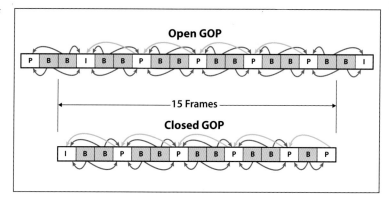

recording. It was developed as an alternative to RGB output which generates more data than can be transmitted over analog signal paths or processed by the technology that existed in the 20th century.

INTRA-FRAME VS. INTER-FRAME

Compression schemes fall into two general categories: *intra-frame* and *inter-frame*. *Intra-frame* deals with each frame independently, without reference to other frames (think of *intramural* sports, where all the teams are from the same school). An alternative is *inter-frame* compression (as in *international*), which compares different frames and deals with them in groups, known as a *GOP* or *Group of Pictures*.

The advantage of intra-frame is that not every frame needs to be completely encoded and decoded as a complete image. Instead *key frames* are identified and groups of subsequent frames are encoded only insofar as they are different from the keyframe. For example, in the case of a static shot of a person moving in front of a plain wall the subframes would only deal with the moving person because the wall remains the same in every frame. It would be different if the shot were handheld, as the wall would be slightly different in each frame. Some codecs combine intra and inter-frame compression. Codecs that employ inter-frame compression do require a substantial amount of processing power as in playback they have to deal with several frames at once rather than just interpreting one frame at a time.

The inter-frame method identifies I-frames which are the reference and are completely encoded (and thus can be decoded without additional information) P-frames, which are "predicted" from the I-frame and B-frames which are "bi-directionally predicted" meaning that they may be encoded in reference to either previous or following frames.

Compression formats that use a GOP structure are not ideal for editing, as they tend to make big demands on the computer processor because not every frame is "complete." These types of camera video are often transcoded to another format before editing. They may be *Open GOP* or *Closed GOP* (Figure 7.3). An *Open GOP* means there is reference to a frame outside the GOP; a *Closed GOP* refers only to itself.

There are *Long GOP* and *Short GOP* formats which is just the number of frames in each group. Since they apply mainly to editing and other aspects of post they are beyond the scope of this book but it is useful for those who work on the set to be familiar with the terminology and understand what it means.

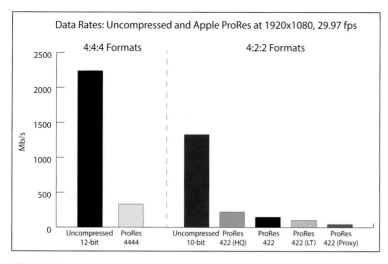

Figure 7.4. Typical target data rates for the different versions of Apple ProRes. Data rate is determined by several factors: the codec itself, frame size, frame rate and amount of image detail.

CODECS

As we previously mentioned, a codec has two parts: compression and decompression. It reminds us that once you compress something, you will often need to reverse the process by undoing that compression or changing it to a different type of compression, which is called *transcoding.*

MPEG AND JPEG

MPEG stands for *Motion Picture Experts Group*, and *JPEG* is an acronym for *Joint Photographic Experts Group*. Various forms of MPEG are used for both video and audio. MPEG-2 and MPEG-4 are widely used as video compression formats. There are variations such as *MPEG-4 Part 2, MPEG-4 Part 10, MPEG-4 AVC* and many others. An example of MPEG-2 compression GOP structures is shown in Figure 7.3.

TIFF/EP

Originally a still photo file format, *TIFF* (*Tagged Image File Format*) or *EP* (*Electronic Photography*). It can be stored uncompressed or with lossy or lossless compression such as *LZW* employed. RAW video is sometimes converted to a series of 8-bit or 16-bit TIFF files (one per frame) for editing or viewing. This was a common procedure before RAW files were readable by editing software systems. Uncompressed TIFF files tend to be very large.

JPEG 2000

Like its predecessor *JPEG*, this codec was developed by the *Joint Photographic Experts Group*, but unlike the earlier standard, which used a *discrete cosine transform* (*DCT*), JPEG 2000 is a wavelet based compression scheme; it can be either lossy or lossless. The filename extension is *.jp2*. While it does have some advantages over JPEG in quality, the main difference is in the versatility of the encoded signal. Because it is wavelet based, compression artifacts are blurring and ringing at edges in the image rather than the familiar blockiness of JPEG.

H.264/MPEG-4/AVC

MPEG-4 is designed for very low bit-rate encoding. It was created in 1998 as an update of MPEG-1 and MPEG-2 (which is still used for DVDs). *H.264/AVC* is an inter-frame codec also known as *MPEG-4 Part 10* or *AVC* (*Advanced Video Coding*). Among other uses, it is the encoding standard for *Blu-Ray discs* (*BD*) and is widely used for internet streaming video and High Def television (*ATSC*). On the set, it is often used to encode compressed video files for dailies, as the director can then view them on a variety of devices. There are several varieties of H.264, not all of which are interchangeable; meaning that a particular decoder/playback device may be capable of playing some variety of H.264 but not others. It is patented and licensed technology.

AVC-Intra

AVC-Intra is an implementation of H.264 — a 10-bit 4:2:2 intra-frame compression format originally developed by Panasonic; it was primarily intended for their I (*ENG*) equipment as the intra-frame recordings are easier to edit than inter-frame video and time is especially important in news video so transcoding is to be avoided. It is used in their *P2* systems. *AVCHD* is also a variety of H.264 that is more consumer oriented.

ProRes

There are five varieties of Apple's ProRes codec as explained in the *Apple ProRes White Paper*:

- ProRes 4444, the highest quality can be used with either 4:4:4 RGB or 4:4:4 YCbCr color space. Even with 12-bit pixel depth, it offers a reasonably low data rate as compared to uncompressed 4:4:4 HD. The fourth "4" is for the *alpha channel* (*transparency data*). Because of its very high color fidelity, it is often used for color grading.
- ProRes 422 (HQ) is a visually lossless codec for HD. It supports full-width 4:2:2 video sources at 10-bit pixel depth. It is often used as an intermediate codec for efficient workflows as it remains visually lossless through several generations of encoding and decoding.
- ProRes 422 offers nearly all the benefits of 422 (HQ) but at a substantially lower data rate. It supports the same 10-bit 4:2:2 but may be more suited to multi-stream real-time editing.
- ProRes 422 (LT) also supports 10-bit 4:2:2 but at an even lower data rate: 100 Mbp/s or less, depending on the video format used.
- ProRes 422 (Proxy) is the lowest data rate of the family, at below 36Mbp/s but still at 10-bit 4:2:2, although as the name makes clear it is strictly a low-res proxy or draft mode format for uses such as offline editing on less powerful computers such as notebooks or where data storage is very limited. Even as a proxy, it still supports full 1920x1080 and 1280x720 HD native frame sizes.

Although ProRes is nominally a variable bit-rate codec, the actual data rate generally doesn't change that much. It may sometimes exceed the target bit rate, but is restricted to no more than 10 percent above the target rate. ProRes is content aware and doesn't add bits to any frame unless it would visually benefit from the additional data. Apple points out that even though the math of a particular codec may look good on paper, the real goal of codecs is the preservation of visual fidelity to the original footage and preservation of maximum image quality. In the end, it is up to the user to evaluate how well a codec is working for them all the way through the workflow.

Format	Avid DNxHD 36	Avid DNxHD 100	Avid DNxHD 145	Avid DNxHD 220	Avid DNxHD 444	DVCPRO HD	HDCAM	HDCAM SR
Bit Depth	8-bit	8-bit	8-bit	8- and 10-bit	10 bit	8-bit	8-bit	10-bit
Sampling	4:2:2	4:2:2	4:2:2	4:2:2	4:4:4	1280 Y samples 4:2:2	1440 Y samples 3:1:1	4:2:2
Bandwidth	36 Mb/sec	100 Mb/sec	145 Mb/sec	220 Mb/sec	440 Mb/sec	100 Mb/sec	135 Mb/sec	440 Mb/sec

FULL FRAME VS. HALF FRAME

Apple makes references to support for *full frame* vs. *half frame* video in their ProRes specifications. Here is their explanation of the difference: "Many video camcorders encode and store video frames at less than the full HD widths of 1920 pixels or 1280 pixels, for 1080-line or 720-line HD formats, respectively. When such formats are displayed, they are upsampled horizontally to full HD widths, but they cannot carry the amount of detail possible with full-width HD formats. All Apple ProRes family members can encode full-width HD video sources (sometimes called "full-raster" video sources) to preserve the maximum possible detail an HD signal can carry. Apple ProRes codecs can also encode partial-width HD sources if desired, thereby averting potential quality and performance degradation that results from upscaling partial-width formats prior to encoding." (*Apple ProRes White Paper*).

DNxHD

DNxHD is a lossy high def codec developed by *Avid*; it stands for *Digital Nonlinear Extensible High Definition* (thank goodness for acronyms!) and is functionally similar to JPEG and each frame is independent but it is a DCT codec. It can be used as both an intermediate for editing or as a presentation/deliverable format. It features selectable bit rates and bit depths (8-bit or 10-bit). Obviously it is compatible with various Avid editing systems, but it can function as a standalone Quicktime codec to create and playback DNxHD video streams. It was designed for reduced storage requirements with optimal image quality and minimal degradation over multiple generations. According to Avid "HD camera compression formats are efficient, but simply aren't engineered to maintain quality during complex post-production effects processing. Uncompressed HD delivers superior image quality, but data rates and file sizes can stop a workflow dead in its tracks." It comes in five "families" each with different data rates from DNxHD 444 (full resolution, 10-bit 4:4:4 RGB and high data rate) down to DNxHD 36 which is intended as a *proxy* format.

From the *Avid DNxHD White Paper*: "Many popular compressed HD formats do not natively support the full HD raster. Horizontal raster downsampling makes HD images easier to compress, but significantly reduces high frequency detail information in the image. As a result, downsampling makes HD images look softer by degrading horizontal resolution in the process. The camera original HD raster's 1920 pixel horizontal resolution has 33% more resolution than a 1440 pixel downsampled image and 50% more than a 1280 pixel downsampled image."

COMPRESSION TECHNOLOGIES

Compression involves some intense mathematics and information theory. Fortunately, as imaging professionals, we don't have to get into the technical side of things in order to use them, but some understanding of what's going on puts us in a better position to evaluate and employ various codecs. Better mathematical theorems and

Table 7.1. The varieties of DNxHD along with some other formats. (Courtesy of Avid).

Figure 7.5. Sometimes with codecs such as wavelet compression, the closer you examine something, the less information you have, as in this iconic scene from *Blowup*.

improved algorithms in compression technologies and implementations are a big part of the incredible advances that have been made in HD and UHD video made in recent years. Also, the software and hardware that use these techniques are increasingly better adapted to employ them efficiently. A part of this is the ongoing shift of image processing from the computer *CPU* (*central processing unit*) to the *GPU* (*graphics processing unit*).

DCT

Discrete Cosine Transform (*DCT*) is used in JPEG, MPEG and several other codecs. It is a lossy compression closely related to a *Fourier Transform*. It works on blocks of 8x8 pixels and applies quantization to reduce file size. DCT is computationally intensive and can result in compression artifacts as well as ringing or blurring at sharp edges. Codecs that use DCT include:

Motion JPEG
MPEG-1
MPEG-2
MPEG-4
H.261
H.263

WAVELET COMPRESSION

Wavelet compression is a relative newcomer to video compression although the mathematical roots for it extend back to the early 20th century. One of its earliest uses was on the Pixar film *A Bug's Life*, where many reviewers commented on the rich detail in the scene. Wavelet compression takes an approach very different from something like DCT (which address the image on a pixel or pixel block basis) in that it deals with the entire image (in our case, a video frame) and does so on a multi-resolution basis. In other words, it can apply different levels of compression to different parts of the image. Wavelet compression is used in *JPEG 2000*, *REDCODE*, *CineForm* and other codecs. One detail is that the wavelet transform itself does not compress the image, it only prepares it for compression, which is handled in a different step of the process called *quantization*, although for practical purposes, it is called *wavelet compression*.

It is also worth noting that "wavelets" have nothing to do with waves as we normally think of them either in surfing or in video, such as we might measure with the waveform monitor. Rather, it refers to the fact that (for those of us who have dim memories from that long ago calculus class) they integrate to zero, meaning that they make little waves above and below the X-axis.

THE FOREST AND THE TREES: WAVELET COMPRESSION

An analogy that is often used in discussing wavelet compression is a view of a forest. If you are flying over a forest, it will appear as pretty much a large swath of slightly differentiated green. If you are driving through the same forest, it will resolve into individual trees and plants. If you walk though the forest, you will see each tree and flower in greater detail and so on until you are viewing an individual leaf through a magnifying glass. It's all the same forest, it's just the resolution of your observation that has changed.

"Wavelet Image Processing enables computers to store an image in many scales of resolutions, thus decomposing an image into various levels and types of details and approximation with different-valued resolutions. Hence, making it possible to zoom in to obtain more detail of the trees, leaves and even a monkey on top of the tree. Wavelets allow one to compress the image using less storage space with more details of the image." (Myung-Sin Song, PhD, *Wavelet Image Compression* in the journal *Contemporary Mathematics*, 2006). It can be thought of as a bit like the David Hemmings character in *Blowup* (Figure 7.5). Antonioni's existential message is simple: the closer you look, the less you see or maybe it's the other way around.

PROPRIETARY CODECS

Proprietary codecs are those developed and used by software or equipment manufacturers, particularly companies that make cameras, editing applications and other types of post-production gear. While these codecs are often part of the "secret sauce" that companies keep secret, there is a growing tendency toward releasing them as *opensource*, meaning that anyone is free to use them.

REDCODERAW

RedcodeRAW is the output from cameras by the Red company. It is RAW video encoded in a proprietary codec. Even though the output is always RAW, it is recorded at various levels of compression, depending primarily on the limitations of the recording media. The compression scheme employed is called REDCode and written as Redcode 28, Redcode 36, Redcode 42; (the numbers represent the *data rates*), or as compression ratios: 10:1, 8:1, 5:1, etc. The lower the compression, the higher the data rate. This has been replaced by a newer system which simply lists the actual degree of compression. It starts at 3:1 as the lowest degree of compression and can go much higher. Red no longer uses the Redcode 28 and other designations; instead they only use compression ratios. RedcodeRAW is a lossy compression, although Red calls it visually lossless. Data compression can range from 3:1 up to 18:1. It is a wavelet-based JPEG 2000 codec. Many consider that 5:1 or 6:1 compression is the "sweet spot" — a good balance between file size and quality of the image.

With all data, the choice of what compression ratio to use is about image quality, the final use of the images (if it's a YouTube video, compression matters less than if it's going to end up as an IMAX presentation), the type of scene but also about reasonable limits of data storage and the processing power of the equipment you're working with, particularly on the set at the DIT cart but in the first stages of post as well.

CineForm

CineForm was formerly a separate company but now is a division of *GoPro* as well as a codec and an integrated system. CineForm advocates the advantages of their format as:

- Full-frame (no blocks) wavelet compression for high image integrity.
- Unrestricted spatial resolution (4K and beyond).
- Up to 12-bit arithmetic precision.
- RGBA, RGB, YUV, and RAW chroma formats.
- Standard wrapper interfaces including AVI and MOV for broadest compatibility.
- CineForm products enable workflow efficiency from camera, through post-production, and into mezzanine or long-term archive. Cross-platform (Windows / Mac) workflows and file compatibility for mixed post environments.
- Compatibility with most AVI or MOV compatible applications including *Final Cut Pro*, *Premiere Pro*, *After Effects*, etc.
- Visual quality equivalent to uncompressed workflows but with much lower cost.
- Performance-optimized compression eliminates need for specialized hardware.

Some professionals call *CineForm* possibly the highest quality compression codec available, with quality equal to or better than the highly respected *HDCAM SR*. CineForm software provides editorial workflows optimized for use with industry-standard tools,.

AVC-Intra

This is a Panasonic format that stores I-frames, which means that there are no GOP structures; it is based on the H.264/MPEG-4 AVC standard. As they note "Compression has become critical for emerging workflows, but compression cannot be considered in isolation to the overall workflow goal. AVC/H.264 is a new generation state-of-the-art codec family with both Intra and Inter-frame compression implementation options. Inter-frame compression, (long GOP) is usually used for content delivery and packaged media; in this mode its efficiency is unequaled. However, any image manipulation or processing will severely degrade the image quality in long GOP compression schemes. By contrast, Intra-frame compression processes the entire image within the boundaries of each video field or frame. There is zero interaction between adjacent frames, so its image quality stands up well to motion and editing. Intra-frame compression is used most often for broadcast and production applications where such image manipulation is normal."

ArriRAW

ArriRAW was developed by Arri for their D-20 and Alexa cameras; it is 12-bit logarithmic uncompressed RAW Bayer data with 2880x1620 pixels or 2880x2160 pixels. Like most camera companies, Arri offers free decoder software for their camera output files; in this case it is *ArriRAW Converter* (*ARC*) which performs deBayering and color science for viewing and processing. They also offer *Arri Meta Extract*, which is a free command line tool for working with the metadata.

ArriRAW supports both automatic and human-readable metadata designed to support production at all stages. In addition to the normal exposure, ISO, gamma, white balance, FPS, date/time data etc., it can also record lens data and tilt and roll information for some of the Alexa models. This extensive metadata is stored in the header with the ArriRAW file.

Alexa Legal vs. Extended

In their Alexa FAQ, Arri states that "An image encoded in 10 bit legal range has a code value range from 64 to 940 (876 code values), and a 10 bit extended range signal has a code value range from 4 to 1019 (1015 code values). Contrary to popular belief, extended range encoding does not provide a higher dynamic range, nor does legal range encoding limit the dynamic range that can be captured. It is only the quantization (the number of lightness steps between the darkest and brightest image parts) that is increased by a marginal amount (about 0.2 bits).

The concept of legal/extended range can be applied to data in 8, 10, or 12-bit. All ProRes/DNxHD materials generated by the Alexa camera are in legal range, meaning that the minimum values are encoded by the number 64 (in 10-bit) or 256 (in 12-bit). The maximum value is 940, or 3760, respectively. Most systems, however, will automatically rescale the data to the more customary value range in computer graphics, which goes from zero to the maximum value allowed by the number of bits used in the system (e.g. 255, 1023, or 4095). FCP will display values outside the legal range ('superblack' and 'superwhite') but as soon as you apply a RGB filter layer, those values are clipped. This handling is the reason why the Alexa camera does not allow recording extended range in ProRes."

Sony RAW

Sony RAW files are stored as MXF files (Figure 7.1). Sony offers a free plug-in to import F65 footage into several editing applications. As is usual, more and more post-production software applications are supporting these files natively.

XAVC

Sony has introduced a new format for some of their cameras. XAVC is a variety of H.264/MPEG-4 AVC. It can support 4K resolution at up to 60 frames per second. XAVC supports color depths of 8-bits, 10-bits, and 12-bits and chroma subsampling can be 4:2:0, 4:2:2, or 4:4:4. MXF can be used for the digital container format. XAVC allows for intra frame recording and long GOP recording. It is an

Figure 7.6. The file structure of the Phantom .CINE file. While hopefully most filmmakers will never need to examine files at this level, it is useful to get a sense of how it works. Source: *The Cine File Format*, Vision Research white paper.

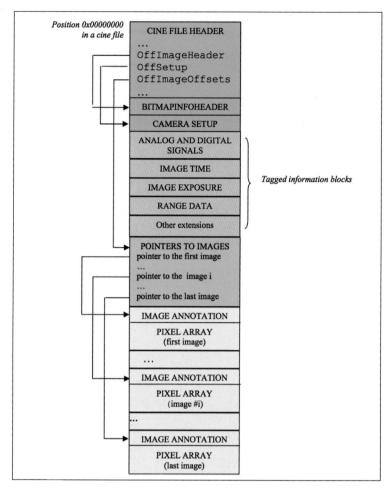

open format that can be licensed by other camera companies. Sony has built these codecs into the F5 and F55 cameras — *XAVC HD/2K* (F5/F55) and *XAVC 4K (QFHD)* (F55 only) — which are designed to be a combination of efficiency and quality and specialized for those cameras. Both are 4:2:2 10-bit, with the HD variety at a bit rate of 100Mbps and the 4K version at 300Mbps.

Canon RMF

Canon's high end cameras output .*RMF* files, which stands for *RAW Media Format*. As noted elsewhere it is a bit different in the way it treats RAW files in that the ISO and white balance are baked in rather than being purely metadata. The Canon Log curve is also applied to these 10-bit files which maximizes the dynamic range. The logic is that by doing some of the processing at the camera level, the stop range above and below middle gray stays constant as the ISO is changed. This is discussed in more detail in the chapter *Linear, Gamma, Log*.

Phantom Cine

High speed *Phantom* cameras from the company *Vision Research* record .*CINE RAW* files. As with most RAW formats, it does require processing in post, such as deBayering. The file structure of .CINE is shown in Figure 7.6. Most filmmakers never need to examine a file at this level, but it is useful to get an idea of what the structure is in order to better understand how to work with it.

CinemaDNG

Adobe has been campaigning for some time to persuade other software and camera companies to attempt some standardization and open formats for both RAW video and still images. In the long run, standardization seems unlikely. *CinemaDNG* (*Digital Negative*) is Adobe's RAW lossless file format for digital cinema files. It is based on the TIFF/EP format and makes significant use of metadata. It supports stereo (for 3D production) and multiple audio channels. DNG files can be either a frame based MXF container file or a sequence of DNG image files in a stack. The two types can be interchanged, which among other things makes for an easier transition of video images to stills, which might apply to producing publicity stills or possibly using a very high resolution DSLR camera for stop motion, as is a common practice. As it is an open format, there are no patents or licensing requirements for its use.

Sony HDCam and SR

HDCam is a Sony proprietary format originally developed for their tape based HD cameras. It is 8-bit DCT compressed with 3:1:1 chroma subsampling. *SR* uses 12-bit or 10-bit format recording in either 4:2:2 or 4:4:4 RGB or YCbCr with a bit rate of 440 Mb/s and *SR Lite* at 220Mb/s. It is also possible to gang two SR video streams for double the bit rate. It also has 12 channels of audio.

XDCam

Another Sony invention, *XDCam* is a format for their series of HD cameras primarily aimed at field production and new gathering. There are four families: *XDCam SD, XDCam HD, XDCam EX* and *XDCam HD422*. Sony pioneered the use of disc-based recording and some early cameras in this line wrote video directly to a disc similar to Blu-Ray for random access playback although these have been supplanted by solid state memory such as the widely used *SxS Card* (Figure 7.8). *IMX* (also known as D10 or MPEG IMX) allows for standard def recording using MPEG-2 with selectable bit rates.

DVCPro

A primary competitor with Sony's HDCam, the *DVCPro* format was developed by Panasonic and uses a similar compression scheme. It comes in a range of resolutions including *DV, DVCPro, DVCPro25, DVCPro50* and *DVCPro-HD*. Some Panasonic professional cameras can record either DVCPro or the newer *AVC-Intra*.

Other File Components

In addition to the actual video data, which is often referred to as video *essence*, video files usually have other components as well. Some of them relate to postproduction, some are for broadcast purposes (such as subtitles) and some are for VFX work.

Metadata

Metadata is just "data about data." It is something we will be coming back to several times as it has become a central issue and key tool in shooting, editing and processing video (see the chapter *Metadata & Timecode*). Where with photochemical film processing and editing, separate paper lists of camera reports, lab reports, data and Keycode numbers had to be maintained, it is now possible to pack all the necessary information (and more) right along with the video/audio files.

CLIP0000003	8.01 GB
CLIP0000003_0000000.rmf	12 MB
CLIP0000003_0000001.rmf	12 MB
CLIP0000003_0000002.rmf	12 MB
CLIP0000003_0000003.rmf	12 MB
CLIP0000003_0000004.rmf	12 MB
CLIP0000003_0000005.rmf	12 MB
CLIP0000003_0000006.rmf	12 MB
CLIP0000003_0000007.rmf	12 MB
CLIP0000003_0000008.rmf	12 MB
CLIP0000003_0000009.rmf	12 MB
CLIP0000003_0000010.rmf	12 MB
CLIP0000003_0000011.rmf	12 MB
CLIP0000003_0000012.rmf	12 MB
CLIP0000003_0000013.rmf	12 MB
CLIP0000003_0000014.rmf	12 MB
CLIP0000003_0000015.rmf	12 MB
CLIP0000003_0000016.rmf	12 MB
CLIP0000003_0000017.rmf	12 MB
CLIP0000003_0000018.rmf	12 MB
CLIP0000003_0000019.rmf	12 MB
CLIP0000003_0000020.rmf	12 MB
CLIP0000003_0000021.rmf	12 MB
CLIP0000003_0000022.rmf	12 MB
CLIP0000003_0000023.rmf	12 MB
CLIP0000003_0000024.rmf	12 MB

Figure 7.7. (Above) This folder is an individual clip from a Canon C500. As with many RAW formats, each *RMF* (*RAW Media Format*) frame is an individual file, in this case 12 MB each, which reminds us why shooting RAW is like drinking from a firehose!

Figure 7.8. A Sony SxS card, in this case a 64GB.

All video files contain *headers*. This is data at the beginning of the file that defines certain basic parameters and informs the software how to handle the data. It might specify information such as frame rate, aspect ratio and other data.

EXTENSIONS

This is the part after the "dot." These are also essential for the software to be able to "read" the video. Examples include: .mov (Quicktime), .r3d (Red camera), .mpg (MPEG compression), .mkv (Matroska video) and so on. Some applications go by the file header rather than the extension. In some few cases, you can get software to accept a file format it doesn't normally recognize by changing the filename extension. For example, *Adobe After Effects* does not normally recognize MPEG files in .vob or .mod formats, but may accept them if the file extension is changed.

FLOATING POINT

When video or still images pass into the processing phase (which can include things done in the camera after the sensor and at the DIT station in addition to postproduction) they move into the world of mathematics. Any time we change an image in some way, be it contrast, color, exposure or whatever, we are basically performing some sort of mathematical operation on the pixels. Fortunately, this is almost entirely automatic but in some cases, we do actually deal with the numbers. *Floating point* is an example of this. It is nearly ubiquitous in computer operations; for example, supercomputers are often rated in how many *FLOPS* they can perform, where a FLOP is *floating operations per second*.

In this context, 8-bit video would be an example of an *integer format*: color values can only be represented as whole numbers: 0, 1, 2, 3, and so on. Floating point, on the other hand, can deal with decimal values, allowing for finer gradations of color/grayscale values.

THIS ONE GOES TO ELEVEN

Film has always had something that only high-end video cameras are beginning to achieve: the ability to record parts of the image that are "beyond pure white." It does this with the built-in compression of the *shoulder* of the film. Some file formats have the ability to capture under and over range data. To go along with the extraordinary dynamic range of these new sensors, file formats need to keep up.

Color values can be written as a decimal with the range of colors going from 0.0000 to 1.0000. Black is 0.0000 in all systems and pure white is 1.0000; the middle value in the normal range is 0.5000. *Floating point* means that the position of the decimal can change when needed. This means that the potential maximum and minimum numbers are huge. The result of this is that you can have values that are "darker" than zero and "brighter" than white; these are the *under-range* and *over-range* values. They can be thought of as being "in reserve" for use when you need them. In effect, it gives you unlimited amounts of *headroom*. In other words, you can have a knob that goes to eleven!

This type of color is commonly called "32-bit float." It offers very high color precision and more flexibility in processing. Where 8-bit can show 255 levels, 16 bit can show 32,768 levels from pure black to pure saturated color.

Half Float

Floating point 32-bit is great but the files can be very large and require a tremendous amount of bandwidth. In response, *half-precision floating point* was devised. It is also called *half-float* and has greater dynamic range than 8-bit or 16-bit integer formats but occupies less computing real estate than full floating point — it is 16 bits (or two bytes) although at the cost of some precision. Half float is supported in *OpenEXR*.

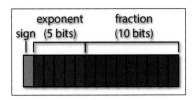

Figure 7.9. Structure of 16 bit floating point: one bit for the sign (plus or minus), 5 bits for the exponent and 10 bits for the fraction (mantissa).

OpenEXR

OpenEXR (extended range) is a format devised by *Industrial Light and Magic* (*ILM*), for use with digital visual effects production files. OpenEXR features 16-bit and 32-bit floating point. EXR files have a higher dynamic range than 8-bit file formats. While 8-bit files feature 20-70 steps per f/stop, EXR files render 1024 steps per f/stop. EXR files are generally compressed using lossless methods, but lossy compression can be used.

ILM developed the format in response to the demand for higher color fidelity in the visual effects industry. When the project began in 2000, ILM evaluated existing file formats, but rejected them for various reasons. According to ILM, these include:

- 8- and 10-bit formats lack the dynamic range necessary to store high-contrast images captured from HDR devices.

- 16-bit integer-based formats typically represent color component values from 0 (black) to 1 (white), but don't account for over-range values (e.g. a chrome highlight) that can be captured by film negative or other HDR devices. For images intended only for display or print reproduction, clamping at "white" may be sufficient; but for image processing in a visual effects house, highlights often need to be preserved in the image data. Preserving over-range values in the source image allows an artist to change the apparent exposure of the image with minimal loss of data, for example.

- 32-bit floating-point TIFF is often overkill for visual effects work. 32-bit FP TIFF provides more than sufficient precision and dynamic range for VFX images, but it comes at the cost of storage, both on disk and in memory. When creating background plates for VFX work, film is usually scanned in at 2k pixels wide but frequently at higher resolutions such as 4K, so background plates are already relatively large.

- OpenEXR supports several lossless compression methods, some of which can achieve compression ratios of about 2:1 for images with film grain. OpenEXR is extensible, so developers can easily add new compression methods (lossless or lossy).

- OpenEXR images can be annotated with an arbitrary number of attributes, e.g. with color balance information from a camera.

Now lest you get too excited about this talk of over, under and extended range, keep in mind that this largely applies to the images in signal processing — after they have been recorded. There are still very real limits to what a sensor can reproduce and what a camera can record; however, camera manufacturers have made some truly amazing advances in the dynamic range of sensors, and then there is HDR photography, which is nothing short of a revolution in digital image reproduction.

From *OpenEXR, An Introduction*: "With this linear relationship established, the question remains, what number is white? The convention employed by OpenEXR is to determine a middle gray object, and assign it the photographic 18% gray value, or 0.18 in the floating point scheme. Other pixel values can be easily determined from there (a stop brighter is 0.36, another stop is 0.72). The value 1.0 has no special significance (it is not a clamping limit, as in other formats); it roughly represents light coming from a 100% reflector (slightly brighter than white paper). However, there are many brighter pixel values available to represent objects such as fire and highlights. The range of normalized 16-bit floating-point numbers can represent thirty stops of information with 1024 steps per stop. We have eighteen and a half stops above middle gray, and eleven and a half below" These values over 1.0 are used for the specular highlights and objects that generate their own light (candle flames, lamps, and so on) that we talked about before.

COMPRESSION ARTIFACTS

While some compression schemes are lossless and some are lossy, all of them aim, at least in theory, at being visually lossless — in other words that even if they are technically lossy, the result is indistinguishable to the human eye. Anyone who has viewed a low quality, highly compressed internet video is familiar with the results of too much compression — the artifacts that result are distortion of some areas and pixelation — where sections of the picture are rendered as large pixel blocks rather than individual pixels.

In general, this blockiness is caused by the fact that DCT treats each image as a collection of 8x8 blocks of 64 pixels each. Individual pixels are compared to their neighbors — if two pixels are "almost" the same, they are rendered with the same color values. This means that after several rounds of compression/decompression and re-compression, an area of the image that was formerly subtly differentiated in color and brightness are now rendered as a uniform block with a resultant annoying appearance. Wavelet compression schemes don't result in the same form of blockiness but most of them are lossy codecs so they degrade in other ways if overcompressed.

image control & grading

So far we've been looking at digital images from a purely technical point-of-view, which is important — if you don't master the technical side of imagemaking, the odds of creating powerful and meaningful shots is slim at best. Now it's time to start thinking creatively, but first a bit more on the technical side — a look at the tools we have available to control images.

In front of the camera:
- Lighting
- Choice of lens
- Filters
- Mechanical effects (smoke, fog, rain, etc.)
- Choosing time of day, direction of the shot, weather, etc.

In the camera:
- Exposure
- Frame rate
- Shutter speed
- Shutter angle
- Gamma
- White balance
- Color space
- Knee control
- Black stretch
- Matrix

And of course, in shooting film, you have the option of choosing the film stock and perhaps altering the processing and changing the look by color correcting during printing. These options are not only available (in different form) when shooting HD or Ultra HD video, we now actually have much more control than before.

As always, we can dramatically change the nature of the image after it has left the camera. This has been true since the early days of film but with digital images, the degree of control later on is even greater. As one cinematographer put it "The degree to which they can really screw up your images in post has increased exponentially." But notice that the first sentence of this paragraph didn't say "in post." The reason for that is there is now an intermediate step.

AT THE DIT CART

A fairly new position on the crew is the *DIT* — *Digital Imaging Technician*; we'll talk about that a good deal in coming chapters. The DIT cart is not really post-production, but it's not "in the camera" either — it's an in-between stage where there are all sorts of options. On some productions, the DIT may in some cases be concerned with nothing more than downloading media files; perhaps also setting up monitors and running cable. On other productions the DIT cart might be a central hub of the creative process where looks are being created, controlled and modified; where camera exposure and lighting balance are being constantly monitored or even directly controlled and where the director, DP and DIT and director are involved in intense conversations and creative back-and-forth concerning all aspects of visual storytelling.

These aspects of the visual image are what we are concerned with in this chapter: they are both camera issues and post-production/color correction issues. In the world of digital imaging, the dividing line of what is "production" and what is "post" is indefinite at best.

WHAT HAPPENS AT THE CART DOESN'T STAY AT THE CART

In some cases, the images from the camera receive no processing at all as they pass through the DIT station, and the process is more clerical and organizational; a matter of downloading, backing up and making shuttle drives to deliver to postproduction, the production company, archives, etc. In other cases, the DIT spends a good deal of time rendering dailies for use by the director, different ones for the editor and a third set for the VFX process. As previously noted, in some instances, there are substantial changes to the look of the image and even color correction and creating a *look*. In short, there are a wide range of functions at the DIT cart and we'll talk about those more in the chapter *Workflow*. In this chapter we're going to talk about only processes that affect the look of the images: in some cases just making them viewable and in other cases, applying creative choices that are part of the visual story.

So let's add to our list of image controls and bring in some of the topics we're going to talk about here:
- Changing *lift*, *gamma* and *gain*
- *Color correction*
- Creating *LUTs* and *Look Files*
- Applying *LUTs* to the camera and set monitors
- Creating *Color Decision Lists* (*CDLs*)

Clearly, some of these processes are the same as controls we have in the camera. The beauty of file-based digital workflow is that there is considerable choice not only in the type of image alterations available to the filmmakers but also a great deal of flexibility in choosing *when* to apply them to the image. Deciding when a look gets "baked in" is something to be thought through carefully and should be agreed to by all parties involved. Another consideration is deciding when the time and conditions are right for certain decisions to be made: sometimes the situation on the set is just not right for making these types of creative decisions, sometimes they are; the same may be true of a first pass color correction or even the editing process — having the latitude to make creative choices without being stuck with them forever is a great thing, it means the creative process can be an ebb and flow of ideas instead of an endless series of relentless high-pressure deadlines.

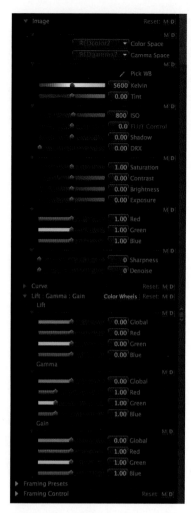

Figure 8.2. (Above) Sliders in *Red-Cine-X Pro* offer control over every aspect of the image. Since Red cameras shoot RAW, controls include ISO, White Balance as well as selections for color space and gamma space; in this example RedColor2 and RedGamma2.

Figure 8.3. (Above, right). The full *DaVinci Resolve* controls setup. (Courtesy of Black Magic Design).

COLOR CORRECTION AND COLOR GRADING

Although most people use the two terms interchangeably, some professionals do make a distinction between what is *color correction* and what is *color grading*.

Color correction is a process where each clip (shot) is adjusted for "correct" exposure, color and gamma. This is a slightly more straightforward process, but is an art form in its own way. The waveform monitor, vectorscope, histograms and other evaluation tools are critical to this step and most editing and color correction software have them built-in. This phase of image control is what is likely to happen at the DIT cart for dailies — there is neither the time nor the proper environment to make fine tuned final decisions about the look on the set, but the DIT will either have LUTs or image guidelines from the DP which he or she will approximate so that the on-the-set monitors and the dailies are not just "whatever comes out of the camera." Even with the most careful controls by the cinematographer and lighting crew, there are bound to be some variations in exposure and color balance; while these cannot be dealt with entirely in production, it is usually desirable to iron out the biggest variations to make the dailies viewable without distraction.

Color grading is a more creative process where decisions are made to further enhance or establish a new visual tone to the project including: introducing new color themes, films stock emulations, color gradients and a slew of other choices — in other words, the final look of the project. Since it is purely creative, there is no wrong or right…only what the DP, director and colorist feel is appropriate for the story. The essential difference is that the first is more or less temporary while the latter is more artistic, creative and final, and by final we mean the *baked-in* result which is sent out for distribution.

CONTROLLERS AND CONTROL SURFACES

Video controls have been around since the earliest days of television; the types of controls we use today date from the introduction of film-to-video transfer which was originally called *film chain* (used for showing film footage and movies on television), but has been replaced by *telecine*, which transfers film to video, usually with color correction. Video to video has always been called *color correction*. In the 80s the front ends of these systems became somewhat standardized with some elements common to all of them, especially the arrangement of three trackballs with surrounding rings.

| Color-A H | Lift C | Gamma C | Gain C | Color-B H |

CONTROL PARAMETERS

All video grading software share some basic features, most prominent among these are the controls. They fall into certain basic groups:

- Lift/Shadows
- Gamma/Midtones
- Gain/Highlights
- Offset

This may seem like a confusing profusion of terminology, and in fact it is — there is no industry wide standardization. Although there are some subtle differences in how various software packages implement them, in practice they are largely the same things with different names. Keep in mind that these controls are separately applicable (in most cases) to each of the color channels.

It is important to remember that all these controls interact with each other to some extent — none of them is "pure" in its ability

Figure 8.4. (Top) The *Tangent Design Element* control surface for color correction. It comes in three separate sections; many DITs start with just the middle section.

Figure 8.5. (Above) Lift, gamma and gain controls in *Assimilate Scratch*. They can be adjusted with the mouse or connected to a control surface.

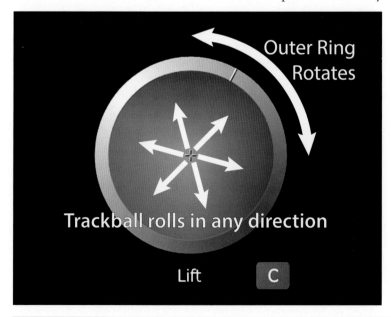

Figure 8.6. How the hue offset wheels operate. This wheel is for Lift, so rotating the outer ring raises or lowers Lift and moving the trackball in the center alters the hue. Moving toward green raises green while lowering red and blue.

Moving toward yellow raises red and green while lowering blue.

Moving toward red raises red while lowering blue and green and so on.

The colors are laid out just as they are on the vectorscope. Now you see why it's so important to understand the color wheel.

image control & grading

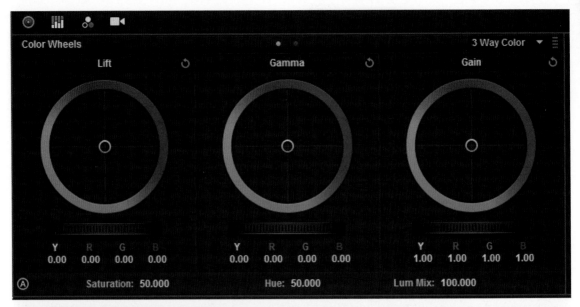

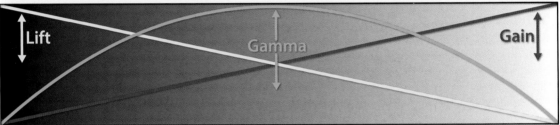

Figure 8.7. (Top) The *Lift*, *Gamma* and *Gain* controls on the *3 Way Color* page of *DaVinci Resolve*.

Figure 8.8. (Above) The effect of *Lift*, *Gamma* and *Gain* controls. Although they affect different aspects of the image, there is always some overlap. Notice the "gate" effect with *Lift* and *Gain* — one end stays anchored while the other end is free to move through the entire range.

to affect only one specific part of the image, except in Log mode, which we'll talk about in a moment. There are methods such as *Power Windows*, *Secondary correction*, *qualifiers* and others which target specific parts of the image or specific color or tonal ranges but those are beyond the scope of this discussion as they are most often used in postproduction — here we are only introducing basic concepts as they might be used on the set at the DIT cart.

LIFT/SHADOWS

These operations affect the darkest areas of the scene; they make the shadows darker or lighter in each color channel. As you can see in Figures 8.9, 8.10 and 8.11, *Lift* raises or lowers the darkest areas while being anchored at the pure white end; this means that it has the ability to take the shadows fully up or down the scale. While it will always have some effect on the midtones, the change it makes to the highlights is minimal.

Think of it like a swinging gate seen from above: the part of the gate attached at the hinge hardly moves at all, while the part of the gate farthest from the hinge has complete range of movement. The same concept applies to other aspects of image control as well, except in *log grading*, as we will see.

GAMMA/MIDTONES

These affect the medium tones of the picture. In practice they can be seen as contrast adjustment. We are already familiar with the concept of gamma or power function from the discussion in the chapter *Linear, Gamma, Log*. As we noted there, the term gamma is used a bit loosely in the video world, but it is largely the same here.

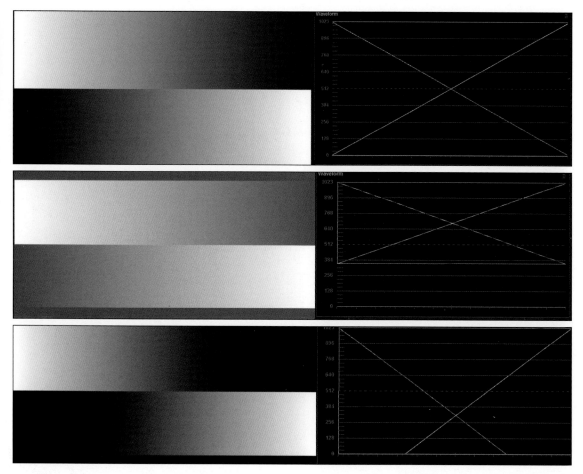

In Figures 8.13 and 8.14 you can see that Gamma/Midtones affects the middle range of the gray scale; it can take these midrange tones up or down while pure black and pure white remain anchored; this give it the bowed shape.

Gain/Highlights

Gain (sometimes called *Highlights*) affects the highlights the most (Figures 8.15 and 8.16). Similar to Lift, it is anchored at the dark end and so has very little effect there, while at the highlight end, it has freedom to range up and down the scale.

Curves

In addition to separate controllers for each segment of the grayscale, most applications allow you to draw curves for the image — to independently manipulate the response curve, usually with Bezier controls. This can be a fast and efficient way to work. Figure 8.22 shows an image adjusted by using Curves in *Assimilate Scratch*. Taking the flat, dull log image and transforming it into a representation closer to how we want it to finally appear involves applying the classic S-curve to the image: crushing the blacks and stretching the whites.

LOG CONTROLS

Some software (particularly *DaVinci Resolve* and *Baselight,* but undoubtedly more in the near future, especially with wider implementation of *ACES Log/Proxy mode*) have a mode called *Log*. In *Resolve,* the Log mode has the controls *Shadow, Midtone, Highlight*

Figure 8.9. (Top) *Lift* at normal — no adjustments made to the crossed grayscale gradients — everything normal.

Figure 8.10. (Middle) Raising *Lift* lightens the shadows but has little effect on the highlights, but some effect on the midtones — middle gray is raised substantially.

Figure 8.11. (Bottom) Lowering *Lift* depresses the dark tones; has some effect on lowering the midtones, but little effect on the highlights; middle gray is lowered.

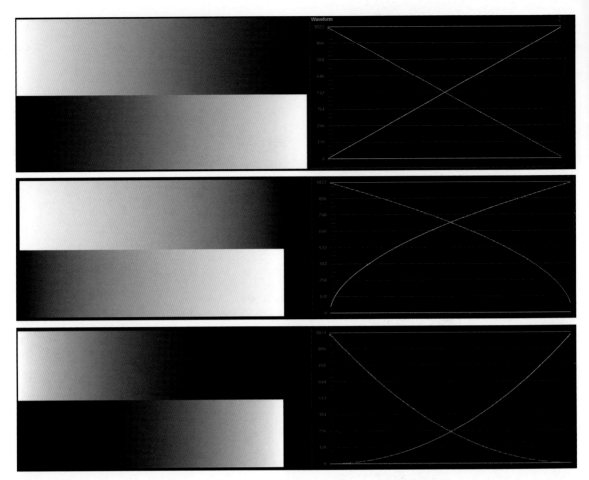

Figure 8.12. (Top) Crossed gray gradient curves with *gamma* at normal. The gradients display normal contrast with even distribution of tones from black to white.

Figure 8.13. (Middle) The same gradients with *gamma* raised; the effect is lower contrast and raised midtones.

Figure 8.14. (Bottom) The gradients with *gamma* lowered; the effect is raised contrast. In both cases, there is still pure black at one end and pure white at the other end, but the midtones are altered significantly.

and *Offset*. It also includes *Low Range/High Range*, *Contrast*, *Pivot*, *Saturation* and *Hue*. (As we have seen, the other mode in Resolve is *Three-Way Color* which includes the wheels *Lift*, *Gamma*, *Gain* and also *Saturation*, *Hue* and *Luma Mix*.)

Three Way Color in Resolve has been described as "painting with a broad brush," while *Log* mode allows much more targeted adjustments with far less overlap between shadows, midtones and highlights. *Low Range* and *High Range* determines where the separation point will be for the shadows, midtones and highlights. The following discussion focuses mostly on DaVinci Resolve — discussing every color correction software in detail is far beyond the scope of this book but the fundamental concepts remain the same, even though there are variations in specific application. Also, since *Resolve Lite* is free, it is easily available for anyone who wants to learn, experiment and test. They also offer some test images for you to work with. There are several other software packages (some free) that offer control over the image parameters we're talking about here.

LOG OFFSET COLOR AND MASTER CONTROLS

The Log controls have one other difference from Lift/Gamma/Gain, and that is a fourth set of color balance and master wheel controls: the *Offset* control, which lets you make adjustments throughout the entire tonal range of the RGB channels (Figures 8.18 and 8.19).

Offset raises or lowers the level of the entire scene equally. Also sometimes called *Setup*, although this is an archaic term that dates back to analog video. Since this means that you could take it into

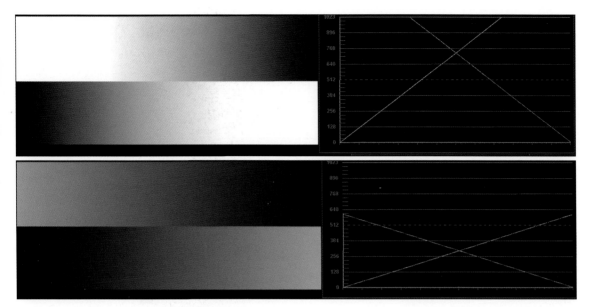

clipping at the top or below zero at the bottom, although as we saw in *Linear, Gamma, Log*, there is headroom and footroom in log. Offset is sometimes accompanied by a *Contrast* control which allows the user to alter the contrast of the signal around a selectable pivot point. In other words, the user can select a center pivot point and stretch or squeeze the entire signal above and below this point to allow for keeping the image within limits while still moving everything up or down with the Offset control.

Low Range moves the border where the Shadows and Midtones meet. Lowering this parameter widens the range affected by the Midtones, and narrows the range affected by the Shadows. Raising this parameter narrows the Midtones and widens the Shadows.

High Range moves the border where the Midtones and Highlights meet. Lowering the High Range parameter narrows the range affected by the Midtones, and widens the range affected by the Highlights. Raising it narrows the Highlights and widens the Midtones.

Figure 8.15. (Top) *Gain* raised; in this case it causes clipping. This is just an example, raising the gain does not always cause clipping, although it is always a danger. Just as with lift, the midtones are also changed.

Figure 8.16. (Above) *Gain* lowered. Highlights become gray. Note that in both examples, middle gray also moves up or down.

Figure 8.17. (Below) The *Log* page in DaVinci Resolve showing all adjustments at neutral with the crossed grayscale gradients.

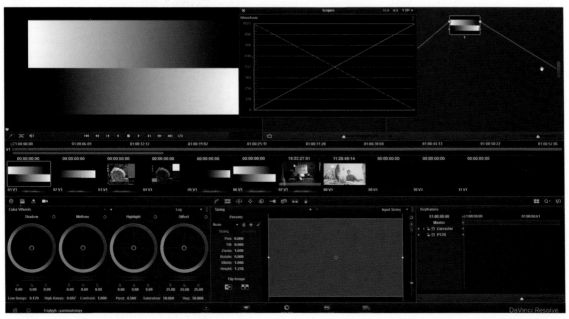

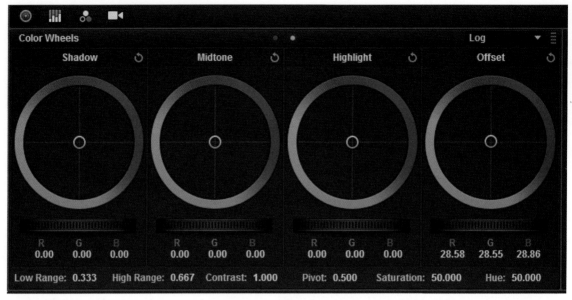

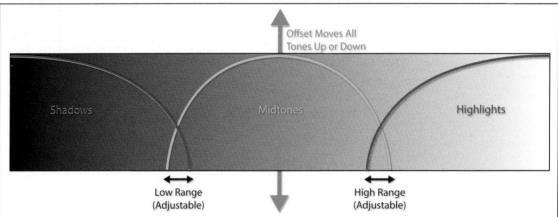

Figure 8.18. (Top) The *Log* controls in *DaVinci Resolve*: *Shadows, Midtones, Highlights* and *Offset* —which raises or lowers all tones at the same time.

Figure 8.19. (Above) How log controls work: there is relatively little overlap between the control areas and how much they overlap is variable. Complete separation between them would leave gaps and create some odd images.

Contrast allows the user to increase or reduce the distance between the darkest and lightest values of an image, raising or lowering image contrast. The effect is similar to using the Lift and Gain master controls to make simultaneous opposing adjustments. Bright and dark parts of the image are pushed apart or brought together around a center point defined by the *Pivot* parameter. Raising the contrast adds the familiar S-curve to the image: raising the highlights and lowering the dark tones while mostly leaving the mid-tones alone.

The *Pivot* control changes the center point around which dark and bright parts of the image are stretched or narrowed during contrast adjustment. Darker images may require a lower Pivot value to avoid crushing the shadows too much when stretching image contrast, while lighter images may benefit from a higher Pivot value to increase shadow density adequately.

Colorist and VFX supervisor Mike Most explains it this way: "The log controls [in Resolve] have nothing to do with linearizing the output. That is a step handled by either a LUT or a curve. The log controls are designed to manipulate information that is coded in a log format, with the expectation that you're viewing the result through a normalizing LUT. The values in a log coded image have different black and white points and a different gamma than video images, and controls need to be scaled differently to allow for

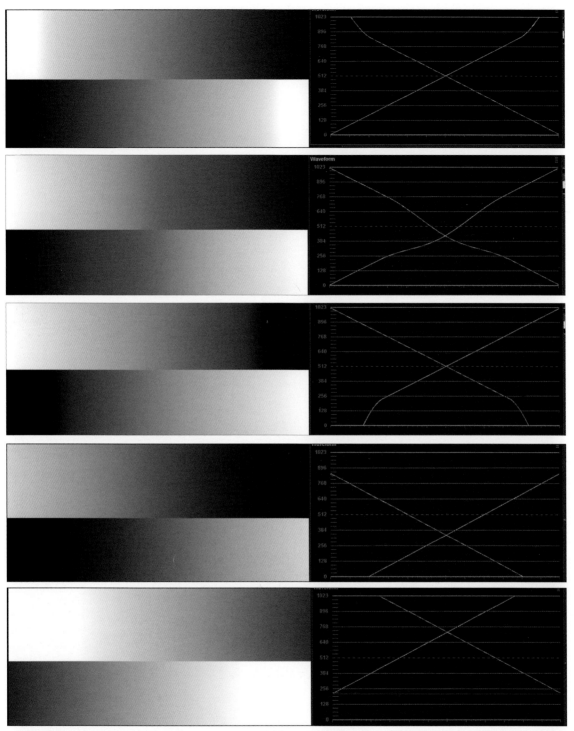

manipulation of those images in a more controllable and predictable way. The most common way of dealing with this, based on the film timing approach, is to use a combination of exposure (implemented here as offset) and contrast to alter the color balance and overall level on the image as a whole and adjust contrast to better match any under or overexposed material to the video display environment. The shadow, mid tone, and highlight controls act on very restricted ranges that are based on the Cineon log black and white points of 95 and 685 rather than 0 and 1023.

Figure 8.20. *Log* controls in *DaVinci Resolve*: (top) *Highlights* raised. (second from top) *Midtones* lowered. (third from top) *Shadows* lowered. (fourth from top) *Offset* lowered. (bottom) *Offset* raised. Note that the three regions are affected with little change to the other parts of the image.

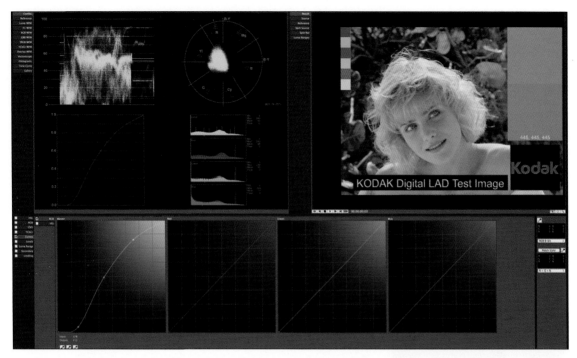

KODAK Digital LAD Test Image

"The result is that you can set up basic balance on an image using purely offset and contrast, then fine tune it using shadows, mid tone, and highlight adjustments. Because of the design of those controls, you'll find that the highlight control, while restricted to input values near or above 685, acts as a sort of variable soft clip rather than a gain control (the gain control has a pivot at 0) so it's sometimes useful even in a non-log grading environment. It is also important to note that the contrast pivot can be very useful in dealing with exposure issues, such as lack of fill or blown out highlights. By raising the pivot, the contrast control affects the darker areas, and begins to feel more like a "black stretch" control. By lowering the pivot, it affects the upper ranges, bringing out more detail in things like overexposed facial highlights and the like. On Resolve, you get a lot of corrective power out of these things because you can implement them separately on different nodes (provided all of those nodes are prior to the output LUT).

"Film DI work has been done using exposure/contrast and log scaled range controls for a long time; in fact, *Lustre* was designed around it, as was the *Film Grade* strip in *Baselight*. Because you're not pulling the picture apart by separating the brightness ranges, the offset/contrast control lets you stay much more true to the original image because once you get the balance right (usually by setting up flesh tones), all of the colors in the scene become what they're supposed to be based on the original photography. It might be counterintuitive to those who have only used lift/gain/gamma control systems, but it's much simpler to come up with something representative of the photography using only one trackball (the offset trackball) than it is using three. You get better color separation and thus a lot more depth. I would suggest experimenting with the log grading controls using this description rather than trying to use them as you would lift, gain, and gamma. I think you'll be surprised at the clean results you can achieve. By lowering the pivot, it affects the upper ranges, bringing out more detail in things like overexposed facial highlights and the like."

Figure 8.21. (Opposite page, top) The Kodak *Marcie* (*LAD*) test chart in log space — dull and low contrast. Note how the waveform monitor (green notation) doesn't reach black on the low end or 100% on the high end. The effect indicator (blue notation) is a straight line showing that no changes have been made. The curve tool (red indicator) is also a straight line. This is in *Assimilate Scratch*.

Figure 8.22. (Opposite page, bottom) The curve tool has been used to create the classic S-curve which takes the shadows down and the highlights up to bring the image back to normal contrast. The waveform (green) now fills the full range from 0% to 100%, the histogram (yellow) is now much wider and the effect indicator (blue) shows the changes that have been made.

Figure 8.23. (Above) The same image in *Color Finesse*. Again, applying an S-curve has brought it back to normal contrast as can be seen in the waveform monitor and histograms.

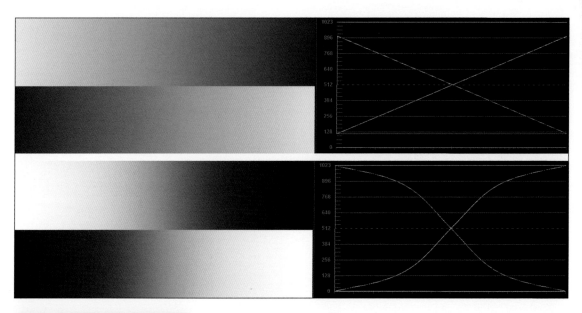

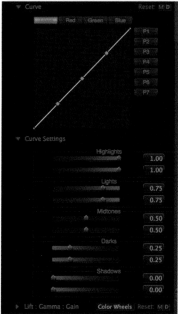

Figure 8.24. (Top) *Contrast* at normal and (Middle) lowered and raised in *DaVinci Resolve Log* controls.

Figure 8.25. (Above) *Curve* controls in *RedCine-X Pro*.

In DaVinci Resolve, *Saturation* and *Hue* are fairly obvious but *Lum Mix*, not so much. Here are some brief descriptions.

Saturation: Increases or decreases overall image saturation. At higher values for this parameter, colors are more intense; while at lower values, color intensity diminishes until, at 0, all color is gone, leaving a grayscale image.

Hue rotates all colors of the image around the color wheel. The default setting of 50 leaves the hues unchanged. Raising or lowering this parameter rotates all hues in the image equally forward or backward along the hue distribution as seen on a color wheel. The important thing is that this controls all colors of the image equally, unlike other individual controls which can target specific color ranges.

According to *Black Magic Design* (the developer of *DaVinci Resolve*): "*Lum Mix* lets you control the balance between YRGB contrast adjustments you've made using the master wheels or ganged Custom Curves, and Y-only adjustments [grayscale luminance] to contrast made using the Y channel Lift/Gamma/Gain controls of the Primary Control palette or the unganged Luma curve. At the default of 100, YRGB and Y-only adjustments to contrast contribute equally. Reducing this value diminishes the effect of Y-only contrast adjustments until, at 0, Y-only contrast adjustments are turned off."

COLOR SPACE

Color space is an important consideration for several reasons, some of which we touched on in the chapter *Digital Color*. Different color spaces have different abilities to convey the full gamut of color. Changing the color space of a project can have unexpected consequences — which is why it's important to consider the entire image chain: if the final product is changed to a different color space it could end up altering the image in undesirable ways. Testing the entire workflow is the best way to guard against these mishaps. Although the tendency is to shoot RAW, many cameras still have a selection of color space options built into the camera, with the capability to accept user input color space decisions as well. In any case, images can't stay RAW forever, they have to be converted to a particular color space at some point and it will be baked in.

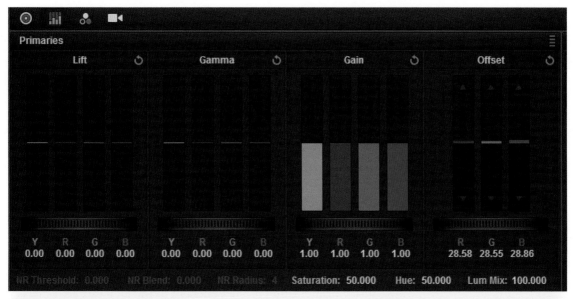

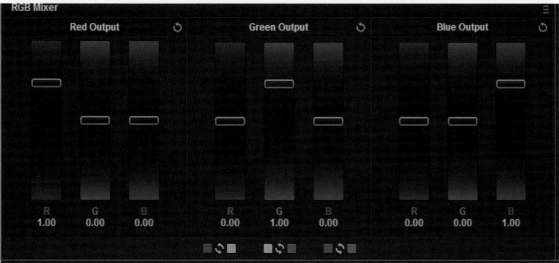

COLOR CONTROL

Primary color correction is any change in the image that affects the entire image. *Secondary color correction* is more specialized and isn't even used at all in many project. It uses the same controls (red, green, blue, saturation, lift, gamma, gain) but they are applied to only certain aspects of the image. Specific colors, saturation levels or brightness values are isolated and manipulated.

Although they are beyond the scope of this book, masks, mattes and power windows can be used to isolated specific areas of the frame and alterations can be made only in those areas. They can be animated and motion tracked so that they move with objects or areas in each frame as the scene progresses.

VECTORS

Vectors are, not surprisingly, associated with the vectorscope. Here, vectors means narrow "wedges" of color as we might see on the vectorscope display. The example shown here (Fig. 8.28) is from *Assimilate Scratch*; the six controls shown here are the primaries: red, green, blue and the secondary colors: magenta, cyan and yellow. However,

Figure 8.26. (Top) Most image control software offers several ways to change the image values. Here are the *Primaries* controls in *Resolve*. It also includes *Offset* controls for individual color channels.

Figure 8.27. (Above) The *RGB Mixer* in *Resolve*.

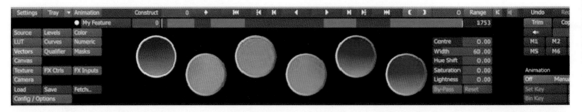

Figure 8.28. The *Vector* controls in *Assimilate Scratch* affect narrow segments of the color wheel.

they are customizable. On the right hand of the window are controls which include center and width. Center refers to the hue/phase selection and width is how wide a wedge you are going to isolate; then within that range you can manipulate hue, saturation and lightness. This means that you could, for example, isolate everything in a shot that is low-saturated blue and change it to deep red.

Although these secondary corrections are extraordinarily powerful and useful, they are something that would rarely be done on the set, except for a quick experiment to see if a particular effect is possible.

EXPORTING AND REUSING GRADES

Image manipulation in the camera or at the DIT cart are generally intended to be non-permanent and more of a rough draft. Given the limitations of time, equipment and viewing conditions to do more than a quick dailies correction would be a risky operation and it is seldom needed anyway. However, since dailies grading is usually going to incorporate the ideas of the DP and director, they need to be exportable and reusable. Exportable so that they can be sent on down the line to dailies for the producers or other parties and to various parties involved in post production — an important factor in keeping everybody "on the same page" for a production. Unprocessed RAW dailies would give essentially no guidance to post houses as to what the DP and director intended for the scene and they might start off in an entirely different direction, which may waste time, resources and possibly lead to creative confusion. The *ASC-CDL* system is an attempt to address this idea of transporting the DP and director's ideas forward through the rest of the process. The ASC-CDL system will be discussed in *Workflow*.

Being reusable is important so that the on-set grading doesn't need to be repeated from day to day or scene to scene; especially useful if only certain types of scenes get a particular color correction, as is typically the case. Repeatability is also necessary because our perception of a particular look can "drift" over time. This is a phenomenon often noticed in color grading a long project such as a feature. The first time a particular type of scene gets graded, the director and DP may go for a fairly extreme look. As the days go by, eyes and brains tend to adjust to that look and the next time that type of scene comes up, it is not unusual for them to want to push it to a more and more extreme look. The result can sometimes be more than they really intended when they first started and worse, can create an inconsistency in the look.

To counteract this most color grading software has the capacity to save *frame still grabs* or *still stores* that can be referenced back to for consistency. In some applications, such as DaVinci Resolve, these frame grabs also contain the parameters of the look, so all that is necessary is to copy the reference frame and drop it onto the current scene and the look is automatically applied. You can always make adjustments to this look at any time.

LUTS AND LOOKS

A *LUT* is a *Look Up Table*, a way to associate (or replace) one value with another value without mathematical calculation. You can think of it as an algorithm for all the pixel values already precalculated and stored in memory. A very simple type of LUT is shown in Table 8.1 — for any value of Celsius temperature you can quickly *look up* the associated value for the same temperature in Fahrenheit.

1D LUTS

This example is a one dimensional (1D) table, meaning that for each input value, there is one and one only output value; interesting but less than useful for video, where we are almost always dealing with at least three values for Red, Green and Blue. A basic type of LUT for video is three 1D LUTs, one for each color channel. There is no interaction between color channels. As an example a 3X (three channels) 1D LUT could be like this:

```
R,G,B
3, 0, 0
5, 2, 1
9, 9, 9
```

This means that:
For input value of 0 for R, G, and B, the output is R=3, G=0, B=0.
For input value of 1 for R, G, and B, the output is R=5, G=2, B=1.
For input value of 3 for R, G, and B, the output is R=9, G=9, B=9.
LUTs consist of long lists of these sets of numbers.

3D LUTS

A 3D LUT is more complex but also allows for more control of the image. 3D LUTs are useful for converting from one color space to another. It applies a transformation to each value of a *color cube* in RGB space (Figures 8.31 and 8.32 show color cubes). 3D LUTs use a more sophisticated method of mapping color values from different color spaces. A 3D LUT provides a way to represent arbitrary color space transformations, as opposed to the 1D LUT where a value of the output color is determined only from the corresponding value of the input color. A 3D LUT allows for *cross-talk* between color channels: a component of the output color is computed from all components of the input color providing the 3D LUT tool with more power and flexibility than the 1D LUT tool.

Because it would be impossibly large to include every single value for each channel, the number of *nodes* is limited. With 17 coordinates per axis (a typical size) there are 4,913 nodes total. Increasing to 257 per axis results in 16,974,593 total. For this reason, only nodes are precisely calculated; between nodes, the value is interpolated, meaning it is less precise.

While 1D LUTs are useful for adjusting contrast and gamma per color channel, 3D LUTs are usually more flexible — 3D LUTs can cross-convert colors between channels, alter saturation, and independently control saturation, brightness, and contrast.

1D LUTs have a 1:1 correspondence between the bit-depth and the number of entries. 3D LUTS must be interpolated from a subset or the LUT could be over a gigabyte in size. LUTs can be integer values or floating point.

- 8x8x8 is too small for most transforms.
- 16x16x16 is a reasonable size for previews.
- 64x64x64 is rendering quality.

Celsisus	Fahrenheit
0°	32°
20°	68°
40°	104°
60°	140°
80°	176°
100°	212°

Table 8.1. A very simple one-dimensional form of *Look Up Table*. In this case, knowing the temperature in Celsius allows you to look up the equivalent in Fahrenheit.

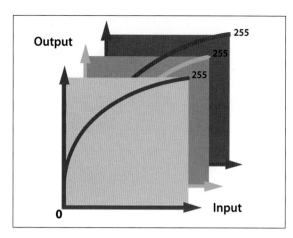

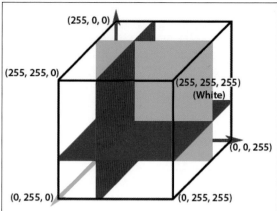

Figure 8.29. (Left) A *1D LUT* has separate tables for each color channel, however for imaging purpose, it is almost always three 1D LUTs; one for each color channel. (Illustration courtesy of Light Illusion.)

Figure 8.30. (Right) A *3D LUT* is a cube or lattice. The values of 0 to 255 in both of these are the digital color values. (Illustration courtesy of Light Illusion.)

Examples of Floating Point LUTS:

- Iridas
- Truelight
- CineSpace

Some might ask if there are *Log* and *Linear* LUTs. The simple answer is no. According to Steve Shaw of *Light Illusion*, "There is actually no such thing as a Log LUT. Any LUT just converts input points to output points, and has no knowledge of the space in which it is working LIN or LOG."

LUT FORMATS

As is typical with new technology, there is little to no standardization between LUTs devised by different parties and so they come in a variety of formats, some of which are mutually compatible and some of which are not. As a result different software packages can read some types of LUTs and not others; although application designers generally strive to be more inclusive with each iteration of their programs.

PROPER USE OF LUTS IN COLOR CORRECTION

Mike Most says this about LUTs: "The LUT approach is often misunderstood by those who feel, for some reason, that what a LUT is supposed to do is yield a 'perfect' starting point for every image. That is not the case. What a LUT does is transform the log curve back to a proper gamma corrected curve based on the particular display device being used, most often a monitor. In the case of an image that is a bit underexposed, this will likely cause the blacks to be crushed by the LUT, and in the case of an overexposed image, it will cause the whites to be clipped. This is where the misunderstanding comes into play. The LUT is not meant to be used as the first correction in a grading pipeline. If you place the LUT after an initial correction, you can then raise the blacks or lower the whites on the original log image prior to it being transformed by the LUT. The LUT will still do what it's supposed to do, and you then have the option of grading prior to the LUT or after it as needed. This is the 'secret' that many professional colorists (especially those who work in the digital intermediate world) know, and few inexperienced ones seem to understand. A LUT is not a color correction, just as a log image is not an image. It is a transform, and the log image is a container. The image needs to be 'processed' by the LUT in order to appear properly to the eye."

VIEWING LUTS

One variety is the *Viewing LUT*, which is designed to make a camera's output look good during shooting or in the case of RAW and log footage to make it viewable in a WYSIWYG mode — that is to say that it makes sense to people who are not accustomed to viewing scenes in RAW or log mode. Often they are as simple as converting a flat, low-contrast S-Log, C-Log or Log-C feed into a normal-looking Rec.709 image, while other LUTs also will reflect the "look" that the DP and director are going for, in other words, they incorporate creative decisions made by the cinematographer. The DIT on or near the set often will create a Viewing LUT for the DP and director's monitors. These LUTs can then be sent to postproduction to create dailies and to give the colorist a starting point for the final grade. Viewing LUTs are usually a 3D LUT because this allows the most possible manipulation and control of the look. Additionally, the DP has the option to create an *ASC-Color Decision List*, which essentially says to post "This is what I intended with this image."

It is important to remember that viewing LUTs, particularly those that convert log to Rec.709 are not going to be perfectly representative of the picture because you are fitting a high dynamic range image into a smaller dynamic range. The reason is obvious: log encoded video is capable of rendering substantially more in the highlight regions than Rec.709 is capable of. While it may make for a pretty picture on the monitor, it may be misleading in terms of exposure and tonal rendering. When viewing a log image without a viewing LUT, unless you have a lot of experience with log space, it can be difficult to evaluate exposure because there is very little contrast in these images and of course even if you have a lot of experience, you will be mentally adjusting for what you see on the screen — another term for this might be *guessing*. The nice thing about log is that it is more forgiving in terms of highlights (which is certainly no excuse for being sloppy about exposure). You still need to ensure an overall baseline for consistency and continuity. Using a LUT as a color space transformation of the log stream to non-destructively put it into a more normal range of contrast is one method of doing this.

Viewing LUTs on the set are very useful tools, not difficult to create and are easy to apply in most situations. The real problem is employing them on the set; in particular getting them to show up on the monitors used by the DP, director and the rest of the crowd at video village. Some cameras allow for the application of a LUT or Look to the monitor output, but frequently, a piece of hardware, called a LUT Box, is used in between the camera and a monitor to insert the LUT into the viewing stream; also, some monitors have built in LUT boxes. More detail about using these rigs on set will be discussed in the Chapter *Workflow*. Examples include *Blackmagic Design HDLink Pro*, *Cine-tal Davio* and *Pandora Pluto*. Software like *Pomfort LiveGrade*, *cineSpace* from *THX* and *Light Illusion LightSpace CMS* can be used to combine Calibration LUTs and Viewing LUTs, which can be a tricky process.

LUTS AND LOOKS: WHAT'S THE DIFFERENCE?

Red and Arri cameras have the ability to load in special files, called *Looks*, that essentially function very much like LUTs. The distinction between a *Look* and a *LUT* is that these *Look Files* are used in-camera, whereas LUTs can generally be applied anywhere in the workflow.

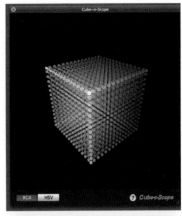

Figure 8.31. (Top) The color cube of an unaffected image as shown in *Pomfort LiveGrade's Cube-O-Scope*.

Figure 8.32. (Above) The same image with a LUT applied. The cube diagram shows how the colors are shifted by the LUT.

Figure 8.33. Pomfort *LiveGrade* is a widely used application for creating and managing LUTs. It can also control devices such as LUT boxes and monitors (panel on the left).

ARRI LOOK FILES

Here is Arri's explanation of their Look file system: "Arri Look Files in the Alexa camera enable DPs to view images on set that convey their full creative intentions. A look file can be previewed on monitors or recorded into the image; either way all the metadata that define the look travel embedded in the media into postproduction. This is a completely new way of handling looks." They continue: "In essence, *Arri Look Files* are a purely creative tool, used within the Alexa camera itself. They might be created by the colorist, or by the DP, but in either case they encourage greater and earlier interaction between production and post, and allow monitors on the set to give a good idea of what the final look for each scene might be."

As generated by the *Arri Look Creator* (free software available from Arri) they are based on a Log C DPX picture grab taken from the Alexa. For a closer look at how this system works, see the chapter *Workflow* for a diagram of how frame grabs are obtained from the Alexa, and sent through the process to generate a Look File that can be re-imported back into the camera. The Alexa camera can load a Look File, generated by the ARRI Look Generator or other software, and its output is adjusted accordingly. That output could even be recorded if the job didn't want to deal with video in the flat Log C mode. The Look File will travel with the metadata of every clip shot on the ALEXA and can be extracted to make a LUT.

ARRI LUTS

A LUT can be created with the online *Arri LUT Generator* (www.arridigital.com), which creates LUTs in many different formats. This LUT can be loaded to create dailies or into a color-grading application for finishing. See the chapter *Workflow* for more details on this process.

RED'S LOOK FILES

Red's look files are called *RMDs* (Red Metadata). With their Red-Cine-X software, a look file can be generated and loaded into the camera. The cameras then can apply the adjustments to the monitor outputs. A *Look* works just like a *LUT*, but is built just for a specific camera and doesn't require external hardware. This type of adjustment then travels through metadata of the recorded clips and can be applied very easily through to post production. This aspect of using LUTs is discussed in more detail in *Workflow*.

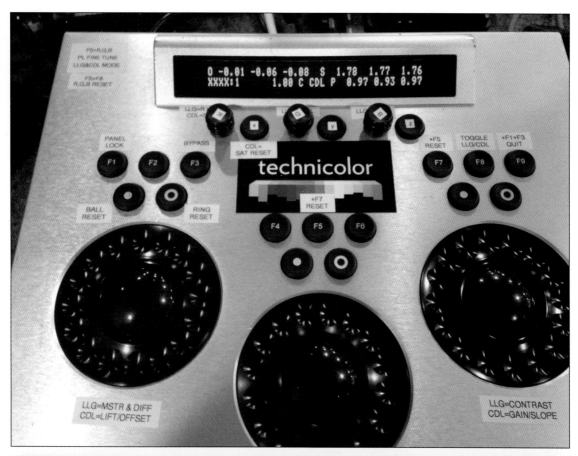

CALIBRATION LUTs

A *Calibration LUT* (sometimes called a display or monitor LUT) is one that compensates for deficiencies or differences in one or more monitors on the set. Of course it's possible to use individual controls on the monitors, but this can be time consuming and not as reliable depending on viewing conditions. They might also be used for scenes where several monitors appear in the scene and need to be matched up for the on-screen look.

WE ALREADY BAKED THIS TURKEY

Although it's rare, there is always a chance that a LUT might inadvertently be applied twice to the same footage; for example a Log to Rec.709 LUT is applied at the DIT cart and then through some

Figure 8.34. (Top) A proprietary system by Technicolor with ASC-CDL in use on the set. (Courtesy of DIT Evan Nesbit).

Figure 8.35. (Below) A closeup of the readings on the panel. (Courtesy of DIT Evan Nesbit).

image control & grading

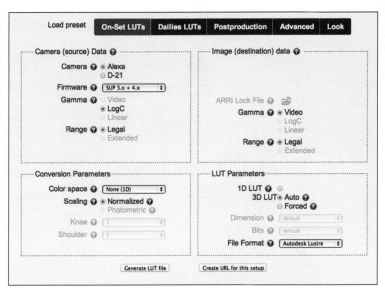

Figure 8.36. (Above) This Sony camera includes a selection for *MLUT*, which is a monitor viewing LUT. In this case, Rec.709 at 800% has been chosen for viewing on the set monitors.

Figure 8.37. (Right) The on-line *Arri LUT Generator*, available at Arri's website.

confusion, the same or a similar LUT gets applied again in post, or as Andy Shipsides puts it "We already baked this turkey." For this reason, many DITs maintain LUT reports which keeps track of what LUTs have been used on the footage. Usually these are just simple spreadsheets.

POYNTON'S FOURTH LAW

We must never forget that "technical" control is subservient to our decisions as artists. Getting things mathematically correct is never as important as telling a story that reaches people at the emotional level. Don't forget *Poynton's Fourth Law* — "After approval and mastering, creative intent cannot be distinguished from faulty production." Charles Poynton, color scientist/mathematician.

the DIT cart

THINGS TO THINK ABOUT IN PLANNING A CART

If you plan to own and operate a DIT cart, there are many things to take into account as you plan the rig. Remember that it will be more than just an equipment holder. It will also be your workspace, your office and your refuge for those inevitable long days on the set. It will also need to be adaptable for different jobs and new technology as it comes along. Some things to think about:

1. What are your transportation conditions? A van?, SUV?, car?, camera truck?
2. Need to travel by air sometimes?
3. What types of productions are you going to be working on? Features? Commercials? 3D? High speed? Multi-camera?
4. Will you be working on the set? Near the set? Off the set?
5. Will you be fairly static (as in long studio shoots) or moving many times a day?
6. Need to go up stairs or hills? Small elevators?
7. Studio conditions (level floors and loading docks) or locations (outdoors, hills, sand, gravel, etc.)
8. Will you be doing dailies? Transcoding? Monitoring the camera with a waveform monitor?
9. What happens when it rains on location? High winds?
10. Will you need a black-out tent or similar setup to give you good viewing conditions on daytime locations?
11. Will there always be AC power available or will you sometimes need battery power or your own putt-putt generator?
12. Real estate. Will you need a work area for a control surface, laptop or card readers? Will a digital loader be working alongside you?

OTHER CONSIDERATIONS

Do you want to set up a "mega-cart" that can handle anything you may encounter, or do you want to be able to change out equipment to suit the job? How often will you need to get inside the computer to make changes? Of course another factor is that equipment changes, is upgraded, needs repair or is replaced, so having the inner workings of your cart accessible is a key factor.

Some DITs reconfigure their setup for nearly every job; changing out PCI cards (such as a *Red Rocket*, for example), hard drives, connectors (such as fibre optic) and RAIDs depending on the type of cameras the job will use, whether the project is 3D, high speed, multi-camera, etc.

Cooling has always been an important factor for computer gear (including digital cameras) and the other side of that coin is that cooling generally creates noise. In some circumstances such as working at a desert location in mid-summer, some DITs even find it necessary to run small air conditioners to keep their computers and hard drives within a reasonable temperature range. Obviously, a rig like this is not going to be welcome near the set if they're recording sound — the audio people would forbid it. While a good deal of cooling capability and access can be accomplished with careful design of the layout and exterior of the cart (such as the removable sides on some carts), there are limits to what can be done.

MOBILITY

Obviously, the equipment is always going to need to travel to the set in some sort of van or truck and this is likely to be different for every job. Some DITs just require that the production company rent a truck to transport the gear; some own their own vans and some use space on the camera truck — something the audio folks have been doing for years with their sound carts. All this means that there has to be a way to get the gear on and off the vehicle — in many cases, especially with a van, this involves portable ramps, which are widely available. They come in types that include rigid, extra light weight and collapsible to make them easier to store. Large cube vans and trucks (such as a typical camera truck) will usually have a lift gate, which greatly simplifies loading and unloading. The size of the wheels is a big factor to consider: larger wheels make it easier to move on rough ground such as on location but might be difficult in a tight location.

Another consideration is whether or not air travel is going to be necessary. In this case, a cart that is designed to close up completely and ruggedly will be necessary, see Figure 9.15 for an example of an air shippable configuration.

Figure 9.1. (Left) DIT Mark Wilenkin runs some footage through *Assimilate Scratch* using the *Wrangler* by *1 Beyond*.

Figure 9.2. (Above) A *Codex Vault* data management system on top of a BigFoot cart. Under the laptop is the control unit for the *Dolby* monitor.

POWER

With the possible exception of downloading a few digital mags on a laptop during a less than full day shoot, you're always going to need a power supply of some sort to run your rig. While computers, hard drives and monitors don't use an enormous amount of power, they do consume their share of current. For years, sound recordists have used heavy duty batteries and DC to AC inverters to power their equipment when other power sources are not available. They often build their own by putting motorcycle batteries in small cases such as those from Pelican and others. One advantage is that DC tends to be "cleaner" than AC power, especially that from a generator.

AC POWER

The simplest way to get power is, of course, plugging into an AC power supply. Most film sets will have some kind of power: either in a studio, on location with a big generator for the lighting, a small putt-putt for just essentials; in extreme cases, a vehicle battery can run an inverter to convert DC to AC. Some trucks are equipped with an extra battery for just this purpose; obviously the danger of using your main vehicle battery to power your rig through an inverter is that you may not be able to start the vehicle later on.

Figure 9.3. (Top) A DP reviewing footage on a 3D feature. The carts are color coded for left and right stereo (3D) cameras.

Figure 9.4. (Below) A different view of the same 3D feature.

Another potential source of power is the RV that is sometimes used for makeup, hair and wardrobe or as a mobile production office. They usually have a small AC generator built in. If noise is a concern, which it is anytime audio is being recorded, the RV will be parked far away from the set, so you'll need plenty of stingers (extension cords) to reach your cart position. Don't count on the RV generator running unless you check with the AD to be sure. Most of the time, it will be running to power the air conditioning and hair dressers dryers and curling irons, but occasionally it will be turned off if the audio department complains. Never assume!

SMALL GENNI

Some DITs carry a small *putt-putt generator* to provide power for their equipment without relying on other sources (Figure 9.26); sometimes just as a backup. It is important to remember that the lighting crew often shuts down the main generator very soon after wrap is called or at the very least, an electrician anxious to get home might go around pulling out plugs without worrying too much about where they are going. The drawback of a generator is, of course, noise. Big movie generators are enclosed in heavy duty sound proof *blimped* housings and even then they are parked as far away from the set as is practical. Small unblimped putt-putt generators are going

Figure 9.5. (Top) Mobility and desk real estate are crucial. This cart has a slide out drawer for a laptop and a top that converts to a side desk to hold monitors and color control panel. (Courtesy of Bertone Visuals).

Figure 9.6. (Bottom) DIT Griff Thomas uses a compact portable system that fits on a dolly. (Courtesy of Griff Thomas).

to make you very unpopular with the sound department so they are really only useful if you are working off the set or if audio isn't being recorded at all; such as on a high-speed or product shot job. Don't think that a couple of *sound blankets* (as they are called on the East Coast) or *furny pads* (as they are called on the West Coast) are going to muffle the sound enough to keep the audio people from coming after you — they won't.

AC CABLES

In most cases, you're going to need to have plenty of AC stingers available for you own use. It's not wise to depend on the lighting department to supply you with them; as previously mentioned they may be pulling up stakes and driving away long before you've finished your work. AC *stingers* on the set are universally black and heavy gauge (#12 wire with double jacketing), so if you use ordinary #14 or #16 orange extensions, they will stand out as being separate from the equipment used by the lighting crew which makes them less likely to get yanked by an overenthusiastic electrician and also less likely to accidently get loaded back onto the lighting truck at the end of the day.

the DIT cart

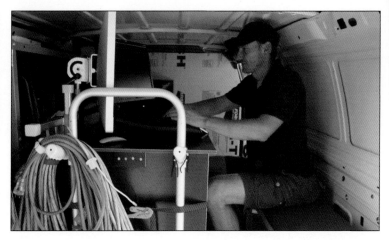

Figure 9.7. (Above) The new round Mac Pro calls for special mounting treatment, as in this solution by Doug Solis of BigFoot. (Courtesy Big-Foot Mobile Carts)

Figure 9.8. (Right) DIT Ben Hopkins in his van; he has devised a system that allows him to work inside the vehicle, where he has systems ready for additional cooling if needed, or he can roll the cart off and work on the set. Another clever aspect of his design is that he can drive home, park the van in the garage and let the computers continue doing time-intensive work such as transcoding.

BACKUP POWER

Even if you supply your own power and cables, something can always go wrong. An inattentive PA tripping over a cable could potentially result in the loss of all or most of the days footage! For this reason, every DIT cart always has a backup power supply which switches online instantaneously. Called *uninterruptable power supplies* (*UPS*), they are battery based and switch online instantly in the event of loss of the main power supply. Most units also include *surge protection* which is obviously of critical importance when dealing with equipment and precious data.

They are heavy and take up a good deal of space on the cart but they are an absolute requirement for any rig that deals with video data. They last long enough to save your data and shut down safely to avoid disaster. Computers that are processing files, card readers that are downloading and other similar gear will often experience fatal and unrepairable errors if there is a sudden unexpected loss of power or a surge. In some cases, entire video files can be lost; this can be disastrous when you're dealing with footage that took hours of hard work and large amounts of money to shoot.

VIDEO AND DATA CABLES

Besides power, you will need a variety of video and data cables. Especially if you are tethered to the camera for instantaneous viewing of the recording signal on the waveform and vectorscope, you will need video cables (Figure 9.12). These are almost always BNC connectors with coax cables and are sometimes provided by the camera crew but you should never depend on that — have backups — and it is certainly something to bring up at *the Meeting,* which should happen in preproduction and involve the DP, line producer or production manager, the DIT, first AC and editor or post production supervisor. These meetings have been known to save the production thousands of dollars and the lack of them has sometimes led to mistakes, confusion and large unnecessary expenditures to make corrections in post that you could have easily avoided with some preproduction coordination and planning. On commercials and smaller projects, an exchange of emails or phone calls may take the place of a sit-down meeting.

BNC video cables are important and as they are frequently a problem, backups are necessary. They might be provided by the camera department but most likely the camera crew is only going to have the length of cables to serve their own needs.

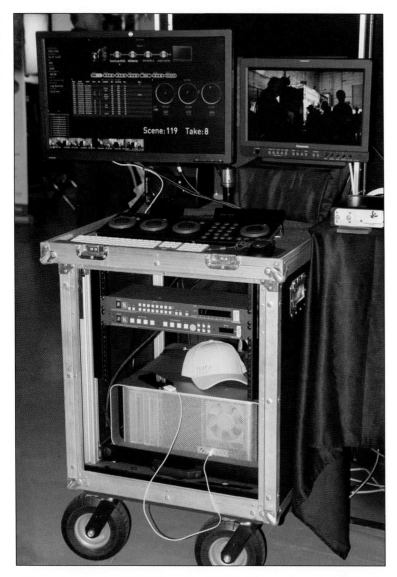

Figure 9.9. A *ColorFront* grading system for use on the set. Turning the Mac Pro sideways makes it *rack mountable.* Many carts incorporate standard 19″ racks for equipment mounting.

You may also need *USB* (2 or 3), *eSATA*, *Firewire* (400 or 800), *Ethernet*, *Thunderbolt* or *fibre optic* cables depending on your equipment. One rule of thumb in video — if something stops working or gets glitchy, the cable and connections are the first things to check. Wiggling the switch may work with electrical cables, but with video and audio connectors, making sure it is securely plugged in is a better idea. Unplugging and replugging will at least assure you that the connector is solidly seated, especially if the cart has been subjected to vibration from being transported or moved from set to set. The same applies to *PCI* cards as well, even though inside a computer or extension chassis. Backups, backups, backups when it comes to cables and connectors!

MOVING AROUND ON THE SET

Beyond just getting to the location as we previously discussed, you need to think about moving around once there. It might be a single location (warehouse, hospital, office building, house) but there might be many different sets within that building. Are there elevators or stairs? Is the second set up a hill, maybe over a gravel drive-

Figure 9.10. (Above, top) Portable light weight ramps make it easy to get the cart into a van, as here in Ben Hopkins' setup.

Figure 9.11. (Above) A drawer specifically made for safely housing a monitor during transport.

Figure 9.12. (Right, top) It's important to have plenty of cables, not only to reach remote places but also as backups; faulty cables are a frequent source of failure.

Figure 9.13. (Right, below) *DIT House* in LA has a number of different carts they use and rent including this large one fully outfitted. The computer is still inside its shipping case.

way? These are things to think about particularly as you select the type of wheels for your cart. It also includes a bicycle type locking hand brake on the handle for better control. For many years, the sound department has made arrangements to park their audio cart on the camera truck, but don't assume that there will be room or that they can accommodate you; however it never hurts to ask.

One thing is universal on sets — everything needs to move fast. If your rig is difficult and slow to move, it's going to be a problem. This is also something to keep in mind when you consider if you need to ask for a digital utility or video utility person on your team; they will be able to help you get around more efficiently, especially when it comes to wrangling all your power and video cable.

FAILOVER

Failover is just another form of backup. For example, many DITs have two computers on their cart; the second one might be used for separate tasks such as transcoding but it also is ready to perform as a failover backup — it can be used as the main computer if the first one fails in some way.

Figure 9.14. (Above) DIT Von Thomas with some key accessories: a bag of BNC cables and a box of every possible type of video connector.

Figure 9.15. (Left, top) A clamshell design and detachable wheels make this cart air shippable for remote locations.

Figure 9.16. (Left, below) A minimized DIT rig mounted on a single shorty C-stand. Very compact and clever, but moving to the next set might be a bit more complicated than with a wheeled rig.

Figure 9.17. (Right, top) Because viewing conditions are critical, DITs often work in a blackout tent on exterior locations. An ordinary white tent would be of little use in these situations as it would cause reflections on the monitors. (Courtesy of Musitelli Film and Video).

Figure 9.18. (Right, below) A well organized cart used by *Swiss Filmmakers*. It has Red camera card readers, a compact flash card reader, RAID, backup power supply and transfer hard drives. At the top of the standard rack mount that holds the shelves is a panel of European style power plugs; on top are a laptop and an iPad. This unit uses square hole rack mount rails. (Courtesy of Swiss Filmmakers).

filmmaker's guide to digital imaging

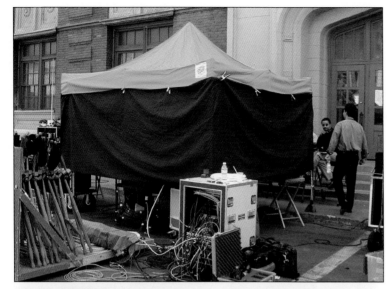

Figure 9.19. (Left, above) A combination DIT tent and video village on a backlot shoot. (Courtesy of DIT Bob Campi).

Figure 9.20. (Left, below) Doug Solis designed this system in a Pelican *Storm Case* for distant location work. The slide out drawer can hold card readers, a Mac Mini or other gear. The monitor is mounted in the case top and the surface can hold a laptop or keyboard. This one has a Red card reader built into the surface. (Courtesy BigFoot Mobile Carts).

RACK MOUNT

Many self-contained carts incorporate standard rackmount rails. This is a standardized system that has been around for quite some time, as shown by the original name for them, *relay racks*. They were first developed by AT&T to house banks of relays, before the phone system became largely digital. They are also called 19" racks based on the spacing of the mounting rails and thus the horizontal size of equipment or shelve that can be mounted in them; 19" translates to 48.26 centimeters. Equipment that fits the specifications (includ-

Figure 9.21. (Above) DIT Von Thomas with his "follow cart" which carries monitor air shipping cases and the all important comfortable director's chair for those long days on the set.

Figure 9.22. (Right, above) A foldout clamshell cart with a drawer for the new round Mac Pro. The top holds the monitor and lifts into position. On the lower right is a compartment for an extension chassis. (Courtesy BigFoot Mobile Carts).

Figure 9.23. (Right, below) The same cart as above but closed up to a compact size for travel. (Courtesy BigFoot Mobile Carts).

ing the size and spacing of mounting holes at the sides) is called *rack mountable*. The racks, have side rails with predrilled and tapped mounting holes (10-24 screws) are specified in terms of height, with the unit being "U." A 1U piece of gear is nominally 1.75 inches high but in practice is usually slightly less to allow some wiggle room. A 2U unit would be nominally 3.5" (88.9 mm). There also rails that have square holes for mounting without screws or bolts (Figure 9.18).

The standardization makes it easy to buy and install a great variety of commonly needed equipment such as power bars, shelves, power backup units and so on.

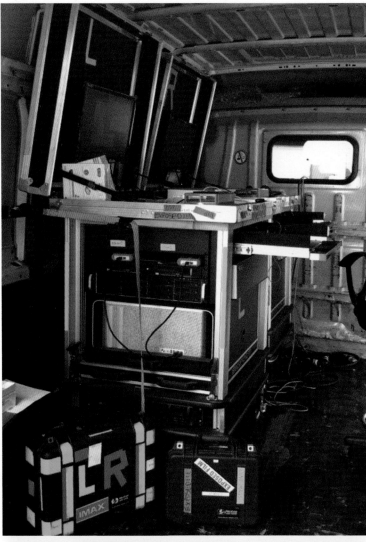

Figure 9.24. (Top) Two carts working inside a van on a 3D shoot. Note how everything is color coded for left and right sides of the stereo cameras for 3D. These carts have slide out shelves on the side for access to the computers (Courtesy of New Media Hollywood).

Figure 9.25. (Below) Another view of the twin DIT carts on a 3D shoot. One note: if you use gaffer tape or camera tape (which is just 1″ wide gaffer tape) for marking, don't leave it on for long periods of time or it will leave a sticky, gooey mess that is difficult to remove. (Courtesy of New Media Hollywood).

the DIT cart

Figure 9.26. (Top) On this studio shoot in Copenhagen, the DIT has set up right next to the set — upper right corner.

Figure 9.27. (Middle) This open cart design allows for easy access to components and cabling.

Figure 9.28. (Bottom). Because of the putt-putt generator, DIT Griff Thomas had to work away from the set. It's lonely at the top! (Courtesy of Griff Thomas).

Figure 9.29. (Above). *LightIron* makes and rents portable systems such as this one.

Figure 9.30. (Left, top) This BigFoot mega cart was designed for the *Universal Virtual Stage*.

Figure 9.31. (Left, middle) The mega cart in use at the *Universal Virtual Stage*. (Courtesy BigFoot Mobile Carts).

Figure 9.32. (Left, bottom). Many DITs consider two computers and at least two monitors the minimum.

Figure 9.33. (Above) A close-up of the two RedMag readers, a USB 3.0 port and slots for various types of flash memory cards. (Courtesy of Swiss Filmmakers).

Figure 9.34. (Right, above). This portable system by Swiss Filmmakers is shown here mounted on a dolly. Note the cooling vents on the lower left side. (Courtesy of Swiss Filmmakers).

Figure 9.35. (Right, below) A top view shows the Mac Book Pro, ingest ports, connectors and two "plug in" hard drives. (Courtesy of Swiss Filmmakers).

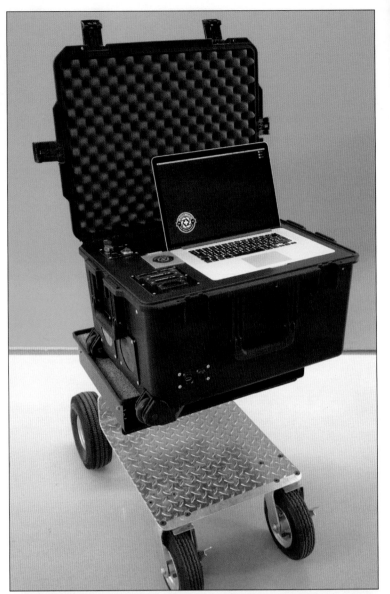

data management

Figure 10.1. (Top) The *Sony ASX card* with reader and onboard module.

Figure 10.2. (Above) SxS cards are flash memory with a transfer rate of 800Mb/s and burst transfer rates of up to 2.5Gb/s. They can be read directly in an ExpressCard slot which is a feature of many notebook computers or can be read with a special SxS card reader with a USB connection. In both cases the Sony driver must be installed. SxS Pro+ is a faster version designed for 4K video production with speeds of 1.3Gb/s and a maximum burst rate of 8Gb/s.

DATA MANAGEMENT

In principle, data management sounds simple: you download the camera media, put it on a hard drive and back it up. In reality, it is a process fraught with danger and rife with chances to mess up badly. Handling the recorded media is an enormous responsibility; a single click can erase an entire day's shooting!

The film industry has spent decades developing methodical and careful processes regarding the handling of exposed film stock; *loaders* (the member of the camera crew who loads the film mags with raw stock and then downloads the exposed footage) are trained in standard methods and procedures; they keep extensive standardized paperwork and prepare the film in a prescribed way for delivery to the film lab, which in turn keeps a thorough paper trail of every roll of film. With digital video, in some ways the job is made more difficult by the fact that we are dealing entirely with computer files. If the DIT is not handling it the crew member who does this is titled *Loader* (the official term) but sometimes called the media manager, data wrangler or any one of a number of similar terms, sometimes depending on what area of the US or what country you are in.

BASIC PRINCIPLES

Certain core principles apply:

- Cover your rear.
- Have a standard procedure and be methodical.
- Maintain all logs.

Let's talk about these in detail.

COVER YOUR REAR

When everything is going OK, people rarely even notice what the Loader is doing; it seems routine and automatic. When something does go wrong, the entire production can turn into a blame machine. You don't want to be the person who ends up bearing responsibility for a major disaster. The most important protection against this is, of course, to not screw up, but it is also important to be able to demonstrate that it wasn't you. Film camera assistants have a long standing tradition of immediately and unreservedly owning up to mistakes they make: DPs, ADs and directors respect them for this. However, if it really wasn't you that messed up, you need to have the procedures and paperwork to show it.

Some people interpret this rule as just being "avoid blame." That's not the point at all. The real issue is make sure nothing goes wrong so that there is no blame to go around. Protect the production from mistakes and you'll be hired again and recommended to others. If you do screw up but immediately own up to it, the DP and production will still know that you are someone who can be trusted as part of the production process: mistakes happen — the point is to fix them and prevent them from happening again.

STANDARD PROCEDURES

As camera assistants have learned over the decades, the number one way to ensure against mistakes is to have a methodical and organized way of doing things and *then do it the same way every time*. Observe any good crew of camera assistants working: there is almost a ritualistic aura to the way they work. They are also very focused and attentive to every detail at all times. Their repetitive actions are practiced and reliable. Their procedures are standardized industry-wide.

FNF LOG 0926														
CARD	DATE	FOLDER	CAM	DL#	FILE	SIZE	CARD	DESCRIPTION	MASTER	✓	SHUTTLE	✓	TOTAL GB	NOTES
P2	9/26/1	FNF 0926	F	01	0001FI	4.26 GB	001	STRATEGY	MASTER 01	✓	SHUTTLE 01	✓	JA	48.34
			F	01	0002NG	4.26 GB	001	STRATEGY	MASTER 01	✓	SHUTTLE 01	✓	JA	
			F	01	0003YU	4.26 GB	001	STRATEGY	MASTER 01	✓	SHUTTLE 01	✓	JA	
			F	01	0004QY	4.26 GB	001	STRATEGY	MASTER 01	✓	SHUTTLE 01	✓	JA	
			F	01	0005VE	4.26 GB	001	STRATEGY	MASTER 01	✓	SHUTTLE 01	✓	JA	
			F	01	0007CI	4.26 GB	001	STRATEGY	MASTER 01	✓	SHUTTLE 01	✓	JA	
			F	01	0008GE	4.26 GB	001	STRATEGY	MASTER 01	✓	SHUTTLE 01	✓	JA	
			F	01	0010N0	4.26 GB	001	STRATEGY	MASTER 01	✓	SHUTTLE 01	✓	JA	
			F	01	0011UY	4.26 GB	001	STRATEGY	MASTER 01	✓	SHUTTLE 01	✓	JA	
			F	01	0012L2	857.3 MB	001	STRATEGY	MASTER 01	✓	SHUTTLE 01	✓	JA	
			F	01	000961	4.26 GB	001	STRATEGY	MASTER 01	✓	SHUTTLE 01	✓	JA	
			F	01	000637	4.26 GB	001	STRATEGY	MASTER 01	✓	SHUTTLE 01	✓	JA	
P2	9/26/1	FNF 0926	E	01	0001GA	370.1 MB	007	STRATEGY	MASTER 01	✓	SHUTTLE 01	✓	JA	48.54
			E	01	0003P8	4.26 GB	007	STRATEGY	MASTER 01	✓	SHUTTLE 01	✓	JA	
			E	01	0004EP	4.26 GB	007	STRATEGY	MASTER 01	✓	SHUTTLE 01	✓	JA	
			E	01	0005L8	4.26 GB	007	STRATEGY	MASTER 01	✓	SHUTTLE 01	✓	JA	
			E	01	0006F5	4.26 GB	007	STRATEGY	MASTER 01	✓	SHUTTLE 01	✓	JA	
			E	01	0007LL	4.26 GB	007	STRATEGY	MASTER 01	✓	SHUTTLE 01	✓	JA	
			E	01	0008E8	383.4 MB	007	STRATEGY	MASTER 01	✓	SHUTTLE 01	✓	JA	
			E	01	0009RZ	2.78 GB	007	STRATEGY	MASTER 01	✓	SHUTTLE 01	✓	JA	
			E	01	0010NR	4.26 GB	007	STRATEGY	MASTER 01	✓	SHUTTLE 01	✓	JA	
			E	01	0011BB	4.26 GB	007	STRATEGY	MASTER 01	✓	SHUTTLE 01	✓	JA	
			E	01	0012QU	4.26 GB	007	STRATEGY	MASTER 01	✓	SHUTTLE 01	✓	JA	

Figure 10.3. DIT Jillian Arnold keeps highly detailed logs for data management. The column labels: *Card* refers to the source (P2 cards in this case).

Date is day of the shoot. *Folder* refers to the parent folder which is in turn labeled with the *Production Name* and *Date*. *DL#* is the chronological download order of that particular card. File is the file name which most cameras generate automatically. *Description* refers to the segment of the show.

Master lists what *Master Drive* the material is ingested to. *Check* is a way to verify that the file made it onto that drive.

Shuttle describes which *Shuttle Drive* the files was transferred to and the check box is for verification. JA are her initials. *Total GB* is the total card/folder size. *Notes* is self-explanatory. She emails this report every night to the producer and post production supervisor. At end of shooting she sends a final comprehensive report.

Jillian's philosophy is "keep the process pure, time stamp everything and be obsessive about the procedures. Producers need to understand that it's a special skill set like loading mags is. You don't just trust anyone with your fresh footage."

Maintain Your Logs

Film camera assistants have quite a few forms that need to be filled out and kept up to date: camera reports, film stock inventories, camera logs and so on. In the digital world, we are lucky that a great deal of this work is done by the camera and the various software applications we use immediately after the camera. Most downloading apps (such as *Shot Put Pro*, *SilverStack*, *Double Data* and others) also create logs that can track the files. Many Loaders also maintain separate logs either handwritten or more commonly as spreadsheets. An example of this type of log prepared by Jillian Arnold is shown in Figure 10.3.

PROCEDURE — BEST PRACTICES

By far the biggest danger is accidently erasing data which has no backup — this fear hangs over any operation where media is handled. Practices vary between different data managers and may be adapted or changed for various productions if the producer or insurance company requires certain procedures but they all have one basic goal: ensuring the safety of recorded data by clearly marking what media is empty and what media has recorded data on it.

One fundamental principle is that there should be one and one only person on the set who is allowed to format the media. This addresses the most basic of all dangers in digital workflow — being absolutely and unfailingly sure that the data has been downloaded and backed up and so it is safe to format. You certainly don't want to have conversations on set like "Is this ready to format? I thought Danny already did that?" There is no room for uncertainty. Designating

Figure 10.4. DITs and Loaders need to be able to handle a variety of media. This Qio card reader can download several types of cards. Readers may also be needed for specific cameras — these may be rentals or may be owned by the DIT as part of the package.

data management

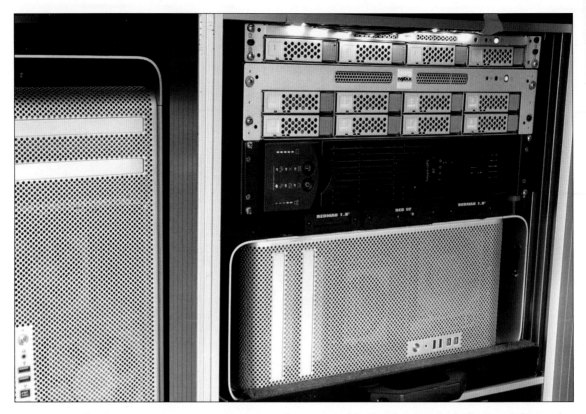

Figure 10.5. The "business" section of Von Thomas' DIT cart includes a large RAID for data ingest and management. He also sometimes networks his Mac Book Pro laptop as well for it's Thunderbolt capability.

one person to be responsible for formatting helps keep this under control. It is not the entire solution of course; a rigid adherence to a standardized procedure is necessary also, just as camera assistants have always done.

LOCKED AND LOADED

One typical method is for the second AC to remove the media (whether SSD or card) from the camera and immediately engaging the *record lock* tab (if there is one). It is delivered to the DIT or Loader locked. After downloading, it is returned to the AC with the record lock still engaged. This way *only* the AC (the designated formatter, in this case) is authorized to disengage the lock, put the media back in the camera and format the card. This is one method only and different DITs and camera crews will have their own way of doing this.

Naturally there are variations on this procedure, such as when the camera crew doesn't want to take the time to format media. This varies by the type of camera you are using. For example, it is very quick and simple to format a drive with the Alexa; on the other hand, formatting media for the Phantom takes quite a bit of time. What is important about this process is not so much who does it as it is that it be an established procedure understood by everyone on the crew and that it be religiously observed at all times: any deviation from procedure is always flirting with danger. Remember the basic religion of being a camera assistant: establish procedures and do it the same way every time — be methodical!

SIGNALS — DISASTER PREVENTION

Without a doubt, the greatest fear is that someone might erase/ format a card or hard drive that has footage on it that has not been stored elsewhere. There is no DIT, loader or camera assistant on

Figure 10.6. A *Sony F3* with a *Ki Pro* mounted between the body and the battery. (Courtesy of Aja).

earth that has not had this nightmare. The protection, as always, is to develop procedures, make sure the whole crew knows what they are and then stick to them.

Is this card ready for formatting? There are many systems but perhaps the most reliable is to use tape. Typically, green means "It's OK to format." Say something like "This drive is ready for formatting." Red tape means "Not Ready for format." Keep the red tape on it until you are absolutely sure it is finished and you have two tested backups. Use paper tape for marking cards and SSDs, not camera tape or gaffer tape. Camera tape can leave a sticky gum residue on the media and who wants to stick that into a camera? There are no hard and fast rules; it is whatever the crew agrees on. The important thing is consistency and communication. Many people make it a practice to not only mark the cards but to add a verbal signal as well, such as "these cards are ready for formatting." Always putting them in a consistent location is important too. This might mean a small box on the DIT cart or something similar.

Always Scrub

Make it a habit to always *scrub through* (preview) the footage, even if only at high speed. A visual check is the only way to be certain the footage is good. You can also be watching for other problems — if you catch something no one else noticed, be sure to let them know. It is always best for a production to know about problems right away, when a reshoot is not a huge problem, as it will become once they have wrapped that location or set.

Do not scrub through the original media. This has two potential problems: one, having done that, you may think that you have downloaded the footage and two, it is what really gets downloaded to the hard drives that matters. It is usually best to use the camera companies software to preview/scrub the footage. This is going to have the least potential for problems. If you use some other software to preview and something doesn't look right, then you can't be sure if it is a problem with the footage or if there is just a playback issue and the material is fine.

Download>Scrub to check>Mark as ready for format.

Figure 10.7. *Double Data* takes a different approach to data ingest. It is designed to manage your data all the way through the process.

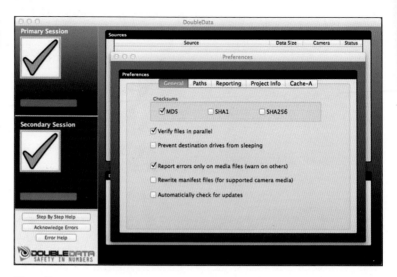

THREE DRIVES

Most DITs consider three copies of the footage to be a minium. Hard drives die; files get corrupted. Backups are your only protection. Hard drives that are used to transfer the footage to post, archives or the production company are called *shuttle drives*. As an example, the hard drives might be:

- One for the editor.
- One backup for the client/producer.
- One backup for you (so you can be the hero when something bad happens).

An alternate process might be:

- All files on the DIT RAID drives.
- A shuttle drive of all files delivered to the producer.
- A shuttle drive of all files delivered to the post house.

The VFX people may also need files delivered. Obviously, the DIT can erase all drives on the DIT cart once the shuttle drives have been delivered to the producer/post house and checked, but many DITs prefer to keep the files live on their hard drives as long as possible (meaning until the next job) just as an emergency backup.

To be prudent, production and the post house should also make backups of all files as soon as they are received; it's just common sense. Archiving to LTO tapes as soon as possible is a sensible method of protecting against unforeseen disasters. We'll talk about LTO tapes in a moment.

Some productions do not allow the media to be erased until it has been confirmed by the post house; often this is a requirement of the insurance company. Some insurance companies will not give clearance to format the media until it has been transferred to LTO tape and stored in a vault. Obviously this requirement has a big effect on the amount of media (SSD drives, Phantom mags, compact flash, SxS cards, and so on) that need to be ordered and also has meaning for the planning of the DIT/post workflow. This again points to the importance of having a pre-production planning meeting which gets all of the parties together to work out the details of how it's going to be done. Since downloading drives takes time, some DITs request that they get the media before it is filled up completely. Some crews make it a practice to only fill up drives half way for this reason.

Figure 10.8. Pomfort's *Silverstack* offers a wide variety of features in addition to ingest: a clip library, transcoding, native playback, metadata search, user metadata and even clipping warnings and focus assist for help when viewing on small screens. It also generates reports as XML, HTML or PDF as well as *Final Cut Pro* XML files.

DO NOT DRAG AND DROP

One principle that is universal no matter what procedures are in play: never "drag and drop." Anyone who uses computers is familiar with the idea of grabbing a folder or file with the mouse and dragging it to a new location. It's simple enough but for a couple of reasons, it is to be avoided with video files. Some cameras produce video files that are far more complex than just "file.one, file.two" etc. There are often associated files in addition to the video clips.

CRC

What is missing when you merely drag-and-drop files is a confirmed check that the copied files exactly match the originals. One method of doing this is *CRC — Cyclic Redundancy Checking*. It sounds complicated, but it's actually simple in principle. Copied files are divided into predetermined lengths that are divided by a fixed number, which results in a remainder, which is appended onto the copied file. When the check is performed, the computer recalculates the remainder and compares it to the transmitted remainder. If the numbers do not match, an error is detected and a warning displayed.

For example, *Double Data* remarks that a prominent feature of their data management software is that a big green check mark appears on screen when the files have been transferred and thoroughly double-checked for accuracy. There is a great value to this. Remember that working on the set is pressured, hectic, chaotic and often involves insanely long hours. There is a great value in having your software give you a clear and understandable signal that all is OK. All professional ingest software includes CRC.

OTHER FILE COPY CHECKS

A far simpler method is *file size comparison*, which is self explanatory — the process merely compares the size of the original file and the copied file — it may be OK for a quick and dirty look but not nearly accurate enough for real verification. Two other widely used methods are *MD5 Checksum* or *Message Digest 5*; it's similar to CRC but a bit more complex. It is an algorithm which creates an alphanumeric string associated with each file that is as unique as a fingerprint. It is commonly used when downloading files from the internet; by comparing the MD5 checksum you calculate against the published checksum of the original file, you can have some assurance that the file that arrives on your hard drive has not been tampered with in some way. This also applies to copying video/audio files. If the two MD5 checksums match up, there is little chance that fatal errors have crept in during the copy process.

Another method is *byte verification,* which takes file size comparison to the next level — it compares every byte of data to make sure the copy exactly matches the original.

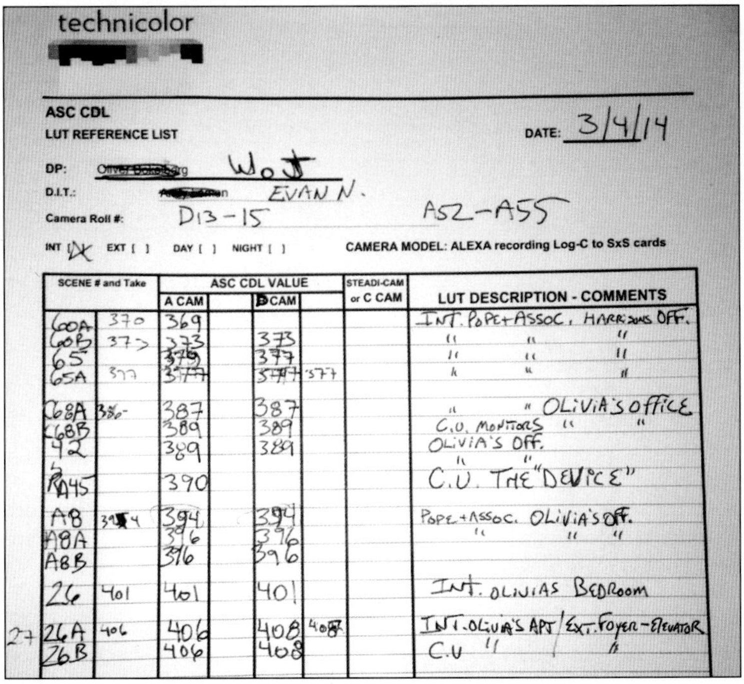

Figure 10.9. A DIT's LUT log sheet for a TV show. Note that in addition to listing scene and take numbers it also has columns to record ASC-CDL numbers for three cameras. (Courtesy of DIT Evan Nesbit).

LOGS

Logs are something you normally don't think about much but they can be very important. Most professional file copy applications can generate logs which record every detail of the copy and backup process: date, time, file size, name of card and so on. Some logs can be remarkably verbose, recording details that you might think you'll never need; however it is this thoroughness that may save your career some day. These are the kinds of things that really differentiate the professional from the wannabe.

Logs usually only come into play when there is a corrupted or lost file; when this happens, it can often turn into a blame game and for a DIT or Loader to lamely say "I'm pretty sure I copied that file," just isn't good enough — the log is your backup and paper trail. In a professional situation, it is critical to have the software generate logs and that you keep them or to make your own. To have the download software do it usually involves a selection in the preferences section of any application, you need to select that the software will generate the logs and that you keep track of what folder they are kept in. You'll want to backup this folder and in many cases, provide copies of the logs to the editor, the producer or even the insurance company. Beyond the computer files downloading software generates, most DITs and loaders maintain separate logs of all operations, either handwritten or on a computer, tablet or even smartphone, as in Figure 10.3.

FILE MANAGEMENT

Download everything — this is crucial; so make sure you have plenty of hard drive space at the start of the shoot (see the hard drive storage calculators elsewhere in this chapter). Picking clips can be dangerous unless you have a specific plan or instructions to dump rejects — in general, it's a very dangerous idea. Retain files structure! Don't change file names or locations, particularly with R3d files. Red files are a good example of why this is important. Notes can be kept in "Read Me" text files.

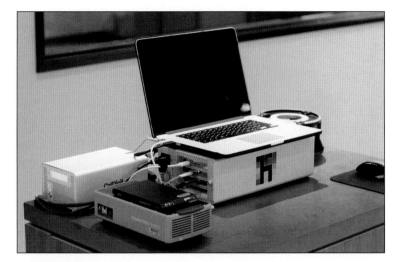

Figure 10.10. 10Gig ThunderStation for Phantom, built by DIT Ben Hopkins. It features a 3TB internal RAID-5 which is capable of downloading a 512GB Phantom mag in 35 minutes or downloading and verifying a 512GB Phantom mag to two external shuttle drives in just 49 minutes. It runs on AC or DC and has the option to add Thunderbolt external RAID storage. (Courtesy DIT Ben Hopkins).

FILE NAMING

It is crucial to establish a consistent file naming convention for every project. The cameras themselves generate file names that are orderly and useful. In the end, the editor is likely to have the final say on file naming as they are the ones who have to deal with the long-term consequences of how the files are named and organized. Again, this shows the importance of that pre-production meeting, phone calls or exchange of emails — the editor and VFX people need to be part of that conversation.

DOWNLOAD/INGEST SOFTWARE

Fortunately, there are several software applications that have been developed specifically for downloading and backing up video/audio files within the specific needs of on-the-set film production for features, commercials, music videos and other types of professional production. In some cases, they can also transcode the files. All of these applications offer redundancy checking; they simply wouldn't be professional use without it. They also offer a range of choices for these checks. Most also allow naming of reels/mags and automatically incrementing those numbers with each download. Some DITs use scripts in Apple's *Terminal* to handle download tasks.

SHOTPUT PRO

This application is widely used for downloading recorded media on the set. It is specifically designed for this purpose and offers all the options a Loader or DIT will normally need: multiple copies to different hard drives, logs and several different methods of file verification. Versions are available for both Mac and Windows operating systems. The company describes it like this: "ShotPut Pro is an automated copy utility application for HD video and photo files. ShotPut Pro is the industry de-facto standard off-loading application for professionals. The simple user interface and robust copy speeds make it indispensable for today's tapeless HD workflows."

SILVERSTACK

Pomfort's *Silverstack* performs media download but also quite a bit more. Silverstack can ingest all camera media types and all file formats. It can do checksum-verified, high-speed backup to multiple destinations. According to Pomfort "Ingesting source material and creating backups of media from a digital film camera is a repetitive, but responsible task. This process just got a whole lot easier, faster

Figure 10.11. (Top) A *Codex Vault* accepts many types of camera media and can record to LTO tapes among other types of outputs. (Courtesy of Codex).

Figure 10.12. (Below, right) A *Codex* record module mounted on a *Canon C500*. (Courtesy of Codex).

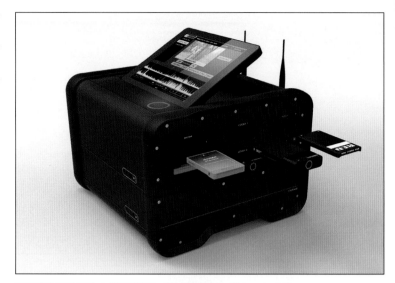

and more secure thanks to Silverstack's accelerated copy feature. Combining the parallel ability to read, verify and write in one operation and leveraging the full bandwidth of your hardware allows you to copy a large amount of files conveniently and securely."

Additionally Silverstack has a full featured clip library and can do transcoding/export, QC (quality control) and native playback (for certain cameras). Finally it can output customized reports for production and post-production.

DOUBLE DATA

Originating as *R3D Data Manager* and its companion *Al3xa Data Manager*, *Double Data* (which combines the two) approaches data management with a definite philosophy. In addition to standard copying with verification, it is capable of what the company calls *Automatic Multiple Sessions Management* which they describe like this: "Double Data takes a different approach to on-set and post data management than other software. The idea is that your workflow involves, or can be split up into, phases. The first phase would be to get your shots off the original camera media to a high-speed RAID or similar device. From there you will copy to slower speed destinations for redundant copies or shuttle/transfer drives.

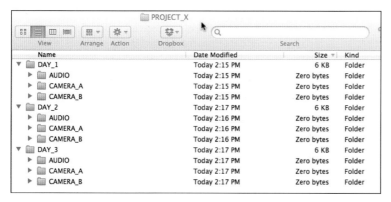

"Double Data has two 'sessions', the idea being that you will quickly offload files in the first session to a primary RAID, then in the second session copy from that primary RAID to other slower destinations. Double Data will keep track of where each camera media is in the process and automate your sequential backups for best performance, for example only copying things in the second session when the first is standing by. Of course, if you would rather just copy to all your destinations at once without using the second session, that is also possible to do. Double Data can write a single camera media to four destinations simultaneously."

It also performs what they call *Intelligent Error Reporting* — "*Double Data* knows the difference between an error in a MOV or R3D file and an error in a XML or RMD file. One is expected to change, one should never change. *Double Data* will warn when non-essential files have changed, but error when essential files don't match." The software can also do some types of recovery for accidently deleted data.

PROPRIETARY DATA MANAGEMENT SOFTWARE

All camera companies make some sort of file transfer software for the types of media their cameras use and they make this software available for free download. Arri, Sony, Red, Canon, Panasonic, Black Magic and others have software applications with various capabilities. Some are basic data management and some, such as RedCine X, have color correction and transcoding as well.

So clearly, opinions about the job and duties of the DIT position are varied and sometimes heated. It is not at all difficult to be a "file monkey," one of the ones who just know the rote mechanical aspects of "take card A and dump it to the hard drive and output a 4:2:2 Pro Res." Let's face it, a monkey could actually do that — it's really not that hard. OK, it would have to be a really smart monkey but we could get one of those.

So, we have seen the vast array of issues that affect the digital image. If you are one of those people who thinks that their only job is to take what the camera crews outputs and make backups and send files to post — well, then you are doomed to being one of those "file monkeys" as you may sometimes hear. It's a dead end job — hardly more than a PA with a laptop.

If, on the other hand, you aspire to be one of those higher end DITs who can work closely with a DP in creating a look, controlling the (multiple) cameras, and properly formatted dailies that shape ideas and then outputting the wide variety of files needed for the post production workflow, then you are on the road to being one of those truly in-demand DITs who work on the big shows and, frankly, pull down the big bucks.

Figure 10.13. (Top) The *Samurai* on-board recorder from *Atomos*. Here it is also being used as a monitor for the camera assistant. (Courtesy of Atomos).

Figure 10.14. (Above) The *Odyssey 7Q*, features recording of 4K RAW, DNxHD and other formats onto a removable SSD; it also supports LUTs. As options, it can also record ArriRAW, Canon 4K RAW and Sony RAW. It is also an OLED monitor which can display either in Rec.709 or DCI-P3 as well as various waveforms and scopes. (Courtesy of Convergent Design).

Figure 10.15. (Left) A folder of dailies for a two camera shoot. Careful labeling of folders and files is essential for good data management. Since separate audio is going to be recorded, it is not specific to either camera as they are both synched with the same slate. If they were operating separately, such as a B Unit, then that audio would require a separate folder.

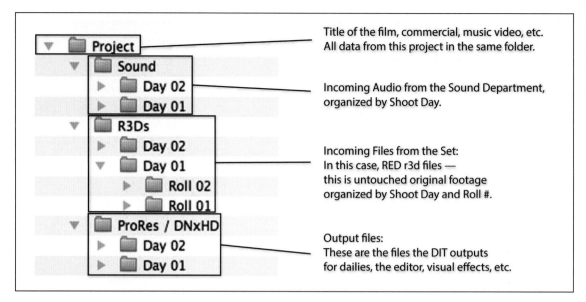

Title of the film, commercial, music video, etc. All data from this project in the same folder.

Incoming Audio from the Sound Department, organized by Shoot Day.

Incoming Files from the Set: In this case, RED r3d files — this is untouched original footage organized by Shoot Day and Roll #.

Output files: These are the files the DIT outputs for dailies, the editor, visual effects, etc.

Figure 10.16. Two days of shooting on a Red, arranged in separate folders for audio, R3Ds and ProRes/DNxHD. Keeping the data organized is an important duty of the Loader or DIT.

EXTERNAL RECORDERS

Most cameras are engineered to record clips internally, although not all of them will record their full resolution in RAW form internally. The original Red, for example, recorded onto Compact Flash cards — just as most high end DSLRs do with RAW files. Sony cameras have long used *SxS cards* which replaced the original XDCam solution of recording onto Blu-Ray DVD. Resolution and frame rates sometimes exceed the capacity of Compact Flash and even SxS cards. The Alexa is a good example of this—only Quicktime files are recorded directly on the camera — directly onto the dual SxS cards which can easily be downloaded onto a laptop and external drives. In order to record ArriRAW files, an off-board recorder is needed. The *Codex* is produced specifically for this purpose and is engineered to be an integral part of the camera. It is fairly small and light and even Steadicam operators find it easy to work with. As with many things in the digital post-HD world, it's new and developing and practically a full time job to keep up with new workflows.

CINEDECK

What is *Cinedeck*? According to the company that makes them: "It is an extremely capable, upgradable, highly rugged, portable, direct-to-disk video recorder designed and built by cinematographers for cinematographers.

It is compatible with HDMI/HD-SDI/LAN cameras and records to the widest choice of formats including Uncompressed 4:4:4 or 4:2:2 HD, Apple ProRes, Avid DNxHD (wrapped in MXF or MOV), Avid Meridien JFIF, and CineForm™ Digital Intermediate files in MOV format via HDMI and single/dual link 3G HD-SDI. It also records to the world's most popular camera and playback formats including AVC-Intra, XDCAM HD, and H.264. This gives you the fastest file-based workflow possible. It has a large 7" high-res preview/focus/playback monitor and physical button interface for all commonly used functions."

A Cinedeck unit combines the ability to monitor, record and play-back a wide variety of video types: ProRes (including 4:4:4:4), AVC-Intra, H.264, DPX, DNxHD, XDCam, DNG and others. The monitor includes waveform, vectorscope, histogram, clipping and edge focus assist. For playback it employs VTR (video tape recorder)

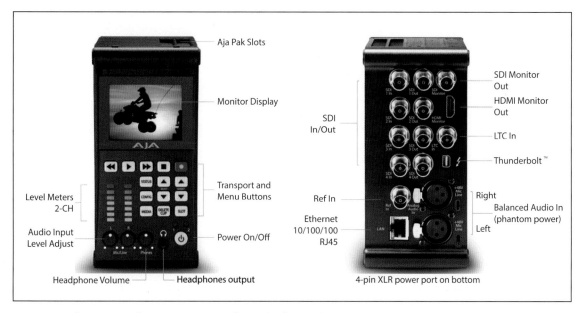

Aja Pak Slots

Monitor Display

Transport and
Menu Buttons

Level Meters
2-CH

Audio Input
Level Adjust

Power On/Off

Headphone Volume — **Headphones output**

SDI
In/Out

SDI Monitor
Out

HDMI Monitor
Out

LTC In

Thunderbolt ™

Ref In

Ethernet
10/100/100
RJ45

Right

Balanced Audio In
(phantom power)

Left

4-pin XLR power port on bottom

type controls on a touchscreen user interface which can also connect to an HD-SDI or HDMI display monitor. It can also perform real time up convert/down convert or cross convert between more than a dozen resolution/frame combination.

It is lightweight and highly mobile, an important consideration for many types of production — it is designed for the rigors of field production. It can also make footage immediately available for editing in Avid, Final Cut Pro, Adobe Premiere and Sony Vegas. Figure 10.19 and 10.20 shows the wide variety of connections it can make, including 3G HD-SDI, HDMI and LAN. It can be controlled via the touchscreen or via a remote system, including, if needed, jog/shuttle devices or traditional RS-422 VTR equipment interface.

Figure 10.17. Front and back of the *Ki-Pro Mini* by Aja. It has connections for SDI, HDMI, LTC timecode, Thunderbolt, audio and ethernet as well as a small monitor for playback. (Courtesy of Aja).

Ki-Pro

Ki-Pro is made by *Aja* pronounced (a-jay-a) and is a widely used external recorder. It records 10-bit Apple ProRes 422 which, says Aja "revolutionized how footage could be moved efficiently from production to editorial," and also DNxHD files. It has removable storage modules (most external recording system do, all of them

Figure 10.18. *CatDV Pro* is a file management and archiving application which features a wide array of methods to catalog, sort and search video files. It can also build timelines of selects for export as an XML to most major editing systems.

Figure 10.19. (Above) The back of a CineDeck RX recorder. (Courtesy of CineDeck).

Figure 10.20. (Right) A Thunderbolt RAID storage unit on the ingest cart. (Courtesy of DIT Evan Nesbit).

are basically solid state hard drives — SSDs). It does up/down and cross conversion between formats and also features SDI, HDMI and analog connections and also RS-422 VTR type control links. The Ki-Pro Mini can be mounted directly on the camera and the company makes a variety of accessories for this purpose.

OTHER ON-BOARD RECORDERS

There are several compact on-board recorders for camera output. Among these are the *Convergent Design Gemini 4:4:4:4* recorder which can handle *ArriRAW* (as an option), *Canon 4K RAW* and other formats. It records to removable *solid state hard drives (SSDs)*. It is small enough to be camera mounted and includes a small monitor for reviewing footage. A small adapter unit is used for downloading footage to hard drives at the DIT station.

CATALOGING SYSTEMS: CATDV PRO

A cataloging system is primarily designed for organizing a searchable index and is less concerned with how and where the material itself is stored. An example of this design is *CatDV Pro* (short for *Catalog of Digital Video*). This type of *DAM* (*Digital Asset Management*) gives the user great freedom, since it is designed to organize any type of content by using XML tags to point to the material. It never touches or changes the content itself and doesn't even care where that content resides, simply allowing the user to organize and search. It is a virtual library, a catalog describing content that can be located anywhere. This can be a great aid in controlling storage costs and physical management, as users do not require access to the actual library of content, because they have access to the virtual and proxy libraries. CatDV Pro interacts with non-linear editing systems, such as Final Cut Pro, allowing the user to find a group of clips and send them to an NLE for editing with the proxies. Two-way communication is also possible, so changes made in the NLE can be reflected back in the catalog metadata.

While CatDV is designed as a system separate from the storage media, there are tie-ins with archiving appliances such as LTO devices. Using these in concert, a complete DAM can be created. Due to its autonomous nature, CatDV is scalable from single user, to a workgroup of four to five people, to an enterprise-server of more

Figure 10.21. A shuttle drive for a TV show. Labeling is critical in data management. (Courtesy of DIT Evan Nesbit).

than 100 users, including the ability to allow remote access to web users. In the past, traditional DAM systems were expensive to start up and maintain, and needed specialized equipment and trained consulting staff. Such systems were always custom installations. CatDV, however, can be started minimally and scaled up as needed.

SONY XDCAM ARCHIVE

Unlike a cataloging system such as CatDV, the heart of an archive system is the content itself. It is primarily a content management system rather than a catalog with an archive component. An example of this is *Sony XDCAM Archive* (*XDA*). However, the system is much more flexible and universal than its name implies, since content can originate from many systems in various formats, including non-Sony formats. Content gets ingested into the XDA system for storage and proxy transcoding. The material maintains its original file structure and can be off-loaded again for access, and proxies are created to allow for searches and off-line use. XDA places media files onto XDCAM optical discs, which are then stored on physical shelves in an organizational system managed by the archive.

HARD DRIVES & RAIDS

In dealing with hard drives, whether spinning drives or solid state, it is important to remember that there are only two types of hard drives: those that have died and those that are going to die. This is what makes backups and redundancy so critical. The same applies to flash storage as well — media fails, it happens all the time. Expect it. Be ready for it. When you calculate how many hard drives you will need for a job, include some redundancy for potential drive failure.

RAID

Most DITs run *RAIDs* (*Redundant Array of Independent Disks*) for immediate storage of video that is downloaded from camera media. There are several reasons for this. They offer a speed advantage and have much greater capacity than a single hard drive is capable of but they also offer built-in back up – that is the redundancy in the name. Even if one of the drives fail, the RAID can continue to function and no data is lost.

TRANSFER/SHUTTLE DRIVES

At the end of the job, the files need to be delivered to the editor, producer, VFX house and other parties. For this purpose, *shuttle* or *transfer drives* are used. Since multiple copies of the day's footage are absolutely a must, these shuttle drives need not be RAID storage. However, many DITs keep the job on their RAID until they have

Figure 10.22. (Top) A RAID array on a DIT cart along with a Sony HDCam SR tape deck.

Figure 10.23. (Below, right) A drawer set up with foam padding for transporting hard drives. Leaving them in a RAID case might not offer sufficient protection during transport.

assurance that post-production, the producer or even the insurance companies have transferred the data to their own systems. Many DITs have achieved hero status by having these files available when production suffered some disaster and thought all was lost.

The DIT will advise production on which hard drives to buy, based on their own experience with reliability and failure rates. It may be necessary to remind production that saving a few bucks on cheaper hard drives is meaningless compared to the cost of lost data.

SHARED STORAGE

Shared storage is simply hard drives (usually a RAID) that can be accessed by one or more operators at the same time. It is essentially a file server. While it is generally not necessary on the set, it is very useful in larger post-production operations where the same files are being used for different processes at the same time.

HOW MUCH STORAGE DO YOU NEED?

Some things are unforgiveable on a film set. In digital filmmaking, they include running out of charged batteries and not having enough storage in the form of camera cards and hard drives. (The list is longer, of course, but these are the things that concern us here.)

How much on-board storage you need for the camera (whether they be P2, Compact Flash, SxS, SD cards, solid state hard drives, etc.) and hard drives for off-loading at the DIT cart depends on many factors: how many days of shooting, how many cameras, whether it's a feature, commercial, music video, industrial or documentary. Budget is always a consideration in film production, but it's more

Figure 10.24. RAID servers for shared storage mounted on a cart.

than just "how many hard drives is production willing to pay for?" There's a big trade off. If a production manager is complaining about the cost of buying hard drives or renting storage for the camera, it is often sufficient to ask them to compare this relatively minor cost with the huge cost that can be incurred by having the entire production come to a halt while the filled up camera cards or drives are downloaded and backed up, a process that can take a surprisingly long time; or to ask them to think about the unacceptable risk of not having all the data properly backed up. This is usually enough to convince even the most tight-fisted producer.

Some DITs have forms to fill out covering what the deliverables are going to be, how many hard drives are to be ordered, what file types and so on — getting it in writing is always the best idea and having the producer, editor and other key people sign off on it is a great way to prevent confusion and short-cut the blame game that sometimes follows a problem on the set.

Another factor in determining hard drive space for the DIT cart is formats and transcoding. In some cases, the media might be in a fairly compact codec to begin with; for example if the camera is recording H.264 or ProRes. At the professional level this is likely to be rare. In most cases, the camera will be shooting RAW and the files will be kept RAW for delivery to post. However, there might be transcoding to a more efficient format for dailies (such as H.264 for the director to review) or to the more space consuming DPX files. As always, a pre-production meeting or at least phone calls and emails are important to determine who needs what.

data management

●●●●○ AT&T 3G
9:26 AM
77%
0
1 Hours
2
3
8
9
10 Minutes
11
12
23.98 FPS
24
25
REDCode RAW 4K (4096x2048)
(Tap to Change Video Format)
1.26 TB
VideoStorage
Audio Settings
About

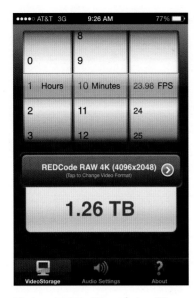

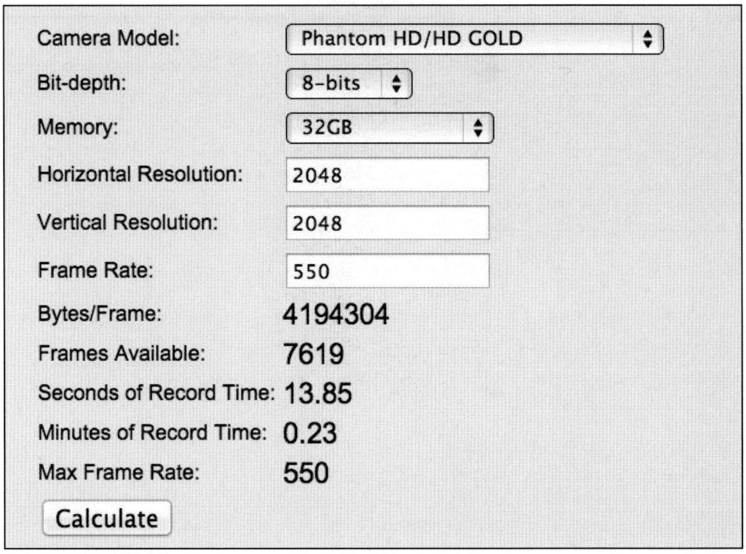

Camera Model:
Phantom HD/HD GOLD
Bit-depth:
8-bits
Memory:
32GB
Horizontal Resolution:
2048
Vertical Resolution:
2048
Frame Rate:
550
Bytes/Frame:
4194304
Frames Available:
7619
Seconds of Record Time:
13.85
Minutes of Record Time:
0.23
Max Frame Rate:
550
Calculate

Figure 10.25. (Above) An iPhone based calculator for video storage requirements; there are many available. Running out of hard drives is as unforgiveable in the digital age as it was to run out of film raw stock in a previous time.

Figure 10.26. (Right) A data calculator for Phantom high speed cameras. (Courtesy of Vision Research).

Frequently, this type of transcoding will take place off-site or perhaps overnight on the set. In any case, it is critical to have enough drive space to handle these transcoded files as well as preserving multiple copies of the original files. In the end, the only practical solution is to use a video space calculator. Fortunately, there are many excellent ones available, both online and as computer, phone and tablet apps. Figure 10.25 shows one of these calculators.

LONG TERM STORAGE

HD/UltraHD video generates very large files and the increased use of 4K, 5K and larger formats has exponentially increased the storage requirements. Keep in mind that for feature films, television shows and other projects, just preserving the final project output is not enough — there is often a need to preserve original footage as well over long periods of time.

Hard drives are not considered stable enough for long term storage and archiving. It is not merely a matter of hard drives failing — which they inevitably do, there is also the issue of the magnetic media "evaporating" — the data will gradually become unreadable over long periods of time at an expected rate of about 1% a year. There is also mechanical failure and environmental conditions. It is possible to deal with this by periodically recording the data onto new media, but this is obviously a stopgap measure at best.

Besides the stability issue there is another important consideration: future accessibility. The types of video formats that are either impossible or nearly impossible to play because there is no longer an installed base of equipment is a long one. Try to find a facility to play back 2" *Quad* tapes or 1" *Type C* video and you'll see the problem. The same applies to floppy disks or Zip drives and other types of computer storage — they are increasingly difficult to find, sometimes impossible.

At the present time, archived video is preserved in much the same way as film negative has been kept for some time: in temperature and humidity controlled fire-proof vaults. The most prominent storage location is a top-secret salt mine in Kansas. Well, it's not really top-secret but it is in Kansas. It has been used by the film industry for quite some time for vaulting negatives and prints and is now used also for video storage.

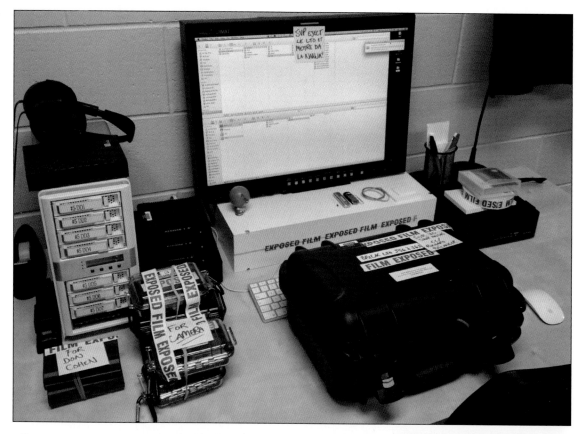

Strange as it may seem, some organizations actually use 35mm film as a long term storage medium: it is stable if properly stored and the technology to play it back is durable, simple, non-electronic and will probably be around for quite some time in one way or another. It is also very high in resolution and color reproduction capability. Methods for storing negative for long periods of time in temperature and humidity controlled fireproof vaults are a well known and trusted technology in the film production business. The *Irony Meter* is still being calibrated for such occasions.

LTO

Probably the archiving method that is closest to being an industry standard is *Linear Tape-Open (LTO)* shown in Figure 10.29. LTO uses magnetic tape for data storage. It was originally developed in the late 1990s as an alternative to the proprietary magnetic tape formats that were available at the time. LTO is now in its 6th generation, the primary difference between generations is the capacity of the tape cartridges

MOVING THE DATA

There are a number of different choices for ingesting and moving the data between hard drives and computers. Moving data as quickly as is safely practical is always a goal but it becomes particularly important in the time-intensive situations that are the norm on film sets. It is especially critical for DITs and Loaders who don't want to be waiting around for hours after the rest of the crew has wrapped for the day, and for producers who want to avoid paying overtime for them to be there.

Figure 10.27. (Above) A Qio card reader and fibre optic connection on a DIT cart.

Figure 10.28. (Top) The importance of proper labeling and an organized work station cannot be overemphasized. (Courtesy of DIT Sean Sweeney).

SDI STANDARDS				
Standard	**Name**	**Bit Rates**	**Color Encoding**	**Coax Distance**
SMPTE 259M	SD-SDI	270 Mb/s, 360 Mb/s	4:2:2 YCbCr	300 meters
SMPTE 292M	HD-SDI	1.485 Gb/s, and 1.485/1.001 Gb/s	High Def	100 meters
SMPTE 372M	Dual Link HD-SDI	2.970 Gb/s, and 2.970/1.001 Gb/s	High Def	100 meters
SMPTE 424M	3G-SDI	2.970 Gb/s, and 2.970/1.001 Gb/s	High Def	100 meters
TBD	6G-SDI	6 Gbit/s	4K	100 meters

Table 10.1. SMPTE standards for various type of SDI output.

INPUT/OUTPUT OPTIONS

Speed listed as "maximum" are in reality a theoretical maximum, in the real world, the actual transfer speeds are usually somewhat lower and may be more or less consistent. The length of the cable may also affect this. Most data formats have a maximum length of cable that can be relied on to deliver the data with minimal errors and dropouts. These maximum lengths are subject to a number of factors which may increase or decrease the usable length that may be used without significant problems. Clearly, when dealing with data on the set, there is little room for dropout and errors in data transmission. The choice of what transmission system to use is influenced by the types of equipment it needs to interface with as well as the DITs preferences. Some DITs have several systems on their cart to be able to adjust to different workflows and different situations.

FIREWIRE 400/800

Firewire 400 is now outdated as *Firewire 800* (IEEE 1394b) runs at a much faster data rate. The copper wire version is most familiar, but Firewire can run on fibre optic and coaxial cables as well. Firewire 800 has a maximum rate of 800 Mbit/s.

SATA/eSATA

SATA stands for *Serial Advanced Technology Attachment*; it is by far the most widely used connection for computer internal hard drives. eSATA is a variant used for external connections. It is a very fast type of connection; eSATA 600 is listed as "up to" 6Gbit/s. A newer version called SATA Express runs at 16 Gbit/s.

USB 3.0/2.0

USB tends to have fairly consistent data rates. USB is familiar to anyone who has used a desk computer or laptop as it is very widely used to connect keyboards, mice, and of course thumb drives or flash drives. USB 3.0 was a great leap forward in data speed with a jump from 480Mbit/s to 5Gbit/s.

THUNDERBOLT 1.0/2.0

As a primarily Apple product, *Thunderbolt* is spreading only slowly through the production world but it has enormous promise as a data management channel. Thunderbolt 2 is an impressive 20 Gbit/s.

SAS

SAS is *Serial Attached SCSI* (*Small Computer System Interface*). It replaces the old parallel SCSI which was phased out of use on hard drives several years ago. Physically, it is very similar to eSATA. SAS is listed at 6 Gbit/s or a newer version at 9.6 Gbit/s.

Figure 10.29. An LTO tape and recorder/reader. (Courtesy of DIT Helmut Kobler).

ETHERNET

GigaBit ethernet is widely used in home networks. It is important to note that it is GigaBit ethernet, not GigaByte. As you might guess, it moves data at a top rate of 1 gigabit per second; 10 Gigabit ethernet operates at 10 times that rate. 40 and 100 Gb ethernet also exist.

FIBRE CHANNEL

Historically, data transmission has operated over copper wire, but fibre optic is now becoming more available. It comes in two versions, which are capable of 6.8 Gbit/s and 12 Gbit/s. It is faster than copper wire, but so far the much higher cost has confined it primarily to large video facilities. However, it does get used on the set.

SDI, DUAL LINK, 3G, QUAD LINK, 6G

Serial Digital Interface runs at 1.485 Gbit/s for a single channel and 2.97 Gbit/s for *Dual Link SDI*. These aren't fast enough for many advanced applications. 3G-SDI is faster but to accommodate data hungry devices such as 4K cameras and monitors, higher rate standards are coming into use. 4K generally needs at least *6G-SDI* connection. *SDI* uses *BNC* connectors on the cables. BNC is by far the most widely used professional connector on cameras, monitors and other devices (Figure 10.31). There is also a mini-BNC connector for tight spaces on cameras.

DVI

DVI (Digital Visual Interface) is based on a common format for video known as *TMDS - Transition-Minimized Differential Signaling*. It consists of three serial data channels: red, blue, and green – plus a fourth channel carrying a *pixel rate clock* for the timing reference to keep the channels synchronized. Each DVI link is essentially a digitized RGB signal, with support for 8 bits per color.

To support different resolution requirements, the DVI standard provides for one or two video links per connector, known as single link or dual link. The maximum pixel rate for single link DVI is 165 MHz, corresponding to 4.95 Gbps, which is sufficient for 1920x1200 and HDTV 1080p/60, at a depth of 8 bits per channel. Dual link DVI handles pixel rates up to 330 MHz and resolutions as high as 3840x2400.

Figure 10.30. (Top) HDMI and mini-HDMI connectors.

Figure 10.31. (Above) BNC connectors are widely used on video equipment.

HDMI

HDMI (High Definition Multi-Media Interface) is a consumer interface, but out of necessity it is reluctantly used in some professional situations. The biggest problem is the plugs, which have no locking device and can easily be pulled or even fall out. All manner of camera tape, rubber bands and clips have been used to make these connections more secure. HDMI runs at 10.2 Gbit/s.

The HDMI interface includes the TMDS video functionality of DVI and extends it to carry digital audio and control information. It consolidates high definition video, audio, and control functions into a single connector and cable. The most common HDMI connector is the 19-pin Type A (Figure 10.30), which contains a single TMDS link. HDMI has gone through several revisions, with the latest on supporting up to 16 bits per channel, which is knows as *Deep Color.*

DISPLAYPORT

DisplayPort is a digital interface between sources and displays that is being positioned as a lower-cost alternate to HDMI for PC equipment manufacturers. DisplayPort uses a digital video transmission scheme that differs from TMDS and is therefore not directly compatible with HDMI and DVI. The 20-pin DisplayPort connector, with characteristics similar to the HDMI Type A and Type C connectors, can be used to carry HDMI signals, provided that the device supports this. For example, if a video source only has a DisplayPort connector, but also has HDMI signaling capability, then it is possible to use a DisplayPort-to-HDMI adapter to connect the source to an HDMI-equipped display.

DisplayPort video and audio signals are carried on four lanes/wires, with each lane running at either 1.62 Gbps or 2.7 Gbps for a maximum data rate of 10.8 Gbps.

workflow

THE DIGITAL CAMERA CREW

In digital production, the crew at the camera is not much different than it was when shooting on film — the idea that you need fewer people on a digital camera crew is largely a producer's fantasy: the *Director of Photography*, the *Camera Operator* (sometimes) and camera assistants, certainly a *First AC* and *Second AC*.

Also like a traditional film crew, there may be a *Loader*. In film-based production, this person loads the raw stock into the magazines and then downloads them and also maintains careful paperwork detailing the process. In digital, it's the same, except obviously the media is different: SSDs (solid state drives), compact flash cards, SxS cards, Red mags, Phantom mags, etc. They still maintain logs, although the forms are not yet as standardized as they were in film.

The *DIT* (*Digital Imaging Technician*) is also part of the camera crew, although they operate a bit more independently. The duties and responsibilities vary widely according to the type of job, the budget and the wishes of the DP; to say that every job is different is an understatement. There are two additional positions that may be part of the crew, although generally only on bigger jobs: *digital utility* and/or *camera utility*.

LOADER

Loader is the official term in the US cinematographer's guild, but other terms sometimes get used. DIT Matt Efsic comments "On different shoots over the past 6-7 years I have been given different titles (often covering much of the same job). My titles have included *Data Loader, Data Wrangler, Digital Asset Manager, Data Asset Manager, Digital Media Manager, Digital Media Tech,* and *Digital Imaging Tech.*

While I have nothing personal against the title 'Data Wrangler,' there are times when higher-ups don't realize the full aspect of the position, thinking it to be 'just drag and drop.' For this reason, I tend to avoid it.

"If I am only doing the secure downloads and backups with bit parity checks and download logs, checking the files against the camera reports, and parsing out stills for the DP, I feel that covers the Data Loader, Data Wrangler, or Digital Media Tech label. I am not altering the files in any way, but am putting them in a secure, organized structure for post and working with the paperwork (not unlike a film loader).

"If I am making any changes to the footage (i.e. changing color temp, adjusting ISO (at the request of the DP), applying a LUT or a one-light grade, or rendering out dailies and possibly transcodes, I would prefer the title *Digital Imaging Technician*, as I am now working with the image."

So when does a Loader get hired? DIT Dane Brehm summarizes — "On features it's pretty regular for a DIT to have a Loader depending on the complexity of the shoot. That Loader may or may not be handling data and be more of a 3rd AC with the ability and knowhow to handle data. On larger pictures north of $25M shooting 3, 4, and 5 or more cameras with the accompaniment of large volumes of data, the skill set of a second DIT may be more appropriate. Therefore my Media Manager will be a DIT in classification but handle the media management exclusively. This is because Loaders don't typically have network, coding, and scripting skills that are required on some shows. It's more of an experience and knowledge solution that's particular to the higher end acquisition formats. On some productions I sometimes get push back from the UPM to not have a

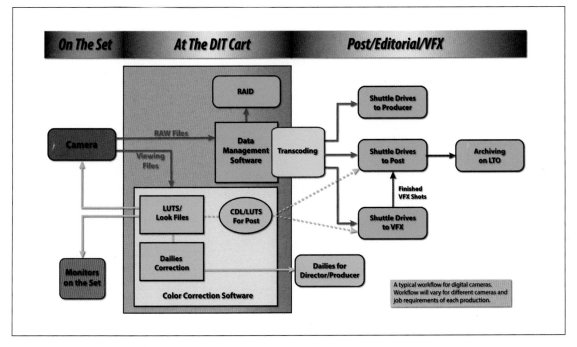

second DIT on payroll so I must hire them as a *Camera Utility* (not *Digital Utility*) as the pay scale is that of a First Assistant. Then I'm not asking other DITs to take such a pay cut for their valuable skill set which often is in demand on other jobs."

UTILITY

Digital Utility assists the DIT with extra monitoring, cables, media inventory, rental house needs, and paperwork in regards to DIT duties. *Camera Utility* can do everything a Camera Assistant/DIT/ Data Manager does minus coloring the image on-set.

THE JOB OF THE DIT

BVK, the *German Society of Cinematographers,* has published a definition of the duties of the DIT. Obviously, circumstances are different for every job and individuals have different specialties and skills so a list like this is never going to be universal, but it is an excellent starting point for understanding the job. Their job description is:

DIGITAL IMAGING TECHNICIAN (DIT)

The increasing digitalization of individual steps, as well as of the whole of the process of image recording or image processing, and the corresponding changes in means and forms of production have an influence on the work of the director of photography that is not to be underestimated. At the same time there is increasing pressure on all departments to produce ever more quickly and efficiently.

Digital production often needs an additional, appropriately specialized person, in the camera department who takes over new additional tasks and advises the team.

If necessary, s/he can carry out preliminary technical quality checks of the recorded material already on location. This does not replace the final technical control of the image material in post-production but can contribute greatly to production safety with the aim of assuring the best possible technical quality of the digital film records. The DIT is an independent specialised technician and adviser of the camera department. S/he supports the camera crew in their technical

Figure 11.1. A typical workflow from cameras on the set to the DIT cart and then on to editorial and VFX. This is an example only, every job, every situation, every camera may be different. For example, some jobs may not require *transcoding* or it may be done off-site. *Shuttle drives* are hard drives or similar digital media that are used to deliver footage to the producer, editor, VFX or secure storage.

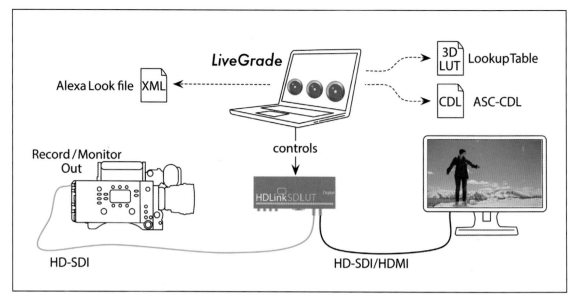

Figure 11.2. A block diagram of using Pomfort *LiveGrade* to provide adjusted, viewable video on the set through an *HDLink LUT* box. Note that it can also be used to produce *Alexa Look* files for use in the camera, as well as LUTs and ASC-CDL metadata. (Courtesy of Pomfort).

creative work using an electronic camera. S/he works during preparation as well as during production and can act as a link between location and post-production.

The DIT has

- Knowledge of the processes of film and TV production, as well as of possible differences in respective production and post-production techniques.
- Extensive knowledge of customary cameras, storage media and their respective possibilities and limitations.
- Basic knowledge of lighting, optics and filters, color theory and technical and creative light exposure.
- In-depth knowledge of video and digital technology and of measurement technology used in practice, such as waveform monitors, vectorscopes, histograms.
- Good knowledge of use of computers and relevant accessories, e.g. to be able to assess the data security of different storage media for image recording or to be able to make camera-specific adjustments.
- Basic knowledge of possibilities and work flow in post-production, e.g. of color correction and transfer to film.

Duties and activities — Preparation:

- Advising the DOP in the choice of the production system.
- Planning the work flow.
- Testing the visual concept of the DOP with respect to its feasibility during production and post-production.
- Intensive testing and preparation of the equipment in collaboration with the first assistant cameraman and post-production.
- If required, calibration and look management of the equipment.
- If required, fine-tuning of data structures/data management in consultation with post-production.
- Assembly and choice of equipment in collaboration with the first assistant cameraman.

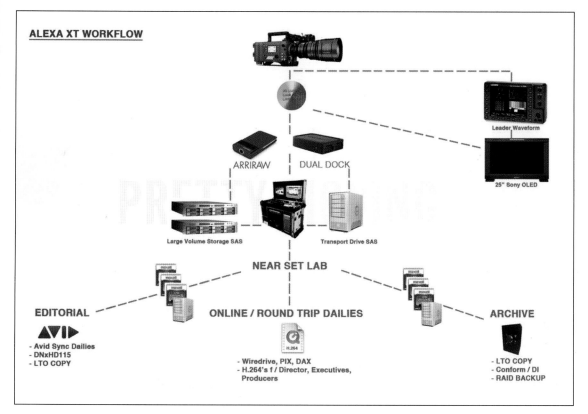

ALEXA XT WORKFLOW

ARRIRAW · DUAL DOCK

Leader Waveform

25" Sony OLED

Large Volume Storage SAS · Transport Drive SAS

NEAR SET LAB

EDITORIAL
- Avid Sync Dailies
- DNxHD115
- LTO COPY

ONLINE / ROUND TRIP DAILIES
- Wiredrive, PIX, DAX
- H.264's f / Director, Executives, Producers

ARCHIVE
- LTO COPY
- Conform / DI
- RAID BACKUP

- Carrying out and if necessary correcting the set-up of the equipment, controlling technical functioning, e.g. adjustment (matching) when working with several cameras.
- Planning and organization of equipment in consultation with the first assistant.

DURING SHOOTING:

The DIT supports the DOP in the implementation of the desired image character using the appropriate technical options.

- First technical checks on location (digital gate check).
- Responsibility for maintenance of the technical work flow during shooting and data storage, during filming at difficult (e.g. high contrast) locations or while working with chroma key (blue/greenscreen).
- Data management on location / checking samples, if necessary data storage.
- Operation of special equipment, e.g. recorders.
- Close collaboration with the first assistant cameraman e.g. for control of focus and exposure, as well as with other departments (e.g. sound).
- Repairing small technical defects, as far as possible.
- Setting up and adjusting the set-up of equipment (video village, measurement technology, monitoring, recording) in collaboration with the first assistant cameraman/video operator.
- Changing the recording parameters for optimizing the desired image characteristics.

Figure 11.3. A workflow designed by DIT Dane Brehm of *Pretty Moving Pictures* for Alexa XT from capture all the way through to archiving on a large feature. Note that the *Near Set Lab* in the diagram is not the DIT cart; it is actually the cart for a 2nd *DIT/Media Manager/Dailies Colorist* doing the *Data/Ingest/Dailies/Deliverables/QC/LTO* archiving. Dane prefers to be close to the camera with his DIT cart, monitoring the image live and working directly with the DP and camera assistants and often doing live grading of the image. Dane also uses a similar cart which the *Loader* works from, but it is much smaller and designated as an *Ingest/Data Wiping Station* where (once the LTOs are verified) the original media is wiped clean. He notes that this workflow would be essentially the same for Red or Canon footage. (Courtesy Dane Brehm of *Pretty Moving Pictures*).

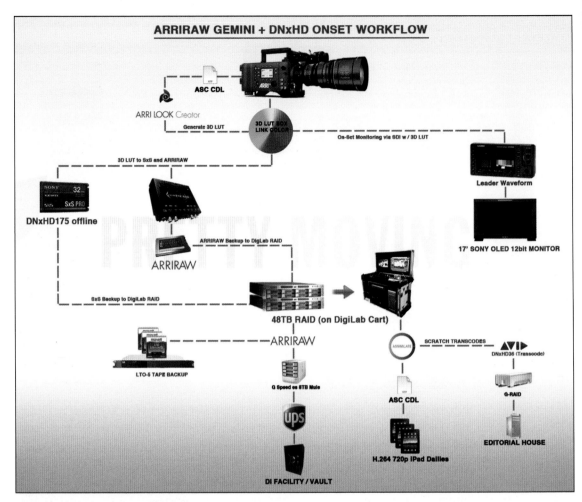

Figure 11.4. Another workflow designed by DIT Dane Brehm for a feature film. Note the LUT box which sends the image to on-set monitors with the selected "look" applied. This workflow also includes an ASC-CDL so the DP's choices can be communicated down the line to post. The process includes H.264 dailies and shipping archives to a vault — often a requirement of the insurance company. (Courtesy of Dane Brehm of *Pretty Moving Pictures*).

Post-production:

- If required, technical/visual check of the image material at the post-production facility using appropriate equipment.
- If desired, preparing the production of dailies/rushes or of working copies or similar in consultation with post.
- Equipment logistics, e.g. for handing the recordings over to post-production, data storage, data transfer, etc.
- Return of equipment in collaboration with the first assistant cameraman.

In the US

Here's a bit more from the contract for US camera union, the *IA Local 600 Camera Guild*, which includes DITs as well as cinematographers and camera assistants:

- Digital Imaging Technician: the DIT may set up and supervise end to end workflow to ensure the integrity of the image from the point of capture through to the hand off to post-production.
- Responsible for all in-camera recording, digital audio acquisition, genlock and timecode processes in the camera with an understanding of how they are integrated into digital acquisition format and post-production environment.
- Responsible for ordering, preparation, set up, operation,

Figure 11.5. The main screen of *Pomfort LiveGrade* in ASC-CDL mode. *LiveGrade* is a widely used tool for on the set LUT creation and management, and also for ASC-CDL creation as shown here. It includes not only controls for creating LUTs but also multiple device control. Note also on the far right lower how it is possible to change the order in which LUTs are applied. This is an important function. Applying LUTs in a different order can create different results. It also records a history of the LUT activity and outputs a report. (Courtesy of Pomfort).

troubleshooting and maintenance of digital cameras (provides oversight of Camera Assistants and Utilities), wave form monitors, down converters (Hi-Def to other formats), monitors, cables, digital recording devices, terminal equipment, driver software and other related equipment.

- Performs advanced coloring/shading of cameras, encompassing traditional Video Controller duties; responsible for color timing including but not limited to: adjusting, balancing, registering and setting timing, matching electronic contrast, brightness, quality and edge definition; matching of cameras, color consistency (RGB) exposure (iris), density (master black), electronic color balance (chroma, hue and saturation), of each camera and its monitor and totally matching camera inputs to the VCU and checking the wave form monitor and the vectorscope.

- Exercises supervisory responsibility for technical acceptability of the image.

The Bottom Line

The exact role of the DIT varies from production to production and from DP to DP or might even shift a bit on a day-to-day basis as dictated by workflow. As anyone who has spent a few years on film sets will tell you — no two shoot days are exactly alike.

As indicated by the quotes above, the job of the DIT ranges from being just a data manager all the way up to working closely with the camera crew in setting up the camera, shooting, monitoring the look and the signal (the DIT almost always has a better monitor and better viewing conditions as well as a waveform/vectorscope). Creating LUTs for specific conditions or even certain scenes, creating dailies, and quality checking the footage are important jobs as well. Beyond that, the DIT is often expected to be the "authority" on

Figure 11.6. (Above) A Qio card reader is built into the *Wrangler*. (Courtesy of 1 Beyond)

Figure 11.7. (Right) The *Wrangler* by *1 Beyond*; a self-contained highly portable DIT station. The red cartridge is an *LTO* tape for archiving. (Courtesy of 1 Beyond)

all things digital on the set. Although it may not be an official part of the job description, many DPs and ACs expect that if they are unsure of a particular camera operation (such as loading a LUT) or a best practices workflow for the files, it is up to the DIT to know the right answer to any question about digital workflow, setup, files and procedures concerning the camera output data and how to handle it. The DIT works closely with the camera crew but is also the producer's best insurance against lost, damaged or corrupted data files which is where all the money ends up in a production.

The bottom line is that you can choose to learn how to copy files to hard drives and call yourself a DIT or you can absorb the whole range of knowledge of the digital signal, the digital image, digital color, file structures, LUTs, file types and so on — it can seem imposing at first but in the end you'll find it's not rocket surgery either. A good memory for three letter acronyms is also important.

Dane Brehm, who works as a DIT and workflow consultant on large studio features and commercials, describes it this way:

- Design the workflow from camera to conform.
- Anticipate storage needs (master+copy) of entire show even up to conform. Cost analyze to achieve desired result.
- Assure unquestionable monitoring for DP, Gaffer, Director, VFX Supervisor, Makeup/Hair to make choices from.
- Facilitate proper exposure based on creative intent of DP and Director.
- Create LUTs or live grade the footage, then pass to lab.
- Manage data (Sound, Camera, Script, Metadata, Lens Data).
- Oversee technical aspects on the set and coordinate with Camera Assistants, DigiLab, Editorial, Transpo, Production, and Post.
- Create transcoded dailies for editorial (two person job).
- Create verified LTO backup of project while on-location.
- Be a charging station for iPad/iPhone/Android/Blackberry of various members of Camera/Makeup/Hair/Props, basically anyone. Good way to make friends.

Conform is the process where edited material is matched back to the original footage. Dane also mentions *Transpo*. Why would the DIT have anything to do with the transportation department? Because hard drives and LTO tapes need to be delivered and that's their area.

DIT Working Alone

Frequently the DIT works alone, handling both the data ingest (downloading of files to hard drives plus backups) and look management: LUTs & look files, color correction of dailies, watching the scopes and so on. The third area — transcoding, may be something the DIT does, or it might be done off site, perhaps by a subcontractor or the post-production facility. It's a lot of different tasks to handle and time-management and a knack for multi-tasking are essential.

Loader Working Alone

Some smaller jobs require nothing more than downloading the data and making backups. In these cases a Loader/Media Manager might work alone or even the second or third AC might handle these duties, although there is always a danger in this — any time someone is trying to do two separate jobs on the set, there is always a risk they will do one or both of those jobs with less than optimum results.

DIT/Loader Team or Two DITs Working Together

This is common for larger jobs, particularly if there is more than one camera involved and when shooting high speed, 3D or other types of shooting which produced very large amounts of data during the day. How they work together and who does what is something they work out themselves. There is always a danger of confusion and safeguards need to be in place to prevent something being missed.

WORKING WITH THE DP

The DIT often functions as a second set of eyes for the DP. This means either live monitoring the feed from the camera or checking the footage to watch for clipping, noise or other exposure problems. In addition, the DIT might be expected to be on the alert for soft focus and other problems that aren't readily apparent with the smaller monitors and less than ideal viewing conditions on the set.

How the DIT works with the DP is, of course, the cinematographer's call. Some want close collaboration and continuous feedback from the DIT; some want less or none — every crew is different, every job is different. New York DIT Ben Schwartz puts it like this: "Particularly in the world of commercials, where I do the bulk of my work, the DIT often represents the DPs best (and sometimes only) chance to impose his/her vision on the final color. Using software such as *Livegrade*, *Scratch Lab*, and *DaVinci Resolve*, the DIT creates LUTs, graded stills, and color-corrected offline material that gets passed on to post. Many DPs — for reasons either financial or schedule-related — don't have the chance to be present for the final DI [color correction], so taking at least a few minutes to work with a DIT on color will benefit all involved. Without impinging on the authorial control over an image, I think the DIT has much to offer the DP in terms of collaborating on color, exposure, and camera settings; I wish more DPs took advantage of that."

Any member of the camera crew will tell you that interpersonal relationships are crucial to getting through the day productively and getting the next job. The DIT is in a particularly delicate position as they are in a position to comment on and make changes to the image; obviously there are many opportunities to step on the wrong toes, particularly those of the Director of Photography. As with anything on a film set, diplomacy is paramount. DIT Ben Cain offers this — "If a DP is having exposure issues or prefers images that are technically problematic, the best approach is to objectively show them the issue and frame the solution as a choice. For example, 'You're picking up a lot of noise here in the low light areas of the shot or the fill side of this face. If you're ok with it, great. If not, here's what we can do.' At that point, you then use the tools at your disposal to offer up the best solution."

LIVE MONITORING AND LIVE GRADING

Many times the DIT works on the set near the camera doing live monitoring. This means that the camera monitoring output is sent directly the DIT cart where it is continuously viewable on a high quality monitor, a waveform monitor and vectorscope. Depending on the wishes of the DP and camera crew, the DIT may or may not give immediate feedback on exposure, clipping, noise, color and even focus. In some cases they communicate via walkie-talkie and in other cases, just whisper a quiet word after the take.

Live grading means the DIT is making adjustments to the look during the day, generally so the DP and director can get an idea of how everything is working together. As mentioned above, live grading applications such as Pomfort *LiveGrade, Scratch Lab, DaVinci Resolve, LinkColor* and *Colorfront* are often used for this although obviously other grading applications can also be employed. Some, such as *Colorfront*, can output dailies to an iPad for the DP who can make changes and send them back to the DIT for further adjustment.

WORKING WITH THE CAMERA CREW

How the DIT will work with the camera crew should be worked out in advance and procedures firmly established before the day begins.

Ben Cain takes this approach, "As members of the camera department, it's a good idea to be an active member of the team and help out wherever you can. In my experience, many focus pullers love having a second set of eyes on their focus. They have one of the hardest jobs on the set and sometimes even with their modern tools; it can be difficult for them to evaluate their focus. A little note from the DIT over the radio during the take can be helpful to nudge them into perfect focus when they need it.

"Digital is all about real-time — real-time color correction, real-time focus and operating, real-time feedback. It's an opportunity for everybody to get it right, but it requires an objective set of eyes scrutinizing the take. Some Directors of Photography are very involved with this whereas others are not and heavily lean on their DIT to help manage the department and catch mistakes."

THE MEETING

Pre-production planning is essential in order to have a smooth running project. More than just avoiding delays and mistakes, it is an important aspect of staying on schedule and on budget. Some people make the mistake of thinking "We've got the camera footage and backed it up — what could go wrong now." The answer is that plenty of things can go wrong in the post shooting phases of any production.

By now, so many people have dealt with computers for so many years that file naming conventions are often second nature; the most important aspect is consistency. Work out your file/folder naming procedures in advance and stick to them — most often it will be the editor who calls the shots on this one. As always, talking to the post-production supervisor, the editor, the VFX house, the DP, first AC and anyone else involved in the digital workflow is critical. Without a doubt the best procedure on a long form project (such as a feature) is to get all these people in the same room for an hour or so, along with the director and producer. It may be inconvenient, but the selling point is that it can potentially save production many thousands of dollars and possible costly delays in the production workflow — most producers take notice when that issue is advanced. On commercials and smaller projects such as short films, it is more common for the key people to talk on the phone or exchange emails.

DIT WORKFLOW

As with just about everything in filmmaking, the duties and responsibilities of the DIT can vary widely depending on the production, the DP, the requirements of post production, etc. The same goes for the workflow. All of this is why The Meeting is so important — issues of who does what, file naming conventions, transcoding dailies, LUTs and labeling of drives absolutely must be worked out before shooting begins. The actual duties will vary from the simplest file management up to consulting with the DP on the look, preparing LUTs, camera prep (in conjunction with the camera assistants), monitoring the signal and other high end duties.

SIMPLE DATA WORKFLOW

Let's start with simplest case.
1. Media is delivered from the camera.
2. DIT or Loader downloads the media and backs it up to at least two separate hard drives or RAIDs — preferably three.
3. DIT scrubs through the shots to make sure everything recorded and downloaded properly.
4. Media is delivered back to the set, ready for camera use.
5. Keep a detailed media log of all operations.

ADVANCED WORKFLOW

Now a slightly more advanced workflow:
1. Media delivered from the set.
2. Downloads and backs up.
3. Scrubs through the shots to make sure everything recorded and downloaded properly.
4. If requested, prepares LUTs for viewing and for the camera or applies previously developed LUTs for reviewing on the set and for dailies.
5. May do slightly more advanced color correction for dailies.
4. Media sent back to the set ready for formatting.
5. Files are transcoded for dailies.
6. Keep a detailed media log of all operations.

INTERFACING WITH OTHER DEPARTMENTS

Working with the camera is a big variable and depends not only on the requirements of the production but also the training and knowledge of the people involved and also what equipment/software is available which may be dictated by the budget. Keep in mind that although a particular DIT may have all equipment and software for any conceivable situation, they are not necessarily going to bring it to every set at the same flat rate. This is just business — DITs make substantial investments in equipment and software and it would be unfair to expect them to just provide everything without the proper compensation. This is also, of course, what makes the difference between a professional DIT and a "PA with a laptop." There may be times (from the producer's point of view) when a PA with a laptop is sufficient and worth the risk. However, think of the time, money and effort that went into creating that footage and then think of how a single mouse click can potentially destroy every bit of it in an instant.

The First and Second AC will physically assemble the camera on the tripod or dolly but when it comes to setting the variables on the camera — shutter speed, ISO, white balance and most of all any Look Files or LUTs — then the DIT may be indirectly or directly involved. In any case, when something goes wrong with a camera, the DIT is expected to know what to do.

MONITOR OUTPUTS

Some cameras have monitoring outputs in addition to unprocessed video. The *Sony F55* has 4K output over 4x HD-SDI. *Canon C500* has 4K output via several of the 4K recorder options. *Phantom Flex 4K* has 4K output over 2x 3G-SDI. Some Sony cameras also include a selection for *MLUT*, which is their monitoring LUT. Some camera-mountable monitors also support LUTs which means that the operator or camera assistant can get a display more suitable for their purposes on the set.

DELIVERABLES

Traditionally in the film world, the term *deliverables* means the contractually obligated set of film or video and audio elements that are to be presented to the client, distributor or broadcaster. Normally, payment is withheld all or in part until these elements have been delivered and quality checked (QCed). In this context, we'll use the term deliverable to mean the elements (generally digital files) that need to be passed on to the next step in the process. Since we are focusing on the work done with digital video/audio files on the set during production, we'll talk about preparing elements to be sent to the editor, the visual effects people, the producer and dailies for the director. An additional requirement may be added by the insurance company, which may set additional checks and backups.

TRANSCODING

Transcoding is, of course, converting the files to another format; either for editorial or for dailies. It is the last item that can be a point of contention; for the simple reason that transcoding can be a time-consuming process. Some DITs charge extra for it and on some productions, transcoding is contracted out to a facility that has faster hardware and perhaps more importantly, isn't on overtime as the processors chug through the hours. Of course the hardware for this processing is constantly improving, the most obvious example being the *Red Rocket or Red Rocket-X* cards — which vastly speeds up the processing of Red RAW files.

ON OR OFF THE SET?

Because of the time factor, many production companies resort to having outside companies (such as subcontractors or the post house) do the transcoding. In reality, it makes little sense to have a highly skilled employee stay behind on set for several hours while the computer grinds through a routine process. It all comes down to the time factor — does the director or producer need transcoded files right away or is there some breathing room before they need to arrive at the post house? Commercials, features, music videos and documentaries will have widely varying time frames and workflows. The

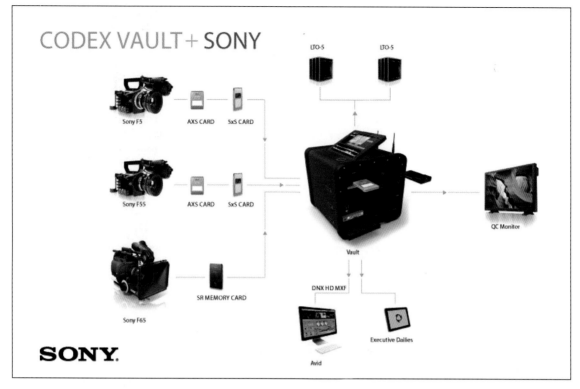

CODEX VAULT + SONY

SONY.

Codex Vault (Figure 11.8) is one solution in that it largely automates transcoding for dailies and delivery elements. Its modules can also include LTO recording for long term archiving and storage.

The *DIT House* in Los Angeles offers this viewpoint, with Alexa as an example: "Although the Alexa can record Apple ProRes 4444 and ArriRAW with the Codex On-Board Recorder, many editorial facilities request smaller offline files so their systems don't slow down. Creating your own dailies on-set saves you money and allows greater control over your images.

- Save time, compared to typical one-light dailies turnaround.
- Save money, compared to typical one-light Dailies costs.
- Rent fewer Sony SxS Cards.
- Preview footage quickly and know you got the shot.
- Communicate your desired looks to post & VFX."

Figure 11.8. *Codex Vault* workflow for Sony capture to dailies and editing plus archiving on LTO tapes. There are similar workflows for Red, Canon, Sony and other cameras. (Courtesy of Codex and Sony).

MULTISTREAM OUTPUT

Fortunately, many software applications are capable of transcoding several output streams simultaneously — depending on the power and number of the computer cores running at the time. The Codex Vault can generate different types of files at the same time.

DAILIES

Dailies are an old tradition in motion pictures. In film-based production, it usually meant that the exposed negative was sent in by midnight. By next day (in an ideal situation) the printed dailies were ready for screening. Over time, this transitioned to the original negative being transferred to video and tapes, DVDs or digital files were used for dailies. You've probably seen scenes of cigar chomping executives sitting in a screening room commenting on the actors, the director, the plot: "I've seen better film on teeth!" That is a part of the need for dailies, but not really the main reason. The primary need

Figure 11.9. (Top) *Arri Look Creator* displaying a LogC encoded Alexa file.

Figure 11.10. (Middle) The same shot with a Rec.709 LUT applied.

Figure 11.11. (Bottom) A separate page in *Arri Look Creator* can create and output *ASC-CDL* files; in this case a warmer look.

was to double check the technical basics: is a magazine scratching? Is a particular lens not focusing? Is the film mis-registered? Things of this type. In fact, an old production rule is that a set was never struck until the dailies had been reviewed, in case a reshoot was needed.

Since review of the actual footage is virtually instant these days, the need for that technical review is a matter that can be dealt with on the set (primarily at the DIT cart). For the creative side, many directors want dailies that they can review every night. Frequently, these are in the form of H.264 transcoded files that can be viewed on an iPad or laptop computer. The DIT may be asked to produce these files or in some cases, they might be farmed out to an off-site company. If they are done on the set, this can lead to some extremely long hours after the rest of the crew has gone home, which is why there is a tendency to have them done off-site or in some other way that doesn't keep the DIT sitting alone on the set, long after wrap. See *The DIT Cart* for another solution — DIT Ben Hopkins keeps his computers in his van so they can keep transcoding while the vehicle is parked in his garage at night. The only drawback is that they may still need to be delivered to the producer the next day if shooting is finished but this can easily be done by messenger or a PA sent from the production office.

FILES FOR POST AND VFX

What files do you need to deliver to post? Whatever they ask for. This is the point of the pre-production meeting — to make sure that everyone in the production understands what is needed by the next stage of the process. For the DIT on set this means understanding what files the editor needs and possibly what the VFX people need.

As an added wrinkle, sometimes the production's insurance company will have specific requirements as well. It is not only a matter of what file types they need: RAW, ProRes, DNxHD, log or whatever; it is also important to know if they need them in a particular container (Quicktime, MXF, etc.) and what type of media they can handle. One example: while Thunderbolt is enormously helpful on the set, it is important to check that the post house can handle drives with Thunderbolt connections. The same applies to any other connectors as well as file formats.

CAMERA SPECIFIC WORKFLOWS

The major camera companies have realized from the beginning that digital image making is about more than just hardware. They have been very active in developing software to go along with their hardware and have also given a good deal of thought to entire workflow of the data output from their cameras. In some situations, it is easier to work with the software that goes along with that camera. Fortunately, the software is in most cases provided free for downloading.

ALEXA

Workflow with the Alexa is a bit more complex if you want to generate and use their *Look Files* with the camera. The camera can record Quicktime ProRes 1080p to internal SxS cards and uncompressed ArriRAW (and other formats) or HD and to an external recorder. It can also output 1920x1080 HD (with or without a user look applied) to monitors. Figures 11.9 through 11.12 shows the sequence of steps involved.

Arri offers these thoughts on workflow: "A Digital Imaging Technician with the Alexa needs to have a proficient working knowledge of the camera: Tasks — Ensure proper monitoring with the various options available. They have to know navigation, setting the various gamma options for recording, monitoring, electric view finder, etc. A DIT doing 'Data Wrangling' on set makes sure the DP/Camera Operator has enough storage in place (SxS Cards for example) and the data is properly being backed up and verified; especially if you are rotating through a limited number of SxS cards. Also preparing dailies, etc.

"It also is good to redundantly check the camera settings on a frequent basis. For example, if you go into the Alexa's High Speed Mode, and want to record in 120 frames per second you cannot

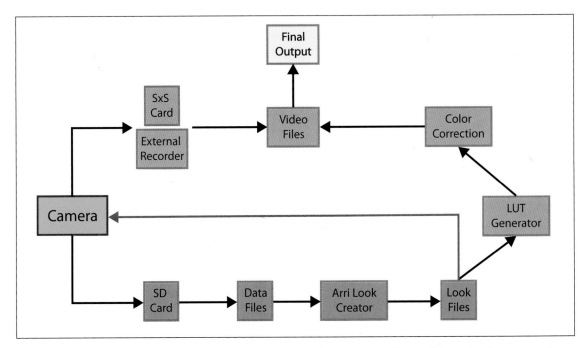

Figure 11.12. The workflow for creating *Arri Look files* (used in the camera) and LUTs. Although LUTs can be created in many ways, this particular method creates them based on *Grab files* (still frames) from the camera.

record in 4:4:4, rather 4:2:2. But if you change the frame rate down to 60 frames per second you can record in 4:4:4 (providing you are using the new 64GB SxS cards). Someone could accidentally change or not realize the SxS cards are recording in Rec.709 vs. LogC, or if the exposure index was left at 1200 vs. 800 from one setup to another, etc."

RED

When new camera formats are introduced, they tend to go through a similar cycle — in the beginning, transcoding and even special software is needed to make them usable in color correction and editing applications, then plug-ins are developed for those applications and eventually the various software packages accept the files natively with no problems. Many editing and color correction applications can ingest Red files natively, but Red also offers *RedCine-X Pro* (Figure 11.13), its own proprietary software; as with most camera company software of this type it is available free online. It is a remarkable application, performing ingest, color correction and a wide range of controls including, of course, selections for deBayering RAW files: ISO, color space, gamma space and color temperature. One of its most clever and useful features is that as you move the cursor around on the image, a small dot appears on the waveform display so you can easily see exactly what part of the picture is being represented on the scope.

CANON

Canon workflow for their cinema cameras is fairly straightforward, however the *.RMF* (*Raw Media Format*) files may need transcoding in some cases. As with ArriRAW and CinemaDNG, they are stacks of images in folders for each clip. As with most camera manufacturers, they also have proprietary software well suited to their files, in this case it is *Canon RAW Development*. It can transcode and export DPX, OpenEXR and ProRes files as needed. They also make plug-ins available for Final Cut X and Avid.

Sony

Sony's high end cameras all have a similar workflow, although they vary slightly in what files they output (Figure 11.14). The F65 can produce 16-bit Linear RAW, S-Log2, S-Log3, Gamma or Rec.709 and can output several flavors of RAW or SR-HQ HD, from 16-bit to 10-bit. Sony say that "The 16-bit linear RAW capture of the F65 is the ideal point of entry into the 16-bit linear ACES workflow." The F55/F5 can output XAVC 4K, SR files, XAVC 2K HD or MPEG2 HD also with RAW, S-Log2, S-Log3 and Rec.709 options. Figure 11.8 shows a typical workflow — the camera files are transcoded to dailies as ProRes or DNxHD for ease of use in editing systems. Grading is then done on the original files which are then reconnected or conformed using XML and AAF.

Panasonic P2

Panasonic has the *P2 CMS* (*Content Management System*) for their P2 MXF files with *AVC-Intra* encoding (see *Codecs & Formats*). Panasonic advises against using the computer operating system to transfer files from the P2 cards (not advised at all on Mac). P2 cards are PCMCIA compatible or you can use a card reader designed for them.

Blackmagic Camera Workflow

Blackmagic Design recommends this typical workflow for their cameras. Of course, this is generic and variations are always possible.

1. Shoot with *Blackmagic Cinema Camera* and record to *CinemaDNG* RAW files.

2. Take the SSD out of the camera and dock it to your computer via an SSD dock with a fast Thunderbolt, USB 3.0 or eSATA connection.

3. Bring the files into *DaVinci Resolve* (after the usual redundant backups).

4. Apply a basic grade in Resolve and render out to Apple ProRes, DNxHD or other formats.

Figure 11.13. *RedCine-X Pro* offers a complete suite of image control tools for Red camera footage.

workflow

247

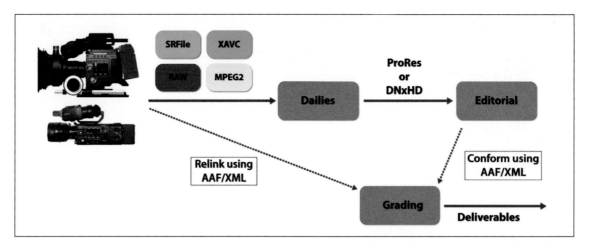

Figure 11.14. Sony camera workflow is similar for the F65, F55 and F5, although they don't all output the same type of files. It is also typical of any workflow where editing is not done with the original camera files. In Sony's case AAF/XML are used to reconnect the original files with the edited versions, a process called *conforming*.

5. Edit the files in popular NLE software such as Apple Final Cut, Avid or Adobe Premiere Pro.

6. When finished editing, export an XML or AAF file.

7. Import the XML or AAF file into Resolve and conform with the original CinemaDNG images for maximum creative control.

8. Grade the edited timeline in Resolve to complete project.

If you have shot and recorded your clips in ProRes using the Film Dynamic Range, you can quickly turn it into Video or Rec.709 using the built in 3D LUT in Resolve.

INDUSTRY STANDARD WORKFLOWS

In addition to workflows designed by camera manufacturers specifically for their data files, there are workflow tools that have been developed by influential industry-wide organizations which are intended to encompass data files from all types of cameras. These industry solutions are efforts by some of the major players in the film industry (such as the ASC), industry consortiums like DCI and the ACES Committee which includes color scientists, industry representatives and people from camera and display companies.

TEN NUMBERS: ASC-CDL

As cinematographers have a great deal at stake with how images are captured, processed, altered and shown, the *American Society of Cinematographers* made an early move to ensure that the director of photography doesn't have to see their images put on a hard drive then just wave goodbye and hope for the best. During production when there is little or no chance of the DP having time available to supervise the production of dailies (either from film or from digital acquisition), they saw a need for an organized system for the cinematographer to convey their ideas to post people in some way other than vague statements such as "this scene was intended to have deep shadows and an overall sepia tone." For years, film cinematographers have communicated with the colorist doing their dailies every night by any means possible: written notes, stills taken on the set, photos torn from magazines — anything they could think of. How well it worked depended on the communications skills of the DP and also on the night shift colorist. Of course, it's not the most experienced people who work the night shift doing dailies. Viewing on the set monitors often involves applying a Rec.709 based LUT, which has a far more restricted gamut than what is actually be recorded.

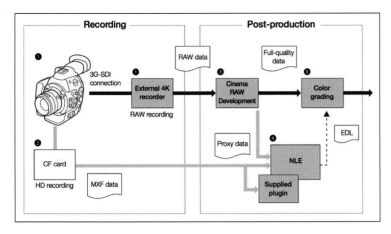

Figure 11.15. Typical Canon 4K workflow using their *Cinema RAW Development* software. (Courtesy of Canon.)

GOODBYE, KNOBS

In large part, this effort to give the cinematographer tools to send their image ideas down the line to the post people is an effort to address the fact that as we move toward cameras that shoot RAW and log, the DP no longer has "the knobs" to make adjustments to the look of the picture in the camera. As we will see, the ACES workflow brings all cameras into a unified color space. Some camera characteristics will still show through due to differing color responses. This doesn't mean that the artistry and creative image making are going to be taken out of filmmaking; it just means that it is going to be done in ways that are different from how they were done in the past, in film and also in traditional HD shooting.

Fortunately, the digital workflow opened up not only new ways for post to screw up our images, it also created new possibilities to maintain some control over our vision of what the image was intended to be. To facilitate control of the image after it leaves the set, the *ASC Technology Committee* under chairman Curtis Clark, devised the *ASC Color Decision List* (*CDL*). In operation, it allows the interchange of basic RGB color-correction information between equipment and applications made by different manufacturers. Although the basic controls of most color-correction systems are similar, they all differ somewhat in specific implementation and in the terminology used to label various controls or aspects of the image. The terms *Lift* (for dark tones), *Gain* (highlights), and *Gamma* (mid-tones) are commonly used by most color-correction systems, but those terms inevitably vary in detail from company to company (Figure 11.16).

To avoid confusion with already existing systems, the committee decided on a set of three functions with unique names: *Offset*, *Slope* (*gain*) and *Power* (*gamma*). Each function uses one number for each color channel so the transfer functions for the three color components can be described by nine parameters. A tenth number was added for *Saturation* and it applies to all channels. ASC-CDL does not specify a color space.

The *ASC Color Decision List* is a system designed to facilitate that "transfer of the idea" — it's about giving the cinematographer the tools to send their decisions about the look down the line to the editor, colorist and other links in the production chain. It addresses the fact that the tools that are used in post-production are not often available on the set and in fact, at the time you're shooting, it might not even be known what those tools are going to be. It's entirely possible that different software and hardware will be used at every step of the process, in reality, it would be very difficult to ensure any

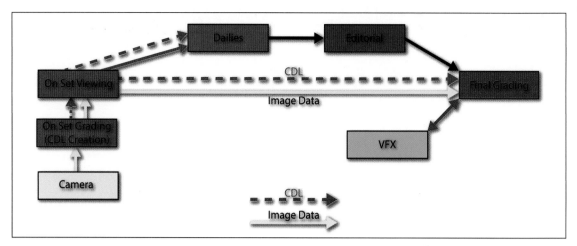

Figure 11.16. Workflow for on-the-set color grading with the ASC-CDL and output for the editors and visual effects people using either *FLEx* or *EDL* data paths. *FLEx* is a separate file that keeps track of the color decisions made on the set. EDL is the *Edit Decision List* that includes the color decisions. Another method is for the EDL to "reference" an external document that contains the record of color decisions.

uniformity of machines or software, particularly in features where dozens of different post houses and effects facilities are involved. Close coordination and supervision is necessary all through the process and that the various tools be capable of working with the CDL data. In order to be effective for a production, it is important to test the workflow before production begins and that the entire team agrees on the color space the CDL is being applied to and used for monitoring. It applies to both log, linear and gamma encoded video.

Primary Correction Only

In order to keep things simple, the ASC-CDL deals only with primary color correction, not secondaries. In practice, this is not the sort of thing that would be done on the set anyway; that kind of secondary, fine tuning correction is far more appropriate in a real color correction situation with proper viewing conditions, time to try alternatives and all the tools we have come to expect in a color correction suite.

Currently, there are two methods of employing the CDL: by piggybacking on existing file formats such as *FLEx*, *ALE* or *CMX EDL* files or by creating a new XML file. FLEx files are a record of the relationship between timecode, KeyKode and audio timecode. Flex files are important in the online editing process.

ALE is *Avid Log Exchange*; it is very similar to a FLEx file in that it is a metadata file that travels with the footage. It records more than 80 types of metadata. ALE can include the ASC-CDL data as well as the headers ASC_SOP (slope, offset, power) and ASC_SAT (saturation). ALE files are text data and can be edited — however, proceed with caution. The ASC-CDL parameters can also be exported as part of *EDLs* (*Edit Decision Lists*); *CMX* is a commonly used type of EDL.

XML files are increasingly used as a standard format. XML stands for *Extensible Markup Language*; in functioning it is similar to a "wrapper file" like Quicktime — it serves as a transport mechanism between different processes. XML is widely used in post production. As with all video technologies, it continues to grow and develop.

DP Mark Weingartner says, "With only these three operators applied to RGB plus saturation, the downside is that you do not have all the different subtle secondary color correction tools at your disposal. However that is perhaps a blessing more than a curse. The beauty of the ASC-CDL is that in theory, if you apply the ASC-CDL to your image file in any of the myriads of color grading systems, it will pop up looking the same... and it will have done so,

```
<ColorDecisionList xmlns='urn:ASC:CDL:v1.01'>
    <ColorDecision>
        <ColorCorrection>
            <SOPNode>
                <Description>WF_CDL</Description>
                <Slope>1.27 1.18 1</Slope>
                <Offset>-0.009 -0.002 0.003</Offset>
                <Power>1 1 1.08</Power>
            </SOPNode>
            <SatNode>
                <Saturation>1.08</Saturation>
            </SatNode>
        </ColorCorrection>
    </ColorDecision>
</ColorDecisionList>
```

Figure 11.17. ASC-CDL code is both machine and human readable and elegant in its simplicity.

effectively, by spinning the balls to the appropriate places... so it provides a great starting point for on-going color correction without having truncated, stretched, or damaged anything as you might if you started by applying a LUT to the files on ingest to the color correction system."

SOP AND S

The ASC-CDL functions *Slope* and *Power* are based on *Gain* and *Gamma*, as discussed in the chapter *Image Control & Grading*. *Offset* is like *Offset* in log grading controls. They are applied to the image in order: slope first, then offset, then power. *Saturation* is an overall function that applies to all channels equally. These controls are in RGB color space and can be used with linear, gamma encoded or log video. Keep in mind that each of the three parameters applies to the three color channels for a total of nine functions plus the tenth, saturation. The *Slope* function alters the slope of the transfer function without shifting the black level. The default is a value of 1.0.

The function *Offset* lowers or raises luminance: the overall brightness of a color channel. It shifts up or down while keeping the slope unchanged. If the video data that is being worked on is in log space, then the *Offset* is an interpretation of printer lights, which is why some cinematographers, especially those with long experience in working with film labs, choose to work primarily or even exclusively with this function while shaping their image. While *Slope* and *Offset* are essentially linear functions, *Power* is non-linear, just as we saw with video gamma. In this function,

$$\text{Output} = \text{input} \wedge \text{power}$$

Figure 11.18. The ASC-CDL control panel from *LightSpace CMS,* a color control and LUT manager software from *Light Illusion.*

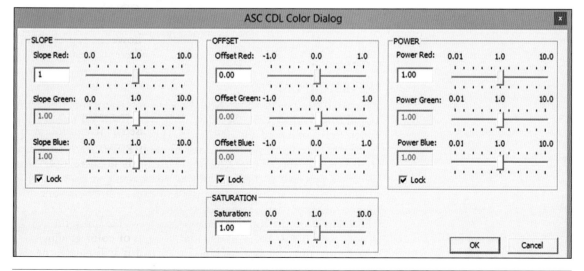

where ^ means "raised to the power of," as in 10^2 is the same as 10^2 which is the same as "ten raised to the power of 2" — all of which equal 100.

Saturation: this system uses the most common industry standard definition of saturation, employing the Rec.709 color weightings. Saturation applies equally to all three color components, so only one number is needed to define it. As an example of how the CDL might appear in the workflow, in a *CMX EDL* (*Edit Decision List*), you might find the following in COMMENTS:

- ASC_SOP (1.0 1.0 1,0) (0.0 0.0 0.0) (1.0 1.0 1.0)
- ASC_SAT 1.0

The first line defines the *Slope*, *Offset* and *Power* for each Red, Green and Blue channel and the second line defines the saturation. In an EDL file, there are two ways of specifying these values: either *inline* or by *xml reference*. Inline means that the CDL values are contained within the EDL and xml reference means they are contained in a separate, referenced xml file.

ACES: WHAT IT IS, WHAT IT DOES

First, here's the official description from the *Academy of Motion Picture Arts and Sciences*: "The *Academy Color Encoding System* is a set of components that facilitates a wide range of motion picture workflows while eliminating the ambiguity of today's file formats. The basic ACES components are:

- A file format specification and open source implementation in the form of an enhanced and 'constrained' version of *OpenEXR*, the popular high dynamic range image file format widely used in CGI applications (SMPTE ST 2065-1:2012 and SMPTE ST 2065-4:2013)
- A portable software programming language designed specifically for color transforms. Called the *Color Transformation Language*, or *CTL*, this technology is now a SMPTE Registered Disclosure Document (SMPTE RDD-15).
- Reference transforms for conversions among ACES-defined encoding schemes.
- A set of reference images and calibration targets for film scanners and recorders.
- Documentation on the architecture and software tools.

ACES is designed to support both all-digital and hybrid film-digital motion picture workflows, and supports custom look development. ACES and ASC-CDL were designed hand-in-hand to complement each other. Some of the same people participated into both development processes."

THE HISTORY OF ACES

We previously talked about Kodak's Cineon system for producing digital intermediates. At the heart of it was *Cineon file format (.cin)* which was contained in *DPX* files (*Digital Picture Exchange*). In developing the Cineon format, one of their primary concerns was preserving the special characteristics that make film look like film. What we perceive as the film look is no accident of chemistry; in addition to color scientists, chemists and experts in *densitometry* (the science of exposure), Kodak also employed many psychologists who focused on the topic of how people perceive images. In order to not lose what is special about film images, the basis of Cineon is *print density*, just as it is in making prints from film negative. It also

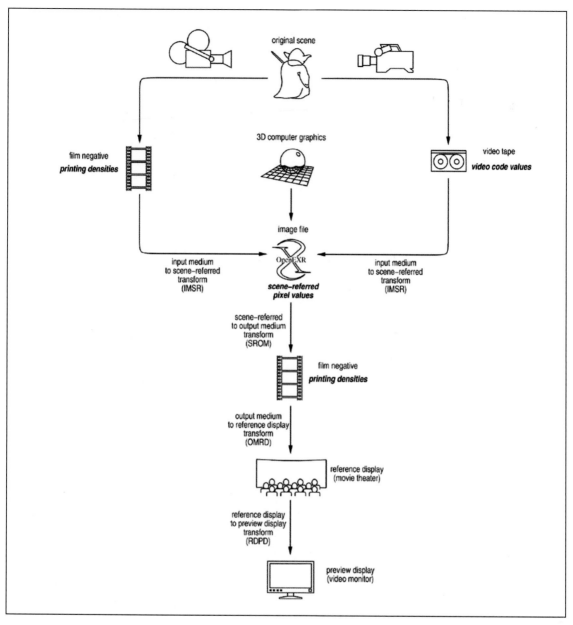

The following labels appear within the figure:

original scene

3D computer graphics

film negative
printing densities

video tape
video code values

image file

OpenEXR
*scene–referred
pixel values*

input medium
to scene–referred
transform
(IMSR)

input medium
to scene–referred
transform
(IMSR)

scene–referred
to output medium
transform
(SROM)

film negative
printing densities

output medium
to reference display
transform
(OMRD)

reference display
(movie theater)

reference display
to preview display
transform
(RDPD)

preview display
(video monitor)

included the characteristics of film gamma and color crosstalk — the tendency of separate color layers to interact with each other. Cineon data is stored in log format corresponding to the density levels of the original negative. Also involved is a process known as *unbuilding*, which interprets the characteristics of the original film negative, which varies according to what film stock was used. As we will see, ACES workflow includes a similar step which, in essence, unbuilds the image characteristics particular to each video camera. For more details on Cineon, in particular the *black point* and *white point* and the concepts of *headroom* and *footroom*, see *Linear, Gamma, Log*.

Kodak retired the system in 1997 but the Cineon file format lives on and has been influential in digital filmmaking. The *DPX* format is also still widely used, but instead of just containing print density values, it can now act as a container for just about any type of image data. It is 10 bits per channel in a 32-bit word (two bits are not used).

Figure 11.19. A critical document in earliest stages of developing the ACES workflow — from the white paper *A Proposal for OpenEXR Color Management* by Florian Kainz of ILM. Although it is different in some ways, we'll see that it is essentially the same overall concept as the ACES workflow.

Figure 11.20. The *ACES/OpenEXR* export settings menu in RedCine-X Pro. More and more software incorporates the ACES workflow.

ILM AND OPENEXR

The next part of the story takes place at *Industrial Light and Magic*, the visual effects house started by George Lucas. ILM has become a cutting edge company in many aspects of filmmaking. As a pioneer in the world of *CGI* (*computer generated images*) and *VFX* (*visual effects*) integrated with live action footage, they soon realized that there were some limitations to the Cineon system. Images shot on film (and indeed on most video cameras) have particular image characteristics. CGI and VFX, on the other hand, are relatively "clean." The problem comes in when you attempt to combine the two. Since Cineon deliberately incorporates film image characteristics, ILM realized they needed a new system. They set out to devise a process that would make it possible to "back out" the particularities of each video camera and make the image neutral enough to be easily combined with computer generated footage.

In his paper *A Proposal for OpenEXR Color Management*, (considered to be one of the "founding documents" of OpenEXR and ACES) Florian Kainz, writes "We propose a practical color management scheme for the OpenEXR image file format as used in a film and visual effects production environment [Figure 11.19]. Our scheme produces predictable results when images from film, video and other sources are converted to the OpenEXR format, processed digitally, and then output onto film or video. Predictable results are possible even when activities like film scanning, image processing and film recording are performed at different companies. The scheme also allows accurate previewing, so that artists working with OpenEXR files can see on their computer monitor what their images will look like when they are presented in a theater."

The fundamental concept behind this is *scene referred* — the idea of recording the actual image without any in-camera processing. Scene referred means that the camera acts essentially as a *photon counter* — if X amount of photons hit the sensor, it produces Y number of electrons; no gamma correction, no knee or shoulder, just the image data as it fell onto the sensor. As Kainz puts it: "OpenEXR images are usually scene-referred: The floating-point red, green and blue values in an image are proportional to the relative amount of light coming from the corresponding objects in the depicted scene. The scene may exist in reality, it may be hypothetical as is the case for 3D computer renderings, or it may be a composite of real and hypothetical elements. In scene-referred images, the data stored in the pixels should not depend much on how the images were acquired. Ideally, if a scene is photographed twice, once on motion picture film, and once with a digital camera, then the corresponding scene-referred image files should contain the same data."

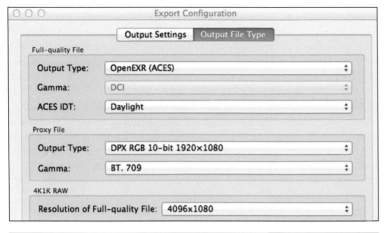

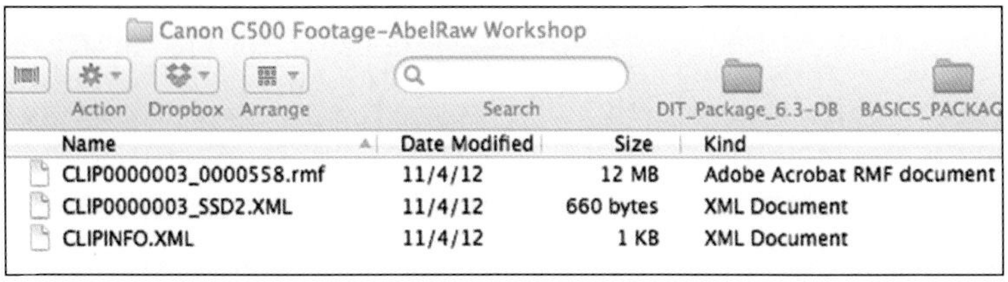

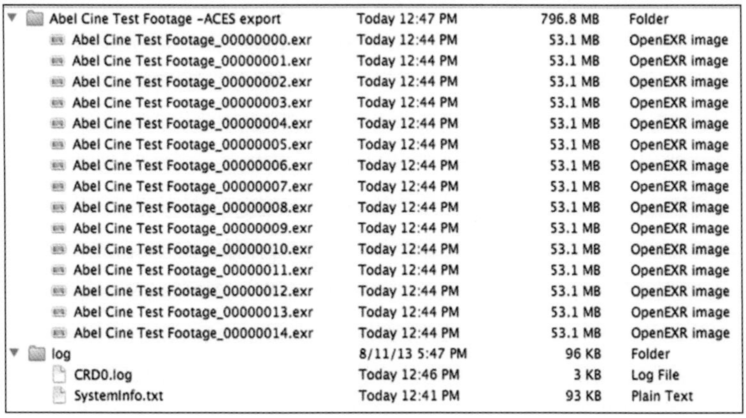

Figure 11.21. (Left, top) The output settings panel of Canon's *Cinema Raw Development*. In this example *ACES OpenEXR* has been selected as the output file type and the *ACES Input Device Transform* (*IDT*) is set for Daylight — that it is Canon footage is inherent in the software. Also note that it will export a proxy file, which in this case is DPX RGB 10-bit 1920x1080 with the BT.709 gamma applied.

Figure 11.22. (Left, middle) The folder containing the original test footage. The *.rmf* file is the actual Canon C500 footage. Also included are two XML files which carry the metadata.

Figure 11.23. (Left, bottom) The ACES OpenEXR output from *Cinema Raw Development*. The number of frames has been reduced for this illustration. This is also an example of files as a *stack* — every frame is an individual file. Note that there are also two log files. The *CRD0.log* is a log of the export and *System info* is a report on the computer hardware. Always preserve these logs for later reference.

Of course, this is an ideal; like film stocks, different sensors have varying artifacts and image particularities that may need to be compensated for, but the ideal of scene referred is that the image coming out of the camera will be linear. Beyond that, every camera manufacturer has different strategies for the processing of the data, even if it is the minimal processing we see in most RAW data. Of course, as we discussed previously, many cameras do log encoding for efficiency, but log encoding is easily *unbuilt* later down the line, unlike other forms of image manipulation that may occur in the camera. To accommodate the data, ILM developed a new file format: *OpenEXR* which introduced the concept of *floating point* which we discussed in *Codecs & Formats*. As you recall from that chapter, floating point permits far greater dynamic range and much finer precision within each step of exposure. ILM refers to it as a *high dynamic range format*. The 32-bit format and the more commonly used half-float 16-bit version are largely possible due to the huge processing power of *GPUs* in modern computers. ILM's concept of "shoot it straight, marry it with VFX and then do your image manipulations" is really the fundamental concept that led to the next stage of the history of this development — the *Academy*.

AMPAS AND ACES

With all the glitz and glamour of the Oscars, it is the *Academy of Motion Picture Arts and Sciences*. Early on in the development of the film industry, the Academy was the organization that standardized such important features as the size and spacing of film sprocket holes, for example. While sprocket holes may seem like a trivial issue, it is in fact an enormous part of the success and spread of filmmaking. We forget the fact that the size of film (35mm in most theatrical cases) and the sprocket holes is what makes film universal. You can shoot a movie in Mumbai, process it in Paris, make release prints in Los Angeles and have your premiere in New York — because the processing equipment, the editing machines and the projectors have all been standardized for many decades.

With the introduction of digital production, post and theatrical release, the Academy understood that there was again a need for some standardization. This is not to be thought of as creative interference — these standards in no way hamper the complete creative control of the director, DP, editor, colorist. A primary goal, according to Jim Houston, chair of the ACES committee, was to "provide a consistent color pipeline." The images from various sources are preserved in a consistent color space for later manipulation at which time the creative team is free to apply whatever artistic/creative decisions they may choose. The idea is that changes are applied nondestructively in the beginning using ASC-CDL or other metadata based color grade files. The entire range of the original camera is always available for manipulation, but they are dealing with footage that isn't causing problems by being in different color spaces, different gammas and so on. According to Houston, "ACES doesn't try to replicate film, but does retain a key design feature of film with a S-shaped tone curve to prevent the appearance of hard-clipping in images. Other than that, ACES tries to retain the exact hue of captured scene colors, something that film never did." In addition to being a consistent color pipeline, the process is also designed to ensure that results will be consistent from facility to facility.

This means that cinematographers have to give up "the knobs" — creative decisions that are baked into the footage at the time of shooting, but in return they get a tremendous degree of creative freedom further down the line. For many DPs this will call for a real philosophical change and perhaps a sense of loss of control of the image. This is where tools such as ASC-CDL come into play. Where in the days of film production the cinematographer had to rely on rough, inaccurate tools to communicate their ideas to the dailies color timer, now there are precise digital methods of sending those ideas down the line. In effect the process potentially gives the DP even greater control over the final image. This is also what makes the DIT such an important part of the process. The DP has specific ideas about what a scene should look like, but the cinematographer is doing several jobs at once — he or she rarely has time to dial in a CDL or work on a look in color correction software. The DIT, can function as the implementer of the DPs vision for the scene by communicating with the cinematographer, perhaps even getting to know their preferences and artistic tendencies; offering them alternate looks to approve or disapprove and then translating that look into a CDL, a LUT or a color grade to make sure that the look of the scene that the DP and director agreed on at the time of shooting is then translated into a form that can pass down the line either as a starting point or guidance or the final color correction process.

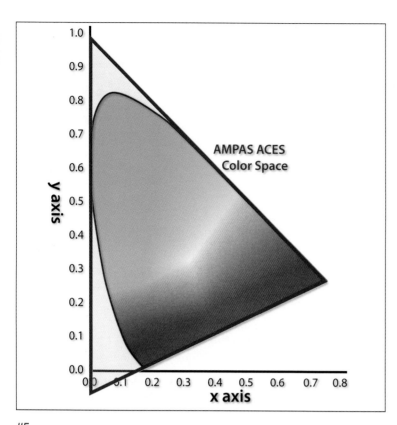

Figure 11.24. As we saw in the chapter *Digital Color,* AMPAS ACES color space has a huge gamut. It is fundamental to the entire ACES workflow in that it "future proofs" the process.

IIF

Their first effort in this area was the *Image Interchange Format.* The interchange refers not only to various stages of the process but also between facilities. Projects pass through a number of different companies: editing, color correction, and possibly several VFX companies. Images must look the same in the editing room, the color correction bay, the VFX house or in final mastering.

The other issue is projection in theaters. Cinema projectors have improved dramatically in a few short years and are likely to continue improving in the color gamut and dynamic range. If standards were to be set, the color scientists and engineers working on this effort felt they should be "future proofed" as much as possible. A big part of this is the ultra wide gamut color space they selected, which we looked at in detail in *Digital Color* (Figure 11.24). They settled on the name *Academy Color Encoding System* or *ACES* for the whole process. It is a method of standardizing camera output by *unbuilding* the various particularities of cameras from different manufacturers by unbuilding the output, putting it into a standardized color space, doing the artistic manipulation and then again standardizing the output so that it will appear the same no matter what projector it is shown on in theaters. The fundamental concept that makes this possible is the idea of *scene referred/linear* image data. Since no camera really outputs truly scene referred image data (due to spectral sensitivities of the sensors and other factors) some adjustment is needed to achieve this goal and also to achieve interchangeability of images from different types of cameras. Because linear images, especially from the latest generation of cameras, may contain images with very high dynamic ranges; the OpenEXR file format, with its range of values and precise image data, is at the heart of the system, which is the legacy of developments by the ILM team.

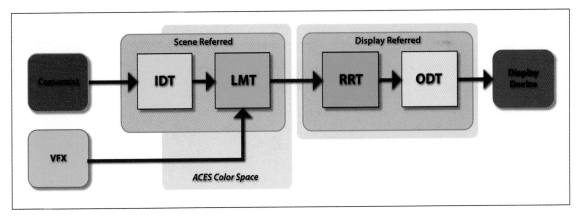

Figure 11.25. Block diagram of the ACES workflow from cameras and VFX to *Input Transform,* then *Look Management,* then to the output stages of *Reference Transform* and *Output Transform.*

THE STAGES

As shown in Figure 11.25, the ACES workflow involves four basic stages in the process, which are defined by their transforms. They are *Input Device Transform, Look Management Transform, Rendering Reference Transform* and *Output Display Transform.* It looks a bit complex but in reality it is rather simple and elegant in its design. Here are some very brief definitions of the primary steps of the workflow. The overall concept of the ACES workflow is much easier to understand once you break it down and look at each individual stage:

• *IDT* — *Input Device Transform.* A calculation to convert a camera or other image sources to the *Academy Color Encoding Specification,* at which point the image will be scene referred and in an RGB floating point format. Each camera will need its own IDT, in most cases provided by the manufacturer

• *LMT* — *Look Modification Transform.* This is where the colorist, DP and director work their artistry, in other words it is color correction. There is often a temporary transform to some kind of log or proxy space (depending on the color correction system). It can be guided by an ASC-CDL decision list, LUT or color grade.

• *RRT* — *Reference Rendering Transform,* A single transform that is designed to be the standard; it is also where *picture rendering* is done. Scene referred images do not look right to the eye, so the RRT converts the image to output referred. The RRT is an important part of making the final image. It also includes *Picture Rendering.*

• *ODT* — The *Output Device Transform,* also referred to as *Electro-Optical Conversion Function,* takes the output of the *RRT* and finishes the process to map data to the actual display devices where the project will be seen at home or in theaters. There are standard ODTs for current displays calibrated to Rec.709, DCI-P3, P3D60 and DCDM(XYZ).

ACES Terminology

Let's go over some fundamental terminology used in describing the ACES workflow.

- *ACES* — The whole system, as based on the *Academy Color Encoding Specification* color space that includes the entire visible spectrum is at the core of this system. ACES uses RGB values that are compatible with most existing image processing systems. The term ACES is also used to refer to the specific color space, as we discussed in *Digital Color*.

- *SMPTE (2065-4)* — The file format for ACES files. It is frame based and a proposed replacement for the .dpx format. ACES is derived from OpenEXR, (developed by *Industrial Light and Magic*) and is a *half float* format that shares the extension .exr. However, ACES files contain a metadata flag that identifies them. All ACES files are .exr, but not all .exr files are ACES.

- *Scene Referred* — ACES images are scene referred meaning that light is recorded as it existed at the camera sensor, regardless of how that might look when viewed in its raw state or independent of any output format or display device.

- *Display Referred* — A color space based on the actual gamut the display device (monitor or projector) is capable of reproducing. Although the front end of ACES is built around scene referred linear data, the back end has to be oriented toward how the images will actually be viewed, which is dependent on what projector or monitor will be used and also what the viewing conditions will be. As we know from the discussion of *picture rendering*, different viewing conditions (with different light levels) require different gamma levels to maintain the appearance of the original scene.

- *ACES* Color Space — This is the *scene referred*, ultra-wide gamut chosen by AMPAS to encompass not only all known current cameras and display devices but also future proofed for new developments since it encompasses all colors the human eye can see and then some. Since it includes every possible color, there is little chance that the color space will be outmoded by new technology.

- *OCES Color Space* — *Output Color Encoding Space*. A technical aspect of the system not essential for users to delve into.

- *ACES Proxy/Log ACES* — A color space based around "the knobs" in the *Look Management Transform (LMT)* stage. ACES color space is so enormous that there isn't really a way to manipulate it with current software/hardware. It is 16-bit integer (like many current grading systems) and it can be floating point as well. The *LMT* stage is where artistic, creative color decisions are made. There are several approaches to this phase of the process and software/hardware manufacturers are implementing this stage in various ways. Undoubtedly this technically difficult task will be evolving for several years as approaches are devised and field tested.

- *ADX* — *Academy Density Exchange Encoding* — A way of outputting film scans to ACES based on print density. ADX recommends a 16-bit integer format to accommodate the full dynamic range available but also defines a 10-bit encoding for compatibility.

- *CTL* — A *Color Transform Language* which is open source software; it is a programing language used for color transforms. For the general practitioner on the set or in post, it won't be necessary to deal with color transforms at this programming level (although they can if they wish to); instead it will be built into the software that is used in production, post production, VFX and mastering. It is primarily a method of enabling developers of post-production software and hardware to incorporate the ACES workflow. Transforms created this way can be converted into C Code and GPU shaders, so it is not necessary to use CTL to incorporate ACES into workflows.

THE TRANSFORMS

These stages of the ACES workflow — IDT, LMT, RRT and ODT are all transforms; fairly straightforward math, but where do they come from? Since *IDTs (Input Transforms)* are particular to each camera, they will be provided by each camera manufacturer, especially if they don't want to reveal the inner workings of their own special *secret sauce*. It is possible, however, to create your own IDT. This can be done in several ways, from as simple as photographing a test chart and plotting the results all the way up to more high-tech methods which require specialized equipment. These methods are outlined in the ACES spec.

Look Modification Transforms (LMT) are largely the province of the developers of the software used in color correction and they are incorporating this into the applications. The *Reference Rendering Transform (RRT)*, on the other hand, is strictly controlled by the ACES Committee. It is intended to be universal and the idea is that it will remain unchanged for long periods. The concept of the RRT is to encompass all of the transforms that are common to all *Output Transforms (ODT)* so that they don't have to be repeated. The *RRT* also includes *Picture Rendering* to adapt it to the viewing environment. *Output Transforms* will be developed by the manufacturers of monitors and of the projection systems used in cinemas. As new technology becomes available, such as laser projectors, *RRTs* and *ODTs* will be necessary for them.

metadata & timecode

Figure 12.1. Basic timecode: hours, minutes, seconds and frames.

Shooting and editing digitally has many advantages and one that is often overlooked is *metadata*. The term simply means "data about data," and in this context it means information within the signal other than the actual images. The concept is not original with digital, but as a concept extends back to the early film era. Whether you call them *clips*, *shots*, *takes*, or *footage*, it is important to keep them organized and easily found. The earliest solution was *slating*, something we still do today. Early slates were chalkboards, which evolved into Plexiglas with erasable markers and although these are still used, the introduction of *timecode slates* was a huge step forward, even though many productions still use the traditional clapper slate.

The next step was fully digital slates which are also available as apps on smart phones and tablets. These have the advantage of not needing the information slots to be erased and rewritten for every take and every shot. For erasing and rewriting on slates, camera assistants have long carried "the mouse" which was an erasable marker with a makeup puff pad taped to the end; a more modern solution is eraser pads that fit onto the ends of a marker.

What goes on a slate:
- Production name
- Date
- Director
- Cinematographer
- Camera (A, B, C, etc.)
- Frame rate
- Scene number
- Take number
- Day or night scene
- Interior or exterior scene
- Whether audio is being recorded or not (called MOS)
- Whether it's Pick Up (PU) shot

Traditionally, the 2nd AC operates the slate and coordinates with *Scripty* (*Continuity Supervisor*) to make sure the information on the slate (particularly scene numbers) are correct. Other notations on the slate might include the letters "PU" after the scene number. This means the take is a *pick up* — that it is being "picked up" from somewhere in the middle of the scene rather than starting the scene from the top. This often happens when the director is satisfied with the first part of a shot in previous takes, but wants the latter part of the take to be redone. This might happen if an actor flubs a line, for example. This is not to be confused with a *pick up day*, which is different. On most long form productions (such as feature films) once editing has begun, the editor and director make list of additional scenes and shots they need in order to do a proper editing job. These scenes are done on the pick up days some time after *principal photography* has concluded. They often involve only a skeleton crew and are sometimes done on a *run-and-gun* basis. On indie films, this may be as minimal as a camera crew and a few key crew members jumping in and out of a van to get shots here and there. Of course, it may also involve much more extensive shooting in a studio or on location.

Figure 12.2 *MovieSlate,* an iPhone/iPad app with all the features of a timecode slate plus extensive logging and reporting.

TIMECODE SLATES

Timecode slates (Figures 12.2 and 12.4) have spaces for the usual information: production name, shot number, take number and so on, but they also include an LED display of the *timecode.* The advantage of this is that it coordinates the film footage with the audio being recorded separately, which is called *double system recording* (one system — the camera — is shooting film while a second system (usually a digital sound recorder) is capturing production audio.

Besides running the slate, the 2nd AC is also responsible for *camera notes,* which keep track of take numbers and footage shot (in film) and sometimes timecode numbers (in video) although this practice varies widely from production to production.

SLATING ON THE SET

Camera assistant Brad Greenspan on syncing timecode on the set: "We make sure there is at least one *Lockit* box available on set [Figure 12.3]. Sometimes the sound mixer owns this, sometimes we get it as part of the camera package. Twice a day (more if they want to), sound jams this for us from their mixer, master clock, or whatever they're using for timecode.

Throughout the day, we jam the camera from the Lockit box. I don't generally like wearing the box on the camera as it's one more piece of hardware hanging from it. I usually keep it in my front box in case there's an issue, as well as for easy access. I jam from the box at the start of the day, after most power-offs (where there have also been no batteries on the camera), after lunch, and after shooting off-speed. If it's been a while and I have a free moment, I'll often jam then as well. I don't make it a big, obvious deal on set, but I do keep it in the back of my mind.

Figure 12.3. The *LockIt Buddy* is for double-system sound on DSLRs. It adjusts the level and impedance for recording timecode on the camera. It can take SMPTE (*LTC*) *Linear Timecode* from a slate, a professional audio recorder or a *Lockit Box* timecode/sync generator; it is shown below along with a *Lockit box* by *Ambient Recording.*

Our downloader is spot-checking for timecode drift as we hand off cards. We also almost always use a timecode slate (a) because it shows the timecode numbers, making it easy to see drift, and (b) it's another backup to make syncing in post faster, saving production money on that end. As far as wearing a wireless hop from sound, that depends on the job and the camera setup, as well as if sound is providing one. I usually don't mind carrying one on the camera if necessary, but it's yet another box to hang from camera. I also prefer it to a hard cable being run, even with the 'break away' connector."

Figure 12.4. A Denecke timecode slate. (Courtesy of Denecke).

TIMECODE GENERATORS

The timecode slate needs to be synchronized to the audio recorder so the slate is most often *jammed* (loaded) from the timecode generated by the audio equipment. In some cases, the timecode might come from a different source, such as a timecode generator; one example is a *Lockit box*. Although there are several software solutions available that can synchronize audio from a pro quality recorder with the sometimes not so good audio recorded on the camera, there are still advantages to having matching timecode on the video and audio; as a result nearly all professional productions use a timecode slate and also use the clapper for sync. Some productions shot on film and even some digital productions still use only the traditional clapboard.

WHAT IS TIMECODE?

Only someone who did editing before timecode was invented can truly appreciate what a huge improvement it brought to production and postproduction. The secret of its power is that it gives a unique, searchable identifier to every single frame of footage; audio will also have a unique timecode for each frame. With modern cameras and audio recorders, timecode is recorded along with every video or audio frame. When the video or audio is played, this data can be read and the appropriate frame number can be displayed. Each frame is uniquely addressed and can be located with precision. The metadata information associated with each frame may have four parts:

- Time in hours, minutes, seconds and frames
- User bits
- Control bits
- Synchronisation word

The time is, in essence the frame number — keep in mind that it may or may not be "real" time: what is considered "zero" might be midnight or (more commonly) it is the beginning of the tape or digital recording. This is a big distinction: timecode can be actual clock time or just the start of shooting as zero. Clock time, called time-of-day timecode, can be useful in some situations, such as documentaries, concerts and events, especially where multiple cameras are shooting at the same time and their footage needs to be synchronized later in post. If multiple cameras can be linked together with hard wire or wireless sync, this may not be necessary.

Figure 12.5. (Top) The timecode panel and controls on a *Sony F900.*

Figure 12.6. (Below) Close up of the controls shows the selections for *Free Run* (*F-Run*) and *Record Run* (*R-Run*) and also *Preset* (which allows the operator to set the beginning time code value) or *Regen*, which regenerates the timecode

TWO NOTES ON TIMECODE

Standard timecode notation is 00:00:00:00 — hours, minutes, seconds, frames separated by a colon. Typing this out every time would be extremely tedious. Most editorial and post production systems allow shortcuts such as typing a period (dot) instead of a colon (which is two handed as it involves the shift key) and it is not necessary to input leading zeros. This means that typing in timecode 00:00:21:15 can just be 21, period, 15 — the software knows how to interpret this correctly by inserting zeros for hours and minutes. Some systems don't even need the periods.

Editors should be aware of a few issues when transferring video to another deck, device, or NLE computer system. The time code will not transfer if you connect via older video systems or HDMI interfaces.

The values range from 00:00:00:00, to the largest number supported by this format; 23:59:59:29, — no more than 23 hours, no minutes or seconds greater than 59, and no frames above the highest allowed by the rate being used (29 in this case for 30 frames per second). This format represents the duration of scene or program material, and makes time calculations easy and direct.

```
------------------------------------------------
Infinite Monkey
------------------------------------------------

CAM  ROLL SCENE TAKE  SLATE  DATE     Timecode IN              Timecode OUT             Duration        FPS     INT  EXT  NITE  MOS

A    3    77A   1     31     3/7/14   14:12:47:22 3/7/14       14:12:55:03              00:00:07:05     23.976          EXT  NITE  MOS

A    3    77    1     30     3/7/14   14:12:26:16 3/7/14       14:12:34:05              00:00:07:13     23.976          EXT  NITE  MOS

A    3    21    2     29     3/7/14   14:11:57:17 3/7/14       14:12:16:18              00:00:19:01     23.976          EXT  NITE  MOS

A    3    21    1     28     3/7/14   14:11:34:14 3/7/14       14:11:50:08              00:00:15:18     23.976          EXT  NITE  MOS

A    3    20    1     27     3/7/14   14:10:53:13 3/7/14       14:11:14:03              00:00:20:14     23.976          EXT  NITE

A    3    19    3     26     3/7/14   14:10:34:23 3/7/14       14:10:44:01              00:00:09:02     23.976          EXT  NITE

A    3    19    2     25     3/7/14   14:10:07:02 3/7/14       14:10:27:01              00:00:19:23     23.976          EXT  NITE

A    3    19    1     24     3/7/14   14:09:29:02 3/7/14       14:10:02:10              00:00:33:08     23.976          EXT  NITE

A    3    27D   2     23     3/7/14   14:08:50:20 3/7/14       14:09:10:16              00:00:19:20     23.976          EXT  NITE
------------------------------------------------
Notes

Production        Roll  Scene Take   Date     Time      Timecode                        Note

Infinite Monkey   3     27    1      3/7/14   2:03 PM   14:02:27:01 - 14:02:44:03       Master at warehouse.

Infinite Monkey   3     27    2      3/7/14   2:03 PM   14:03:04:18 - 14:03:18:06       Sirens in BG.

Infinite Monkey   3     27A   1      3/7/14   2:04 PM   14:04:08:06 - 14:04:19:06       Coverage on him.

Infinite Monkey   3     27C   1      3/7/14   2:07 PM   14:06:49:23 - 14:07:02:10       Coverage on her.

Infinite Monkey   3     27C   2      3/7/14   2:08 PM   14:07:26:13 - 14:07:39:11       Sirens in BG.

Infinite Monkey   3     27D   1      3/7/14   2:09 PM   14:08:23:07 - 14:08:38:21       Handheld.

Infinite Monkey   3     27D   2      3/7/14   2:09 PM   14:08:58:19 - 14:09:08:15       Handheld.
```

Figure 12.7. A logging report emailed from *MovieSlate*. This is in plain text; it can also send reports as Avid ALE and Final Cut Pro XML.

VIDEO FRAME RATE

The frame is the smallest unit of measure in SMPTE Timecode and is a direct reference to the individual picture of film or video. The rate is the number of times per second pictures are displayed to provide motion. There are four standard frame rates (frames per second) that apply to SMPTE: 24, 25, 29.7, and 30.

- 24 FPS (film, ATSC, 2k, 4k, 5k, and 8K)
- 25 FPS based on European motion picture film and video, also known as SMPTE EBU PAL (Europe, Uruguay, Argentina, Australia), SECAM, DVB, ATSC)
- 29.97 FPS (30 ÷ 1.001)
- 30 FPS

The frames figure advances one count for every frame of film or video, allowing the user to time events down to 1/24th, 1/25th, or 1/30th of a second. Unless you have an application that specifically calls out one of the above frame rates, it doesn't matter which timecode is used as long it is consistent.

RECORD RUN AND FREE RUN

Most cameras offer the option of recording timecode in either *Record Run* or *Free Run*. Record Run advances the timecode only when the camera is recording. This means that there are no gaps in timecode between takes. Free Run advances the timecode all the time, whether the camera is recording or not; in most cases the timecode advances even if the camera is powered down.

Free Run can also be set up to coordinate with actual clock time — often called *time-of-day timecode*. This can be useful in situations where it is useful to keep a record of when the recording was done. More commonly, in documentary production or concert shooting where multiple cameras are used, having all cameras record synchronized timecode will make editing much easier. This can be accomplished by *jam syncing* all the cameras from the same source (or from a master camera) or by having a timecode generator running to all cameras, either wired or wireless. Some thing you may still encounter is called *Keycode*. This is a method of associating individual film frames with the timecode of any video derived from that original film. It is useful when video editing something shot on film. Keycode is embedded in the film emulsion at the time of manufacture and is machine readable.

REPORTS

Reports and logs are an important part of filmmaking whether you are shooting film or digital. There are several apps for reporting information for each shot (Figure 12.7). Some ACs still prefer handwritten reports. AC Brad Greenspan: "I am still firmly in the camp of paper reports. I've got a template that I like. I can get a box of them made in carbonless copies (3 or 4) depending on production, and it's enough to get through the show.

"There are two main reasons I don't like filling out digital ones: (1) It requires a device whose batteries will stay powered all day. If it's hour 16, I have a feeling my iPad won't have that much power left if it's been used for reports/logs. A piece of paper will always work. (2) I can't find an app that's as fast to fill out as a report and log book.

"With more demands being placed on my 2nd AC these days, anything that can potentially slow them down is a problem. Also, separate report sheets and logbooks for each camera (like in film days) is easier, in my experience, than entering it in an app. *Scripty* [the *continuity supervisor*] gets reports after each reload, loader gets them after. I had one data manager scan them into Acrobat, and emailed them out at the end of the day, as well as included them on the shuttle drive. I had another who copied them into Excel. They also would all mark the circled takes for post." For a more detailed discussion of camera reports and logs see *Cinematography: Theory and Practice* by the same author.

OTHER TYPES OF METADATA

The metadata associated with a particular video clip or still photo has the capacity to store a wide range of information — and these uses are constantly growing, especially in the areas of VFX, motion control and 3D. This data can be generated automatically by the camera (*source metadata*), or added at any stage along the way to final output (*added metadata*). There is also a category called *derived metadata*; this would include things the software can perform on its own such as face and speech recognition.

Some examples of metadata:
- Shooting date and time
- Camera
- Location
- Lens Focal Length
- Camera tilt angle
- F/stop
- ISO
- File size
- Audio channels

And many, many more. Some types of data are highly specialized; for example, some camera heads can record the speed and direction of a pan or tilt. This information is vital if the shot is part of a motion control or VFX shot.

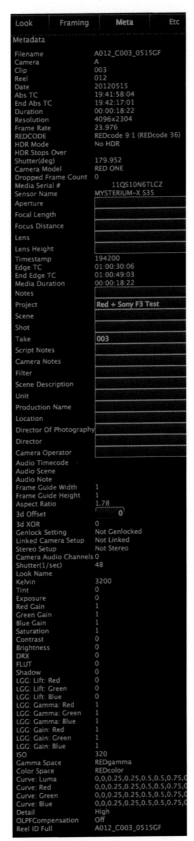

Metadata	
Look	**Framing**	**Meta**	**Etc**

Metadata	
Filename	A012_C003_0515GF
Camera	A
Clip	003
Reel	012
Date	20120515
Abs TC	19:41:58:04
End Abs TC	19:42:17:01
Duration	00:00:18:22
Resolution	4096x2304
Frame Rate	23.976
REDCODE	REDcode 9:1 (REDcode 36)
HDR Mode	No HDR
HDR Stops Over	
Shutter(deg)	179.952
Camera Model	RED ONE
Dropped Frame Count	0
Media Serial #	11QS10N6TLCZ
Sensor Name	MYSTERIUM-X S35
Aperture	
Focal Length	
Focus Distance	
Lens	
Lens Height	
Timestamp	194200
Edge TC	01:00:30:06
End Edge TC	01:00:49:03
Media Duration	00:00:18:22
Notes	
Project	Red + Sony F3 Test
Scene	
Shot	
Take	003
Script Notes	
Camera Notes	
Filter	
Scene Description	
Unit	
Production Name	
Location	
Director Of Photography	
Director	
Camera Operator	
Audio Timecode	
Audio Scene	
Audio Note	
Frame Guide Width	1
Frame Guide Height	1
Aspect Ratio	1.78
3d Offset	0
3d XOR	0
Genlock Setting	Not Genlocked
Linked Camera Setup	Not Linked
Stereo Setup	Not Stereo
Camera Audio Channels	0
Shutter(1/sec)	48
Look Name	
Kelvin	3200
Tint	0
Exposure	0
Red Gain	1
Green Gain	1
Blue Gain	1
Saturation	1
Contrast	0
Brightness	0
DRX	0
FLUT	0
Shadow	0
LGG: Lift: Red	0
LGG: Lift: Green	0
LGG: Lift: Blue	0
LGG: Gamma: Red	1
LGG: Gamma: Green	1
LGG: Gamma: Blue	1
LGG: Gain: Red	1
LGG: Gain: Green	1
LGG: Gain: Blue	1
ISO	320
Gamma Space	REDgamma
Color Space	REDcolor
Curve: Luma	0,0,0.25,0.25,0.5,0.5,0.75,0
Curve: Red	0,0,0.25,0.25,0.5,0.5,0.75,0
Curve: Green	0,0,0.25,0.25,0.5,0.5,0.75,0
Curve: Blue	0,0,0.25,0.25,0.5,0.5,0.75,0
Detail	High
OLPFCompensation	Off
Reel ID Full	A012_C003_0515GF

Figure 12.8. The metadata panel in RedCine-X Pro.

Additional metadata can be added on the set, such as camera notes, production notes, comments and so on, or at the DIT cart or in editing, such as keywords, notes, etc. While film production people are constantly finding new and valuable uses for metadata, one of the most widely used is keywords. In fact some editing software is largely built around the use of keywords to organize, sort and classify video clips. The great advantage of metadata is that it is searchable and can be sorted in any number of ways. This means that what may appear to be nothing more than a *bin* of video clips is in fact a *database*. The advantages for editing, post-production and archiving are enormous. Using metadata is simple, but there are some issues to be aware of.

Not all metadata schemes are compatible and interoperable. There some different standards, including *Dublin Core* (DC), *Public Broadcasting Core* (*PB Core*) and *Motion Picture Experts Group* (*MPEG7*). The term "core" simply refers to the idea of core metadata for generic resource descriptions. As with many aspects of digital video, it is a still developing field and is subject to change, growth and sometimes conflicting standards. There is no one "universal standard" for metadata but at the moment, the *Dublin Core* (formally known as the *Dublin Core Metadata Initiative*) comes closest to being universally exchangeable. It is also possible to classify metadata into four general types:

- Structural metadata: describing the metadata record and its relationship to the digital video resource.
- Descriptive metadata: Summarizes the content of the digital video.
- Administrative metadata: Which can include rights metadata, information about original analogue sources of the video and archiving metadata.
- Technical metadata: Administrative metadata which describes the properties of the video file itself. Also includes information about opening and handling the file, which is useful to the applications in which the data will be handled.

XML

XML stands for *eXtensible Markup Language*. It is a human-readable, plain language method of storing and transferring metadata. It is extensively used in website encoding and is very similar to HTML as it serves much the same purpose. HTML was developed as a standard which makes it possible for many different types of computers and operating systems to not only read text and image data but also to display it as intended — we could think of it as a "translator" which enable the transfer of data to dissimilar environments. Also, both HTML and XML work by *tagging* elements.

XML is actually the result of an evolving set of standards all aimed at data interchange: originally, there was *EDL* (*Edit Decision List*), followed by *OMF* (*Open Media Framework*), and *AAF* (*Advanced Authoring Format*) and *MXF* (*Material eXchange Format*), which is a container format that combines the data (essence) together with the metadata (Figure 12.9).

In video we need the same sort of capability: video data almost never stays on one machine or in one system — it is always on the move from the camera to the DIT cart to various postproduction facilities. XML serves as a method of transferring the metadata along with the video files. For example, XML can be used to transfer edited sequences from an editing program to a color correction application

AN EXAMPLE OF AVID GENERATED XML

```xml
<FilmScribeFile Version="1.0" Date="Oct. 25, 2012">
<AssembleList>
<ListHead>
<Title>SCENE 76</Title>
<Tracks>V1</Tracks>
<EventCount>26</EventCount>
<OpticalCount>0</OpticalCount>
<DupeCount>0</DupeCount>
<MasterDuration>
<FrameCount>2394</FrameCount>
<Edgecode Type="35mm 4p">0149+10</Edgecode>
<Timecode Type="TC1">00:01:39:21</Timecode>
</MasterDuration>
<SourceDuration/>
<MediaFile/>
<VideoConform>KN Start</VideoConform>
<AudioConform>Aux Ink</AudioConform>
<LFOA>
<Edgecode Type="35mm 4p">0149+10</Edgecode>
</LFOA>
<EditRate>24</EditRate>
<Resolution>24</Resolution>
</ListHead>
<Events>
<Event Num="1" Type="Cut" Length="75" SourceCount="1">
<Master>
<Reel/>
<Start>
<Timecode Type="TC1">01:00:00:00</Timecode>
<Pullin>A</Pullin>
<Edgecode Type="35mm 4p">5010+08</Edgecode>
<Frame>80168</Frame>
<FrameImage/>
</Start>
<End>
<Timecode Type="TC1">01:00:03:03</Timecode>
<Pullin>C</Pullin>
<Edgecode Type="35mm 4p">5015+02</Edgecode>
<Frame>80242</Frame>
<FrameImage/>
</End>
</Master>
```

Figure 12.9. An example of XML code generated by Avid.

and then back again — this is called *round tripping*.

Editors and color correction artists have been exchanging files for a long time but often that involved *rendering* the files, which can be an extremely time consuming process, not to mention the demands it places on the hardware. This is a bigger deal than it might seem. In digital workflows, it is very common to have several parts of the production process (both hardware and software) "talk" about the same footage. Most often, all of these operations rely on a central repository of the footage — a server where all video files and documents are consolidated and backed up. Applications such as cataloging and archiving software, editing, color correction, visual effects, etc. need to be able to access and process these video and audio components. While XML and other interchange languages can facilitate this workflow, there are still glitches and problems to smooth out.

METADATA FROM RIGS

Metadata can be generated from sources other than the camera. Some camera heads and cranes (including 3-axis heads) also record data such as tilt and rotation angles. This is extremely valuable for use in compositing with other shots, greenscreen and VFX work. Most of these rigs can also record GPS data as well, so any time that location, height of camera above the ground, tilt and rotation, time of day and related data come into play, they are recordable, searchable and usable in post. Much of this data used to be recorded manually, by camera assistants or VFX specialists measuring and writing down the data; without this metadata, writing it down is still necessary. This type of recording was pioneered by DP David Stump who won a technical Academy Award for it.

METADATA AT THE DIT CART

Most download and processing software allows the user to add or alter some metadata. The most obvious is Reel #, Mag or Media #, name of production/director/DP, etc. These are an important part of keeping track of data and preparing it for the editorial process. Of course, metadata for editing purposes will be done at the request of the editorial team and to their specifications — one of the most important things to be worked out in preproduction meetings. Some cameras, such as the Black Magic, allow for direct input of metadata.

references

Adams, Ansel. *The Negative*. Little, Brown & Company. 1976.

Adams, Ansel. *The Print*. Little, Brown & Company. 1976.

Adams, Art. *Hitting the Exposure Sweet Spot*. ProVideo Coalition. 2012.

Adams, Art. *What are Incident Light Meters Really Good For, Anyway?* ProVideoCoalition.com. 2012.

Adams, Art. *Log vs. Raw: The Simple Version*. ProVideo Coalition. 2013.

Adams, Art. *The Not-So-Technical Guide to S-Log and Log Gamma Curves*. ProVideoCoalition.com. 2013.

Apple. *Apple ProRes White Paper*. Apple. 2009.

ARIB. *Multiformat Color Bar — ARIB Standard STD-B28 V1*. Association of Radio Industries and Businesses. 2002.

Arri. *ARRI Look Files for ALEXA*. Arri White Paper. 2011.

Arri. *ARRI Look File Low Contrast Curve*. Arri White Paper. 2011.

Arri. *MXF/DNxHD With Alexa*. Arri White Paper. 2012.

Avid. *Avid DNxHD Technology*. Avid White Paper. 2012.

Behar, Suny. *Best Practices Guide to Digital Cinematography Using Panasonic Professional HD Cameras*. Panasonic Broadcast. 2009.

Brendel, Harald. *Alexa LogC Curve, Usage in VFX*. Arri White Paper. 2006.

Brown, Blain. *Motion Picture and Video Lighting*, 2nd Edition. Focal Press. 2007.

Brown, Blain. *Cinematography: Theory and Practice*, 2nd Edition. Focal Press. 2011.

Cain, Ben. *Arri Alexa — Legal vs. Extended*. NegativeSpaces.com. 2012.

CineForm. *CineForm RAW Technology Overview*. CineForm White Paper. 2007.

Cioni, Michael. *Best Practices for Data Management*. Canon White Paper. 2012.

Clark, Curtis; Kawada, Norihiko; Patel, Dhanendra; Osaki, Yuki; Endo, Kazuo. *S-Log White Paper*, Version 1.12.3. Sony White Paper. 2009.

Dunthorn, David. *Film Gamma Versus Video Gamma*, CF Systems. 2004.

Extron. *The ABC's of Digital Video Signals*. Extron Video White Paper. 2009.

Gaggioni, Hugo; Patel, Dhanendra; Yamashita, Jin; Kawada, N. Endo; K, Clark Curtis. *S-Log: A New LUT For Digital Production Mastering and Interchange Applications*. Sony White Paper. 2011.

Galt, John and Pearman, James. *Perceptually Uniform Grayscale Coding In the Panavision Genesis Electronic Cinematography System*. Panavision. 2009.

Goldstone, Joseph. *Usage of Test Charts With the Alexa Camera — Workflow Guideline*. Arri. 2011.

Grimaldi, Jean-Luc. *Using 1D and 3D LUTS for Color Correction*. TCube. 2012.

International Telecommunication Union. *Recommendation ITU-R BT.709-5: Parameter Values for the HDTV Standards for Production and International Programme Exchange*. ITU-R Publication. 2002.

Iwaki, Yasuharu and Uchida, Mitsuhiro. *Next Generation of Digital Motion Picture Making Procedure: The Technological Contribution of AMPAS-IIF*. FujiFilm Research & Development #56-2011, FujiFilm Corporation. 2011.

Kainz, Florian. *A Proposal for OpenEXR Color Management*. Industrial Light & Magic. 2004.

Kainz, Florian. *Using OpenEXR and the Color Transformation Language in Digital Motion Picture Production*. Industrial Light & Magic/The Academy of Motion Picture Arts & Sciences, Science and Technology Council Image Interchange Framework Committee. 2007.

Kainz, Florian; Bogart, Rod; Stanczyk, Piotr. *Technical Introduction to OpenEXR*. Industrial Light & Magic. 2013.

Kodak. *Conversion of 10-Bit Log Film Data to 8-Bit Linear or Video Data for the Cineon Digital Film System*. Kodak White Paper. 1995.

Lejeune, Cedric. *Using ASC-CDL in a Digital Cinema Workflow*. Workflowers. 2009.

Most, Michael. *Scratch and Red Raw: The Red Color Workflow v2.0*. Assimilate White Paper. 2010.

Oran, Andrew and Roth, Vince. *Color Space Basics*. Association of Moving Image Archivists Tech Review. 2012.

Parra, Alfonso. *Color Modifications in Sony CineAlta Cameras*. White Paper. 2008.

Poynton, Charles. *High Definition Television and Desktop Computing*. Sun Microsystems, Proceedings of the International Technical Workshop on Multimedia Technologies in HDTV, IEEE CES Tokyo. 1993.

Poynton, Charles. *A Technical Introduction to Digital Video*. John Wiley and Sons. 1996.

Poynton, Charles. *A Guided Tour of Color Space*. New Foundations for Video Technology. SMPTE. 1997.

Poynton, Charles. *Frequently Asked Questions About Gamma*. www.poynton.com. 1998

Poynton, Charles. *Brightness and Contrast*. www.poynton.com. 2002.

Poynton, Charles. *Merging Computing With Studio Video: Converting Between R'G'B' and 4:2:2*. Discreet Logic. 2004.

Poynton, Charles. *Picture Rendering, Image State and BT.709*. www.poynton.com. 2010.

Poynton, Charles. *Digital Video and HD Algorithms and Interfaces,* 2nd Edition. Elsevier/Morgan Kaufman. 2012.

Quantel. *The Quantel Guide to Digital Intermediate*. Quantel White Paper. 2003.

Rodriquez, Jason. *RAW Workflows: From Camera to Post*. Silicon Imaging. 2007.

Roush Media. *Digital Cinema Mastering 101*. Roush Media. 2013.

Selan, Jeremy. *Cinematic Color From Your Monitor to the Big Screen*. Siggraph 2012 Course Notes. Sony Pictures Imageworks. 2012

Selan, Jeremy. *Cinematic Color: From Your Monitor to the Big Screen*. Visual Effects Society White Paper. 2012.

Shaw, Kevin. *The Beauty of Aces*. Final Color, Ltd. White Paper. 2012.

Shaw, Steve. *Digital Intermediate — A Real World Guide to the DI Process*. Light Illusion. 2009.

Shipsides, Andy. *HDTV Standards: Looking Under the Hood of Rec.709*. HDVideoPro.com. 2013.

Sony. *Digital Cinematography with Hypergamma*. Sony White Paper. 2013.

Sony. *4K Workflow With CineAlta F5, F55, F65*. Sony White Paper. 2013.

Sony. *Technical Summary for S-Gamut3, Cine/S-Log3 and S-Gamut3/S-Log3*. Sony White Paper. 2014.

Sullivan, Jim. *Superior Color Video Images Through Multi-Dimensional Color Tables*. Entertainment Experience. White Paper. 2010.

Thorpe, Larry. *Canon-Log Transfer Characteristics*, Canon White Paper. 2012.

Vision Research. *The Phantom CINE File Format*. Vision Research, 2007.

Wong, Ping Wah and Lu, Yu Hua. *A Method For the Evaluation of Wide Dynamic Range Cameras*. Proceedings of SPIE, Digital Photography VIII, 2012.

acknowledgements

SPECIAL THANKS

I want to acknowledge the many people who have made this research and writing possible: Art Adams, Adam Wilt and Charles Poynton among many others. Their research, careful methodology and thorough methods of testing have paved the way for many of us. Geoff Boyle's *Cinematographer's Mailing List* is the go-to place for professional cinematographers and DITs who have questions. And especially David and Susan Corley at *DSC Labs* for their assistance.

Thanks to Art Adams, Ben Cain and Nick Shaw, who read the manuscript. Thanks also to Adam Wilt, Joseph Goldstone, Jim Houston, Mike Sipple, Ben Schwartz and Graeme Nattress who read individual chapters. They all made many helpful comments and suggestions. Any errors that remain are entirely my responsibility. I invite comments, suggestions, corrections and debates. I can be contacted at hawk-handsaw@charter.net.

ACKNOWLEDGEMENTS

Abel Cine Tech. *Abelcine.com*

Adam Wilt, Inventor and Consultant. *Adamwilt.com*

Andy Shipsides, Director of Education at *Abel Cine Tech — LA. Abelcine.com*

Arri. *Arri.com*

Art Adams, DP and writer. *Artadamsdp.com*

Ben Hopkins, DIT. *Huemaninterest.com*

Ben Schwartz, DIT

Blackmagic. *Blackmagic.com*

Bob Campi, DIT

Canon. *Canon.com*

Charles Poynton, Color Scientist, consultant, writer. *Poynton.com*

Dane Brehm, DIT, Workflow Consultant. *Prettymovingpictures.com*

DSC Labs, David and Susan Corley. *DSClabs.com*

Doug Solis, *BigFoot Mobile Carts. Bigfootmobilecarts.com*

Evan Luzi, Camera assistant. *Theblackandblue.com*

Evan Nesbit, DIT

Geoff Boyle, DP and founder of the *Cinematographer's Mailing List*

Graeme Nattress, Image processing software. *Nattress.com*

Jim Houston, Colorist and ACES Committee Chair. *Starwatcher Digital*

Joseph Goldstone, Image Scientist. *Arri.*

Mark Wilenkin, DIT. *Markwilenkin.com*

Micha van Hove, *NoFilmSchool.com*

Mike Sipple, Director of Engineering. *Fletcher Camera*

Nick Shaw, Colorist and Workflow Consultant, Antler Post. *Antlerpost.com*

Steve Shaw, Light Illusion. *Lightillusion.com*

Panasonic. *Panasonic.com*

Panavision. *Panavision.com*

Pomfort. *Pomfort.com*

Sacha Riviere, DIT. *Thedithouse.com*

Sony. *Sony.com*

Von Thomas, DIT. *Digitaltechnyc.com*

ABOUT THE AUTHOR

Blain Brown has worked in the motion picture industry for over 25 years as a cinematographer, and also as a director, screenwriter and producer. He was educated at C.W. Post College, MIT, and Harvard Graduate School of Design.

Cover Photos — Top: Colleen Mlvezia, Bottom: Blain and Ada Brown.
Book and cover design by the author.

index

References to figures are shown in *italics*. References to tables are shown in **bold**.

2K video 30, 31

3D feature DIT carts *196*

3G-SDI 33

4K Production Cameras (Blackmagic Design) 125

4K video 30, 31, 32, 33, 143

8K sensors 14

8K video 143

18% gray *see* middle (18%) gray

19" racks (or rack mounts or relay racks) *202*, 203–204

45 degree rule (diffuse white) 123

75% color bars (SMPTE) 50, *51–53*, 52–53, 57

85 correction filters 134

100% Color Bars (or RGB pattern) 52, 53, 57

Academy Density Exchange Encoding (ADX) 259

Academy of Motion Picture Arts and Sciences (AMPAS) 144, 252, 256; *see also* ACES (Academy Color Encoding System)

ACES (Academy Color Encoding System): color spaces 142, 144, *145*, *257*, 259; components of system 252; digital negative 114; headroom/footroom 76, 253; history of (AMPAS and ACES 256; Cineon system (Kodak) 252–253; ILM and OpenEXR 76, 118, 169–170, 252, *253–255*, 254–255, 257; Image Interchange Format (IIF) 257); picture rendering 95; Reference Rendering Transforms (RRTs) 260; scene-referred method 71, 254–255, 257, 259; SMPTE ACES file format 259; terminology 259; workflow stages 258, *258*

Adams, Ansel 58, 118, 127

Adams, Art: bits per stop 81; deBayering 12; diffuse white (45 degree rule) 123; DSC Labs OneShot charts 63–64; expose to the right (ETTR) 123; incident and reflectance (spot) meters 119–120; matrix 145–146; middle (18%) gray 121–122; native ISO 20–21; putting black at black 122-123; RAW concept 25–26; S-curve 72; Sony S-Log 86; waveform monitors and LUTs 120–121; zebras 124

ADC (Analog-to-Digital Converter) 2, 3

additive color 130

Adobe: CinemaDNG 28, 89, 157, 167; Flash Video (FLV, F4V) 154; and frame rates 34; Lightroom 125; Photoshop 125, 133

Advanced Systems Format (ASF) (Microsoft) 154

Advanced Video Coding (AVC) 159–160

ADX (Academy Density Exchange Encoding) 259

AIFF (Audio Interchange File Format, Apple) 154

Aja, Ki-Pro *213*, 221–222, *221*

ALE (Avid Log Exchange) files 250

Alexa cameras *see* Arri

algebra, linear algebra 37

aliasing 7–8, *8*

alpha channel 29, 32

Ambient, LockIt box *46*, *263*

American National Standards Institute (ANSI) 90

American Society of Cinematographers (ASC) 248; *see also* ASC-CDL (Color Decision List)

American Standards Organization (ASA) 99

AMPAS (Academy of Motion Picture Arts and Sciences) *see* Academy of Motion Picture Arts and Sciences (AMPAS)

amplitude (video signal) 42

Analog-to-Digital Converter (ADC or A-to-D Converter) 2, 3

angstroms 38

ANSI (American National Standards Institute) 90

anti-aliasing filters 7–8, *8*

Antonioni, Michelangelo, *Blowup 162*, 163

aperture (or iris) 99, 100

aperture mask 13

Apple: AIFF (Audio Interchange File Format) 154; iPhone-based video storage calculator *226*; MovieSlate *263*, *266*; ProRes codecs *159*, 160–161, 165; QuickTime format 154, 220; Terminal 217; *see also* Thunderbolt cables

ARIB (Association of Radio Industries and Businesses) 53, 74

Arnold, Jillian 211

Arri: Alexa (ArriRAW 11, 157, 165; camera tests set-up *4*; drive formatting 212; dynamic range 69; false colors 115; file folder *223*; f/stops on waveform 108; HDR (High Dynamic Range) 128; Log C 87–88, 121–122; Looks 190, *191*, *192*, *244*, *245*, *246*; middle (18%) gray 91; output options *76*; and Quicktime files 220; sensors 15–18; stacks format 154; workflow *235*, *244*, *245*–246, *246*); Arri Meta Extract

sensitivity 20–21, *21*; *see also* ISO levels

sensors: and color balance (Arri *Alexa*'s approach 15–18; Canon's approach 15, *17*; color correction 15); digital sensors (back-illuminated CMOS 9; CCD (Charge Coupled Device) 8–9; CMOS (Complementary Metal Oxide Semiconductor) 9, 19; Foveon sensors 9, *9*; frame transfer CCD 9; Junction Field Effect Transistors (JFET) 9; LBCAST (Lateral Buried Charge Accumulator) 9; three-chip sensors 9, *9*, *10*; three main types *9*); and IR/hot mirror filters 21–22; and ISO (sensitivity) levels 20–21, *21*; and OLPF (Optical Low Pass Filters) 7–8, *8*; sensor saturation 70, 117; sensor size and depth-of-field 18; sensor substrate 11; and shutters 18–19; *see also* cameras; deBayering/demosaicing; digital signal path/processor (DSP); noise; photosites; pixels

separation, and exposure 118

Serial Digital Interface (SDI) *see* SDI (Serial Digital Interface)

Serial Attached SCSI (SAS) connectors 228

setup/pedestal level 46

S-Gamut (Sony) 87

shadows 175, 176, *176*, *177*

Shaw, Nick 94

Shaw, Steve 81

shift register design 8–9

Shipsides, Andy 75, 157, 192

ShotPut Pro 211, *216*, 217

Showscan 34

shutters 18–19; global shutters 19; rolling shutters 19; rotating shutters 101; shutter angles 99, 101, 107; shutter speed 99, 101; spinning mirrors 19

shuttle/transfer drives 214, 223

Siemens Star *63*

signals: dark current signal 14; digital signal path/processor (DSP) 2, 3, *3*, 5, 8, 99; RGB signals 16, 28, 229; *see also* legal video

Signal to Noise ratio (S/N or SNR) 20

silent aperture 31

Silverstack (Pomfort) 211, *215*, 217–218

SI metric system 37, 38

Sippel, Mike 52

skin tone 52, *61*, *63*, 64–65

slating 262–264

S-Log (Sony) 86, *86*, **87**, *87*, *93*

Smith, George 8–9

SMPTE (Society of Motion Picture & Television Engineers): 75% color bars 50, *51–53*, 52–53, 57; 372M dual link interface standard 33; ACES file format 259; Color Transformation Language (CTL) 252; gamut 142; OpenEXR 252; SDI output **228**; SMPTE EBU PAL frame rates 266; standard-setting organization 74

S/N or SNR (Signal to Noise ratio) 20

software *see* download/ingest software

solid state hard drives (SSDs) 222

Solis, Doug *203*

Song, Myung-Sin 163

Sony: ASX cards *210*; back-illuminated CMOS 9; Black Gamma 78, *78*; Camera Control Unit (Paintbox) 25; CineAlta cameras 24, *134*, 148; and Codex Vault *243*; data management software 219; F3 cameras 147, 148, *149*, *213*; F5 cameras 157, 166, 247; F55 cameras *18*, 157, 166, 242, 247; F65 cameras 14, *14*, *15*, *16*, 157, 165, 247; F900 cameras 24, *25*, *265*; HDCam 29, 167; HDCam SR 167, *224*; HyperGamma 78–80, *79*, 108; LUTs (conversion) 87; MLUTs *18*, *192*, 242; S-Gamut 87; S-Log 86, *86*, **87**, *87*, *93*; Sony RAW 165; Sony Rec.709 *93*, 94; SRMaster recording 28; SxS cards 24, 167, *167*, *210*, 220; workflow 247, *248*; XAVC 165–166; XDCam 24, 167; XDCAM Archive (XDA) 223; zebras 110, *110*

sound blankets (or furny pads) 197

spectral colors 131

Spectra light meters 37; Spectra Professional 8, *9*

spectral locus 139, *140*, *141*

specular highlights 83, 118

spinning mirrors 19

split diamond displays 57, *57*

spot (reflectance) meters 90, 106, 107, 119–120, 121

sRGB 143

SRMaster recording (Sony) 28

SSDs (solid state hard drives) 222

stacks format 154

still stores 186

stops (or f/stops) 100, 108

storage (data management): hard drives and RAIDs 222, 223–224, *224*, *225*; long-term storage 226–227; LTO (Linear Tape-Open) tapes 214, 222, 227, 229, 243, *243*; storage needs 224–226; video space calculators 226, *226*

studio-swing 46, 76, *76*

Stump, David 270

sub-pixels 11

subtractive color 130

superblack 46, 58, 165

superwhite 46, 58, 83–84, *83*, *84*, 165

surge protection 198

sweet spot 66, 88

Swiss Filmmakers, DIT carts *202*, *208*

SxS cards (Sony) 24, 167, *167*, *210*, 220

sync generator 45–46, *46*

sync sound, and frame rates 33

Tangent Design Element *175*

tapeless recording 4

Technicolor film 69

Tektronix 42–43, 44, 57

telecine 174

Terminal (Apple) 217

termination (scopes) 45

test charts: and 100% saturation 56; calibration charts (DSC Labs Cavi-Black charts *60*, *63*, 123, *124*; DSC Labs ChromaDuMonde™ charts *60*, *61*, 62–63, 118, 122, *147*; DSC Labs OneShot charts *62*, 63–64; Macbeth/xRite ColorChecker *63*, 64, 141, *146*, *149*; skin tone 52, *61*, *63*, 64–65; warm cards 65); and camera setup 54; neutral gray cards 58–59, *58*, 60–62 (*see also* middle (18%) gray)

test methodology 44–47

test patterns 54, 56

textured black 118

texture/detail, and exposure 118, *119*

textured white 118, 123

Theora format 154

thick/thin images 119

Thomas, Griff *197*, *206*, *212*

Thomas, Von *201*, *204*

Thompson, Viper Filmstream 4, 69

Thorpe, Larry 89

three-chip sensors 9, *9*, *10*

Thunderbolt cables 199, 228

THX, cineSpace 188, 189

TIFF (Tagged Image File Format) 28, 154, 155, 157, 159

timecodes: functions *262*, 264; record run and free run 266–267; reports *266*, 267; timecode panel *265*; timecode slates 262, 263, *263*, *264*; time-of-day timecodes 266; two notes 265; video frame rates 266

time measurement 38

tint (or magenta/green axis or CC) 138

TMDS (Transition-Minimized Differential Signaling) 229, 230

"to the power of" function *see* power function

traffic lights (Red) 110, 111–112, *112*

transcoding 159, 160, 242–243, *243*

transfer function: modulation transfer function 66, *66*; Rec.709 transfer function 75–76, **75**, *75*; and video gamma 73; *see also* power function

transfer/shuttle drives 214, 223

transforms: and ACES workflow 260; Color Correction Matrix transform 2; color transforms 144, *144*; DCTs (Discrete Cosine Transforms) 159, 162; IDTs (Input Transforms) 260; LMTs (Look Modification Transforms) 260; matrix transforms 142; ODTs (Output Transforms) 260

Transition-Minimized Differential Signaling (TMDS) 229, 230

Transmission stops (T/stops) 100

transparency (or reversal or positive) film 102–103

tristimulus values 141, *146*, 149

True Color 32

Truelight 188

Trumbull, Douglas 34

T/stops (Transmission stops) 100

tungsten balance 15, 16, 17–18, 56, 134, *135*, 138

UHD (Ultra High Definition): definition 2, 30–32, *31*; digital HD history 24; and knee control 78; and Rec.709 74, 143; and square pixels 6; UHD/RAW 25; *see also* HD (High Definition)

ultra high speed cameras 34, *35*